CW01080249

Soviet Internationalism after Stalin

The Soviet Union is often presented as a largely isolated and idiosyncratic state. *Soviet Internationalism after Stalin* challenges this view by telling the story of Soviet and Latin American intellectuals, students, political figures and artists, and their encounters with the 'other' from the 1950s through the 1980s. In this first multi-archival study of Soviet relations with Latin America, Tobias Rupprecht reveals that, for people in the Second and Third Worlds, the Cold War meant not only confrontation with an ideological enemy, but also increased interconnectedness with distant world regions. He shows that the Soviet Union looked quite different from a southern rather than a western point of view, and he also charts the impact of this new internationalism on the Soviet Union itself in terms of popular perceptions of the USSR's place in the world and its political, scientific, intellectual and cultural reintegration into the global community.

TOBIAS RUPPRECHT is Lecturer in Latin American and Caribbean History at the University of Exeter.

Soviet Internationalism after Stalin

Interaction and Exchange between the USSR and Latin America during the Cold War

Tobias Rupprecht

CAMBRIDGE
UNIVERSITY PRESS

CAMBRIDGE
UNIVERSITY PRESS

University Printing House, Cambridge CB2 8BS, United Kingdom

Cambridge University Press is part of the University of Cambridge.

It furthers the University's mission by disseminating knowledge in the pursuit of
education, learning and research at the highest international levels of excellence.

www.cambridge.org
Information on this title: www.cambridge.org/9781107102880

© Tobias Rupprecht 2015

This publication is in copyright. Subject to statutory exception
and to the provisions of relevant collective licensing agreements,
no reproduction of any part may take place without the written
permission of Cambridge University Press.

First published 2015

Printed in the United Kingdom by Clays, St Ives plc

A catalogue record for this publication is available from the British Library

ISBN 978-1-107-10288-0 Hardback

Cambridge University Press has no responsibility for the persistence or accuracy
of URLs for external or third-party internet websites referred to in this publication,
and does not guarantee that any content on such websites is, or will remain,
accurate or appropriate.

Contents

Preface and acknowledgements   *page* vii

Introduction: the end of Soviet isolationism after 1953   1

1   A modern image for the USSR: Soviet self-representation
    towards Latin Americans   22

2   Moscow learns the mambo: Latin America and
    internationalism in Soviet popular culture   73

3   Paradise lost and found: Latin American intellectuals
    in and on the Soviet Union   128

4   From Russia with a diploma: Latin American students
    in the Soviet Union   191

5   Desk revolutionaries: Soviet Latin Americanists and
    internationalism in the late Soviet Union   230

Conclusion: Soviet internationalism after Stalin and its
domestic and foreign audiences   284

Postface: legacies of Soviet internationalism in Latin America
and Russia   291
Bibliography   298
Index   323

Preface and acknowledgements

Historians should be aware of the fallacies of individual memory and retroactive construction of traditions and origins. Yet I am pretty sure that the first vague idea for this book dates back to 1 May 2006. Fidel Castro gave what turned out to be his last May Day speech on Havana's Plaza de la Revolución. Coincidentally, I was travelling in Cuba with a friend, and we decided to join the huge crowd, brought together by hundreds of school buses from the entire island to the sweltering heat of that huge square. The midday sun was soon unbearable, and so was Castro's lengthy speech about the achievements of his revolution and the on-going evil-doings of imperialism. After half an hour or so, we left. The lasting impression from this somewhat atavistic spectacle was that of a group, standing next to us just in front of the stage, waving a big banner of the PDS (Partei des Demokratischen Sozialismus), the successor organisation of the East German communist party. Their pink wristbands gave them away as guests of one of the many all-inclusive beach-side holiday resorts, territory off-limits to ordinary Cubans. We had gotten a vivid picture of poverty and repression on the island in the weeks before and felt somewhere between amused and embarrassed about our compatriots. Our Cuban hosts had not understood why we wanted to go to the silly rally in the first place. As we got back to their home two hours later, we could see live on Cuban state television that Castro was still blustering and bragging, and selected European visitors were still endorsing him, about the bright future of socialism. Our friends' television set, just like their Minsk refrigerator and many cars in the street, was Soviet-produced.

These curious fragments of self-benefiting leftist romanticising of Latin America and the flotsam of Soviet internationalism in the Third World stuck in my head when I got back to Tübingen, where I had to come up with a topic for my final paper in contemporary history. I wondered whether Soviet citizens had a similarly idealised view of Latin American revolutions-cum-nice tropical amenities. There had been extensive contacts with Cuba, and to a lesser extent with Chile and Nicaragua, after all. I realised that we know quite a bit about the ramifications of the grand geo-political conflict of the second half of the twentieth century on the lives of people in the West, but basically nothing about what this Cold War meant for people in the Second and Third Worlds. Did Soviet citizens partake in the global activities of their state? And what did Latin Americans actually think of the former Soviet Union and its activities in the hemisphere during the Cold War?

Almost nine years passed from these very first ideas about a research project on the Soviet Union and Latin America until the book entered final production. The list of people who have accompanied it and contributed to its genesis is accordingly long, and I have incurred a fair amount of intellectual and personal debt. Klaus Gestwa in Tübingen was a staunch supporter from the very beginning; I am very thankful for his personal and enthusiastic commitment, especially in the dire straits of the early phase. It was in Ute Planert's lively seminar on trans-national historiography that I first heard of global history – and, the impressions from Cuba still on my mind, noticed the conspicuous absence of both Russia and Latin America from the debates. After graduation, appositely celebrated with rum and vodka, Jannis Panagiotidis provided the link from Tübingen to Florence. In the fantastic academic and culinary setting of the European University Institute, Steve Smith was a great supervisor for my Ph.D thesis and a very generous donator of many a *pranzo*. Dietrich Beyrau, Sebastian Conrad, Kiran Klaus Patel, Philipp Ther, Federico Romero, Antonella Romano and Daria Bocharnikova all provided useful advice and important input at various stages of the process of research, conceptualising and writing.

Ruth Gbikpi and Alex Howarth from the EUI library proved dedicated hunters for all sorts of literature, no matter how obscure or hard to find. Edurne Iraizoz and Maria-José Chousal were wonderful language teachers. Phil Jakes took over the big task of proof-reading and moulding the language of this book into something akin to idiomatic English. José Guillermo Londoño gave a very precious hint about Latin American alumni from Soviet universities and was, together with his wife Lucero, a consummate host in Medellín. Antonella Fazio provided the Florence–Bogotá link; her family put me up and kept me well fed and very safe in Colombia. I am deeply indebted to Hugo Fazio for his generosity and commitment to my research. Carlos Tapias and Luis Eduardo Bosemberg in Bogotá and Maíra Ervolino Mendes in Brasília alleviated the process of research in South America, which included unforgettable moments as well as ones of serious sweating, cursing and desperation.

Rumour has it that historians evaluate Russia according to their first personal experience there. If I present Soviet internationalism in too rosy a light in this book, Anton Lebedev and Gabriel Fogaça, who were close friends through many adventures in crazy Moscow, are partly to blame. Aleksandr Sizonenko, Katya Samsonkino, Yelitza Marcela Avila, Ingrid Schierle and Marc Elie all helped under different circumstances. Fellow archive rats Pia Koivunen, Claus Bech Hansen, Manfred Zeller, Moritz Florin, Victoria Smolkin, Markus Berg and Vladislav Drilenko were wonderful company and much appreciated for many discussions over after-work beers. Sergio del Castillo provided links to his native Peru; I was devastated to hear he died tragically on New Year's Eve 2010 in Moscow.

Round tables of historians of eastern Europe at Moscow's German Historical Institute (DHI) as well as the Universities of Cologne, Tübingen, Bremen, Munich, Bochum, Göttingen, Berlin and Bonn displayed varying degrees of enthusiasm as for the contribution of global history to the way we think about the Soviet Union. In every case, I appreciated the opportunity to present my work. At several international workshops and conferences of Latin America and Cold War historians in Florence, Rio de Janeiro, Princeton, Jyväskülä, Boston and Paris, the feedback was usually more benign – thanks to the exotic Soviet topic, I assume. I am grateful to Jeremy Adelman, Leslie Bethell, David Engerman, Michael Goebel, Delia Gonzales de Reufels, Anne Gorsuch, James Mark, Nicola Miller, Dina Odnopozova, Balázs Trencsényi, Arne Westad, Vladislav Zubok and anyone else who gave input and commented on my presentations at these and other occasions.

This final typescript has profited greatly from two anonymous reviewers with the rare ability to couch trenchant points of criticism and advice in words of enthusiastic encouragement. I would also like to express my appreciation to Karen Anderson Howes, who did a great job giving the final touches to the text during the copy-editing process.

As a sad and oft-bemoaned matter of fact, working conditions in academia in most European states allow usually only those young scholars who have the backing of their families to pursue careers. The original transcription of Ph.D ('Parents have Doubts') may hold true also for *i miei*, but they never made me feel their scepticism. For this and many other reasons, this book is dedicated to them.

The Russian, Spanish and English versions of Wikipedia as well as the online English translator dict.cc saved enormous amounts of time, which older generations would have spent, often in vain, browsing through thick paper encyclopaedias and dictionaries. The DHI Moscow and the EUI Florence gave lavish funding to realise my research in distant areas of the world. I never made it back to Cuba though: Castro may no longer rant for hours on May Day, but he and the political system he created are alive and grant no access to most foreign researchers.

The transliteration of Russian follows the international scientific ISO 9 standard, with the exception of commonly known personal names and terms in the main corpus of the text, but not in the apparatus. Institutions, organisations and groups are rendered in their Spanish original names, which I assume are comprehensible to the English reader. The Russian ones are referred to in their original terms upon first mention, and in their English translations only subsequently.

Introduction: the end of Soviet isolationism after 1953

Late Stalinism, the period between the end of the Second World War and the death of the dictator in 1953, was the most isolated period of Soviet history. The political leaders saw the world as divided into two parts, and everything outside their own camp as ruled by unalterably hostile capitalist and imperialist war-mongers, eager to annihilate the Soviet Union. Internationalism, once a fundamental Bolshevik principle, had long been subordinated to the political goals of 'socialism in one country' after Lenin's death and Trotsky's ousting; foreign contacts had abated from the mid 1930s. While the Second World War had forced a specific form of violent interaction with the world abroad upon Soviet citizens, the USSR, with the onset of the Cold War in 1947, isolated itself more than ever from foreign countries beyond the control of the Soviet Army. Scholars were cut off from most international scientific discourse, and compliant writers claimed any notable invention to be of Russian origin. 'Cosmopolitanism' came to be a perilous reproach during a renewed terror against the populations of now both the Soviet Union and its new satellite states and annexed territories in eastern Europe.

A 'myth of encirclement'[1] was to bond together Soviet citizens, devastated and traumatised by the war, behind their leaders. Only their wise policies, they claimed, could provide the peace and stability people so desperately wanted. By the late 1940s, the cultural and intellectual – if not the economic – isolation of the post-war Soviet Union was almost complete. Even international marriages were illegal. Western observers such as Isaiah Berlin noticed the complete ignorance of the Soviet intelligentsia about contemporary cultural life abroad.[2] For ordinary Soviet citizens, Vladislav Zubok wrote, 'meeting a foreigner was less likely than

---

[1] Elena Zubkova, *Russia after the War: Hopes, Illusions, and Disappointments, 1945–1957* (Armonk: Sharpe, 1998), pp. 84–7.

[2] Vladislav Zubok, *Zhivago's Children: The Last Russian Intelligentsia* (Cambridge, MA: Belknap Press of Harvard University Press, 2009), p. 14.

1

seeing a total solar eclipse. Foreign travel was unimaginable. Comparison between the Soviet experience and life in other countries was almost impossible.'[3] While some not very extensive contacts with the people's democracies in eastern Europe were established and the offspring of the urban elites had access to scattered western cultural products, the bulk of the Soviet population remained isolated from the rest of the world and had a very hazy idea of what was 'out there'.[4]

This book, an entangled history of the Soviet Union and Latin America during the Cold War, explores how this extreme isolationism ended after the death of Stalin. The Soviet political and intellectual elite now harked back ideologically to what they saw as unspoiled Leninist socialism of the 1920s, and thus rekindled internationalism as an integral ideational component of the Soviet project. This cautious opening to the world brought Soviet intellectuals and citizens back into selected realms of contemporary world culture. At the same time, the northern hemisphere was politically divided into two hostile camps; both the United States and the Soviet Union tried to present their model of modern society in a good light to the emerging Third World, and culture was an pivotal battlefield of this struggle for hearts and minds. It was in the context of this tension between international cultural integration and political delimitation from the West that Soviet contacts with distant Latin America (re-)emerged at different levels. In five chapters, this book sheds spotlights on five zones of interaction between Soviet and Latin American societies, cultures and individual agents through the period of the Cold War; they all explore how what is called here 'Soviet internationalism after Stalin' was designed and how it was received by internal and external addressees.

In order to understand how the Soviet Union continued to function after the death of Stalin and the end of his terror regime, we need to consider more what could be called the 'appeal of the empire'. Time and again, western observers have underlined the shortcomings, faults and inner contradictions within the Soviet Union to an extent that makes it difficult to understand why this system actually prevailed for so long and, through the late 1980s, enjoyed at least the passive support of the overwhelming majority of its population and the respect of many political

---

[3] *Ibid.*, p. 21.
[4] Jan C. Behrends, *Die erfundene Freundschaft: Propaganda für die Sowjetunion in Polen und in der DDR* (Cologne: Böhlau, 2006); Ellen Brun and Jacques Hersh, *Soviet–Third World Relations in a Capitalist World: The Political Economy of Broken Promises* (New York: St Martin's Press, 1990), p. 36; Wolfgang Kasack, 'Kulturelle Außenpolitik', in Oskar Anweiler and Karl-Heinz Ruffmann (eds.), *Kulturpolitik der Sowjetunion* (Stuttgart: Kröner, 1973), pp. 345–92.

leaders and intellectuals in the Third World. This book argues that Soviet contacts with the Third World were an integrative moment within the Soviet Union after Stalin. Internationalism was not only an empty political catchphrase, but an ideal that many Soviet scholars, intellectuals, cultural figures, political decision makers and, through the consumption of internationalist cultural products, ordinary citizens actually subscribed to. The admiration for the USSR expressed by many visitors from the global South only confirmed to many Soviet politicians, intellectuals and the wider public the ostensible superiority of their own system. Soviet internationalism after Stalin was a source of legitimisation for the new Soviet political elite and an integrative idea within Soviet society during the turmoil of de-Stalinisation and through much of the period under the rule of Leonid Brezhnev that has been labelled the Era of Stagnation. Even early perestroika witnessed an upsurge of pro-Third World sentiments, before its failure initiated the dismantling of the USSR and thus of Soviet internationalism after Stalin.

The world's first socialist state has been critically analysed almost exclusively from European or North American points of view. Scholars have outlined its economic and moral inferiority to the western, liberal-capitalist model of modern society in all facets. Looking at the second half of its history from a southern perspective, this book tries to reconstruct and comprehend – though not justify or whitewash – the attractive and thus cohesive factors of this system. Unlike a recurring concept in historiography that sees the late Soviet Union as driven by pragmatist imperialism, *Realpolitik* or materialist rational choice, it takes ideas, convictions and emotions seriously. Looking at the impact of internationalist ideals, rekindled with explicit reference to the 1920s and early 1930s, reveals that ideology changed after the death of Stalin, but still framed the political horizon of the elites in politics and culture in the Soviet Union.

Soviet contacts with Latin America are particularly suitable for elucidating the role of convictions and ideology, as opposed to geo-strategic considerations, for, throughout the history of Soviet foreign policy, Latin America was usually of lowest priority. Geographic factors – the proximity to the overpowering United States on the one side, the huge distance to the USSR on the other – determined expectations of Moscow's foreign policy makers. But Latin America was interesting for many Soviet communists, as it was there where the first communist party outside Russia was founded (in Mexico); it was where, for the first time since the October Revolution, a socialist revolution took place without interference of the USSR (in Cuba); and it was a Latin American country that firstly voted democratically for a Marxist president (in Chile). Agitating the

United States in its proclaimed back yard was a bonus, but not the main motivation to support political parties in every single state of the region. Latin America was interesting not so much for geo-politics, but for its homemade socialism.[5] Mounting a Latin American lens to study Soviet internationalism after Stalin offers yet another advantage: recurring references to contacts in the 1920s and 1930s between the young Soviet state and leftist movements in the Hispanic world (contacts that had not existed with such other Third World regions as sub-Saharan Africa or the Middle East) make this book's case that Soviet internationalism after Stalin rekindled similar sentiments from the inter-war period.

This book tells the story of Soviet internationalism after Stalin as an intertwined history with selected groups from Latin America, mostly intellectuals, students and political and public figures. It looks at interactions below state level, it goes beyond the purely political dimension of international relations, and it underlines the role played by cultural exchange and cultural currents in the development of the late Soviet Union. This trans-national dimension makes clear how, also in the Soviet case, the domestic and the foreign were intertwined: internationalism was directed to audiences at home as much as abroad. There can be no talk of hermetical isolation or autarky of the Soviet Union from the rest of the world. In many respects, Soviet society was in tune with global developments from the mid 1950s, and in the realm of culture even more so than in economics or politics. Giving room to a foreign perspective on the Soviet Union thus allows for a reconsideration of the successes and shortcomings of Soviet advances to the Third World. Back home, the opening up of the Soviet state to the world had no undermining effect on its society. If anything, the selective perception and presentation of world developments created a coherent world-view that seemed to prove to many Soviet politicians, cultural figures and common citizens that the Soviet Union was still the global trail-blazer of modern society.

The opening up to the world under Khrushchev and Russia in global history

Much ink has been spilled by historians of the Cold War on Soviet foreign relations under Stalin's successor Nikita Khrushchev; they can be summed up here briefly. The Kremlin withdrew the Soviet Army from

---

[5] Ilya Prizel, *Latin America through Soviet Eyes: The Evolution of Soviet Perceptions during the Brezhnev Era 1964–1982* (Cambridge: Cambridge University Press, 1990), p. ix; Cole Blasier, *The Giant's Rival: The USSR and Latin America* (Pittsburgh: University of Pittsburgh Press, 1983), p. 68.

Austria and Finland, relinquished claims on Turkish territory and, conceding that there were different paths to socialism, reconciled with Yugoslavia. In the wake of the 1955 Bandung Conference, many Third World leaders sought contact with Moscow and raised high hopes there for anti-imperialist collaboration. Propagating a peaceful path to socialism, Khrushchev travelled to India, Burma and Afghanistan, later to Egypt and Indonesia, and altogether to thirty-five countries. The Soviet Party boss and the leading politicians who accompanied him (often including Ekaterina Furceva, Soviet minister of culture and the only woman in the Politburo), journalists and intellectuals offered Soviet assistance and friendship.[6] Beyond these state-to-state contacts, the USSR became a member of more than 200 international organisations, from the Red Cross and the International Olympic Committee to many sub-organisations of the United Nations which it had previously boycotted, such as the International Labour Organization (ILO), UNESCO (both in 1954) and the World Health Organization (WHO, in 1957).[7]

While these integrative tendencies at political level are fairly well studied, this book seeks to explore how the opening up of the Soviet Union also concerned cultural figures, intellectuals and ordinary people. Soviets citizens were still restricted in their freedom of movement, and peasants were not free to travel even within the Soviet Union until the early 1970s – in essence, a continuation of serfdom. But interacting with the 'foreign', in personal contacts as much as through representations, was much more of an everyday experience, at least for educated city dwellers, than during late Stalinism. The country that, in 1953, had still officially claimed to have invented the steam engine, the light bulb and television hosted, five years later, twenty international scientific conferences. Soviet academics and artists, most notably architects, could travel abroad again, for inspiration or to attend conferences in their field – or even for symbolic gatherings for the sake of international co-operation such as the 1957 Pugwash Conference in Canada. In the early 1960s, some 1,500 Soviet doctors were sent abroad every year. Soviet radio broadcast 2,000 hours weekly from 147 stations to all parts of the world by 1956 and expanded this programme for years to come. Soviet publishing houses had an average of 100 million books per year printed for

---

[6] Aleksej Adshubej, *Gestürzte Hoffnung: Meine Erinnerungen an Chrustschow* (Berlin: Henschel, 1990), p. 250.

[7] Chris Osakwe, *The Participation of the Soviet Union in Universal International Organizations: A Political and Legal Analysis of Soviet Strategies and Aspirations inside ILO, UNESCO and WHO* (Leiden: Brill, 1972).

the outside world.[8] There were already 2 million Soviet citizens travelling abroad from 1956 to 1958, and 1.5 million foreigners visited the USSR. By 1964, the yearly number of foreign tourists who flocked into the Soviet Union had surpassed 1 million. In 1955–8 alone, 20,000 Soviet artists were sent to 60 countries around the world, more than half of them to non-socialist parts of the world. The number rose to an impressive 80,000 Soviet artists abroad and about the same number of foreign artists in the Soviet Union from 1961 to 1965.[9]

The history of the Soviet Union was not determined only by authoritarian politicians and subservient apparatchiks. After the death of Stalin and the revelation of his crimes, a new generation of mostly young and urban Soviet citizens, later called the *šestidesjatniki* ('the '60ers'), strove for socialism with a human face. Referring to a glorified notion of Lenin and of leftist culture of the 1920s, they longed for revolutionary activity and displayed an 'idealistic sense of social and moral justice'.[10] With this reference, they, too, revived the socialist internationalism of the early Soviet Union. In its specific form after 1953, internationalism was not merely a political concept, but an officially promoted attitude that was adopted by large parts of the intelligentsia and the population. While contacts with foreigners and the world abroad were always subject to restrictive Soviet laws and official fears – particularly of western influence – they would increase steadily in number and importance in the years to come. By the end of the 1960s, no fewer than 40 million Soviet citizens were members of international friendship societies.[11]

Historians of eastern Europe have long shunned an analysis of these 'trans-national' contacts and focused on the inner history of both Russia and the Soviet Union. 'Global' historians did not care much about Russia, either. In their stories of migrant networks, trans-continental

---

[8] Richard Stites, 'Heaven and Hell: Soviet Propaganda Constructs the World', in Gary Rawnsley (ed.), *Cold War Propaganda in the 1950s* (Basingstoke: Macmillan, 1999), p. 88; Sergej Romanovskij (ed.), *Meždunarodnye naučnye i kul'turnye svjazi SSSR* (Moscow: Gosizdat, 1966), pp. 135–6, 101–7, 234–7; Spravka o kul'turnich svjazjach Sovetskogo Sojuza s zarubežnymi stranami, undated, GARF f.9518 op.1 d. 343 ll.169–173.

[9] Romanovskij, *Meždunarodnye naučnye i kul'turnye svjazi SSSR*, pp. 47–8, 128.

[10] Zubok, *Zhivago's Children*; Vladislav Zubok, *A Failed Empire: The Soviet Union in the Cold War from Stalin to Gorbachev* (Chapel Hill: University of North Carolina Press, 2007), p. 191; Juliane Fürst, 'The Arrival of Spring? Changes and Continuities in Soviet Youth Culture and Policy between Stalin and Khrushchev', in Polly Jones (ed.), *The Dilemmas of De-Stalinization: Negotiating Cultural and Social Change in the Khrushchev Era* (London: Routledge, 2007), p. 141; Petr Vajl' and Aleksandr Genis, *60-e: mir sovetskogo čeloveka* (Moscow: Novoe Literaturnoe Obozrenie, 2001).

[11] Anon., 'Im Namen von 40 Millionen', *Kultur und Leben* 11 (1971), 18–20; Nina Popowa, 'Über die Tätigkeit und die Aufgaben des Verbandes der Freundschaftsgesellschaften', *Kultur und Leben* 4 (1962), 6–9.

connections, the global spread of commodities or ideas and the impact of 'global moments' on different societies, they have questioned not only the central role of the nation state as the given entity of analysis, but also the ostensibly all-encompassing and mono-directional influence of the West on the history of the rest of the world and its interpretation. However, they have predominantly implemented their theoretical approach through a historiography of eighteenth- and nineteenth-century South-East Asia, China, India and sometimes Africa. Latin America, once prominent in the Marxist world system and dependency theories, is conspicuously under-represented in recent debates. The region shares this marginal position with the Russian-dominated sphere.[12]

This absence is surprising for a Russian empire that, in the nineteenth century, spread from Swedish-speaking Finland until just short of San Francisco, and included territory from the Arctic Ocean to today's Turkey and China. It boasted an unequalled variety of languages and ethnicities and huge numbers of believers from all world religions. In the twentieth century not only did Russia style itself as the global trail-blazer of an alternative modern society, but it also experienced unmatched immigration and emigration streams. After the Second World War, the Soviet Union contributed to the foundation of the most important international organisations, and it expanded its direct influence from the Elbe to some miles off the coast of Florida, and from large parts of Eurasia to the Horn of Africa. 'The Soviet Union has become the centre of the civilised world', bragged the 1958 issue of the *Great Soviet Encyclopaedia* in its foreword. Moscow now supported influential political groups in essentially every single state on earth and was active in the Antarctic, the seven seas and outer space.

Russia's inappropriate absence from the debates of global history has been acknowledged and deplored enough times – and relief has been

---

[12] For a sense of the field, see Matthias Middell and Katja Naumann, 'Global History 2008–2010: Empirische Erträge, konzeptionelle Debatten, neue Synthesen', *Comparativ* 6 (2010), 93–133; Pamela Kyle Crossley, *What Is Global History?* (Cambridge: Polity Press, 2008); Ulrike Freitag (ed.), *Globalgeschichte: Theorien, Ansätze, Themen* (Frankfurt am Main: Campus Verlag, 2007); Bruce Mazlish, *The New Global History* (New York: Routledge, 2006); Anthony Hopkins, *Global History: Interactions between the Universal and the Local* (Basingstoke: Palgrave Macmillan, 2006). The classics include Immanuel Wallerstein, *The Capitalist World-Economy: Essays* (Cambridge: Cambridge University Press, 1979); James Theberge, *Latin America in the World System: The Limits of Internationalism* (Beverly Hills: Sage Publications, 1975); Andre Gunder Frank, *Capitalism and Underdevelopment in Latin America: Historical Studies of Chile and Brazil* (New York: Monthly Review Press, 1969); Raúl Prebisch, *Hacia una dinámica del desarrollo latinoamericano* (Montevideo: Ediciones de la Banda Oriental, 1967).

produced.[13] Yet in much of what has been written subsequently on Soviet participation in world integrative processes, there is a tendency to emphasise the shortcomings of the Soviet model compared to western global integration, an approach that contrasts with the core demand of global history not to take the West as a conceptual norm.[14] With a degree of cynicism, one might actually say that communist eastern Europe and the Soviet Union are predestined for the analysis of a global historian. On the one hand, the 'global' was always an immensely important point of reference for Party leaders and theoreticians. They drew their legitimacy from processes in world history as they perceived them, and they constantly claimed that their type of state and their concept of modern society served as a role model for the rest of the world.[15] Citizens, on the other hand, were, by and large, confined to where they lived, locked up in states that restricted foreign travel severely. Proponents of global history have emphasised that they are interested in the manifestation of global phenomena in a local context.[16] Communist eastern Europe offers, in a pure form, such cases of the local meeting the global. There is another epistemological and theoretical reason to include the East and

---

[13] Authors who have pointed out this lacuna in scholarship include Martin Aust (ed.), *Globalisierung imperial und sozialistisch: Russland und die Sowjetunion in der Globalgeschichte 1851–1991* (Frankfurt am Main: Campus, 2013), p. 26; Michael David-Fox, *Showcasing the Great Experiment: Cultural Diplomacy and Western Visitors to the Soviet Union, 1921–1941* (Oxford: Oxford University Press, 2012), p. 313; Jürgen Osterhammel, *Die Verwandlung der Welt: Eine Geschichte des 19. Jahrhunderts* (Munich: Beck, 2011), p. 1286. A selection of studies on the Soviet Union and the Third World includes Andreas Hilger (ed.), *Die Sowjetunion und die Dritte Welt: UdSSR, Staatssozialismus und Antikolonialismus im Kalten Krieg 1945–1991* (Munich: Oldenbourg, 2009); Vladimir Shubin, *The Hot Cold War: The USSR in Southern Africa* (London: Pluto Press, 2008); Ragna Boden, *Die Grenzen der Weltmacht: Sowjetische Indonesienpolitik von Stalin bis Brežnev* (Stuttgart: Steiner, 2006); Maxim Matusevich, *No Easy Row for a Russian Hoe: Ideology and Pragmatism in Nigerian–Soviet Relations, 1960–1991* (Trenton: Africa World Press, 2003). For a broader overview, see David Engerman, 'The Second World's Third World', *Kritika* 1 (2011), 183–211; Tobias Rupprecht, 'Die sowjetische Gesellschaft in der Welt des Kalten Kriegs: Neue Forschungsperspektiven', *Jahrbücher für Geschichte Osteuropas* 58 (2010), 381–99.

[14] Examples include accounts in which the Soviet model lacks economic competitiveness, money and/or lacking right of assembly. See Oscar Sanchez-Sibony, *Red Globalization: The Political Economy of the Soviet Cold War from Stalin to Khrushchev* (Cambridge: Cambridge University Press, 2014); Stephen Kotkin, 'The Kiss of Debt: The East Bloc Goes Borrowing', in Niall Ferguson (ed.), *The Shock of the Global: The 1970s in Perspective* (Cambridge, MA: Belknap Press of Harvard University Press, 2010), pp. 80–93; Frederick Starr, 'The Third Sector in the Second World', in Bruce Mazlish and Akira Iriye (eds.), *The Global History Reader* (New York: Routledge, 2005), pp. 191–200.

[15] Jan C. Behrends, 'Vom Panslavismus zum Friedenskampf: Außenpolitik, Herrschaftslegitimation und Massenmobilisierung im sowjetischen Nachkriegsimperium', *Jahrbücher für Geschichte Osteuropas* 56/1 (2008), 27.

[16] Kenneth Pomeranz, 'Social History and World History: From Daily Life to Patterns of Change', *Journal of World History* 1 (2007), 69–98.

its relations with the Third World in the debates on global history: most historians who give a voice to non-western actors usually still do so with reference to Europe or the United States. Comparisons and shared histories of different non-western countries add a perspective that puts the pivotal role of the West in world history in perspective. Not all worldwide entanglements were predestined to finally merge into free markets and liberal democracies.

Terminology: internationalism, USSR, Latin America, Third World, (cultural) Cold War

'Internationalism' in this book follows Akira Iriye's definition of 'cultural internationalism' as 'attempts to build cultural understanding, international co-operation, and a sense of shared values across national borders through cultural, scientific or student exchanges'. Iriye has hinted at the impact that communist internationalism had on his concept of a 'global community' from early on, but he has himself, like most global historians, otherwise concentrated on Asian and western activities.[17] This book fills the gap by putting the entangled history of the Soviet Union and Latin America in the context of a multi-polar history of the Cold War. International integrative developments in the history of the second half of the twentieth century were engendered not just by the West and under western terms.

Internationalism in the Soviet Union has so far been studied only in institutional histories of the Comintern and Cominform, and thus only for the first half of Soviet history.[18] Stalin's successors announced a return to *proletarian* (in relation to international communist parties in power) and *socialist* internationalism (towards the rest of the world), but in fact they did not simply warm up the old model of spreading world revolution and Soviet communism. The Soviet Union after 1953 combined ideas of socialist internationalism of the 1920s with the 'cultural internationalism' of the 1950s. The new Soviet leadership opened the country to the world in order to spread, if much more cautiously than the

---

[17] Akira Iriye, *Cultural Internationalism and World Order* (Baltimore: Johns Hopkins University Press, 1997), p. 34; see also Martin H. Geyer and Johannes Paulmann, *The Mechanics of Internationalism: Culture, Society, and Politics from the 1840s to the First World War* (Oxford: Oxford University Press, 2008); Carsten Holbraad, *Internationalism and Nationalism in European Political Thought* (New York: Palgrave Macmillan, 2003); Kjell Goldmann, *The Logic of Internationalism: Coercion and Accommodation* (New York: Routledge, 2001).

[18] E.g. Michael Buckmiller and Klaus Meschkat (eds.), *Biographisches Handbuch zur Geschichte der Kommunistischen Internationale: Ein deutsch-russisches Forschungsprojekt* (Berlin: Akademie-Verlag, 2007).

early Bolsheviks, their model of society across the globe. At the same time, the end of isolation meant a re-integration of the Soviet Union, on political, scientific, intellectual and cultural levels, into a global community under the conditions of the Cold War. It is this specific conglomeration of revolutionary and integrative ideals that this book defines as 'Soviet internationalism after Stalin'.

The definition of 'USSR', is rather straightforward: interchangeably with 'Soviet Union', and occasionally 'the Soviets', it refers to the Soviet state and Soviet society, the latter with a focus on urban areas with a Slavic majority. 'Latin America' requires more explanation, possibly even justification: for the purpose of this book, it encompasses all countries of the American continents and the Caribbean except the United States and Canada. The more geographically rooted concepts of 'North' and 'South America', separated at the isthmus by the Panama Canal, represent today's political and mental maps. In the context of the Cold War, they are of less avail. To diminish tedious repetitions, the book occasionally – semantically and geographically not perfectly correctly – refers to Latin America as a 'subcontinent' and to Latin Americans as 'Latinos' (a term that, in the United States, refers to US citizens of Hispanic or Brazilian origin, whereas in Latin America and continental Europe it is simply a short form of 'Latin Americans'). The English language continues another pretension often criticised by Spanish and Portuguese speakers, as it claims the adjective 'American' for the United States only. In order to avoid offence or confusion, the abbreviation 'US' is used instead, and 'the Americas' replaces 'America' whenever the entire continent is concerned.

Cultural macro-histories, by conservative scholars such as Samuel Huntington and liberals such as Shmuel Eisenstadt alike, have been criticised for their large-scale construction of ostensibly homogeneous world cultures. Latin America is of course not homogeneous. Socioeconomic, ethnic and cultural/language differences are tremendous between white settler colonies such as Argentina or southern Brazil and countries with an indigenous majority such as Bolivia or Guatemala. Dutch-, English- and French-speaking states in and around the Caribbean have little in common with Mexico or Uruguay. Exactly the same criticism, however, could be applied to the analysis of one specific nation: ethnic and class differences often vary to the same extent within a single Latin American country. For a global history that is not primarily interested in political relations of national governments, but in interactions of agency groups and individuals between different world regions, the nation state is just as questionable a category as the cultural unit 'Latin America'. A short history of the concept, and its application by Latin

American travellers to the Soviet Union, will go into more detail on this issue in Chapter 3. For now, suffice it to say that 'Latin America' is a reasonable analytic term because was a meaningful category for contemporaries from both the USSR and the Americas during the Cold War.

As for the generalising concept of Latin America, there has been some criticism of the usage of 'Third World', as it ostensibly constructs a normative gradient to the leading First and Second Worlds. The term 'Third World' was coined in the early 1950s by the French historian Alfred Sauvy, based on the *Tiers état*, for all those parts of the planet that were not part of the western and eastern camps of the Cold War. In the West, it replaced the term 'underdeveloped countries' from the 1960s. Soviet official discourse was actually quite similar: the old expression *narody vostoka* ('peoples of the East') was geographically outdated when Africa and Latin America joined forces with Asia. The Soviets now referred to the *narody Azii, Afriki i Latinskoj Ameriki* ('peoples of Asia, Africa and Latin America'), and after decolonisation also interchangeably to the *razvivajuščiesja strany* ('developing countries') and *slaborazvitye strany* ('poorly developed countries'), or sometimes simply to *novye gosudarstva* ('new states') or *molodye nacii* ('young nations'). From the 1970s, Soviet scholars also used the term *tretij mir* ('Third World'), albeit initially always in quotation marks to distance themselves from its western originators.[19]

The term 'Third World' is used in this book for the same pragmatic reasons as 'Latin America'. Interchangeably with 'global South', it means all countries of Asia, Africa and Latin America with the exception of Soviet territory, China and Japan. For one thing, it was a meaningful category for contemporaries of the Cold War and thus needs some concept that refers to it in the historical analysis. For another, the alternatives that include the word 'developing' are much more explicitly normative.

Soviet contacts with the rest of the world, at the political as much as at other levels, invariably happened against the backdrop of the geopolitical constellation of the Cold War. Recent scholarship has included the perspectives of the East and many Third World countries, which had long been lacking.[20] As for Soviet foreign policy during the Cold War, it

---

[19] Boden, *Die Grenzen der Weltmacht*, p. 31; A. Šestopal, 'Koncepcii social'no-ekonomičeskogo razvitija stran "tret'ego mira"', *Latinskaja Amerika* 3 (1977); A. Šul'govskij, 'Opyt rešenija nacional'nogo voprosa v SSSR i ideologičeskaja bor'ba v Latinskoj Amerike', *Latinskaja Amerika* 8 (1972), 15; Michail Lavričenko, *Ekonomičeskoe sotrudničestvo SSSR so stranami Azii, Afriki i Latinskoj Ameriki* (Moscow: Gosizdat Političeskoj Literatury, 1961), p. 2.

[20] Federico Romero, *Storia della guerra fredda: l'ultimo conflitto per l'Europa* (Turin: Giulio Einaudi, 2009); Odd Arne Westad underlines the active role of many Third World

is a long-standing question whether it was driven by imperial interests and political realism – or by communist ideology.[21] Arne Westad, in line with a historiography that took ideas and convictions more seriously than a generation before, saw Soviet Third World policy as a Marxist continuation of old Russian missionary-imperialist thought and as a continuation of late European imperialism: 'its objectives were not exploitation or subjection, but control and improvement.'[22] Shaped by these *longue durée* ideas, Soviet political leaders also had concrete geo-political and security interests and sought recognition as a world super-power. With his 'revolutionary-imperialist paradigm', Vladislav Zubok has offered a workable concept to reconcile ideas and power.[23] In his history of the Soviet Union in the Cold War, he argues convincingly that there is actually no contradiction between geo-political interests and their interpretation in categories of Marxist-Leninist ideology.

Zubok's book is also interesting for dedicating a chapter to the Soviet home front. Most other accounts of the Cold War remain at the level of high politics and diplomacy; only a few include the impact of the conflict on societies. If they do so, they usually introduce the perspective of the United States alone.[24] For people in the West, the Cold War meant isolation from the other camp and threat of nuclear annihilation on the

---

leaders in *The Global Cold War: Third World Interventions and the Making of Our Times* (Cambridge: Cambridge University Press, 2007); William Wohlforth, 'Superpowers, Interventions and the Third World', *Cold War History* 6/3 (2006), 365–71; Odd Arne Westad, *Reviewing the Cold War: Approaches, Interpretations, Theory* (London: Cass, 2006); Bernd Greiner (ed.), *Heiße Kriege im Kalten Krieg* (Hamburg: Hamburger Edition, 2006); Roger E. Kanet, 'The Superpower Quest for Empire: Cold War and Soviet Support for "Wars of National Liberation"', *Cold War History* 6/3 (2006), 331–52; Christopher Andrew and Vasili Mitrokhin, *The World Was Going Our Way: The KGB and the Battle for the Third World* (New York: Basic Books, 2005); Tony Smith, 'New Bottles for New Wine: A Pericentric Framework for the Study of the Cold War', *Diplomatic History* 24 (2000), 567–91. Aleksandr Fursenko provides a good analysis of the Soviet perspective in *Prezidium CK KPSS: 1954–1964* (Moscow: Rossijskaja Političeskaja Enciklopedija, 2003) as does John Lewis Gaddis (if in an unabashedly triumphalist pro-Western tone) in *We Now Know: Rethinking Cold War History* (Oxford: Oxford University Press, 1998).

[21] Steve Smith, 'Two Cheers for the "Return of Ideology"', *Revolutionary Russia* 17/2 (2004), 119–35. The 'Realist' approach has become fashionable again as of late. Oscar Sanchez-Sibony's book on the political economy of the post-war Soviet Union uses a rational-choice approach that entirely dismisses the realm of ideas and convictions. Sanchez rightly calls the Cold War a 'discursive construction' (*Red Globalization*, p. 253), but it is telling of his hard-core materialist approach that he contrasts it to the 'encompassing reality of the second half of the twentieth century'. The Cold War discourse, and its geo-political consequences, did shape this reality to a great extent.

[22] Westad, *The Global Cold War*, p. 5.   [23] Zubok, *A Failed Empire*.

[24] Notable exceptions are Bernd Stöver, *Der Kalte Krieg 1947–1991: Geschichte eines radikalen Zeitalters* (Munich: Beck, 2007); Marshall T. Poe, *The Russian Moment in World History* (Princeton: Princeton University Press, 2003), p. 90; Patrick Major and

one hand, but also an increased presence of Third World matters in the wake of decolonisation on the other. The same goes for people on the eastern side of the Iron Curtain, but we know significantly less about the implications of the Cold War on Soviet culture, everyday life and mentalities.

The concept of 'Cold War' altogether has recently come under attack from several sides. An analysis of economic and social developments during the ideological conflict raises the question of to what extent these actually belonged to the geo-political realm of the Cold War. The rise of international social, non-governmental and inter-governmental organisations has led some scholars to believe that, in the long run, the Cold War was a mere sideshow of historical development in the second half of the twentieth century, overshadowed by the forces of globalisation.[25] Others state that, for large parts of the world's population, the Cold War was neither cold nor was it a single war; they favour replacing the name with 'East–West conflict'.[26]

The latter concept, however, is misleading: it blurs the differences between a rivalry between the United States and Russia that dates back to the mid nineteenth century, and the concrete geo-political constellation as it emerged after the Second World War. 'Cold War' in this book thus refers to a world historical epoch roughly between the end of the Second World War and the end of state socialism in eastern Europe. Many political processes worldwide that were originally independent of the Cold War were polarised through the conflict between East and West. Other phenomena, especially socio-cultural ones outside the East–West axis, proceeded, also during the era of the Cold War, without noteworthy impact of the grand ideological foes in Washington and Moscow.

This definition is in line with recent usage by most European and North American scholars. Also in Latin America, the common concept of the *Guerra Fría* today refers to a period from 1947, when both the Tratado Interamericano de Asistencia Recíproca (TIAR) and the Organization of American States (OAS) were founded, until 1989–91, when not only the socialist regimes of eastern Europe, but also the last military juntas in Chile and Paraguay came to a close. The concept of *cholodnaja vojna* ('cold war') in the Soviet Union usually referred only to the short

---

Rana Mitter, 'East Is East and West Is West? Towards a Comparative Socio-Cultural History of the Cold War', *Cold War History* 4/1 (2003), 3.

[25] Akira Iriye, *Global Community: The Role of International Organizations in the Making of the Contemporary World* (Berkeley: University of California Press, 2004); Iriye, *Cultural Internationalism and World Order*.

[26] Jost Dülfer, *Europa im Ost–West-Konflikt: 1945–1990* (Munich: Oldenbourg, 2004).

period from late Stalinism to the Cuban missile crisis. recently, younger Russian scholars, too, have used it to describe the entire period until the end of the USSR.

The renewed interest in the ideational roots of the Cold War and the influence of cultural studies on historiography in general have led some scholars to assess the Cold War from entirely new perspectives. Instead of looking, from above, at policies and diplomatic documents, they based their analyses, bottom up, on cultural artefacts. The superpowers, they claimed, sought hegemony at not only the geo-political, but also the cultural level, and cultural representations were used to mobilise internal and external audiences. The United States as much as the Soviet Union put enormous efforts into proving to the world the superiority of their respective systems through complex programmes of what is sometimes called 'cultural warfare'.[27] The bulk of studies concentrate on US activities and their results on a passively receiving Soviet Union. The Iron Curtain was finally raised, or parted, so the grand narrative goes, thanks to US consumer culture in the Soviet Union.[28]

What in retrospect may look like a story of one-directional influence, however, started out from a much more contingent situation in the mid 1950s.[29] Most of what is known about Soviet activities in the cultural Cold War on a global scale is still written with a certain bias towards western contemporaries, who wrote their books not with an exclusively

---

[27] Laura Belmonte, *Selling the American Way: US Propaganda and the Cold War* (Philadelphia: University of Pennsylvania Press, 2008); Hugh Wilford, *The Mighty Wurlitzer: How the CIA Played America* (Cambridge, MA: Harvard University Press, 2008); David Caute, *The Dancer Defects: The Struggle for Cultural Supremacy during the Cold War* (Oxford: Oxford University Press, 2003); Frances Stonor Saunders, *Who Paid the Piper? The CIA and the Cultural Cold War* (London: Granta Books, 2000); Rawnsley (ed.), *Cold War Propaganda in the 1950s*.

[28] Yale Richmond, *Cultural Exchange and the Cold War: Raising the Iron Curtain* (University Park: Penn State University Press, 2003); Walter L. Hixson, *Parting the Curtain: Propaganda, Culture, and the Cold War, 1945–1961* (New York: St Martin's Griffin, 1998). For a similar view, see Alan M. Ball, *Imagining America: Influence and Images in Twentieth-Century Russia* (Lanham, MD: Rowman & Littlefield, 2003). See also Marilyn Kushner, 'Exhibiting Art at the American National Exhibition in Moscow, 1959: Domestic Politics and Cultural Diplomacy', *Journal of Cold War Studies* 4/1 (2002), 6–26; Pamela Kachurin, 'The ROCI Road to Peace: Robert Rauschenberg, Perestroika and the End of the Cold War', *Journal of Cold War Studies* 4/1 (2002), 27–44; Dmitri Sarab'yanov and John Bowlt, 'Keepers of the Flame: An Exchange of Art and Western Cultural Influences in the USSR after World War II', *Journal of Cold War Studies* 4/1 (2002), 81–7.

[29] Nigel Gould-Davies, 'The Logic of Soviet Cultural Diplomacy', *Diplomatic History* 27/2 (2003), 193–214. Some research has been done lately, but still focuses on late Stalinism and geographically on Europe: Behrends, *Die erfundene Freundschaft*; Thomas Lindenberger (ed.), *Massenmedien im Kalten Krieg: Akteure, Bilder Resonanzen* (Cologne: Böhlau, 2006); Stites, 'Heaven and Hell', p. 88.

academic interest, but as warnings against communist infiltration. Yet what they saw as a gigantic totalitarian PR campaign[30] was in fact often quite similar to activities of their own governments. What is more, the cultural history of the Cold War was not limited to an antagonistic 'cultural Cold War'. In order to avoid the impression that culture was something that always followed political trends and was disseminated only from West to East, or from North to South, this book shuns the term 'cultural Cold War' and speaks of 'cultural transfer' instead.

Historians' assessments of Soviet–Latin American relations

The boom in comparative and trans-national approaches in historiography notwithstanding, there has been very little academic interest in Russian–Latin American affairs in the past two decades, which is conspicuous, considering the many parallels in Russia's and Latin America's modern history. In both vast spaces on the fringes of Europe, which these areas traditionally supplied with raw materials, the old autocratically ruling European elite proved unable to cope with the challenges of a modern society at the beginning of the twentieth century. Bolshevism in Russia and populism in Latin America took over with the promise to involve the peasants as well as the socially and ethnically marginalised in their fundamental reforms. Both the Soviet Union and most Latin American states, predominantly agrarian societies with weak democratic institutions, embarked on state-initiated or corporatist modernisation projects based on a mobilisation of the masses (and mass terror in the Soviet case). The Soviet command economy as well as Latin American import substitution were to provide independence from the world economy – and created the basis of authoritarian rule. After overcoming these dictatorships in the mid 1950s, both the Soviet Union and Latin America experienced a decade of political and economic confidence. The ambitious and bustling modernisation programmes came to a halt in the mid 1960s, when conservative autocrats replaced populist reformers in the USSR and a number of the most important Latin American states. Their rule in turn ended in the 1980s, when their economic models proved unable to cope with the necessary transition to post-industrial societies. Deregulated markets boosted the economic development of

---

[30] Frederic C. Barghoorn, *Soviet Foreign Propaganda* (Princeton: Princeton University Press, 1964); for a similar view, see Clive Rose, *The Soviet Propaganda Network: A Directory of Organisations Serving Soviet Foreign Policy* (London: Pinter, 1988); Anweiler and Ruffmann (eds.), *Kulturpolitik der Sowjetunion*.

both post-communist Russia and many Latin American states in the 1990s, but created social imbalances between the haves and have-nots as well as serious financial crises including state bankruptcies in Russia and Argentina, by the end of the decade.

What has been written on Soviet–Latin American relations beyond this comparative sketch was bound to depend on the authors' historical and political context. The first approaches from the 1950s focused more on the activities of international communism than on the Soviet state. Considering the tense political atmosphere (especially in US academia) at the time, these early accounts were astonishingly nuanced. While obviously anti-communist, they made clear that the Americas were never a Soviet geo-political top priority, and underlined how little influence party communism had, in most countries, outside small circles of artists and intellectuals.[31] From the 1960s, western scholars discerned in a series of well-balanced studies that the post-Stalinist Soviet Union also had interests as a state in Latin America, interests that were not necessarily in line with communist aspirations.[32] What has been written on Soviet political relations with Castro's Cuba is notably more polarised, with political leanings depending on the author's background. Assessments hover between harshly critical studies by renegades and victims of the revolution and much more relaxed, usually European or Canadian rather than US studies that sometimes cannot hide a degree of sympathy for the tropical David fighting the imperialist Goliath.[33]

Soviet scholars did conduct some valuable research on Latin American history; their books on contemporary relations between the USSR and Latin America, however, tended to be positivistic chronicles or

[31] Boris Goldenberg, *Kommunismus in Lateinamerika* (Stuttgart: Kohlhammer, 1971); Rollie Poppino, *International Communism in Latin America: A History of the Movement 1917–1963* (Glencoe: Free Press of Glencoe, 1964);Robert J. Alexander, 'Soviet and Communist Activities in Latin America', *Problems of Communism* 10/1 (1961), 8–13; Robert J. Alexander, *Communism in Latin America* (New Brunswick: Rutgers University Press, 1957).

[32] Wolfgang Berner, 'Die Sowjetunion und Lateinamerika', in Dietrich Geyer (ed.), *Osteuropa-Handbuch: Sowjetische Außenpolitik Band II* (Cologne: Böhlau, 1976), pp. 844–78; Herbert Goldhamer, *The Foreign Powers in Latin America* (Princeton: Princeton University Press, 1972); Joseph Gregory Oswald and Anthony Strover (eds.), *The Soviet Union and Latin America* (New York: Praeger, 1970); Herbert Dinerstein, 'Soviet Policy in Latin America', *American Political Science Review* 1 (1967), 83.

[33] The literature is abundant; examples include Yuri Pavlov, *Soviet–Cuban Alliance, 1959–1991* (Miami: North–South Center Press, University of Miami, 1996); Néstor Carbonell, *And the Russians Stayed: The Sovietization of Cuba. A Personal Portrait* (New York: William Morrow & Co., 1989); Jacques Lévesque, *The USSR and the Cuban Revolution: Soviet Ideological and Strategical Perspectives, 1959–1977* (New York: Praeger, 1978).

somewhat schematic ideological treatises.[34] Just as biased, and with a drive that was clearly more political than academic, was a series of US studies written in the wake of the leftist revolutions in Central America from the late 1970s. Drastically overestimating Soviet activities in their 'back yard', political and intelligence analysts spread paranoia of overall communist subversion, and linked it, in their academic work, with denouncements of political liberalism in the United States, demands for an end of *détente*, and outright calls to arms.[35]

Many academics without political aspirations, and especially in the increasingly more relaxed atmosphere of early perestroika, defied this US paranoia. The most thorough and comprehensive analyses of Soviet–Latin American relations were all written in the mid to late 1980s. They painted Soviet activities in the Americas not as those of an aggressive and perfectly orchestrated evil empire, but rather pointed at the multi-layered economic and political contacts, at limited Soviet influence and, especially, at the lack of co-ordination that different Soviet organs displayed in their activities abroad.[36]

All this literature from the 1950s to the 1980s has analysed Soviet–Latin American relations within a traditional political history framework. It focused on the activities of communist parties on the one side, and on political, military, economic and sometimes cultural relations on a bipolar inter-state level on the other. During times of high *détente* realism in the mid 1970s, some scholars abandoned ideology completely and compared the US and Soviet empires based on systems theory. They drew parallels between Soviet methods of control and influence in eastern Europe and those of the United States in Latin America, compared Poland and Mexico in their position as dependent direct neighbours of the superpowers, or pointed out commonalities of adaptation and

---

[34] Aleksandr Sizonenko, *Sovetskij Sojuz i Latinskaja Amerika: sovremennyj etap otnošenij* (Kiev: Politizdat Ukrainy, 1976); Viktor Vol'skij, *SSSR i Latinskaja Amerika: 1917–1967* (Moscow: Meždunarodnye Otnošenija, 1967).

[35] Timothy Ashby, *The Bear in the Back Yard: Moscow's Caribbean Strategy* (Lexington, MA: Lexington Books, 1987); Dennis L. Bark, *The Red Orchestra* (Stanford: Hoover Institution Press, 1986); Leon Goure and Morris Rothenberg, *Soviet Penetration of Latin America* (Miami: Center for Advanced International Studies, University of Miami, 1975).

[36] Prizel, *Latin America through Soviet Eyes*; Nicola Miller, *Soviet Relations with Latin America, 1959–1987* (Cambridge: Cambridge University Press, 1989); Eusebio Mujal-León (ed.), *The USSR and Latin America: A Developing Relationship* (Boston: Unwin Hyman, 1989); Carlos Rivas, *América Latina, Unión Soviética: relaciones económicas y comerciales* (Bogotá: Ediciones Librería del Profesional, 1989); Augusto Varas (ed.), *Soviet–Latin American Relations in the 1980s* (Boulder: Westview, 1987); Blasier, *The Giant's Rival*.

resistance that Romania or Yugoslavia on the one side and Cuba or Peru on the other built up against the dominance of their respective hegemons.[37]

Irrespective of their analytical and political perspective, all assessments of Soviet–Latin American relations before 1990 had in common two characteristics: firstly, the authors had no access to Soviet archival material. Secondly, as a common and necessary first step in international history, they focused on the sphere of political relations, as did a series of studies on separate Latin American states that were undertaken from the 1980s.[38]

Since 1991, many Russian archives have become accessible, but so far no one has used them to re-examine relations between the Soviets and Latin America. The temporary lack of political interest in Latin America has also seized many academics. Those historians professionally engaged with Latin America, like back in the 1950s, have focused again on communism, and not so much on the Soviet state: the Comintern's activities on the subcontinent have been revisited.[39] Communism's Latin American crimes found a prosecutor in renegade secret agent Vasili Mitrokhin and a judge in Pascal Fontain in a chapter of the *Livre noir*.[40] The Soviet state, however, is absent in overviews of Latin American history.[41] And, more

---

[37] Jan Triska (ed.), *Dominant Powers and Subordinate States: The United States in Latin America and the Soviet Union in Eastern Europe* (Durham: Duke University Press, 1986); Edy Kaufman, *The Superpowers and Their Spheres of Influence: The United States and the Soviet Union in Eastern Europe and Latin America* (London: Croom Helm, 1976). A rare exception that goes beyond international relations is a comparison between the Zapatista movement in Mexico and the Ukrainian peasant revolt *machnovščina*: Dittmar Dahlmann, *Land und Freiheit: Machnovščina und Zapatismo als Beispiele agrarrevolutionärer Bewegungen* (Stuttgart: Steiner, 1986).

[38] Ruben Berríos and Cole Blasier, 'Peru and the Soviet Union 1969–1989: Distant Partners', *Journal of Latin American Studies* 23 (1991), 365–84; Mario Rapoport, 'Argentina and the Soviet Union: History of Political and Economic Relations, 1917–1955', *Hispanic American Historical Review* 2 (1986), 239–85; Isabel Turrent, *La Unión Soviética en América Latina: el caso de la Unidad Popular Chilena, 1970–1973* (Mexico City: Centro de Estudios Internacionales, 1984); Joseph Nogee, 'Allende's Chile and the Soviet Union: A Policy Lesson for Latin American Nations Seeking Autonomy', *Journal of Interamerican Studies and World Affairs* 21 (1979), 339–68.

[39] Klaus Meschkat, 'Die Komintern in Lateinamerika: Biographien als Schlüssel zum Verständnis einer Weltorganisation', in Buckmiller and Meschkat (eds.), *Biographisches Handbuch zur Geschichte der Kommunistischen Internationale*, pp. 111–26; Michael Löwy and Michael Pearlman (eds.), *Marxism in Latin America from 1909 to the Present: An Anthology* (Atlantic Highlands: Humanities Press, 1992).

[40] Andrew and Mitrokhin, *The World Was Going Our Way*; Stéphane Courtois, Nicolas Wert and Jean-Louis Panné (eds.), *Le Livre noir du communisme: crimes, terreur, répression* (Paris: Éditions Robert Laffont, 1997).

[41] Leslie Bethell (ed.), *Latin America: Politics and Society since 1930* (Cambridge: Cambridge University Press, 1998); Leslie Bethell and Ian Roxborough (eds.), *Latin*

conspicuously, it is all but absent in many new histories of Latin America in the Cold War.[42]

Scenes from a long-distance relationship: theories, narrative structure and theses

While this book can build on the existing literature on Soviet–Latin American relations, it is the first to apply a trans-national perspective, looking at interactions between the two rather than conducting macro-historical comparisons, and it is the first one that is based on Soviet archival material. There is extensive and accessible documentation on officially organised cultural, intellectual and scientific exchanges in Russian state and Communist Party archives. Interviews as well as published memoirs, travelogues, scientific and popular journals, newspapers, fiction, plays, poetry, songs and films from Russian, Latin American and western archives, libraries and the internet have provided a much larger source base than previous scholars of Soviet–Latin American relations have had at their disposal. Instead of adding yet another study of Cold War politics, *Soviet Internationalism after Stalin* seeks to fathom possibilities to combine a global history of the Cold War with its home fronts in the Soviet Union and, to a lesser extent, in Latin America. The new impacts of the world abroad on the USSR after years of isolation did not initially weaken the Soviets' belief in the superiority of their own system, as contacts with the Western world did in the long run. As long as they were directed towards the Third World and especially Latin America, the first contacts actually supported and enforced the ideas the Soviets had about themselves in the world. Soviet internationalism after Stalin was a

---

America between the Second World War and the Cold War: Crisis and Containment, 1944–1948 (Cambridge: Cambridge University Press, 1997).

[42] Michael Grow, *US Presidents and Latin American Interventions: Pursuing Regime Change in the Cold War* (Lawrence: University Press of Kansas, 2008); Leslie Bethell and Ian Roxborough, 'The Impact of the Cold War on Latin America', in Melvyn Leffler (ed.), *Origins of the Cold War: An International History* (New York: Routledge, 2007), pp. 293–316; Sewall Menzel, *Dictators, Drugs and Revolution: Cold War Campaigning in Latin America 1965–1989* (Bloomington: AuthorHouse, 2006); Greg Grandin, *The Last Colonial Massacre: Latin America in the Cold War* (Chicago: University of Chicago Press, 2004); Jean Franco, *The Decline and Fall of the Lettered City: Latin America in the Cold War* (Cambridge, MA: Harvard University Press, 2002); Jorge G. Castañeda, *Utopia Unarmed: The Latin American Left after the Cold War* (New York: Vintage, 1994). A notable exception is Hal Brands's book, *Latin America's Cold War* (Cambridge, MA: Harvard University Press, 2010). Yet, while convincing in interpretation and style, his all-encompassing account remains at the level of traditional political Cold War history and does not include either cultural, intellectual and micro-historical aspects or new archival material from Russia.

combination of old socialist internationalism and the new impacts from worldwide cultural internationalism. With this combination of ideas, the Soviets revived and expanded their interactions with Latin America from the mid 1950s.

The first chapter looks at Soviet self-representation towards Latin Americans. A discursive analysis of a range of cultural diplomacy and other exchange activities asks not so much whether Soviet propaganda was true or misleading (a question rather easy to answer), but reconstructs the image that the Soviet Union after Stalin meant to create of itself abroad. In the second chapter, the perspective changes to the impact of Latin America on Soviet popular culture, music, cinema and literature. The appeal of these arts pre-dated but was again boosted by the Cuban Revolution, and it helped inculcate internationalist sentiments among Soviet artists, intellectuals and many ordinary citizens. Chapters 3 and 4 are dedicated to Latin American students and intellectuals as target groups of Soviet advances and carriers of certain ideas about the Soviet Union that went beyond communist ideology. Travelogues and memoirs by writers who visited the USSR are revealing about two aspects: firstly about how Latin American intellectuals perceived, after the revelations about Stalin's dictatorship, what many once considered a socialist paradise; secondly about how Soviet organisations still managed to keep them interested in the USSR. Interviews with alumni from Soviet universities add the recollections of Latin Americans who spent five to seven years of their youth, fully funded, in Soviet cities. Their perception of the Soviet Union, a recurrent topic of this book, was quite different from the western one. The fifth chapter switches back to Soviet agents and looks at Moscow's regional experts who dealt with Latin America. While roped in for political ends, they broadened scholarly knowledge on the world abroad and brought their internationalist idealism into organisations of the Soviet state.

In a composition that could be called 'scenes from a long-distance relationship', these five chapters constitute somewhat independent and self-contained stories, set into a chronological framework of political events from late Stalinism until the disintegration of the Soviet Union, with occasional recourses to the inter-war period. This build-up takes some inspiration from the construction kit of historical writing offered by *histoire croisée*: it overlaps two geographical areas and analyses how people from both sides interact. The focus is always on ideas, people and groups crossing from one side to the other, and on the ways in which these contacts shaped perceptions of the other and the self.[43]

---

[43] Michael Werner and Bénédicte Zimmermann, 'Histoire Croisée and the Challenge of Reflexivity', *History and Theory* 45/1 (2006), 30–50.

This conception, which looks at cultural products as indicators for political affairs, excludes topics that some may expect to be more in the foreground of a history set in the Cold War. Political economy and military crises are mentioned, yet they are not the focus of this book. The Cuban Revolution and, for that matter, the Chilean Frente Popular government under Salvador Allende appear only insofar as their repercussions in the Soviet Union are concerned. The Cuban Crisis is considered to be the best researched single episode in history; just as for the Sovietisation of the island from the late 1960s, there is little new to tell until archives in Havana become accessible. Cuban domestic developments and Soviet–Cuban relations of the 1970s and 1980s will require their separate, archive-based assessment in the future.

This book, instead, explores the re-opening of the Soviet Union to the world after the isolation of late Stalinism. The revival of internationalism within the framework of the Cold War proved, for a while, a rather successful contribution to the relaunching of the Soviet project, both towards internal and external audiences. Similar to the victory in the Second World War and the technological feats of the 1950s and 1960s, these successes were a source of legitimisation for the Soviet elite and an integrative ideational moment for Soviet society. The chronological focus of the first chapters of this book is on the period of the late 1950s and early 1960s, when Soviet internationalism after Stalin was first rekindled and acquired its strongest vogue. The idea of internationalism, however, lingered on through the 1970s and 1980s until it was finally buried during late perestroika. The final chapters also examine what internationalism meant in the late Soviet Union, when the optimism of the immediate post-Stalin years had given way to a more sober analysis of geo-politics. The analysis of Soviet internationalism after Stalin should thus contribute to a deeper understanding of both the second half of the history of the Soviet Union and the history of the Cold War from a southern perspective.

1 A modern image for the USSR: Soviet self-representation towards Latin Americans

A society is, above all, the idea it forms of itself.

Emile Durkheim, *The Elementary Forms of Religious Life*

As self-representation we shall consider the production of a text or functional equivalents of a text, with which and through which the organisation identifies itself.

Jürgen Habermas and Nikolas Luhmann, *Theorie der Gesellschaft oder Sozialtechnologie*

The cautious reconnecting of the Soviet Union with Latin America during the Thaw

One of the crucial characteristics of the changes in the mid 1950s, studied more by historians of the Cold War than by those of the Soviet Union, was that the new leadership under Nikita Khrushchev ended the extreme isolationism and fear of everything foreign that had prevailed during late Stalinism.[1] At the 20th Party Congress in 1956, Khrushchev announced that the Soviet Union sought a peaceful coexistence of the superpowers and spoke at length about the awakening of the colonial peoples and national liberation movements, including in Latin America. War between the ideological antagonists was no longer considered inevitable; international contacts with states of different social systems should

---

[1] The literature on the social history of the Thaw is abundant, but references to the international dimension are very scant. See Melanie Ilic (ed.), *Soviet State and Society under Nikita Khrushchev* (London: Routledge, 2009); Miriam Dobson, *Khrushchev's Cold Summer: Gulag Returnees, Crime, and the Fate of Reform after Stalin* (Ithaca: Cornell University Press, 2009); Jones (ed.), *The Dilemmas of De-Stalinization*; Ronald Grigor Suny, *The Cambridge History of Russia*, vol. III, *The Twentieth Century* (Cambridge: Cambridge University Press, 2006); Carsten Goehrke, *Sowjetische Moderne und Umbruch* (Zürich: Chronos, 2005); Melanie Ilic, Susan Emily Reid and Lynne Attwood (eds.), *Women in the Khrushchev Era* (Basingstoke: Palgrave Macmillan, 2004); Christoph Bluth, Stefan Plaggenborg and Manfred Hellmann, *Handbuch der Geschichte Russlands: 1945–1991. Vom Ende des Zweiten Weltkriegs bis zum Zusammenbruch der Sowjetunion* (Stuttgart: Hiersemann, 2003).

be established on political, cultural and scientific levels.[2] The Politburo confirmed this new foreign policy and it was suggested as general strategy at the first World Congress of Communist and Labour Parties in Moscow in November 1957.[3] The participants, including representatives from twenty Latin American countries, stated in what came to be known the Moscow Declaration. 'peaceful coexistence does not mean abandonment of class struggle ... it is a form of class struggle between socialism and capitalism. Peaceful coexistence offers good conditions for the national liberation movements of the peoples of the colonial and dependent countries.'[4]

The declaration found its way into the Communist Party of the Soviet Union (CPSU) programme draft of 1961, and at the 22nd Party Congress in 1962, Khrushchev specified four criteria for Soviet help: the national-democratic states, as the potentially Soviet-friendly non-communist countries in the global South were now called, were to refrain from joining military blocs and should not permit the establishment of military bases on their soil. They had to concede democratic rights for progressive organisations, labour unions and communist parties. They should confront or restrict western economic interests, and, finally, they should introduce reforms that aimed at improving social conditions in their countries. In fact, the Kremlin never cared about any of these criteria but the first.[5]

The notion of a categorically hostile capitalist world abroad was challenged. Before 1953, Soviet ideologists had considered Latin American presidents and dictators alike as class enemies and stooges of imperialism. Now they were lumped together with the heads of African and South Asian states as potential anti-imperialist allies of the Soviet Union in the peace camp. This new stance of the Soviet Union needed to be communicated to the old and potentially new friends of the USSR and, to this end, the Soviet Union invested more than US $2 billion a year in tremendously expanded foreign propaganda.[6]

The first advances to India, Egypt and a number of African countries from the mid 1950s were considered great successes, but in Latin America things still looked less promising for the Soviet Union. Most

---

[2] *Pravda*, 15 Feb. 1956.
[3] Fursenko, *Prezidium CK KPSS: 1954–1964*, p. 138; Barghoorn, *Soviet Foreign Propaganda*, p. 30.
[4] *New York Times*, 7 Dec. 1960.
[5] Brun and Hersh, *Soviet–Third World Relations in a Capitalist World*, pp. 39–40; Poppino, *International Communism in Latin America*, p. 169; Boris Ponomarev, 'O gosudarstve nacional'noj demokratii', *Kommunist* 8 (1961), 33–48.
[6] Belmonte, *Selling the American Way*, p. 67.

states had cut diplomatic ties with Moscow from 1947 under pressure from Washington. In 1954, the US Central Intelligence Agency (CIA) helped topple the Guatemalan president Jacobo Arbenz, who had legalised the communist Partido Guatemalteco del Trabajo (Guatemalan Party of Labour) and had admitted a small number of communists into his cabinet. In the tense geo-political situation, Guatemalan conservatives found it easy to paint a picture of international communist conspiracy, and the sale of some dysfunctional German weaponry by Czechoslovakia was enough to construct an account of Arbenz's Soviet ties that needed to be repelled.[7] Accordingly cautious were the allegations the following year by Soviet premier Nikolaj Bulganin in an interview to the Latin American journal *Visión* (found much later to be CIA-sponsored), in which he announced Soviet interest in interacting economically, politically and culturally with all states in the Americas without interference into their inner affairs.[8] Even so, Bulganin managed to get some contracts signed on economic and cultural collaboration with a series of South American states beginning with Argentina and Brazil. But Khrushchev wanted a bigger audience for Soviet internationalism in Latin America.

This first chapter will subject the ensuing Soviet self-representation towards Latin Americans to critical scrutiny, and it starts with a letter that Oleg Ignat'ev, head of the Soviet news agency Sovinformbjuro in Argentina, wrote to his superiors in Moscow in March 1957. In more than forty 'suggestions for the strengthening of Soviet propaganda in Latin America', Ignat'ev demanded more professional and more efficient Soviet activities. More modern technologies were to be used, and the focus should not be on political issues, but on Soviet literature, culture and geography instead. Customs of the western press should be considered, one's own shortcomings and hardships mentioned. The slow-moving behemoth Telegrafnoe Agenstvo Sovetskogo Sojuza (TASS), having failed so obviously in conveying to the world the 'necessity of the invasion of Hungary' the year before, should be replaced with a news agency that appealed also to non-communist 'progressive circles'. To ensure that the Soviet content was still recognised in the new form, Ignat'ev suggested that all staff of Soviet institutions be Soviets, most importantly the lower ranks such as translators and drivers. They were to show Soviet films on Soviet projectors and everyone was to be obliged to

[7] Brands, *Latin America's Cold War*, pp. 16–17.
[8] Welles Hangen, 'Soviet Makes Bid to Latin America for Economic Tie: Bulganin Offers Trade Deals and Aid on Pattern Set in Asia and Mideast. Foothold Believed Aim', *New York Times*, 17 Jan. 1956.

wear Soviet watches, write with Soviet pens, drive Soviet cars and smoke Soviet cigarettes.[9] Finally, Ignat'ev suggested something that would probably have cost him his job (or his head) just a few years earlier: to learn from the more successful enemy. The United States, he reported, had numerous staff in their embassies dealing solely with cultural affairs, they issued a colourful brochure about life in the United States, and they broadcast their Voice of America daily in Spanish. Thanks to private holdings such as those of the United Press, the 'Yankees' also exerted considerable influence on the bulk of Latin American media and news agencies.

Ignat'ev gained support for his appeal when a Soviet cultural delegation to Uruguay later that year reported, in a very similar vein, on the predominance of US cultural diplomacy and its effectiveness in establishing the United States as a role model. After their return to Moscow, they listed the US activities in detail, explained how their libraries and language classes functioned and which periodicals they distributed – and reported that they encouraged youngsters to study in the United States.[10] The Soviet delegation suggested learning from the US programmes and found open ears for their call in the Moscow headquarters of the Vsesojuznoe Obščestvo Kul'turnoj Svjazi s Zagranicej (All-Union Organisation for Cultural Contacts, VOKS), the official Soviet authority for cultural exchange, which agreed to using all the information gathered on US cultural diplomacy for Soviet interests.[11]

As a result, ever higher numbers of copies of Soviet print media were sent to the Americas, and expanding hours of Soviet radio broadcasts reached most of their territories. Soviet artists, intellectuals and political representatives travelled across the South Atlantic on official missions. Large exhibitions were held in Argentina, Uruguay, Mexico, Cuba and Brazil. Ever more Latin Americans were invited, for officially staged short visits as well as for lengthy stays, to the Soviet Union, which now turned especially to the youth of the global South. This chapter analyses the image of itself the Soviet Union tried to convey through all these activities. In order to reach its broadened target groups, it will become obvious, the Soviet Union downplayed the communist character of its political system remarkably and instead flaunted its cultural and technological achievements. This self-representation drew on elements of

---

[9] O. Ignat'ev G. Žukovu v GKKS. Predloženija po usilenju našej propagandy v stranach Latinskoj Ameriki, 8 Mar. 1957, GARF f.9518 op.1 d.39 ll.168–184.
[10] Spravka ob Amerikano-Urugvajskom Kul'turnom Al'janse, 5 May 1958, GARF f.9518 op.1 d.398 ll.35–38.
[11] 11 Feb. 1958, GARF f.9576 op.8 d.4 ll.149.

socialist internationalism of the 1920s and 1930s, with its foreign propaganda on the one hand and the experience of the modernisation of the Central Asian and Caucasian inner periphery on the other. But the references to the United States made it clear: Soviet cultural advances to the Third World from the 1950s stood also in the context of quite similar activities of the ideological foes in the West (and, to a lesser extent, of China). In the field of cultural diplomacy, the Soviet Union and the United States not only competed, but also mutually influenced each other's self-representation, and in doing so shaped a great deal of what Akira Iriye has called 'cultural internationalism' under the conditions of the global Cold War.[12]

Cultural activities of the Soviet state are usually referred to as 'propaganda', but the word carries heavy semantic ballast. Harking back to papal missions in the sixteenth century, the term has been given a distinctly pejorative connotation in today's common parlance by virtue of Nazi and Stalinist propaganda. Yet both sides of the Cold War used the word extensively. The Soviets did so decidedly affirmatively: '"propaganda"', a *Sovinformbjuro* member recalled later, 'means simply what 'public diplomacy' does in western terminology'.[13] But westerners used 'propaganda' as well, usually derogatorily for Soviet activities, but indeed also as an analytical term.[14] And, as a former high-ranking member of the United States Information Agency (USIA) explained, they even used it in an affirmative sense for their own activities: 'propaganda, that is to distribute information, selectively but credibly, with the aim of making other peoples think and act according to [US-] American interest.'[15]

To avoid this normativity, the terms 'cultural diplomacy' and 'public diplomacy' seem more useful than 'propaganda' as analytical categories. They have been defined as attempts to 'portray a country to another country's people in order to help achieve certain foreign policy goals. This self-portrayal includes the transfer and exchange of cultural media and representatives as well as the exchange of students, teachers, professors, government representatives and others, as long as it is at least directed and sponsored in part by government offices.'[16] Yet cultural

---

[12] Iriye, *Cultural Internationalism and World Order.*

[13] Karen Chačaturov, *Tri znaka vremeni: polveka v meždunarodnoj žurnalistike* (Moscow: Meždunarodnye Otnošenija, 2002), p. 10.

[14] E.g. Belmonte, *Selling the American Way*; Nicolas Cull, *The Cold War and the United States Information Agency: American Propaganda and Public Diplomacy, 1945–1989* (Cambridge: Cambridge University Press, 2008).

[15] Thomas Sorensen, *The Word War: The Story of American Propaganda* (New York: Harper & Row, 1968), p. 17.

[16] Manuela Aguilar, *Cultural Diplomacy and Foreign Policy: German–American Relations 1955–1968* (New York: Peter Lang, 1996), p. 8.

diplomacy and public diplomacy are not perfectly adequate terms either for the activities presented in this chapter for two reasons. Firstly, it is impossible to separate reliably where cultural/public diplomacy ends and propaganda begins.[17] Secondly, 'cultural diplomacy' is confined to a more or less immediate political purpose – 'in order to help achieve certain policy goals.' While the political dimension is important, this functionalistic perspective of cultural/public diplomacy includes only parts of a larger set of activities of Soviet 'self-representation'.

In any renewed contact with the world abroad, the Soviets presented a certain image of themselves. This image can be defined as an idealised version of the world that Soviet internationalists believed themselves to live in – or as they believed it should be. It reflected their political imagination, their world-view, their intellectual horizon, their conception of the state they lived in, and the role they were to play in it. By conveying this image to foreigners, these internationalists tried to mould actively what the rest of the world thought of the Soviet Union.

Image – and this is applicable also to similar activities of western states at the time – did not necessarily directly reflect a reality behind it: the term 'self-representation' goes beyond questions of deceit and truth, and captures the ideational, or 'discursive', basis of agency and power instead. That Soviet realities did not comply with their beautified depictions abroad is hardly surprising. In this chapter, Soviet self-representation will be taken at face value, not for the 'real content' behind the signs, but for the signs themselves. Shortcomings and discrepancies – and downright lies – behind the official picture will be pointed out occasionally, but the main interest is the official discourse itself.

Soviet cultural activities in the Third World, which began after the death of Stalin, took place in a complex web of Soviet conditions, local circumstances and US activities. Not only did it influence the target audience and finally also the US adversary, but it had its impacts on the Soviet Union itself, its politicians, its intellectuals and indeed the entire population. What is called here 'Soviet self-representation' defines not just one co-ordinated arm of foreign policy, but the sum of all

---

[17] There is absolutely no coherent concept of the terms 'propaganda' and 'cultural/public diplomacy' in the literature. Some scholars differentiate normatively between the ideal types 'non-reliable, non-transparent, short term' vs 'reliable, transparent, long-ranging', or 'offensive, ideological goals' vs 'decent, humble goals'. Others see 'cultural diplomacy' as only a 'euphemism for "propaganda"'; or they differentiate 'black propaganda' as deliberate misinformation from 'white propaganda' that merely cultivates a certain state image. See Johannes Paulmann (ed.), *Auswärtige Repräsentationen: Deutsche Kulturdiplomatie nach 1945* (Cologne: Böhlau, 2005), p. 4.

endeavours, from different institutions and people, which were to convey a certain image of the Soviet state. This chapter will analyse how the Soviet Union strove to present itself to the outer world. This politically initiated self-representation to foreigners was one integral part of Soviet internationalism after Stalin, and it opened up spaces of interaction between the Soviet Union and Latin America that, in the long run, went beyond the control of the state.

Predecessors and new institutions

Both the idea of peaceful coexistence and the efforts to present oneself in a positive light to the world abroad were not entirely new to the Soviets. Seeking ideological orientation, Soviet theorists in the mid 1950s could find inspiration not only from the contemporary world abroad, but also from their own past: in the early days of Soviet Russia, the Bolsheviks were already seeking to stabilise their power through a number of pragmatic ideological adjustments. Alignments with non-communist but anti-imperialist states should counterbalance western hostility against the Soviets at the international level. The concept of a *nekapitalističeskij put' razvitija* (non-capitalist path of development), which justified collaboration with countries that did not have a socialist revolution, was applied to Mongolia first and later to a number of other states, such as nascent Turkey and nationalist China. National political freedom, the theory had it, was the first precondition for utter independence, which could come only at a later stage, when western economic dominance would be overcome. The Soviets renounced this policy after Chiang Kai-shek had tens of thousands of Chinese communists killed in a 1927 massacre. From 1930, the theory of non-capitalist development was taken out of the Comintern statutes, and it was revived only under Khrushchev. 'Peaceful coexistence', though, was not created by Khrushchev: in October 1952, CPSU secretary Georgij Malenkov, replacing the ailing Stalin at the 19th Congress, had already hinted at a possibility of *mirnoe sosuščestvovanie* ('peaceful coexistence'). Stalin himself had repeated this to a visiting Argentine economic delegation later that month.[18]

As for making themselves heard in the Americas, the Soviets certainly had some experience as well. The Comintern had opened a regional office in Montevideo in 1929, and two attempts at spreading world revolution to the Americas failed shortly thereafter: in a 1932 insurrection

---

[18] Brun and Hersh, *Soviet–Third World Relations in a Capitalist World*, p. 37; James Richard Carter, *The Net Cost of Soviet Foreign Aid* (New York: Praeger, 1969), p. 5.

in El Salvador, the local communist party under Farabundo Martí joined an on-going peasant revolt that was soon to be crushed in a bloody massacre. The only Comintern-conducted attempt at revolution in the Americas took place in Brazil in 1935, when communists reacted to the oppression of the union movement, proclaimed Luis Carlos Prestes president and were finally defeated, had their party declared illegal and began to be persecuted.

By the mid 1930s, the Comintern had learned the lesson that the revolutionary potential of the Americas was much more limited than they had hoped for. Not only were the proletariat small and the structures predominantly agrarian (which had been the case, too, in Russia in 1917); more importantly, the area was under the unchallengeable influence of the United States. The new policy was thus to follow the parliamentary path and seek to form popular fronts with other parties, in order to avoid sinking into insignificance. In their internal structures, the Latin American communist parties, like many others worldwide during Stalinism, went through a process of bureaucratisation, hierarchisation, enacting servile obedience to Moscow's orders and the exclusion of real or ostensible 'Trotskyites'. Most notably, the muralist painter Diego Rivera had to leave the Communist Party of Mexico as early as 1929. He later hosted Leon Trotsky in his Mexico City house, where the latter was murdered in 1942.

From the mid 1920s, however, the Soviet Union was not only already supporting the structures of international communism in Latin America, but also seeking to establish 'normal' relations at state level. Mexico, with its own recent revolutionary past, was the first state in the Americas to officially recognise the Soviets in 1924; the feminist and Marxist thinker Aleksandra Kollontaj was sent as the first Soviet representative (and the world's first female ambassador) to Mexico City, where she enjoyed an excellent reputation. In Uruguay, the USSR organised its trade with all South America from its Montevideo Južamtorg (the Russian acronym for 'South American trade') office and established diplomatic relations in 1926. Colombia, without exchanging diplomats, recognised the Soviet government in 1935. Mexico and Uruguay temporarily interrupted their relations, but the Second World War brought Latin America and the Soviet Union closer than ever: thirteen states, all the major ones except Peru and Nicaragua, recognised diplomatically what was now their ally in the war against the Axis powers. During this time, and for the first time in many Latin American states, communism found a broad following also beyond small circles of intellectuals and artists, and the reputation of the Soviets was at an all-time high. It did not last long.

With the onset of the Cold War from 1947, the US State Department demanded Latin American governments break relations with Moscow; all but Mexico, Uruguay and Argentina did. Statements by high-ranking communists that they would, in the event of war, rather support the Soviet Union than their own countries, did not endear the communist parties to a broader public. In the early 1950s, they were banned in most states; with the exceptions of Cuba and Chile, party communism had ceased to play a serious role in Latin American politics.[19] During late Stalinism, Moscow leaders, if they had any idea of the world abroad at all, saw Latin America as again dominated by a strong oligarchy, backed by a conservative church and reactionary armies, and heavily dependent on the United States.[20] The Bucharest-based Cominform, the puny successor of the disbanded Comintern, opened an office in Buenos Aires, which circulated commands to the Latin American communist parties. Beyond that, Latin America all but disappeared from Moscow's radar.

After the end of Stalinism, however, Soviet 'propaganda' had a new target group. No longer did it attempt to win people over to party communism (as it still did in eastern Europe). The Soviet state now presented itself to the Third World as a role model of non-western development and as an altruistic helper with its own model of fast modernisation. But in order to more successfully address non-communist political leaders and entire populations on a truly global scale, the Soviet Union urgently needed to refurbish its methods and therefore its institutions.

The Cominform was replaced with a publishing board of the multi-language journal *Problemy mira i socializma* (Problems of Peace and Socialism, *World Marxist Review* in the English edition) in Prague. The Comintern apparatus had already been re-organised within the Central Committee of the Communist Party. The organ changed its name and leadership several times until, from 1955, Boris Ponomarev headed what was called the 'International Department of the Central Committee'. It oversaw the work of several front organisations and institutions that were to promote the Soviet way of life abroad. The conduct of cultural relations was now under direct Party control.[21] Having secured its tight grip

---

[19] Bethell and Roxborough, 'The Impact of the Cold War on Latin America', p. 315; Goldenberg, *Kommunismus in Lateinamerika*, pp. 121–6; Poppino, *International Communism in Latin America*, p. 32.

[20] Prizel, *Latin America through Soviet Eyes*, p. 1.

[21] Jurij Poljakov, 'Posle rospuska Kominterna', *Novaja i Novejšaja Istorija* 1 (2003), 106–16; Gould-Davies, 'The Logic of Soviet Cultural Diplomacy', 203.

on these institutions, the Party concealed this influence in their presentation to the outer world.

From the 1920s, VOKS had organised much of the Soviet Union's foreign propaganda, most notably the notorious visits of hundreds of foreign intellectuals. Its name, somewhat discredited internationally, was changed to Sojuz Sovetskich Obščestv Družby (Union of Soviet Friendship Societies, SSOD) in early 1958. While VOKS had only had one department for the United States and Latin America together, the SSOD quickly developed a refined regional differentiation. In 1959, SSOD deputy Viktor Goršakov invited the ambassadors of Argentina, Mexico and Uruguay and many Soviet artists to the founding ceremony of the Soviet–Latin American Friendship Association. He drew parallels between the fight against the Spanish monarchy in the Americas and the Soviets' struggle against the tsar; instead of communist innuendos, there was talk about Russian scientists in the Americas in the nineteenth century. The Armenian composer Aram Khachaturian was elected president of the association and gave a long, rambling speech on Soviet enthusiasm about Latin America: 'never will the tropical exoticism, palms and orchids, parrots and alligators keep us from acknowledging the pride of the Latin American peoples, their diligence, their fight, their history, culture, their pursuits and dreams'.[22]

Friendship societies came into being with most states on earth. By 1964, these circles were already showing the allegedly peaceful nature and the cultural, scientific and technological advances of the Soviet Union in fourteen Latin American countries, and their numbers grew until the 1980s. They distributed books, journals, newspapers and scientific literature, organised the exchange of delegations and students, and held photo exhibitions or Russian tea afternoons.[23]

Several groups and organisations that were founded independently by Latin Americans came under the umbrella of SSOD, too. The first had been founded by the Mexican writer José Mancisidor as early as the 1920s; in 1944, the liberal Colombian president Alfonso López Pumarejo not only established diplomatic relations with the war ally USSR, but also supported the foundation of the Instituto Cultural Colombo-Soviético. Run by local intellectuals in La Candelaria, the old centre of Bogotá, it soon opened local branches in the Colombian cities of

---

[22] Vladimir Pechatnov, 'Exercise in Frustration: Soviet Foreign Propaganda in the Early Cold War', *Cold War History* 1/2 (2000), 16; Stenogramma sobranija učreditelej Sovetskoj associacii družby i kul'turnogo sotrudničestva so stranami Latinskoj Ameriki, 22 Nov. 1959, GARF f.9676 op.2 d.109 ll.21–32.

[23] Anon., 'Auf Freundschaftsbahnen', *Kultur und Leben* 12 (1971), 38; Poppino, *International Communism in Latin America*, p. 136.

Medellín and Cali. A similar institution, the Instituto Cubano-Soviético, came into being the year after in Havana. Like the Instituto Argentina–URSS in Buenos Aires and several other Argentine towns, they all boasted their own libraries, offered Russian language classes, staged plays, supported the translation of literature, edited their own journals and attracted huge crowds with their regularly screened Soviet documentary and feature films – almost half a million people saw films at the Buenos Aires branch in 1958 alone. Deeply impressed after a visit to Argentina, the poet Pablo Neruda went back to replicate the local structure of the association in his native Chile. In Mexico, Diego Rivera headed a similar organisation from 1944.[24]

All these groups, loosely based around the communist parties, leftists and liberals, appointed their chairmen autonomously, organised events and even maintained direct contact with other branches in Soviet republics and all over the world without explicit command from Moscow. But they of course depended heavily on its financial and material resources. For the Soviet Union, they proved a relatively cheap and uncomplicated means of promoting its goals abroad without directly involving the politically problematic communist parties.[25]

The local friendship societies had their counterparts within the Soviet Union, which were under the direct control of the SSOD. By the end of the 1960s, the Dom Družby (House of Friendship), the SSOD headquarters in the Arbat, co-ordinated 56 of these institutes with 745 branches all over the Soviet Union. Around 17,000 co-operative members (Workers' Collective of the Čeljabinsk Institute of Mechanisation, Sovkhoz Družba in Ivanovo etc.) and an impressive number of 40 million plus Soviet citizens were at least nominally members of these international clubs. This does not tell us too much about the amount of activity and motivation all these people displayed, but it does give an idea of how important the Soviet state considered a proper internationalist stance among its population.[26]

As for the image these clubs were to send abroad, it is interesting to note that their chairmen were usually internationally renowned Soviet celebrities, not communist politicians. The film-maker Lev Kulidžanov was the long-time president of the Soviet–Mexican society; Aram Khachaturian headed the umbrella organisation and often appeared

[24] Vera Kutejščikova, *Moskva-Meksiko-Moskva: doroga dlinoju v žizn'* (Moscow: AkademProekt, 2000), p. 144.
[25] Romanovskij, *Meždunarodnye naučnye i kul'turnye svjazi SSSR*, p. 115; Popowa, 'Über die Tätigkeit und die Aufgaben des Verbandes der Freundschaftsgesellschaften'.
[26] Anon., 'Reiz des Exotischen, Fernen', *Kultur und Leben* 4 (1965), 36–7; Margarita Fadeicheva, 'Friends from All Countries Meet Here', *Moscow News* 26 (1962), 8–9.

publicly with his fellow members, the violinist David Ojstrach and the cosmonaut Valentina Tereškova. When the Soviet–Cuban Friendship Society was inaugurated in 1964, no less a figure than superhero Yuri Gagarin served as president, and the Azeri composer Raúf Gadžiev served as his deputy in the Baku branch.[27] While popular figures represented Soviet internationalism externally, orders were still given in the International Department of the Central Committee.

In addition to the structures of the SSOD, the Gosudarstvennyj Komitet Kul'turnych Svjazej (State Committee for Cultural Relations, GKKS. came into being in 1957. The GKKS was responsible for the final implementation of most cultural foreign representational activities in the ten years of its existence. Its officials did collaborate with local communist parties, but whenever they negotiated with foreign authorities in Soviet missions and embassies they were supposed to show a certain distance from the CPSU and to represent the Soviet state. Officially, the administration of international radio broadcasts, the publication of literature in foreign languages and news agencies were subject to the GKKS. But, as acknowledged by its first chairman Georgij Žukov, the ones really pulling the strings sat in the Central Committee. The preface of its charter states clearly that the GKKS had no discretionary rights and was purely an executive organ for information and propaganda. The Ministry of Foreign Affairs, *id est* the Soviet state, had indeed no say in the matter – a source of continuing friction, until the GKKS was finally disbanded in 1967, and the foreign ministry got its own Cultural Department. The GKKS, too, came to be subdivided into regional departments. From 1959, the future ambassador to Cuba and Argentina Aleksandr Alekseev, a former NKVD agent, was in charge of Latin American affairs.[28]

The GKKS employees had to report to the Central Committee of the CPSU, the foreign ministry and the ministry of culture. When the latter two suggested activities, however, they needed the approval of either the International or the Cultural Department of the Central Committee of the Party.[29] This caused impressive amounts of bureaucratic paperwork and rivalry between the downgraded ministries. Considering the highly centralised character of the Soviet political system, it is striking how

---

[27] Stenogramma sobranija učreditelej obščestva sovetsko-kubinskoj družby, 2 Nov. 1964, GARF f.9576 op.2 d.187 ll.1–16.

[28] Gould-Davies, 'The Logic of Soviet Cultural Diplomacy', 206; Kasack, 'Kulturelle Außenpolitik', p. 386; Correspondence between the GKKS and the Communist Party of Brazil, 9 Mar. 1961, RGANI f.5 op.36 d.136 ll.27–29; O sozdanii GKKS pri Soveta Ministrov, 4 Mar. 1957, GARF f.5446 op.1 d.662 l.236.

[29] One representative example can be found in Ministerstvo Kul'tury Central'nomu Komitetu KPSS, 21 Dec. 1959, RGANI f.5 op.36 d.102.

cultural diplomacy was fragmented among various competing organs.[30] The GKKS and the SSOD took on the bulk of the tasks and will be in the foreground of this chapter's analyses. But in addition several more front organisations contributed to foreign propaganda. Numerous anti-fascist committees, women's associations, the central committee of the trades unions, publishing houses and radio committees had their international departments for the various parts of the world. All of them were explicitly required to propagate Soviet achievements abroad.

Alongside the long-established news agency TASS, the Sovinformb-juro in particular was in charge of news provision for the foreign non-communist audience. In 1961, it was given the more neutral and modern name Novosti (or Agenstvo Pečati 'Novosti', Press Agency 'News', APN) and given the official status of a non-Party affiliated public organ-isation. The Sovinformbjuro had already set up an office in Mexico back in 1954. Officials there complained that a lack of co-ordination between the responsible organs limited the vast range of opportunities for the Soviet Union in Latin America. Anti-imperialist thought also prevailed in the bourgeoisie, they reported. Many national-liberation and democra-tisation movements would be susceptible to Moscow's approaches.[31] So Moscow approached.

A modern idyll: the image of the USSR in Soviet media in Latin America

Soviet self-representation in Latin America began with the longest-lasting Soviet global propaganda activity, the distribution of journals. The few English or French samples of VOKS magazine that may have reached Latin America from the 1930s entertained their fairly narrow range of – predominantly communist – international readers with articles such as 'Capital Setup in Soviet Agriculture' and much ideology and statistics. Other internationally distributed journals included *Soviet Cul-ture in the Making*, *USSR* and *Literature in the Soviet Union*. They had in common an almost exclusive focus on Soviet issues, with some asides on the iniquities of western capitalism.

During the great reforms of Soviet media from the mid 1950s, these international publications changed their face.[32] For one thing, they were

---

[30] Pechatnov, 'Exercise in Frustration', 7.
[31] Otčet o rabote predstavitelja SIB v Meksike tov. V. Masjukeviča, undated, GARF f.9518 op.1 d.343 ll.20–27.
[32] Thomas Wolfe, *Governing Soviet Journalism: The Press and the Socialist Person after Stalin* (Bloomington: Indiana University Press, 2005); Mark W. Hopkins, *Mass Media in the Soviet Union* (New York: Pegasus, 1970), pp. 265–96.

translated into ever more foreign languages, including Spanish and later Portuguese. With the advent of decolonisation, they increasingly covered Third World stories, and the layout became more and more appealing. The grey and highly ideologised political journal *War and the Working Class* became the colourful *New Times*, one of the most popular Soviet international monthly illustrated reviews, which, from the mid 1950s, was also translated into Spanish (*Nuevos Tiempos*) and sent to Latin America. By 1954, it had been joined by three more translated magazines: *USSR* became *Unión Soviética*; Soviet literature now presented itself in *Literatura Soviética*; and Latin American women could join the internationalist feminist call by reading *Mujér Soviética*, the translation of *Soviet Woman*.[33] In regular evaluations, the Cultural Department of the Central Committee usually commended the editors, but demanded journals address a broader – not purely communist – readership by 'adapting to local customs'. According to the Soviet officials responsible, this meant the 'frequent use of terms such as *elections, decision* and *resolution*' as well as 'more humour and modern language'.[34] An entire series of reports called for the further improvement and more accessibility of Soviet journals for an international readership. The Soviet embassy in Mexico suggested to the foreign ministry in Moscow that the layout of the magazines should be further refined. More illustrations and photos were necessary; articles should be less about politics and more about technology and science, culture, sports, women and children.[35] In a long letter in the same vein to the GKKS, they repeated their suggestions and added samples of similar brochures distributed by the Japanese, British and US embassies.[36]

Besides the GKKS magazines, local dependencies of the friendship societies and the embassies themselves also began to publish bulletins in large print runs – Argentines, for example, had a choice between *Novedades de la Unión Soviética* (News from the Soviet Union) twice a week and a *Bulletin Argentina–URSS* with 20,000 copies weekly.[37] The monthly *Kul'tura i žizn'* (Culture and Life), with an inglorious past in the forefront of the anti-cosmopolitan campaigns in the late 1940s, was available from 1957 as *Cultura y Vida* firstly in Argentina, Mexico and

---

[33] Spisok sovetskich žurnalov v Latinskoj Amerike v 1954g., undated, GARF f.5283 op.14 d.631 l.30.

[34] El. Romanova: O žurnale Sovetskoj Literaturoj, 2 Feb. 1957, RGANI f.5 op.36 d.36 l.2.

[35] 13 May 1957, GARF f.9518 op.1 d.343 ll.2–4.

[36] 12 Jun. 1957, GARF f.9518 op.1 d.343 ll.4–45. Very similar is an entire series of suggestions from the Sovinformbjuro in Mexico, RGANI f.5 op.36 d.194 ll.285–297.

[37] Spravka SSOD, 11 Feb. 1958, GARF f.9576 op.8 d.4 l.149.

Brazil, and later all over the continent – now with a focus on internationalist topics.[38] With many photos and rather similar to *Nuevos Tiempos*, it
conceptualised a positive, colourful image of the Soviet Union. From
July 1962, the editing house Meždunarodnaja Kniga (The International
Book) sent its own newspaper to Chile, Uruguay, Brazil and Cuba.
Moscow News, the oldest Soviet newspaper for an international audience,
had been shut down in 1949, and its Jewish editor Michail Borodin had
been sent to die in the Gulag. In 1956, the paper was relaunched and,
with an additional Spanish edition, *Novedades de Moscú*, also reached
readers all across the Americas, featuring many photos and articles on
cultural exchanges, visits and travel to the Soviet Union, friendship
between peoples, student exchange, sport, cars, technology, the cosmos,
stories of ordinary Soviet people and the development of the Soviet
periphery.

Eventually, some twenty Soviet magazines regularly found their way to
all Latin American countries, first in Spanish and later also in Portuguese. Some provided specialist literature or still discussed Marxist
theory (*Ciencias Sociales, Comercio Exterior, América Latina, Problemas
del Extremo Oriente, Revista Militar Soviética, Socialismo: Teoría y Practica*
and *Problemas del Paz y del Socialismo*). Yet to a much broader audience,
*Nuevos Tiempos, Cultura y Vida, El Teatro Soviético, El Siglo XX y la Paz,
El Libro y el Arte en la URSS, Film Soviético, Deporte en el URSS* and
Sputnik presented an idealised version of every walk of Soviet life. They
were all shipped first through diplomatic and communist party channels,
mainly via Mexico City and Buenos Aires, and later through Havana.
Fiction and technical literature joined the periodicals in increasing
numbers. US contemporary observers estimated the number of Soviet
publications available in Latin America at more than 400 already in
1957. The annual cost of more than US$ 100 million was usually
covered by trade agreements, lest hard foreign exchange had to be
spent.[39]

The immediate impact of these journals should not be overestimated.
Other than some cultural institutions, libraries and universities, only a
few people actually subscribed to them.[40] Added to that, in numerous
right-wing military dictatorships, the postal service tried to prevent the

---

[38] Ilja Ehrenburg, *Menschen, Jahre, Leben: Memoiren* (Berlin: Volk und Welt, 1977), pp. iii,
258.
[39] Poppino, *International Communism in Latin America*, p. 170; Alexander, *Communism in
Latin America*, p. 42.
[40] As late as 1972, for instance, there were no more than 200 private subscriptions in
Ecuador: Spisok periodičeskich izdanij dlja Ekvadora (avia), undated [1972], GARF
f.9576 op.10 d.164 ll.112–114.

distribution of Soviet print media. Officials in Moscow regularly received letters of complaint about journals that had not arrived.[41] In some cases, people faced persecution simply for reading Soviet material, as a Bolivian told Khachaturian in a letter – from prison.[42] What makes these journals interesting, regardless, is the way in which the Soviet Union represented itself in them: modelled on US journals such as *Life* and *Look*, these new Soviet glossy journals combined reports on high culture, technology, sports, scientific achievements, fashion, folklore and the private lives of stars and heroes. They mainly presented an ostensibly harmonious view of Soviet everyday life and gave some information on the worldwide struggle for development and against imperialism. The virgin lands campaign in Kazakhstan, and the Soviet inner periphery of Central Asia and the Caucasus overall, occupied much space in these new journals. Having undergone a socialist development programme directed by Moscow, they were presented as role models for the modernisation of the Third World. Modern agriculture, industry, water supply and housing compounds as well as science, health care and even theatres and the arts were allegedly blossoming everywhere in Central Asia. Between all these photos of young and active people, happy children and smiling girls with flowers, the absence of politics and even of the word 'communism' is striking. Through its international journals, the Soviet Union gave itself the image of an industrialised, independent, modern, idyllic state with a healthy and happy population.

Moscow speaking Quechua

Just like the journals, Soviet international radio had its predecessors in the 1930s. As early as 1932, Radio Moscow broadcast its very first programme in Spanish to Spain and Latin America, a first Portuguese one following in 1935. On a regular basis, however, broadcasting to the Americas started only in the year of Stalin's death. The 33 hours per week in 1953 increased to 219 hours plus 130 hours from Cuba in 1961.[43] The Soviets now even made the considerable effort to conceptualise shows in indigenous languages of South America, in Quechua, Guaraní and Aymara. Soviet radio, too, now tried to appeal to a larger audience. Political news was not abandoned, but 'Moscow Radio Informs and Comments' was only a fifteen-minute opener to the daily

---

[41] One example of many is Luis Herida, president of Bolivian association of authors, complaining to SSOD, 25 Nov. 1965, GARF f.9576 op.10 d.56 l.23.

[42] Aurelio Angulo to Aram Chačaturian, 7 May 1967, GARF f.9576 op.10 d.73.

[43] Boris Volov, 'Aquí Moscú: con motivo del 50 aniversario de Radio Moscú en español', *América Latina* 9 (1982), 97–111; Bayram Riza and Catherine Quirk, 'Cultural Relations between the Soviet Union and Latin America', *Studies on the Soviet Union* 2 (1968), 32.

show 'Sobesednik'. The rest of the programme was devoted to the scientific, economic and cultural achievements of the Soviet Union and eastern Europe's peoples' democracies. The virgin lands campaigns, Siberian landscapes, travels to the cosmos and the modernisation of Central Asia were typical segments. A Portuguese-language show in January 1959 looked like this: the head of a boarding school in Tashkent gave an account of the changes in the educational system of his native Uzbekistan, whose pre-revolutionary history was compared, unfavourably, to its progress under Soviet rule. Next came a feature on the evildoings of US imperialism in Panama, followed by reports about Soviet agriculture, medicine and energy production.[44] Finally, letters to Moscow were read – hence the title 'Dialogue Partner'.

The success of the radio shows is difficult to estimate. Numbers of listeners are hardly measurable, and the Soviets seem not to have tried to find out who was actually tuning in. Yet, as with the printed media, an interesting change took place in the mid 1950s. For one thing, the great effort to broadcast a full programme in several rare languages in order to inform the other part of the world about its achievements indicates something about the considerable extent of Soviet self-confidence of that time. In 1964, a new Moscow radio station started to broadcast exclusively to the Americas: Radio Progreso was founded on the initiative of the SSOD and put under the direction of Anatolij Sofronov.[45] Moreover, like the journals, Soviet radio smartened up its appearance. Some shows still featured debates on Marxist theory, the falsifications of the western media or Lenin's legacy on Soviet–Latin American relations. But 'peace', 'progress' and 'development' ousted 'revolution' and 'communism' as catchphrases. Reports on tourism to the Soviet Union, on technological feats, cultural events, sports news and the Sunday afternoon show on philately added completely apolitical elements, as did a weekly show by Latin American students at Soviet universities, who shared their experiences with their compatriots back home.[46]

Finally, films also conveyed this new image of the USSR to Latin America. Sovexportfilm, the state-run film distributer, opened a permanent office in Buenos Aires in the 1950s.[47] The Soviet ambassador to

[44] Govorit Moskva, Komitet po radioveščeniju, otdel Latinskaja Amerika, 14 Jan. 1959, GARF f.6903 op.24 d.242 ll.37–59.
[45] *Izvestija*, 24 Jul. 1964.
[46] Anon., 'Escuche diariamente Radio Moscú', *Boletín del Instituto Cultural Colombo Soviético* 5–6 (1974), 7; L. Novikov, 'Golos Mira: k 40-letiju radioveščanija na Latinskuju Ameriku', *Latinskaja Amerika* 9 (1972), 144.
[47] Posol'stvo SSSR v Argentine, GKKS (1965), undated, GARF f.9518 op.1 d.321 l.1; Ministr Kul'tury CK, 28 Nov. 1959, RGANI f.5 op.36 d.114 l.99.

Argentina, Aleksandr Alekseev, reported in the mid 1960s that Soviet films were seen by an average of 2 million Argentines alone. Soviet film-makers again produced internationally competitive films that gained attention and respect. Michail Kalatozov's *Letjat žuravli* (The Cranes Are Flying), to pick but the most famous example, had won the Palme d'Or in Cannes in 1958 and also touched an audience of millions in Latin America with its tragic love story set during the Second World War. Modernisation, human interest stories and the depiction of the USSR as a successful, cultured and idyllic modern state had replaced communism and class struggle in Soviet media abroad.

Don't mention communism! Technology and high-brow culture in Soviet self-representation

It was not just paper, celluloid and airwaves that were to transmit the new Soviet image. In a move towards rather more conventional European cultural diplomacy, the Kremlin began sending artists and sportspeople of all kinds abroad. In April 1956, the famous violinists David Ojstrach and Leonid Kogan travelled with pianist Tatjana Nikolaeva to Argentina, Chile and Uruguay. In Buenos Aires alone, an audience of 3,000 was enthralled by their performances. Igor' Bezrodnyj followed later that year. Together with pianist Evgenij Malinin and the Armenian mezzo-soprano Zara Dolukhanova, he gave sixty concerts in Uruguay, Argentina, Ecuador, Peru, Costa Rica, Mexico and Cuba. Pianist Sergej Dorenskij played Chopin and Rachmaninoff in Rio de Janeiro. Coming back to tour Latin America many times, they all played standard works of classical music, Bach, Tchaikovsky or Vivaldi, but also pieces by Soviet composers Dmitri Shostakovich and Sergei Prokofiev, which were heard for the first time in the Americas on these occasions. Shostakovich himself went to play in Mexico in early 1959 and again in 1962.[48] Aram Khachaturian, third of the big three of Soviet composers, was also head of the Latin American section of the SSOD. He toured Mexico, Venezuela, Colombia and Cuba in early 1960 and again in 1962.[49] It is telling of this new Soviet cultural diplomacy that, in the preparation for his trips, all organisations tried hard to make sure he was perceived only as an artist, not as a Soviet official.[50]

---

[48] S. Dorenski, 'In Brasilien', *Kultur und Leben* 1 (1960), 53–5; Igor Besrodny, 'Von Argentinien bis Kuba', *Neue Zeit* 51 (1956), 28–31; Igor Bezrodny, 'Seventy-Five Days in Latin America', *Moscow News* 94 (1956).

[49] Spravka o sostojanii i perspektivach razvitija kul'turnich i naučnich svjazej meždu SSSR i Meksikoj, 28 Nov. 1963, GARF f.9518 op.1 d.344 ll.139–141.

[50] Posol'stvo SSSR v Meksike, CK, 3 Sep. 1959, RGANI f.5 op.36 d.102 ll.106–107.

In addition to music, which even included a tour of the Red Army Choir in 1961, ballet was the long-running figurehead of Soviet cultural diplomacy. In 1958, the Bolshoi Theatre performed in Montevideo, Buenos Aires and Rio de Janeiro, and repeated their trip many times throughout the late 1950s and the 1960s. The company's trips were always a guaranteed success. Prima ballerina Violeta Bovt and her partner Evgenij Kuz'min once danced six consecutive evenings in a sold-out venue in Rio.[51] Another ballerina, Irina Tichomirovna, gave a proud account after her tour across the Americas, which had taken her to Cuba, Venezuela, Colombia, Mexico, Brazil, Chile, Argentina and Jamaica, in *Culture and Life*: they had given forty-two shows with an audience of 140,000 and were received everywhere with great enthusiasm. In São Paulo, the congestion was so great that they had to move into the football stadium and, after the show, give autographs for hours. As is typical of many similar reports of the time, she firstly confirmed that everyone loved the Soviet Union and that Soviet artists were well known and popular. Secondly, there always had to be a reference to the great people of their host country – and their lack of development due to the imperialists.[52]

After the Bolshoi, Igor' Moiseev's ballet company played Latin America in 1961 and 1963. The latter tour alone drew a remarkable 400,000 spectators to their shows.[53] And besides the *haute volée* of Soviet ballet dancers and classic musicians, chess players were used to favourably represent their Soviet homeland abroad, too. David Bronstein, Boris Spassky, Viktor Korchnoj, Tigran Petrosjan, Paul Keres and many more went to several Latin American countries and played – usually very successfully – in friendly matches and tournaments.[54]

Soviet athletes, who were now included in the international charm offensive, proved not quite so triumphant. When, in July 1956, a Soviet basketball team was sent to South America, they lost their matches against the hosting Uruguayan and Brazilian teams. A victory against a team from Buenos Aires, which had already played in Moscow the year before, smoothed ruffled feelings.[55] These sporting events were

---

[51] Dorenski, 'In Brasilien'; A. Gukasov, 'Sovetskij balet v stranach Južnoj Ameriki', *Teatr* 19/5 (1958), 164–5.

[52] Irina Tichomirnova, 'Sem'desjat dnej v Latinskoj Amerike', *Muzykal'naja Žizn'* 14 (1960), 13–15; a similar article is L. Trunina, 'Sovetskij balet v Latinskoj Amerike', *Teatr* 23/1 (1962), 182.

[53] Riza and Quirk, 'Cultural Relations between the Soviet Union and Latin America', 35.

[54] Nikolai Leonov, *Licholet'e: sekretnye missii* (Moscow: Meždunarodnye Otnošenija, 1995), p. 100.

[55] Sergei Bessonov, 'Soviet Basketballers in South America', *Moscow News* 58 (1956), 8.

remarkable for two aspects: for one thing, they took place in a framework of hospitality and friendship – the coverage in Soviet media was respectful to both the players and their home countries. Secondly, with all sporting fairness, this was still the Cold War: when the Soviet team beat the United States at the 1959 world championship in Chile, newspapers all over the world reported that defeat prominently. 'When it comes to shooting at the moon or at a basket, the United States cannot keep up with Russia', headlined the Chilean newspaper *Ultima Hora*. The *New York Times* stated that the United States (as such, not the sports team) had suffered needless damage to prestige. But the Cold War also ruined the Soviet team's success: they refused to play nationalist China/Taiwan in the next game and were suspended from the competition, losing the secure title of world champion.[56]

International sports were used in the Cold War home front as well: an Uzbek football team toured Argentina, Brazil, Chile, Peru and Uruguay, and a little booklet was made of their trip, combining geographical and cultural information on South American countries with their football strategies. Addressed to a young readership, it also conveyed a political message through the attractive story. On their trip, the sportsmen meet an exiled Armenian in Chile, who bitterly regrets having fled his homeland, 'following the rumours about sweet life in the West'.[57] The message to the young Soviets was clear: compared to the rest of the world, their home country was thriving.

To a certain extent, these elements of traditional cultural diplomacy, high culture and sports, had already been used in the 1920s and 1930s to win over western intellectuals to the Soviet cause. These predecessors, however, were on a much smaller scale than the efforts and the global reach of the new cultural foreign policy from the 1950s, which operated in a context of quite similar endeavours by the United States and some west European states. For the USSR, these activities offered a double advantage: they reached an audience far beyond left or communist circles and presented the Soviet Union as haven of arts and sports. Soviet officials knew of the old Latin American upper classes' predilection for European high-brow culture.[58] To what extent the bourgeois audience actually identified the performances of Russian and European classical high culture with the achievements of the Soviet Union was, however, a

---

[56] Juan de Onis, 'Soviet Five Balks at Taiwan Game: Russians Rout US Team But Face Loss if They Don't Play Chinese', *New York Times*, 30 Jan. 1959.

[57] Gennadij Krasnickij, *Ot Rio-de-Žanejro do Montevideo* (Tashkent: Gosizdat UzSSR, 1964).

[58] E.g. Carlos Sapata and L. Kulidžanov, 'Luče znat' drug druga', *Latinskaja Amerika* 9 (1977), 160.

moot point. Hence, another perk of sending the Bolshoi was a less ideological one: it brought hard currency. When, years later, representatives of Soviet popular music, Iosif Kobzon and Vladimir Vysockij to name two very different examples, also found their way to the Americas, the financial gain remained a motivating factor. This seems to have been an issue of some debate for the internationalist organisations. On several occasions, responsible officials called this practice counterproductive. As so often, reference to the United States was crucial: while they delivered complimentary films, records and literature and had famous musicians play in the name of the United States and for very little money, the Soviets charged too much for their shows, the Soviet embassy in Uruguay complained.[59] Likewise, the Brazilian institute for friendship with the Soviet Union found fault with the commercial character of some artists' performances. They should be used much more to increase the institute's influence on Brazilian politics and society. A counter-model here predated an upcoming conflict: when the Chinese had sent their opera in 1956, the Brazilian friends of the Soviet Union reported, they had given one-third of the seats to members of the Brazilian–Chinese Friendship Society, who in turn were able to act politically upon the ordinary visitors.[60]

Even though all Soviet cultural representatives were presented as non-political, their travels abroad were political issues indeed. They always used their trips to establish and maintain contacts with local intellectuals and 'progressive circles'. And they were always accompanied by KGB-affiliated Soviet embassy staff. But, at least on the surface, the new traditional Soviet cultural diplomacy presented the USSR to the Latin American public as a modern and especially cultured European state.[61]

The 'Columbus of the cosmos'

A completely new and probably the single most successful element of Soviet self-representation abroad was the space programme. Technology had always played a key role in Soviet self-conception. 'Communism is Soviet power plus the electrification of the country', Lenin had declared back in the 1920s. Tractors and combine harvesters for the backward peasants, submarines and airplanes, canals and hydroelectric power plants, and the profession of the engineer were important elements of a

---

[59] Sovetskij Posol'stvo Urugvaj GKKS, 19 Mar. 1965, GARF f.9518 op.1 d.399 l.23.
[60] Zapis' besedy členov delegacii Verchovnogo soveta SSSR s rukovodstvom Instituta kul'turnych svjazej 'Brazilija–SSSR', 4 Aug. 1958, GARF f.9518 op.1 d.322 l.84.
[61] Leonov, *Licholet'e*, pp. 96–100.

cult of progressive technology during Stalinism and beyond. When, from the mid 1950s, the Soviets toned down the communist element in their rhetoric towards the world abroad, the technological feats and scientific advances provided excellent themes for Soviet self-representation. The flight of Sputnik in 1957 impressed many ordinary Latin Americans; some recalled it as the first time they ever heard of the Soviet Union.[62] The new Mexican ambassador to Moscow, presenting his credentials, commended Sputnik's success at great length, concluding with: 'the Russians have paved the way to the stars!'[63] Augustín Nieto Caballero, a Colombian Christian publicist, told his acquaintances during a trip to Moscow about the 'cosmic resonances' the Russian space programme had on the popular concept of the Soviet Union. Old ideas about the USSR had 'burst like soap bubbles'.[64] The Muscovite journalist Aleksej Adžubej reported from Argentina that people were overwhelmed and stunned by the flights of the Soviet satellites.[65] Newspapers from the Rio Grande to Tierra del Fuego and from Chile to the Caribbean led with reports on the space programme. And in Jamaica a group of young jazz musicians baptised themselves the Satellites, later changed the name to the Skatellites and became the founding fathers of ska music – the Soviet Union hence contributed to the name of one of the most influential styles of modern pop music.

Ska music would not make it into the Soviet Union until much later, but news about the repercussions of the space programme did immediately. Yuri Gagarin's flight became *the* success story of Soviet modernity.[66] An Argentine observer felt 'highly emotional' to see the first man in space, his wife allegedly got goosebumps, and they both decided to share that experience in one of many other similarly sounding letters to the SSOD in Moscow.[67] From all over Latin America, telegrams arrived that expressed their admiration for the Soviet triumph.[68] Gagarin became, in

---

[62] Luis Soto, 'Un verano en Siberia' (unpublished article, 2008; druzhba.se/druzhba/vivencias/unveranoensiberia), p. 30.

[63] 15 Oct. 1957, RGANI f.5 op.36 d.43 l.81.

[64] Agustín Nieto, *El secreto de Rusia* (Bogotá: Antares, 1960), p. 11.

[65] Adshubej, *Gestürzte Hoffnung*, p. 217.

[66] Klaus Gestwa, 'Kolumbus des Kosmos: Der Kult um Jurij Gagarin', Osteuropa 10 (2009), 121–51.

[67] Preserved in GARF f.9576 op.8 d.85 l.104.

[68] E.g.: 13 Apr. 1961, Pozdravitel'noe pis'mo edinogo centra trudjaščichsja Čili predsedatelju VCSPS po povodu pervogo poleta v kosmos sovetskogo čeloveka – Jurija Gagarina, and 24 Aug. 1961, Pozdravitel'noe pis'mo profsojuza švejnikov štata Guanabara (Brazilija) v VCSPS po povodu poleta v kosmos Germana Titova, both in N. Isaev (ed.), *Dokumenty proletarskoj solidarnosti: sbornik dokumentov o sodružestve trudjaščichsja Sovetskogo Sojuza s trudjaščimisja stran Azii, Afriki i Latinskoj Ameriki v 1918–1961 godach* (Moscow: Profizdat, 1962), pp. 174–8.

a somewhat double-edged comparison, the 'Columbus of the cosmos'[69] – and went on to conquer the Americas: in July 1961, shortly after his successful space flight, he arrived in Cuba, where a cheering crowd received him in his motorcade and for a reception on Havana's Revolution Square.[70] Gagarin's meetings with the heroes of the Cuban Revolution, hugging Castro and grinning with Guevara, gave priceless photo opportunities and inspired Yevgeny Yevtushenko, at the time lingering on the island, to a series of turgid poems (see Chapter 2). Gagarin went on to Brazil to enjoy the same spectacle with President Jânio Quadros, who decorated him with the state's highest order of merit, the Ordem Nacional do Cruzeiro do Sul.[71] These events caught on with a broad public and were repeated with the next generation of cosmonauts. Andrijan Nikolaev and Pavel Popovič went to Brazil in March 1963 and, in October, Gagarin and the first woman in space, Valentina Tereškova, visited Cuba and Mexico. Tereškova, on a second trip to Argentina in 1966, was hosted by the Sovietophile US singer Dean Reed in his local television show. These public appearances were enacted most carefully by Soviet officials in the background: allegedly, an entire press conference in Mexico had to be repeated when a waiter crossed the cameras carrying a Coca-Cola bottle.[72]

Exhibitions

Soviet feats in technology and high culture were central features, too, in a series of exhibitions the Soviets held in the Americas. In May 1955, accompanying the renewal of a first trade agreement from 1953, a Soviet trade fair was held in Buenos Aires. Across 11,000m², Soviet harvesting machines, lorries, coal seam cutters and portable oil well drilling equipment could be examined and bought. The show, opened by the Soviet ambassador and the Argentine minister of trade, was primarily addressed to potential business partners, but the echo it found went well beyond that. The exhibition drew an unexpected number of 2.3 million curious visitors in forty days, and media all over the Americas covered it in detail.[73] Soviet film-maker Igor' Bessarabov was sent

[69] Krasnickij, *Ot Rio-de-Žanejro do Montevideo*, p. 58.
[70] Gagarin na Kube, undated photograph, RGAKFD #0-309204.
[71] N. Denisov, 'Na orbite mira i družby', *Sovetskaja Pečat'* 10 (1961), 38–42.
[72] Leopold Grün, *The Red Elvis: The Dean Reed Story* (2007); Andrew and Mitrokhin, *The World Was Going Our Way*, p. 20.
[73] Ivan Bol'šakov, 'Uspech sovetskich vystavok v stranach Latinskoj Ameriki', in Ivan Bol'šakov (ed.), *Na vsech kontinentov mira* (Moscow: Pravda, 1962), pp. 87–8; anon.,

to Buenos Aires to capture the success, and the host country, on celluloid.[74]

The fair proved so popular that the Soviets repeated it in Uruguay – and decided to use it also as a means to convey an idealised image of their entire society, a concept that traced back to nineteenth-century world fairs, which promised universal prosperity to the masses. In the context of the Cold War rivalry, the United States had also begun to use exhibitions from 1950 with a fair called 'Frontiers of Freedom', which over the course of the decade was held in ninety-seven venues worldwide. As early as 1955, however, the State Department registered that the Soviets had followed suit with a large number of exhibitions themselves, including the particularly successful one in Buenos Aires.[75] As for Latin America, it was Washington's turn to react. Their exhibition, which explicitly referred now to the Soviets even in the title 'People's Capitalism', opened in Bolivia, Chile, Colombia, Guatemala and Mexico in 1956 – but did not find nearly as many visitors as the Soviet one.[76]

In the head-to-head record, the Soviet Union was defeated famously, when, during a temporary rapprochement in 1959, both sides held exhibitions in the opponent's country.[77] Yet the Soviet one was held not only in New York, but also in Mexico City afterwards. No longer called a trade fair, the 'Exhibition of Soviet Achievements in Science, Technology and Culture' was now organised with the help of the GKKS.[78] Within twenty-five days, it again drew almost 1 million visitors, which made it the biggest in the history of the country. Anastas Mikojan flew in from Moscow to open the exhibition with Mexican president Adolfo López Mateos and both his foreign and trade ministers. Alongside Soviet machinery, this time 16,000 exhibits presented all walks of Soviet life, from information stalls on Soviet geography, health care and the educational system, to urban construction, the (ostensibly) shortest working hours on earth, industrial and agricultural output, and scientific discoveries. Technology remained an important issue with models of ships, of the Sputniks and of a nuclear power plant on display. Of especial interest was a photograph of the back of the moon – an absolute novelty at the time.

'Argentina, Russia Sign: Trade Agreement Is Renewed as Soviet Opens Big Exhibit', *New York Times*, 20 May 1955.

[74] Sovetskaja Vystavka v Argentine (1955), RGAKFD #10283.

[75] Robert H. Haddow, *Pavilions of Plenty: Exhibiting American Culture Abroad in the 1950s* (Washington, DC: Smithsonian Institute Press, 1997), pp. 3, 39.

[76] Belmonte, *Selling the American Way*, p. 133.

[77] Kushner, 'Exhibiting Art at the American National Exhibition in Moscow, 1959'.

[78] GARF f.9518 op.1; GARF f.9518 op.3.

Obviously, the exhibition was no longer addressed simply to potential trade partners, but to as broad an audience as possible. To that end, the organisers also combined it with elements from the cultural diplomacy programme. Stalls with classic Russian literature and contemporary Soviet authors, oil paintings and sculptures added cultural aspects. Soviet films were shown, Shostakovich played a concert, and the Bolshoi performed and rounded off what was considered a major success from the Soviet side.[79]

Undoubtedly impressed were a group of Cuban officials at the fair. They asked the Soviets to put it on in Cuba as well. In February 1960, Mikojan again, accompanied by Khachaturian, opened the Exposición Soviética in Havana in the presence of the entire crew of bearded revolutionaries.[80] Fidel Castro, President Osvaldo Dorticós, Camilo Cienfuegos and Che Guevara leant in their combat dress over models of Soviet factories, power plants, Sputniks and food products, smoked their cigars and dreamt of the industrialisation of Cuba. 'Almost everything we see here is new to us', they allegedly said, impressed. Tables of statistics at the exhibition explained why a planned economy guaranteed steady, fast and secure development. Mikojan made his famous offer to buy 1 million tons of sugar annually above world market price, and gave credit of US $100 million to buy Soviet goods. Not only did the revolutionary leaders revel in Soviet generosity and achievements, but 800,000 Cubans – one in eight inhabitants of the island – also visited the exposition, making it more popular than Carnival, as the *New York Times* observed warily.[81] Their scepticism proved justified: these early cultural contacts became the basis for decades of Soviet presence in the United States' Caribbean back yard. Aleksandr Alekseev accompanied the exhibition as a GKKS official and made friends with the revolutionaries, who nicknamed him Don Alejandro – and, by their request, he became Soviet ambassador to the island.[82]

---

[79] Bol'šakov, 'Uspech sovetskich vystavok v stranach Latinskoi Ameriki', pp. 90–1; M. Meščerjakov, 'Sovetskaja vystavka v Meksike', *Vnešnjaja Torgovlja* 1 (1960), 5–7; Plan propagandy i informacii Sovinformbjuro v svjazi s vystavkoj dostiženij nauki, techniki i kul'tury SSSR v gor. Meksiko/Meksika, 3 Sep. 1959, GARF f.9518 op.1 d.343 l.155; *Pravda*, 30 Nov. 1959; anon., 'Mikoyan Leaves Mexico for Home: His Trip Is Generally Held a Success though Press Comment Was Hostile', *New York Times*, 29 Nov. 1959; *Pravda*, 24 Nov. 1959.

[80] Sergej Mikojan, *Anatomija Karibskogo krizisa* (Moscow: Izdatel'stvo Academia, 2006), p. 624.

[81] Bol'šakov, 'Uspech sovetskich vystavok v stranach Latinskoi Ameriki', pp. 93–4; *New York Times*, 24 Feb. 1960; *Pravda*, 7 Feb. 1960.

[82] Alicia Alted, Encarna Nicolás and Roger González, *Los niños de la guerra de España en la Unión Soviética: de la evacuación al retorno (1937–1999)* (Madrid: Fundación Largo Caballero, 1999), pp. 211–32.

The next Soviet exhibition in the Americas took place in Rio de Janeiro in May 1962. On the opening day, Nikolaj Patoličev, Soviet minister of foreign trade, and Carlos Lacerda, the militantly anti-communist governor of the state of Guanabara, signed a trade contract. Trade volume was increased from US$ 100 million to US$ 140 million, but effectively remained at the level of barter transactions for oil and coffee – nothing that would have justified an exhibition of that scope. According to Soviet sources the largest ever held in Latin America, it reflected many aspects of a highly optimistic Soviet Union some months before the Cuban Crisis. In his welcome article, Khrushchev explained magnanimously that the Soviet Union had also once started from the level of Brazil, which, after national independence, was yet to reach economic autonomy. The Soviets were glad to offer a role model for further development. They themselves would reach, by 1980, the state of full communism with free apartments, free transport and free health care, and the economy would have increased sixfold. The Soviet Union, as Khrushchev presented it to the Brazilians, represented the future and the power of peace and development, and the exhibition would give a first glimpse of it.[83]

To see this state of affairs, visitors could fly from downtown Rio in a Soviet helicopter squadron to admire elaborate models of the Bratsk hydroelectric power plant, of Soviet aircraft and the nuclear-powered ice-breaker *Lenin*. An entire section was dedicated to the space programme, now that Gagarin had made his flight to the outer space (and one to Brazil the year before). Models of the spaceships Vostok 1, Vostok 2 and Sputnik were displayed, and the handsome cosmonauts smiled at the visitors from huge posters. Detailed models and interactive panels explained electrification and energy supply in the USSR. President Goulart, shown around and filmed by a group of Soviet personnel, marvelled at a pair of robotic arms that struck and doused matches in front of his eyes. Like their president, the 500,000 visiting Brazilians could admire cutting-edge machinery, pretentious watches, up-market private cars and tractors at the expo. For ordinary Soviet citizens, these goods were, it goes without saying, as readily available as the beautiful Russian models who wore Soviet-produced short skirts at a fashion show – a gimmick copied from US fairs from the mid 1950s. Brazilian men were visibly impressed in one scene of the Soviet film, which was shot in the fair area and around Rio de Janeiro, 'the most beautiful city in Latin America'.

---

[83] Nikita Chruščev, 'Poslanie k posetiteljam sovetskoj vystavki v Rio-de-Žanejro', *Vnešnjaja Torgovlja* 6 (1962), 3–5.

The Soviet audience back home, in most cases without fancy watches and cars, could at least delight in the beauty of exotic Brazil – and the ostensible global admiration of their country.[84]

Reactions on the Latin American side were twofold: for one thing, hundreds of letters reached the organisers and, while many inquired about the lack of freedom of religion in the Soviet Union, the overwhelming majority commented positively. The average commentator expressed first admiration for the exhibits, then his wish usually to study in the USSR or to get medical treatment or technical literature. The second type of reaction was less positive: already on the second day, the Soviet exhibition had to shut its doors temporarily, after an anti-communist group of army officers had planted a bomb that would have destroyed the entire fair but was found before it went off. In its anti-imperialist rhetoric and friend–foe schema, the Soviet media could not but take this conspiracy as a prime example of the evil-doings of the frequently invoked reactionary circles.[85]

Soviet cultural diplomacy, with its musicians and sportspeople as well as with the depiction of its technological feats, hardly ever mentioned the communist political system of the Soviet state. To be sure, behind the colourful façade of cutting-edge technology and high-brow culture still stood a deep belief in the prospects of a de-Stalinised socialism. Yet the Soviets had learnt that, in order to reach a broad worldwide audience and to interact with 'bourgeois nationalist governments', they had to tone down their rhetoric. Internal documents show that, in the run-up to the exhibition in Rio de Janeiro, long conversations were held with east European experts from the Brazilian foreign ministry.[86] All designated publications and exhibits had to be proof-read and authorised by Brazilian officials. A galley in the GKKS documents demonstrates how that happened: the term 'communist' was replaced with 'Soviet', 'the CPSU' with 'the Soviet government', and all references to the Cold War (such as 'overtaking the capitalist countries in twenty years') were completely cut out. A big Lenin bust in the entrance hall was the only remaining trace of ideology in the exhibition.

[84] Sovetskaja Vystavka v Rio-de-Žanejro (1962), RGAKFD #19909.
[85] Posol'stvo SSSR v Brazilii GKKS, Ob izdanii vystavočnoj literatury, 3 Mar. 1962, GARF f.9518 op.1 d.223 ll.13–15; anon., 'Soviet Exposition Opened in Brazil: Diversified Show Is Russia's Biggest in Latin America', New York Times, 4 May 1962; Bol'šakov, 'Uspech sovetskich vystakov v stranach Latinskoi Ameriki', pp. 96–7; Iu. Dubinina, 'Sovetskij Sojuz v Rio-de-Žanejro', Ogonek 20 (1962), 2.
[86] Reatamento de relaçoes diplomáticas com a União Soviética, Jorge de Cervalho e Silva, Ministro, Chefe da Divisão da Europa Oriental to Secretario-Geral Adjunto para Asuntos da Europa Oriental e Asia, 5 Dec. 1961, AMRE 920.1 (42) (74).

Parliamentary delegations

In another new sphere of interaction, which can be considered part of post-Stalinist Soviet self-representation, the Soviet Union made itself out to be not only a trail-blazer for the future of mankind, but also a modern state which played according to the rules of the political world system: among the tasks of the GKKS was the organisation of exchanges of parliamentary delegations with Third World countries. Four Soviet groups toured Latin America in 1954.[87] Members of the Supreme Soviet were sent to the inauguration of President Arturo Frondizi in Argentina in May 1958 and arranged some cultural and economic contacts.[88] Another large delegation of the Supreme Soviet followed some weeks later to Brazil, where they discussed student and scientific exchanges and took part in an international congress of parliamentarians that debated (unsuccessfully) common resolutions on geo-political issues.[89] They went to see the Brazilian Academy of Sciences, visited factories and power plants and the construction site of the future capital Brasília. After meeting several Brazilian politicians, including President Juscelino Kubitschek and both of his future successors, Governor Quadros and the head of the workers' party João Goulart, they finally signed a cultural treaty between their countries.[90]

When the GKKS invited (non-communist) parliamentary delegations to the USSR, they tried to convey the same image as in their self-representation abroad. As many as twenty-six Latin American delegations had already toured the Soviet Union by 1954.[91] In 1957, fifty Brazilian federal and state parliamentarians were invited to the cheerful Moscow Youth Festival – strictly as private citizens, as the Brazilian foreign ministry rushed to declare.[92] By the end of the 1950s, Third World parliamentarians, including from most Latin American countries, flocked in almost weekly. A Peruvian delegation of parliamentarians and journalists, to name but two fairly typical examples, marvelled at Ukrainian kolkhozes in May 1959. And twelve Colombian senators and congresspeople spent three summer weeks on a paid trip through the USSR,

[87] Kasack, 'Kulturelle Außenpolitik', p. 371.

[88] Stephen Clissold (ed.), *Soviet Relations with Latin America, 1918–1968: A Documentary Survey* (London: Oxford University Press, 1970), pp. 182–3.

[89] Zapis' besedy členov delegacii Verchovnogo soveta SSSR s rukovodstvom Instituta kul'turnych svjazej 'Brazilija–SSSR', 4 Aug. 1958, GARF f.9518 op.1 d.322 ll.82–85.

[90] Otčet o poezdke delegacii Parlamentskoj gruppy SSSR v Braziliju na 47-ju Konferenciju Mežparlamentskogo Sojuza (1958), undated, GARF f.9518 op.1 d.322 ll.56–72.

[91] Kasack, 'Kulturelle Außenpolitik', p. 371.

[92] Undated, RGASPI f.3M op.15 d.271.53/204; Itamaraty to the Brazilian mission at the UN, Viagens de brasileiros a União Soviética, 7 Aug. 1957, AMRE 920.1 (42) (74).

going to the Caucasus and several Soviet cities, seeing factories and academies and visiting theatres and museums.[93] In their own countries, these guests were usually political backbenchers; in the USSR, they were given paid holidays, and they were often accorded the honour of meeting the highest representatives of the Soviet state, Khrushchev or Mikojan, or Soviet celebrities such as the cosmonauts. As a result, many of these ensnared parliamentarians, while not harbouring serious sympathies for communism, upon their return found the Soviet Union quite a nice place.[94]

By the early 1960s, western observers were noting that most of this political tourism was kept separate from any operations of the communist parties.[95] These visits and invitations of lower-ranking political delegations did not primarily serve the establishment of cultural relations or the preparation of diplomatic ones. In fact, members of the Supreme Soviet had hardly any political influence. They were, however, used in Soviet internal and external self-representation. On the one hand, they were supposed to present the Soviet Union as a normal state actor in international politics, with a dash of Third World solidarity. On the other hand, just like all other Soviet activities abroad, they had a self-confirmative purpose and were covered broadly in all Soviet media. In late 1960, when yet another delegation of the Supreme Soviet travelled to Bolivia, Chile, Argentina and Brazil, a colourful booklet with many photographs was composed for the Soviet readership.[96] And when, in August 1961, Michail Georgadze, secretary of the Supreme Soviet, led a delegation through Brazil, Ecuador, Mexico and Cuba, a Soviet film team followed them at every turn and showed how they were received by the most high-ranking and illustrious hosts. The Soviet audience could thus revel in the global importance of their socialist homeland.[97] At the same time, the foreign political guests could learn of the normality and inoffensiveness of the Soviet Union. In its official self-representation towards politicians and the public in Latin America, the Soviet Union was no longer the cradle of world revolution, but a technologically

---

[93] Gustavo Valcárcel, *Reportaje al futuro: crónicas de un viaje a la URSS* (Lima: Perú Nuevo, 1963), pp. 160–2; undated, GARF f.9518 op.1 d.339 ll.119–120.

[94] Anon., 'Parlamentarios colombianos en la URSS', *Boletín del Instituto Cultural Colombo Soviético* 3–4 (1967), 3; Valcárcel, *Reportaje al futuro*, pp. 160–2; Otčet o rabote s byvšim Ministrom vnutrennich del, vidnym političeskim dejatelem Ekvadora Manuelem Araucho Idal'go, 23 Aug. 1962, GARF f.9518 op.1. d.341 ll.28–31; anon., 'Grupo de parlamentarios bolivianos visita Rusia', *Presencia*, 3 Jul. 1960.

[95] Alexander, 'Soviet and Communist Activities in Latin America', 10.

[96] N. Rodionov, *V strane Inkov: putevye očerki* (Alma-Ata: Kazgoslitizdat, 1963).

[97] Riza and Quirk, 'Cultural Relations between the Soviet Union and Latin America', 34; Poezdka M. P. Georgadze v strany Latinskoj Ameriki (1961), RGAKFD #22357.

advanced and cultivated European state with a highly educated and happily consuming population.

Courting the world's youth: the image conveyed to young Latin Americans

Soviet attempts at creating a favourable image of themselves throughout the Third World included more than just activities abroad. Foreigners went to the Soviet Union in increasing numbers, too, in order to follow different programmes set up by official organs. From the mid 1950s, the Soviets made considerable efforts to win over young people especially – who were, after all, the future of mankind – from Third World countries as friends of the Soviet Union. State-controlled receptions of Latin Americans in the USSR were part of Soviet self-representation to the Americas. In the same way as for the activities abroad, examining how the Soviets presented themselves and their state to their foreign guests allows us to draw conclusions that go beyond the categories of propaganda and deceit: the carefully mounted and beautified versions of Soviet life give an understanding of the self-conception of Soviet internationalists and their role towards the Third World. Three elements of this programme will be examined: the reception of Latin Americans at the 1957 Moscow Youth Festival, higher education in the USSR and youth tourism. As before, the focus of the survey will be on the representative character of these events and institutions and the image of the Soviet Union they were to convey to the visitors.

Latin Americans at the World Youth Festival in Moscow

In the summer of 1957, more than 30,000 young people from all over the world flocked into the USSR in order to attend the Sixth World Youth Festival in Moscow. After years of planning, the 'new' Soviet Union wanted to present itself to the youth of the world with openness and a spirit of optimism. The foreign guests were invited to attend artistic, cultural and sports programmes, and to debate at international meetings of students and workers.

The festival is fairly well researched but, as with so many aspects of cultural exchange during the Cold War, there is a certain bias: the focus is almost exclusively on how the festival opened a gateway for western consumer goods and values and thus undermined its very purpose. Yet the 1957 festival – and this fact tends to be a bit neglected – was directed not least to the youth of the global South. Analysing the projected image of the Soviet Union and the interactions between Soviet officials, their

Latin American guests and ordinary Soviet youngsters who attended the festival offers a more balanced view of the cultural transfers and influences that happened in the summer of '57. How did the Soviet Union present itself specifically to the Latin American guests and how did the Soviet population react to these 'exotic' people? As argued for other aspects of Soviet official internationalist activities, the addressees were not only the foreigners, but also the Soviet population itself. Western visitors to the USSR may have received an ambiguous impression of the socialist world, but the effects on Latin Americans and young Soviet citizens were much more successful from a Soviet point of view than is usually acknowledged.

While the CPSU and the communist youth organisation Komsomol actually supervised the organisation of the festival, the World Federation of Democratic Youth and the International Union of Students were presented as the organisers of a preparatory committee in Budapest. The public image of the Moscow youth festival they conveyed differed clearly from former festivals of that kind. It was supposed to appear apolitical: young people were to participate irrespective of their political conviction, race and even religion, as was emphasised in all brochures and posters that were sent around the world. The official slogan 'For peace and friendship' was hazy enough to be agreed on by almost everyone. In contrast to former festivals, political symbols had disappeared in official self-representation, both in advertisements and in Moscow during the festival. Flowers, colours and Picasso's peace dove replaced the iconography of Stalin or Mao. Communist parties worldwide were instructed to send as many non-communists as possible.[98] For two weeks, Moscow presented itself at its best, not as a grim communist capital, but as a modern, colourful city of youth, peace and solidarity. During the festival, all cinemas, circuses, exhibitions, sporting events and public transport were free. Radio Moscow established a round-the-clock 'Festival Radio' that also broadcast shows in Spanish with topics tailored for the Latin American audience. One programme, 'Latin American Youth at the Moscow Festival', featured Latin American music, often presented by prominent artists and intellectuals such as the Argentine singer Horacio Guarany or the Venezuelan poet Carlos Augusto León.

[98] Pia Koivunen, 'The 1957 Moscow Youth Festival: Propagating a New, Peaceful Image of the Soviet Union', in Ilic (ed.), *Soviet State and Society under Nikita Khrushchev*, pp. 46–65; Kristin Roth-Ey, '"Loose Girls" on the Loose? Sex, Propaganda and the 1957 Youth Festival', in Ilic, Reid and Attwood (eds.), *Women in the Khrushchev Era*, pp. 75–95.

On organised excursions, the young visitors could get to know the entire Soviet Union, and these trips had an interesting Third World twist: while guests from the western countries were sent primarily to the European cities of Leningrad or Kiev, youngsters from the Third World could marvel at Soviet achievements in the modernisation of Central Asia and the Caucasus. It was probably no coincidence that Latin Americans tended to be sent to Christian Georgia and Arabic youths predominantly to Muslim Uzbekistan.[99]

While in theory the festival was open to every young person, most visitors were, in fact, dependent on scholarships. Even though the Soviets invested 600 million rubles in the festival, most guests had to cover their own travel expenses. Just the flight to Moscow, however, remarked one Chilean visitor, cost as much as a craftsman in his country would earn in a year.[100] Even under these difficult circumstances, about 850 participants from all Latin American countries arrived at the festival – the only exception was Panama, whose entire delegation was immediately arrested at the airport by the Panamanian authorities. The Mexican painters David Siqueiros and Diego Rivera endowed some of their works in support of the delegates. Communist parties distributed the proceeds among preparatory committees that had been organised in most Latin American countries. Yet fewer than one-third of the Latinos were communists or sympathisers, and many of them were completely apolitical. In Chile, a beauty queen contest sent that year's winner to Moscow; in Bolivia, the best national folklore[101] group in a contest got the trip to the festival paid.

For one year, a Spanish-language edition of the newspaper *Festival'* was circulated all around the Americas. Nonetheless, most participants went without any notion of what awaited them in Moscow. All Central Americans were in the Soviet Union for the first time, and, according to their translators, had no precise idea what the USSR actually was (in contrast, some of the 133 delegates from Argentina did have a very precise idea of the Soviet Union: half of them were Jewish emigrants who seized the opportunity to visit relatives – under the suspicious gaze of the Soviet authorities). Many Latin American students who at the time were attending west European universities asked to be invited to Moscow. Hundreds of letters from West Germany and France but also

[99] Ob ekskursii delegaciij na VI. Festival molodeži, undated, RGASPI f.3M op.15 d.37 ll.9–11.
[100] Héctor Campo, 'Das 6. Weltjugendfestival: Die Jugend trifft sich in Moskau', *Neue Zeit* 15/26 (1957), 18–19.
[101] See p. 91 for more discussion of this term.

Prague and Belgrade arrived at the organising committees, where many were declined because officials did not know how to handle their visa procedures.[102] Yet some of them managed to join their compatriots, who made a stopover in Europe on their way to Moscow. Gabriel García Márquez was at the time a young newspaper correspondent in Paris. Though an unknown but staunch communist, he was declined a visa to visit the USSR four times. His friend Manuel Zapata Olivella – a Afro-Colombian author who would go on to become quite famous – had a folklore combo with his sister Delia Zapata, which was to play in Moscow. García Márquez and his colleague Plinio Mendoza seized their chance, passed themselves off as accordion players and singers, joined the group and finally made it behind the Iron Curtain.[103] In the course of the festival, dozens of similar Latin folklore bands played hundreds of concerts that were always overcrowded. Los Caballeros from Paraguay alone played fourteen concerts, and the Argentine composer Ariel Ramírez went with his Compañía de Folklore. The Uruguayan folk singer Roberto Sagor, Bolivian Carnival ensembles and many more interpreters of indigenous, black, shepherd and religious music laid the foundation for a long-standing fascination with Latin folklore (which will be examined further in Chapter 2). Not only music, but also art from the Americas was on display during the festival: paintings at an exhibition depicted the despair and dignity of ordinary Latin American people in their daily lives.

An interesting aspect is that many of the invited guests could not – even in a generous definition – be considered young. A remarkable number of (older) Latin American intellectuals went to Moscow. The writers Pablo Neruda (53 years old at the time), Nicolás Guillén (55), Miguel Angel Asturias (57), Jorge Amado (44), María Rosa Oliver (58) and composer Gilardo Gilardi (68) were the vanguard of leftist Latin American intellectuals, playwrights, poets and musicians, and happily accepted invitations to the Moscow Youth Festival. Hitherto unknown but later influential figures at the festival included the sneaky García Márquez, but also a young Cuban teacher called Antonio Núñez Jiménez. Together with compatriot students from Norway, he rallied for solidarity with oppressed Cuba. Only three years later, he would return as the first official envoy of revolutionary

---

[102] O sostave i pribyvanij delegacij Latinskoj Ameriki na Vsemirnom festival'e molodeži, undated, RGASPI f.3M op.15 d.204, here: ll.52–142; Materialy o podgotovke VI. Vsemirnogo festivalja v stranach Lat. Ameriki, RGASPI f.3M op.15 d.77. All documents, usually untitled and undated, hereafter are from the RGASPI Komsomol holdings (f.3M op.15) on the World Youth Festival; the titles in most cases refer to entire files, not single documents.

[103] Dasso Saldívar, *García Márquez: el viaje a la semilla, la biografía* (Barcelona: Folio, 2005), pp. 354–8.

Cuba. Carlos Fonseca, the future leader of the Nicaraguan Sandinista movement, started his half-year stay in the Soviet Union with the festival. According to unverified allegations by KGB renegade Vasili Mitrokhin, he was lured by the Soviet secret service to be an agent on this occasion.[104] The bulk of ordinary visitors, though, were not celebrities or future spies. The participants in the Moscow Youth Festival were presented with a modern Soviet Union and met young Soviets who seemed to care honestly about their home countries and their hardships as well as their artistic and intellectual abilities.[105]

The official depiction, however, was only one side of the coin. Behind the scenes, before the festival, unwanted persons who did not comply with the spirit of optimism were 'cleaned' off the streets. In order to show the city only at its best, the Moscow police arrested or deported prostitutes, gypsies and the homeless for the duration of the festival. Nor does the apolitical character of the festival withstand closer examination. In the official discourse, the Soviet organisers underlined their politically neutral stance towards their Latin American guests. Posters and brochures, distributed in Spanish a year in advance in the Americas, promised 'no political or philosophical or religious tendencies'. An internal paper by the preparatory committee, however, reveals that 'in the official programme, some measures with propaganda intention are not included.' These were, for example, fifty to sixty daily meetings of specially trained young Soviet citizens with foreigners in Moscow or on excursions. What they were expected to say was considerably more traditional and less colourful and liberal than the official discourse. The document laments serious deficiencies in the political training of these Soviet youngsters up to that time – they needed to be more prepared in the spirit of proletarian internationalism and to show Soviet patriotism by proudly praising the USSR's achievements.[106] The young guides and translators had to write reports on their work that included questions about the political orientation of their guests.[107]

[104] Andrew and Mitrokhin, *The World Was Going Our Way*, p. 82; Carlos Fonseca, *Un nicaragüense en Moscú* (Managua: Secretaría Nacional de Propaganda y Educación Política, 1980).

[105] I. Golomštok and I. Karetnikova, *Iskusstvo stran Latinskoj Ameriki* (Moscow: Iskusstvo, 1959); Meždunarodnyj podgotovytel'nyj komitet VI. Vsemirnogo festivalja, RGASPI f.3M op.15 d.27, here in particular: ll.17, 53, 144–151 and 204; RGASPI f.3M op.15 d.192 ll.64–129; O radiovešćenie na VI. Vsemirnom festival'e, RGASPI f.3M op.15 d.263 l.395; Besedy o podgotovke VI. Vsemirnogo festivalja v stranach Lat. Ameriki, RGASPI f.3M op.15 d.76, here in particular: ll.153–161.

[106] O podgotovie VI. Vsemirnogo festivalja molodeži i studentov za mir i družbu, 16 Feb. 1957, RGASPI f.3M op.15 d.90 ll.87–100.

[107] Radiovešćenie, RGASPI f.3M op.15 d.263 ll.334–433; Meždunarodnyj podgotovytel'nyj komitet, RGASPI f.3M op.15 d.23–26; Otčety gido-perevočikov o

Moreover, during the festival, all 830 Latin Americans from all 19 countries (and the Caribbean group in an extra session) were asked to participate in a meeting behind closed doors. Here, the objective was distinctly political: 'to strengthen Latin American brotherhood and anti-[US-] Americanism'. Komsomol activists realised the dangers of such an endeavour, but stated that it was 'important to do this, even though the enemy will milk it in their counterpropaganda'.[108] How petty the supervision *could* be is shown by an anonymous report about three Uruguayans who made themselves conspicuous only by not smiling and applauding in the stadium.[109] But the bulk of reports on the Latin American visitors, written mostly by their guides and translators, were very genial, and the guests were usually described as pleasant and friendly. Some Peruvians tended to be more interested in Soviet girls than in politics, which according to one translator made them the exact opposite of the delegates from the German Democratic Republic (GDR). Stereotypes existed among the young Soviets – or were created quickly: 'due to the South American tendency towards anarchy and casualness, these people do not understand the organisational bases and the subordination of the younger to the elder', wrote one particularly fussy guide, after his charges had complained about the unbearable bureaucratic hierarchies they were confronted with. Yet these were exceptions rather than the rule. When, towards the end of the festival, the guides asked their guests about their impressions, they usually got positive answers, and themselves added how much they liked the work with their newly found friends. And even in the more political measures not made public, the goal was never to incite revolutions or convert people to communism.[110]

After the festival, Latin American participants who were considered reliable wrote in the Soviet media about their profound impressions in Moscow.[111] Their reports, written for an exclusively Soviet audience, elucidate again how much the festival was also directed towards the Soviet population itself. Soviet television broadcast ten hours daily from the festival and spread the new images all over the country. The ostensible or real enthusiasm of their guests reinforced a spirit of optimism and

rabote s delegaciej iz stran Latinskoj Ameriki na VI. Festival'e molodeži, RGASPI f.3M op.15 d.205 and d.235. Most reports are very favourable though.

[108] RGASPI f.3M op.15 d.191 ll.74–79.

[109] Spiski učastnikov Latinskoj Ameriki, RGASPI f.3M op.15 d.205, here: l.79.

[110] RGASPI f.3M op.15 d.205, e.g. O robote s delegaciej Peru na VI. Festival'e molodeži ll.29–36; or Otčet o robote s delegaciej Paragvaja na VI. Festival'e molodeži i studentov, 23 ijulja–15 avgusta, l. 45–51.

[111] So did, for example, the head of the leftist Mexican group People's Youth: Rafael Estrada, 'Moe mnenie o VI festivale', *Molodež' Mira* 7 (1957), 6.

a sense of the Soviet Union as an altruistic friend of the peoples of the world. In their underlining of how interested important intellectuals from all over the world apparently were in their country, but also in the folklor-isation of their guests' cultures (while Soviet musicians, again, played classical European music),[112] a certain sense of cultural superiority reson-ated. But the effect on many a young Soviet was indeed a sense of solidarity with his or her contemporaries from the Third World, which reinforced their belief in, and their country's leading role in the global struggle for, socialism. The impact of (after all, apolitical) western consumer goods need not be at odds with the fact that young people observed an aspect of Soviet internationalism and liked what they saw. True enough, the Soviets did hear many less enthusiastic comments as well. Most of them had spent their entire lives under Stalinism, and hence were isolated from the world and from outspoken criticism about their country and its political system. The young foreign visitors now openly remarked on negative aspects such as the oppression of religion, Stalin's crimes, boring architecture and annoying bureaucracy. Yet this was, in most cases, a west European point of view. In relation to the Third World, the festival proved a success. Many Latin Americans, admittedly mostly those with leftist leanings, liked what they saw in Moscow and the rest of the USSR, and Soviet front organisa-tions received letters of commendation by the sackload. Soviet official internationalists once more received proof that they were doing something right.

Universities

While the Moscow Youth Festival was limited to two weeks in 1957, the Soviets found another field through which to present their state positively in the long term: higher education. Moskovskij gosudarstvennyj univer-sitet (Moscow State University, MGU) began to establish contacts with Latin America in 1955 and, from 1957, regularly interacted with the Latin American Association of Universities. Already by 1960, some 200 profes-sors from Argentina (most notably Risieri Frondizi, philosopher, head of Buenos Aires University and brother of Arturo, Argentina's left-leaning, reformist president), Brazil, Chile, Cuba, Peru and Uruguay had been received as guests and were shown the prosperity of the Soviet education system.[113] And students from the Third World increasingly attended universities all over the Soviet Union.

---

[112] As the programme bills for the festival reveal: RGASPI f.3M op.15 d.92.
[113] Predloženija po passíreniju svjazej Moskovskogo universiteta s universitetami stran Latinskoj Ameriki, 31 Mar. 1960, GARF f.9518 op.1 d.339 ll.237–242.

The number of Latin American students at Soviet universities until the late 1950s was almost negligible. In January 1959, there were seven, and even five years later, after years of active Third World engagement, Moscow State University hosted only twenty-seven Latinos.[114] Universities in Leningrad, Kiev, Odessa and Minsk also had their growing but always small share of Latin American students. In contrast to their fellow students from Asia or Africa, the majority of Latin American students in the Soviet Union attended one particular institution in Moscow: in 1960, Khrushchev instigated the foundation of a university in Moscow purely for students from the Third World. Named after the late Congolese prime minister from 1961, the Universitet družby narodov im. Patrisa Lumumby (Patrice Lumumba University of the Friendship of the Peoples) provided, in the 1960s alone, some 2,500 young Latin Americans with higher education during their fully funded five- to seven-year stays in Moscow.[115] Their points of view, their expectations, experiences, further careers and memories will be examined in Chapter 4. Here, in line with the perspective of this chapter, an analysis of the official Soviet discourse will examine higher education, and in particular Lumumba University, as a component of Soviet self-representation to potential and arriving students and visiting foreigners.

In clear distinction from former endeavours of the 1920s and 1930s, when communist cadres from all over the world got their ideological education in several Soviet institutions, Lumumba University, officially, did not address itself to communist youth. Its credos were no longer class struggle and revolution, but internationalism, anti-colonialism and support for economic progress and national independence.[116] The choice of the name is telling: the first head of government of an independent Congo had recently been tortured to death with the assistance of the Belgian and US secret services. He was an icon of African anti-imperialism, but not a communist. A new type of missionary thought now prevailed in the Soviet Union. In a quite similar way to the West, the USSR presented itself as a generous benefactor, sharing its own achievements with the backward rest of the world. '[Students] come from far

[114] O kaličestve studentov-inostrancev iz kapitalističestkich i kolonial'nych stran obučajuščichsja v vuzach SSSR, 1 Jan. 1959, RGASPI f.1M op.46 d.248 l.12.
[115] Tobias Rupprecht, 'Gestrandetes Flaggschiff: Die Universität der Völkerfreundschaft in Moskau', *Osteuropa* 1 (2010), 95–114; communist Cuba, however, was no longer put in the category of 'developing countries' from the early 1960s, so their numerous students (about 1,000 in Moscow alone as of 1964) were not allowed to attend Lumumba University and do not appear in statistics for the Third World.
[116] V. Stanis, 'Kuznica kadrov dlja razvivajuiščichsja stran', *Latinskaja Amerika* 7 (1972), 118.

away to study in our country. They come from Asia and Europe, from Africa and America, to the land of space ships and nuclear power plants, to drink from the inexhaustible source of knowledge the Soviet people has amassed', *Izvestija* put it straightforwardly.[117]

In every official statement, Lumumba University emphasised its non-political character and its spirit of internationalism and patriotism.[118] The initiative, it was proclaimed, came from 'progressive circles in the Soviet Union and abroad'. Contacts with the Communist Party allegedly did not exist. On the occasion of the opening ceremony, which was monitored by and palpably addressed to the world public, both the designated head Sergej Rumjancev and Khrushchev himself again under-lined the absence of ideology and politics from the curriculum.[119] As a matter of fact, throughout the early 1960s, Lumumba University was the only institute of higher learning in the Soviet Union without the obliga-tory classes in Marxism-Leninism. Its faculties focused on subjects that were of immediate use in Third World countries. Agriculture, medicine and engineering were the most popular subject areas.

In their self-representation towards the world, the Soviet state used Lumumba University to establish its image as an altruistic friend of the peoples of the world. Student representatives were expected to collaborate with the friendship societies of the SSOD. From the very first class, Soviet news agencies, journals and newspapers employed students to praise Soviet achievements and generosity in their respective languages.[120] In weekly accounts of their lives, selected students were to convey this mes-sage to the world on Radio Moscow's foreign-language programme.[121] A guided tour of the campus, sometimes accompanied by internationally known and popular public figures, Gagarin among them, was a fundamen-tal part of itineraries when Third World delegations went to Moscow.[122]

---

[117] 'V Universitete Družby Narodov', *Izvestija*, 21 Aug. 1963.

[118] N. Sofinskij, 'Pomošč v podgotovke kadrov', *Latinskaja Amerika* 5 (1977), 127; Alexandre Fradkine (ed.), *Le monde sous un même toit: documents sur les études et la vie des étudiants de l'Université de l'amitié des peuples Patrice Lumumba à Moscou* (Moscow: Novosti, 1973).

[119] Bert Dirnecker, 'Die "Patrice Lumumba-Universität für Völkerfreundschaft" in Moskau', *Moderne Welt* 3 (1961/2), 217; *Pravda*, 24 Mar. 1960; Rešenie Soveta Ministrov, Ob organizacij Universiteta Družby Narodov, 5 Feb. 1960, GARF f.5446 op.1 d.698 l.698.

[120] Anon., 'Das lateinamerikanische Seminar in Moskau', *Kultur und Leben* 4 (1969), 32; Sobre el seminario permanente de estudiantes latinoamericanos en la URRS, undated, RGASPI f.1M op.39 d.399 ll.17–143.

[121] Stanis, 'Kuznica kadrov dlja razvivajuiščichsja stran', 122.

[122] Alvin Rubinstein, 'Lumumba University: An Assessment', *Problems of Communism* 20/6 (1971), 65; Alberto Dangond, *Mi diario en la Unión Soviética: un conservador en la URSS* (Bogotá: Ediciones Suramerica, 1968), pp. 334–6.

This advertising was also directed towards the students themselves. This meant first of all free education, food and accommodation during the academic year in Moscow, but included also their leisure activities. During their long summer breaks, students could voluntarily join camps that the university organised in the periphery of the Union. In Moldavia, students could work for three to four hours a day in local kolkhozes and follow seminars on the 'developing countries' and a recreation programme of sports and music afterwards. Similar projects were held in Central Asia and all around the Black Sea. In a summer study camp in Abkhazia in July and August 1965, an 'internship in tropical agriculture' presented Georgia as a role model of how the guests should engage in farming back home. At night, the Latin American students, together with fellows from the GDR, Iraq and Africa, discussed the socio-economic situation on their continent with high-ranking lecturers including the Chilean ambassador to Moscow. These additional seminars had, no doubt, a certain political bias, but never did they call to arms or have the aspiration to mould communists. Indeed, many leftist Latin American students kept asking for *more* political education during their summer holidays.[123]

Outside the classroom, there were continuous attempts to present Soviet cultural and technological progress during spare-time activities. Seemingly purely recreational tourist trips usually included some Soviet achievement to marvel at. Popular destinations for students as well as for foreign short-term visitors were schools and universities, factories, canals and hydroelectric power plants, as one student recalls remarkably enthusiastically.[124] The official image the Soviet Union tried to convey of itself towards its students was the same as the one it sent abroad directly: that of a culturally and technologically superior modern nation. Devoted to the friendship of the peoples, to international peace and economic and cultural progress, in this picture it was an altruistic USSR that let the rest of the non-western world partake of its achievements.

Practice did not, in this case, differ much from the official discourse. To keep control of the students, the heads of student councils were appointed by the university – which ensured that they were usually members of their respective communist parties. Soviet students at Lumumba University were all CPSU or Komsomol members and were

---

[123] Stanis, 'Kuznica kadrov dlja razvivajuiščichsja stran', 121; O meroprijatach po letnemu otdychu studentov Universiteta Družby Narodov im. Patrisa Lumumby 1968g., undated, RGASPI f.1M op.39 d.143 ll.50–52; letters to Komsomol, RGASPI f.1M op.39 d.138.

[124] Soto, 'Un verano en Siberia', pp. 201–2.

to keep an eye on their fellow students.[125] But there were no systematic attempts to influence the foreign students ideologically. The reports to the Komsomol were in most cases not on individuals, but on national groups, which were classified according to Cold War categories. Anti-Soviet sentiment was hardly ever encountered. To be sure, students were not all free to say and act as they wished without getting into conflict with the ever-conspicuous Soviet authorities. During times of peaceful coexistence and later the schism with China, however, the ideological front lines changed. The greatest concern now were Maoist sentiments among the students. Just like western policy makers, Soviet officials were mostly afraid of a propagation of a violent revolutionary path.

Tourism

In addition to possibilities in education, Radio Moscú regularly told its young listeners in Latin America about the great holiday opportunities in the Soviet Union, sightseeing in new and old cities, spectacular museums, cultural centres, sports and landscapes. The SSOD allegedly sponsored these trips lavishly with scholarships.[126] In June 1958, the Komsomol created the youth travel organisation Sputnik. In the five years to come, it organised short stays in the Soviet Union for some 60,000 young tourists and sent 40,000 young Soviets abroad.[127] Yet the bulk of them came from and went to the people's democracies in eastern Europe. As for the Third World, (youth) tourism is a telling example of the financial limits that constrained Soviet internationalists, and of the gap between talking big and acting small that characterised many Soviet promises to the global South. To Latin American youngsters, Sputnik made a lot of promises that it was at no point able to keep. Hundreds of youngsters applied to the SSOD. If they received any reply at all, it was a rejection. Two letters from 1959 exemplify many other similar ones: a young Colombian had heard of the invitations for travel in the radio show 'El buscón del oyente' (Listener's Corner). And a Peruvian reported that he and all his friends had heard about the Soviet Union on Radio Moscú. Now they wanted to come to the promised paradise, see all the fantastic kolkhozes, factories, universities and sights, and possibly stay, work and

---

[125] O situacii studentov iz Latinskoj Ameriki v SSSR, 13 May 1966, RGASPI f.1M op.39 d.30 ll.1–14; Položenie v zemljačestvach studentov iz stran Latinskoj Ameriki i o sostojanii raboty s etim kontingentom inostrannych učaščichsia v SSSR, 13 May 1969, RGASPI f.1M op.39 d.231 ll.53–79.

[126] Sapata and Kulidžanov, 'Luče znat' drug druga'; Romanovskij, *Meždunarodnye naučnye i kul'turnye svjazi SSSR*, pp. 47–8.

[127] Internal report by Sputnik, undated, RGASPI f.1M op.31 d.42 ll.12–15.

die in the USSR.[128] Most of the many requests of this kind did not get an answer. If someone in the SSOD bothered, they would usually refer to other institutions or decline politely. In no way did the Soviets have the means to meet the appeals that people sent.

But Soviet public diplomacy, even in such a faraway area of the world as Latin America, had shown its effects. People had tuned in to Radio Moscú and had believed what they heard. One remarkable effect of the new self-representation as a modern state was that most of the letters the Soviet authorities received now were by non-communists. Often they made this clear explicitly in their letters, as in 'I am by no means a communist, but I am deeply impressed by the achievements of the Soviet people', or – as in most cases – communist vocabulary is simply not used at all. Yet the Soviet Union did not want and probably could not afford to pay for all the interest in it.

From the mid 1960s, Sputnik's policy changed somewhat. Still without the means to pay for the trips, and with other Soviet institutions reluctant to step in, they started to run their agency as a business. Most letters were answered now, but the supplicants were presented with a bill: the standard tour of Moscow and Leningrad cost US$76 in cash, even without the travel to Europe. The translator/guides still had to write their reports that were mostly featureless to vaguely positive. The only remarkable aspect about them is that now the guests, mostly still with somewhat leftish leanings, began to complain about the complete lack of 'talks on social issues'. Even at this late point in the mid 1960s, the number of young Latin American (excluding Cuban) tourists to the Soviet Union stood at around only 200 to 300 per year. When the Komsomol and Soviet embassies in the region noted that all west European countries were building closer ties to Latin America and therefore asked for an expansion of the invitations to young people to the USSR for free or heavily reduced prices, Sputnik could only refer to its empty tills.[129] They now actively promoted commercial tourism to the Soviet Union via the front organisations. In a letter to the Soviet–Colombian Friendship Association, Sputnik offered itineraries through old Russian cities, the capitals of the republics or cruises on the Black Sea – for the stiff price of 150 rubles.[130]

---

[128] Letters to Sputnik, RGASPI f.5M op.1 d.50, here: 10 Mar. 1960, l.13; 18 Jan. 1959, l.16.

[129] Otčety gido-perevočikov o pribynanij v SSSR turističeskich grupp iz Argentiny, Brazilii, Urugvaja, Čili, 1965–8, RGASPI f.5M op.1 d.633; internal reports of Sputnik and Argentine co-organisation Turismo Mundial, 23 Sep. 1968, RGASPI f.5M op.1 d.556 ll.4–15.

[130] Letter by Sputnik to the Soviet–Colombian Friendship Association, undated, around 1970, Archive of the Instituto Cultural Colombo-Soviético.

The failure of tourism as an element of Soviet cultural diplomacy towards the Third World shows the financial limits of Soviet abilities to present itself as favourably as possible on a global level and is characteristic of the increasing pragmatism it displayed from the late 1960s. It also reveals that the activities of cultural foreign policy did find a curious audience, which went – as designed by Soviet authorities – beyond the usual circles of communists. Tourism was indeed kept utterly separate from the operations of the local communist parties.[131] Foreigners still went for political tourism in the form of delegations from societal groups. Yet an Intourist brochure for Spanish-speaking guests illustrates what the bulk of ordinary tourists were able to see in the USSR: from the sights, monuments and museums of old Moscow ('city of eight centuries') and the Golden Ring of cities around the capital, to ballet and sports performances. Modern Moscow's treats were its architecture and the memorial sites of the space programme. Finally, organised tours to Leningrad, Irkutsk, the hydroelectric power plant of Bratsk, Tashkent, Tbilisi, Erevan and Baku were on offer. The word communism does not appear once.[132]

Space: the inner periphery as a template; time: Stalinist legacies

In Soviet self-representation towards Latin Americans, the regions of the inner Soviet periphery played an important role. The Soviet stance towards the Third World had one of its ideational roots in the state-induced modernisation of Central Asia and the Caucasus. The spatial perception of the outer world, with the rise of the new internationalism from the 1950s, was framed by this experience of socialist internationalism within their own empire from the 1920s. Before summarising what was new in Soviet self-representation to the world abroad, it is worthwhile recalling some continuities and old categories of thought that had prevailed over time.

In the mid nineteenth century, Russia's political elites had already regarded the colonial project in Central Asia as their entrance ticket to the circle of European colonial states. The rhetoric changed from inner colonialism to proletarian internationalism after the October Revolution. But, in fact, the Bolsheviks basically continued the project of a 'civilising mission' – including an old sense of Europe's cultural superiority.[133]

---

[131] Alexander, 'Soviet and Communist Activities in Latin America', 10.
[132] Intourist, *Moscú: Intourist* (Moscow: Intourist, n.d.).
[133] Eva Maria Stolberg, 'Transnationale Forschungsansätze in der Osteuropäischen Geschichte', geschichte.transnational.clio-online.net/forum/2005-03-002 (last accessed

At the bottom of the Soviet courting of the Third World thus lay a paradox. It claimed to be the non-imperialist alternative to European modernity. By the same token, however, it presented the Moscow-led modernisation in its inner periphery as a model to be followed. From the mid 1950s, the Soviets perceived the largely unknown Third World countries as something similar to what they felt they already knew from their non-European Central Asian and Caucasian, 'backward' parts of the empire.

The experience of the 'inner Third World' and its allegedly positive development indeed dominated Soviet self-representation towards Latin Americans. Journals and radio broadcasts reported broadly on the progress of the Soviet republics. Soviet exhibitions featured large tables on industrialisation and effective agriculture in Kazakhstan or Kyrgyzstan. Visitors to the 1957 Youth Festival, tourists and hundreds of delegations of teachers, doctors and engineers were shown around Tbilisi, Baku and Tashkent. Students of Lumumba University spent their summers in work and study camps in Georgia and Turkmenistan. The journal *Problems of the Far East* was translated into Spanish.[134] Also interesting is the choice of representative heads of delegations and friendship societies. The group of the Supreme Soviet that travelled to Bolivia in 1960 was led by the Kazakh Communist Party boss, the next group to Brazil, Cuba, Ecuador and Mexico by the head of the Supreme Soviet, Georgadze, who happened to be Georgian.[135] The Tajik author Mirso Tursun-Sadeh became chairman of the Soviet Committee for Solidarity with the Afro-Asian countries and organised both a 1958 film festival with African and Asian film-makers and a congress for Third World intellectuals – in Tashkent. The Armenian composer Aram Khachaturian headed the Soviet–Latin American Friendship Society, the Azeri Raúf Gadžiev the Cuban–Soviet Institute. In a talk with a Cuban journalist in 1963, Khrushchev explained once more how the Soviet Union provided a role model for development. He also pointed out why he made Mikojan his 'agent for Cuba': he was a native-born Armenian and he had experience in the 'modernisation' of the Caucasus.[136] Mikojan himself also referred to his provenance on his trips to Mexico and Cuba – and declared to the Mexican minister of education, while elucidating wall charts of the Soviet

9 Mar. 2008); Jürgen Osterhammel, 'The Great Work of Uplifting Mankind', in Boris Barth and Jürgen Osterhammel (eds.), *Zivilisierungsmissionen: Imperiale Weltverbesserung seit dem 18. Jahrhundert* (Konstanz: UVK, 2005), pp. 396–9.

[134] Blasier, *The Giant's Rival*, p. 215.

[135] Riza and Quirk, 'Cultural Relations between the Soviet Union and Latin America', 34; Rodionov, *V strane Inkov*.

[136] Fursenko, *Prezidium CK KPSS: 1954–1964*, pp. 884–903.

exhibition in Mexico City. 'education and training of cadres are the keys to development. We learnt that after the civil war in Central Asia and the Caucasus.'[137]

Even in the late 1960s, Soviet regional experts underlined the parallels between the 'Soviet East' and Latin America in scientific treatises. A 1969 talk at an international conference in Frunze, Kyrgyzstan, confirmed the theory of the non-violent path to socialism. Central Asia, after all, it was argued there, did not have a violent revolution either and had skipped – thanks to help from Moscow – the capitalist phase of development. The contributor emphasised that there was no reason to demonise different paths to socialism, as the Maoists did, and that there was no antagonism between city and countryside, as proven by the marvellous conditions in the Central Asian Soviet republics. Marxism-Leninism, he finished in a telling example of Soviet missionary thought, is 'the feeling of historic optimism and the experience of the peoples of the Soviet Union. Only they can teach the right path.'[138]

At the same conference, several representatives from Bolivia, Chile, Panama and Venezuela gave talks on how similar the conditions in their countries were to Kazakhstan in the 1920s.[139] More Latin American intellectuals – albeit usually members of communist parties – took over this colonial attitude readily: Rodolfo Ghioldi, an Argentine journalist, travelled to Uzbekistan in 1956. In his book *Uzbekistan: el espejo* (Uzbekistan: The Mirror) he described the recent history of Central Asia as a straightforward, direct model of what needed to happen in his homeland.[140] The Paraguayan Efraín Morel went to the Caucasus the same year. The ancient advanced civilisations that had fallen victim to imperialism reminded him of his own people, and the solution of socialism apparently found his approval.[141] And the Peruvian Gustavo Valcárcel dedicated one chapter of his travelogue to Central Asia. 'Kasajstan, un ejemplo para América Latina' ('Kazakhstan, an Example for Latin America') depicted the modernisation of Kazakhstan as a model for Latin American development.[142]

---

[137] 19 Nov. 1959, GARF f.9518 op.1 d.343 l.177.
[138] Šul'govskij, 'Opyt rešenija nacional'nogo voprosa v SSSR', 13; A. Šul'govskij, 'Latinskaja Amerika i opyt respublik Sovetskogo Vostoka', *Latinskaja Amerika* 5 (1970), 82–9.
[139] R. Pučkov, 'Opyt Sovetskogo Vostok i razvivajuščiesja strany', *Latinskaja Amerika* 6 (1970), 171–5.
[140] Rodolfo Ghioldi, *Uzbekistan: el espejo* (Buenos Aires: Editorial Fundamentos, 1956).
[141] 10 May 1956, RGANI f.5 op.28 d.439 l.201.
[142] Gustavo Valcárcel, *Medio siglo de revolución invencible: segunda parte de 'Reportaje al futuro'* (Lima: Ediciones 'Unidad', 1967), pp. 50–64.

Another issue on which many Latin Americans agreed with the official Soviet view was contempt for US popular culture. Claiming to speak for all Latin Americans, many leftish and communist intellectuals felt the need to share their anti-US views with the Soviets. 'While Soviet youth care about the progress of their nation and their studies, youth in the United States care about rock-and-roll, youth criminality, racial discrimination, which means, every youngster from the United States is a threat to the world, because, in spite of all their lack of cultivation, they still consider themselves a superior race. [We Latin Americans are] against the sexual criminal novel in the US style', wrote a young Cuban in a personal letter to Khrushchev.[143] Julieta Campusano, member of the Communist Party of Chile, deplored the 'increasing flood of films, books, records and concerts of so-called stars such as Paul Anka ... who are supposed to woo our youth to a path of vice and amusement'.[144] The Brazilian writer Eneida de Moraes, in her talk at the Third Congress of Soviet Writers in Moscow in 1959, was, for a communist, quite defeatist about the youth as such: 'those whom we call the Coca-Cola generation wear "Texas shirts", dance to rock-and-roll, chew North American gum and imitate everything from the Yankees. These boys and girls no longer say *sí*, but *okey*. They do not know our composers nor do they love our beautiful music, but they are crazy about jazz and know all the famous stars of Hollywood and Broadway ... They are victims of the corrosive impact of US films and those hideous North American criminal novels ... Our intellectuals, however, still know the Russian authors of the past. We follow the political life, the scientific discoveries and the cultural achievements of the Soviet Union.'[145]

These views fit perfectly with Soviet cultural policy. On a regular basis, Soviet publications, internal as well as international ones, underlined their own cultural superiority by fiercely attacking US popular culture. Soviet journals presented US literature as a blend of worthless pornography and gangster comics, its films as capitalist propaganda and its abstract paintings as a sign of the decay and the decadence of the contemporary United States. Over and over again, all media repeated Soviet achievements in education. Before the revolution, one typical line of argument went, 46 million books existed in Russia. Now more than 400,000 libraries offered 1.5 billion volumes for free.[146]

---

[143] Letter to Chruščev by a young Cuban, 28 Mar. 1960, RGASPI f.1M op.30 d.258 ll.1–3.
[144] J. Campusano, 'Die Kommunisten und die Jugend', *Probleme des Friedens und des Sozialismus* 1 (1962), 69–70.
[145] Enaida Morais, 'Mein Brasilien', *Neue Zeit* 25 (1959), 19.
[146] Alexej Surkov, 'Interv'ju', *Sovetskaja Literatura* 8 (1961), 175.

Like the reference to the space of the inner periphery, this cultural superiority complex goes back to the time of the 1920s and 1930s. 'Conservative-puritan mass culture'[147] on the one hand and the constant defamation of *nekul'turnye* ('uncultivated') US citizens on the other maintained the continuity of the Stalinist *kul'turnost'* concept and were hence a Stalinist legacy projected on to the Third World. High culture had been propagated among the non-Russian population as a measure of social discipline. After the destruction of their traditional social structures in the years of revolution and civil war, open violence, vandalism, alcoholism and all kinds of deviant behaviour were the order of the day. The propagation of 'cultivated behaviour' was an attempt to stabilise the country and to form 'backwards' peasants and nomads into members of modern socialist society.[148] This *kul'turnost'* concept was now transferred, although not explicitly, on the 'backwards' countries of the Third World. As the internationalist ideological journal *World Marxist Review* put it: 'the creative activity of the masses, including those of the countries of non-capitalist development, is an important factor of progress. Raising their cultural level and awareness is a necessity. The masses of the people have to grow culturally ... The fight for culture is also a fight against western mass culture.'[149]

In their propagating of the notion of culture as a third plank of progress, alongside a planned economy and technology, the Soviets, in the mid 1960s, unwittingly continued perceiving the world in Stalinist categories developed a generation before them. The term 'friendship of the peoples', too, widely used in Soviet national and international media, had already been introduced by Stalin in 1935. It essentialised the concept of the nation and folklorised everything non-Russian. Only 'truly national art, flamingly patriotic, helps prevent the blind mimicry of decadent foreign role models', Soviet cultural officials were still advising artists in Latin America in the 1950s.[150]

Folklorisation or exoticisation of other ethnic groups constructed a cultural gradient, whether they were Uzbeks in their colourful traditional garments or Latinos with their guitars and moustaches (see Chapter 2). In the same spirit, the rehabilitated great Russian past and its high culture

[147] Caute, *The Dancer Defects*, p. 8.
[148] Vadim Volkov, 'The Concept of Kulturnost: Notes on the Stalinist Civilization Process', in Sheila Fitzpatrick (ed.), *Stalinism: New Directions* (London: Routledge, 2000), pp. 210–30.
[149] Georges Batal, Zerewijn Dawagsuren and Pedro Motta Lima, 'Oktoberrevolution und Fortschritt', *Probleme des Friedens und des Sozialismus* 11 (1966), 845–51.
[150] Vera Kutejščikova and Lev Ospovat, 'Progressivnaja Kul'tura Latinskoj Ameriki', *Sovetskaja Literatura* 6 (1956), 212.

were used in Soviet self-representation. In the early 1920s, this attitude would have been criticised heavily as chauvinistic; from the 1930s, it was acceptable again; and, from the 1950s, Russian high culture and folk-lorised versions of other traditions dominated in Soviet cultural relations with the Third World.[151]

While these interactions with distant parts of the planet were indeed new, a certain mistrust of foreigners and the world abroad, if never as strong towards the global South as towards the West, still prevailed. A small but increasing number of Soviet artists and intellectuals were now allowed to leave the country, but they were still monitored closely. Documents reveal numerous examples of travellers being ordered back to the Soviet Union and interrogated because they aroused suspicion with major crimes such as 'leaving the group for more than an hour'.[152]

The Soviet elite of the 1950s claimed optimistically to be back on the path of Leninism. The political concepts were indeed adapted accordingly. Yet they still carried some ballast of Stalinist thought. Internally, the new leadership did denounce terror and the personality cult. In their self-representation abroad, the Soviets nonetheless still celebrated the rise of the Soviet Union to an industrial superpower within only thirty years as a role model for the Third World. That this enforced progress had been intrinsically linked with Stalinist state terror was discreetly overlooked. In the end, it was not only Leninist socialist internationalism, but also legacies of Stalinism that now pre-shaped interactions with the Third World.

Peace and friendship: Soviet self-representation and internationalism from the 1950s

Soviet self-representation to Latin Americans from the mid 1950s had its ideational roots in Leninist internationalism and in Stalinist categories of thought. Yet, as this chapter has outlined, the way the Soviet Union after Stalin wanted to be perceived by the global South was indeed very different from before. Anti-imperialism and the support of non-communist national leaders did refer to older Leninist concepts but, for the first time, Latin American states and populations were targets of Soviet activities on a large scale. Tremendous changes happened in the

---

[151] Terry Martin, *The Affirmative Action Empire: Nations and Nationalism in the Soviet Union, 1923–1939* (Ithaca: Cornell University Press, 2001), pp. 443–4; Stites, 'Heaven and Hell', p. 92.

[152] E.g. on a trip to Chile: KGB Central'nomu Komitetu, 14 Jun. 1963, RGANI f.5 op.55 d.28 ll.117–118.

institutional structuring and implementation of 'propaganda', and these changes opened up spaces of interaction between the Soviet and Latin American societies. While the International Department of the Central Committee of the CPSU, internally, kept direct control of most activities, a number of newly founded organs were to convey the impression that it was the Soviet state, not the Communist Party, that was in charge of cultural affairs.

Relations with Moscow-oriented communist parties continued, and some journals, the *World Marxist Review* in the forefront, still chewed over ideological questions of socialism. But more visible was now a self-representation that, by and large, dropped the topos of communism. Soviet media and international cultural activities became increasingly more colourful and appealing to a broad audience. They presented Soviet achievements in the fields of high-brow culture, education and health care and placed a strong focus on industry and science as motors of this progress. In this image, new cities and factories, with their energy supplied by new hydroelectric and nuclear power plants, were the habitat of the modern Soviet man. Technological and scientific feats had paved the way for social advancement: atomic energy and space travel, both intrinsically linked to military purposes also in the Soviet Union, were always embedded in a rhetoric of peace and happiness – and contrasted to the military rockets that imperialists installed everywhere on earth or atomic bombs that they dropped on defenceless people. The US interventions in Guatemala and the Cuban Bay of Pigs, the quasi-colonial US presence in Guantánamo Bay, Panama and Puerto Rico, and their support for the anti-communist military dictators were contrasted with an altruistic image of the USSR. In this picture of the new Soviet Union, harmony prevailed: there was social justice, free education and health care, and its peoples lived together peacefully and happily.

The catchphrases of this new Soviet internationalism were *mir* (peace) and *družba* (friendship); its iconography boasted Picasso's peace dove and shaking hands of different skin colours. The Soviet Union of the Thaw period presented itself to the world as the trail-blazer of the modern world, with a healthy, educated and happily consuming population. This harmonious *status quo* had ostensibly been achieved quickly and without the hardships of capitalism, the pauperisation of the masses or the exploitation of the Third World. Within the Soviet Union, to be sure, the non-modern and non-idyllic phenomena of nepotism, corruption, less-than-adequate health care and a dire consumer situation prevailed. Even though, remarkably enough, the Sovinformbjuro head Ignat'ev had suggested also mentioning their own shortcomings, there was never a trace of self-criticism, let alone of the terrible consequences the Soviet path to modernity had had for millions of people; the famines, purges and bloodily repressed revolts that accompanied it were not allowed to tarnish the harmonious image.

In many respects, this attitude – pushing the recent past to the back of the mind and looking to the future optimistically – was not only a Soviet characteristic, but a child of its times and shared by many other peoples worldwide in the 1950s and 1960s. Most Europeans, with good or bad consciences, wanted to forget the world wars behind them. An undiluted belief in the benefits of technology and optimism in historical progress had captured large parts of the planet regardless of political orientation in the Cold War. And Soviet internationalists were very much in tune with this global spirit. No longer did they pursue old Marxist questions of alienation of the human being, on man–nature relations or on the structural deformation of North–South economic relations as had been done back in the 1920s. Instead, they echoed the global enthusiasm for industrial development and modernisation.

Soviet self-representation, as presented in this chapter, was, first and foremost, an image campaign that conveyed an idealised depiction of the new USSR. There were, initially, few distinctions made between different addressees of this charm offensive within the global South. Only from the mid 1960s did the perception of the entire global South as a homogeneous bloc give way to more reflections on the specificities of distinctive parts of the Third World. Chapter 5 will examine how Soviet internationalists overcame the gap in knowledge about different world areas after years of international isolation. But, even then, Soviet media and agents of self-representation did not make many concrete suggestions on how to improve life in Latin America – or for that matter in any other part of the Third World. Questions of how to precisely organise land reforms, government planning and nationalisations were not discussed in Soviet glossy magazines and cultural diplomacy activities with cosmonauts and violin players.

Yet the shortcomings and generalisations of Soviet self-representation towards Latin Americans did not mean that it had no impact. In times of the Cold War and decolonisation, Soviet rhetoric that emphasised peace, international solidarity and anti-imperialism did find an audience. From the mid 1950s, the Soviets succeeded, with relatively modest efforts, in making themselves heard in the Americas. Left reformers in Argentina and Brazil, in their desire to modernise their countries quickly and through state-induced initiatives, had a strong interest in certain aspects of the Soviet concept and readily collaborated with the USSR in many of its activities. Millions of Latin Americans flocked to Soviet exhibitions, venerated the Sputnik satellite and Gagarin, or marvelled at their ballet performances. In the long run, attempts at presenting the Soviet Union as a peace-loving state and reliable partner paved, from the late 1960s, the way for the (re-)establishment of diplomatic relations with most Latin American countries, which had no interest in communism, but a lot in development and integration into the global system of states instead of disadvantageous unilateral relations with the United States. In terms of Cold War rivalry, if this is to be considered a success, the Soviets also managed to scare the United States with activities in their 'back yard'. Questions of success and shortcomings of Soviet advances will be reconsidered with a closer examination of Latin American target groups of Soviet advances, in Chapter 3 on intellectuals and in Chapter 4 on students in Soviet higher education.

After a few years of Soviet activities in Latin America, the Cuban Revolution seemed to validate the Soviet conception of the course of world history. Fidel Castro's victory therefore boosted the prevailing Soviet optimism in their prospects in Latin America, where Soviet internationalists were most active in the years between 1959 and 1962. To some extent, the enthusiasm waned again, after the Cuban Crisis showed the limits of Soviet influence and the dangers linked with it. A 1963 report does still list many Soviet cultural activities in Latin America, but the tone of optimism that characterised former writings had given way to a rather sober analysis and references to the 'difficult political conditions'.[153]

This chapter has looked at Soviet self-representation towards Latin Americans as part of a renewed internationalism after 1953. Drawing on elements of socialist internationalism of the 1920s and 1930s as well as on developments of cultural internationalism from the 1950s, the Soviets presented their country as a highly developed modern state with idyllic and harmonious living conditions for its peoples. Formulating and propagating one's path externally has a lot do with affirming one's own identity internally by way of dissociating from some and expressing solidarity with others. What Frederick Cooper and Jane Burbank have attributed to the European empires of the nineteenth century also holds true for the Soviet Union: it 'had to provide publics at home with an acceptable view of the state they lived in'.[154] Many cultural activities directed towards foreigners also reached the Soviet public back home, which participated in their state's global activities through all media

---

[153] SSOD, Otčet o rabote na strany Latinskoj Ameriki za 1963 god, 17 Oct. 1963, GARF f.9576 op.10 d.1 ll.1–27.
[154] Frederick Cooper and Jane Burbank, *Empires in World History: Power and the Politics of Difference* (Princeton: Princeton University Press, 2010), p. 20.

channels. It is striking how dominant the renewed internationalism was, too, in media that were directed to an exclusively Soviet readership. They could revel in their country's global importance and obtained ostensible proof that they were on the technologically, culturally and morally superior side of the conflict. Chapter 2 will explore how the new contacts with the Third World, politically instigated but not limited to state-led activities, initially did more to support Soviet citizens' belief in the state they were living in than to question it.

2 Moscow learns the mambo: Latin America and internationalism in Soviet popular culture

The frontiers oppress me.
I feel it awkward
Not knowing Buenos Aires,
New York.
I want to wander
As much as I like
In London,
To talk, however brokenly,
With everybody ...
      Yevgeny Yevtushenko, 1958[1]

Revolucii
nužen
ritmi!
      Yevgeny Yevtushenko, 1962[2]

Reconnecting: Soviet culture after the death of Stalin

Soviet contacts with Latin America as they re-emerged from the mid 1950s had their origin in political attempts to convey a certain image of the post-Stalinist USSR in the Third World. As Chapter 1 has argued, much of Soviet self-representation to the world abroad was also directed towards Soviet citizens and meant to assure them of the global vanguard role of their socialist home country. Yet the encounter of the ordinary Soviet man or woman with internationalism in general, and Latin America in particular, was more extensive and less one-dimensionally politically determined. To see the world outside the Soviet Union was still a rare privilege, and hardly anyone ever got to go to the Americas. But representations of foreign countries mushroomed in Soviet culture from

---

[1] Anon., 'A Longing for Truth: Russia's New Generation', *Time*, 13 Apr. 1962.

[2] 'The revolution needs rhythms!', in Evgenij Evtušenko, *Nežnost'* (Moscow: Sovetskij Pisatel', 1962), p. 135.

the mid 1950s. Through the consumption of cultural products, all Soviet citizens participated in the Soviet Union's reconnecting to the world; and it was representations of Latin America that made Soviet internationalism after Stalin palatable to many of them.

Late Stalinist culture had been dull, and this was to do with repression of artists on the one hand, and self-isolation from world culture on the other. The ageing dictator was tightening the strings on Soviet cultural life; terror and international isolation, which had to some extent slackened during the war, were resurgent. The man in charge of cultural affairs was Andrej Ždanov, a veteran of the Great Terror of the 1930s, who led a vendetta against everything foreign. Even though he died in 1948, his policy, the *Ždanovščina*, prevailed until the death of the dictator in 1953. Anti-cosmopolitanism campaigns hit artists particularly hard. All poets, painters and musicians who displayed any foreign influence risked serious persecution. Travels abroad were unthinkable for most. Even the Pushkin Museum, with its western art, was closed for years.

Things changed quickly and dramatically after Stalin's death as Soviet artists demanded an immediate and complete change of cultural policy. In October 1953, Ilya Ehrenburg in the reformist journal *Novyj mir* (New World), in November, Aram Khachaturian in *Sovetskaja muzyka* (Soviet Music) and, finally, in December, Vladimir Pomerancev again in *Novyj mir* accused the state of interfering massively in their work, with the result that Soviet artists had become boring and meaningless.[3] The Second Congress of Soviet Writers in 1954 reiterated this accusation and declared an end to the dogma of socialist realism. In the years that followed, the empty heroism of Stalinist art was replaced by a more authentic style.[4] Vladimir Dudincev's *Not by Bread Alone* (1956) and Alexander Solzhenitsyn's *One Day in the Life of Ivan Denisovich* (1962) were the outstanding literary examples of the epoch, and depicted ordinary men in their struggle against bureaucracy and for survival in the Gulag respectively. Authors now criticised not only their personal artistic restrictions, but the moral and social norms of a widely prevailing Stalinism.

This chapter looks at the re-internationalisation of Soviet cultural life from the mid 1950s, and it uses the impact of Latin American culture as perhaps the most illuminating example of this process. Historians have long acknowledged the diversification of cultural life, of literature, music,

---

[3] Ilya Ehrenburg, Aram Khachaturian and Vladimir Pomerantsev, 'Three Soviet Artists on the Present Needs of Soviet Art', *Soviet Studies* 4 (1954), 412–45.

[4] Johannes Holthusen, *Russische Literatur im 20. Jahrhundert* (Tübingen: Francke, 1992), p. 177.

theatre, and film, after 1953. Culture was the field in which the departure from Stalinism was most pronounced and dynamic. Yet one important aspect of the changes in Soviet cultural production has often been overlooked: for writers and artists, the death of Stalin also meant the end of a stultifying international cultural isolation and the chance for Russia to resume its rightful place in world culture. Richard Stites has described the 'new era of contacts with the West' in Russian cultural history, but he, as most other scholars, all but ignored the impact of the entire rest of the world.[5] In order to get a more comprehensive picture of Soviet culture after 1953, this chapter takes the example of one part of the global South to look at the reflection of a new geo-political awareness in aesthetics, and at the cultural adaptation of what Edward Said has called 'previously unreachable temporal and cultural frontiers'. What he claimed for west Europeans of the colonial age describes just as well the Soviet conception of the world after years of Stalinist isolation: 'a very unrigorous idea of what is "out there", beyond one's own territory. All kinds of suppositions, associations, and fictions appear to crowd the unfamiliar space outside one's own.'[6]

Andrei Yurchak is one of the few scholars who have written about the Thaw generation's fascination with exotic worlds, real and imagined (albeit only in a side note on the story of their children's generation). He found an 'explosion of interest in the 1960s in various cultural and intellectual pursuits based on the experience of a faraway elsewhere'.[7] In their search for self-assurance and orientation, Soviet intellectuals and artists, and with them the recipients of their art and writings, now set their sights on hitherto unknown, difficult to reach and therefore exotic places beyond their present horizon. They began with the periphery of the gigantic Soviet Union itself: from the 1950s, the exotic yearning found expression in travelogues from the more distant parts of the Soviet Union, the Far East, Kamchatka and the Arctic. The Ukrainian-Russian painter Igor' Savickij was enthralled by the region of Karakalpakstan by the Aral Sea, eventually moved there and began his huge collection of Russian and Uzbek avant-garde art.[8] Long before the Beatles conquered

---

[5] Richard Stites, *Russian Popular Culture: Entertainment and Society since 1900* (Cambridge: Cambridge University Press, 2000), pp. 116–23; Catriona Kelly and David G. Shepherd (eds.), *Russian Cultural Studies: An Introduction* (Oxford: Oxford University Press, 1998). A notable exception is Sudha Rajagopalan, *Leave Disco Dancer Alone! Indian Cinema and Soviet Movie-Going after Stalin* (New Delhi: Yoda Press, 2008).

[6] Edward Said, *Orientalism* (London: Penguin Books, 2007), pp. 12, 54, 120.

[7] Alexei Yurchak, *Everything Was Forever, until It Was No More: The Last Soviet Generation* (Princeton: Princeton University Press, 2006), p. 160.

[8] Tobias Rupprecht, 'Musenkuss in Nukus: Sowjetische Avantgarde-Kunst in der usbekischen Provinz', *Osteuropa* 3 (2012), 159–71.

the USSR, popular but still official musicians played with the exoticism of their own peripheries of empire, as did the Azerbaijani Muslim Magomaev and Edita Piecha, who – even though fluent in Russian – always kept an artificial Polish accent in her songs.[9] Later in the 1960s, the bard Jurij Vizbor lost his heart in the Tajik Fan Mountains ('Ja serce ostavil v Fanskich gorach'), and millions of Soviet cinema-goers were blinded by Vladimir Motyl'''s *Beloe solnce pustyni*, the white sun of the Turkmen desert.

Soon, this yearning for 'other', 'exotic' places and people included countries from outside the socialist world; travelogues were published from Scandinavia, Australia and the Middle East.[10] Yevgeny Yevtushenko, whose poems preface this chapter, published his *Stichi o zagranice* (Poems about the Outland) in 1962.[11] Many Soviet films of the Thaw feature foreign, usually Asian, tourists in prominent roles.[12] And Latin America, as this chapter will elaborate, inspired Soviet poets, writers, film-makers and musicians as much as it fascinated a broad audience throughout the USSR.

The internationalisation of Soviet culture after 1953, underplayed in most literature on the history of the Thaw, allowed Soviet artists and writers to reconnect to colleagues and trends worldwide, and it fostered the fascination of a broad public with faraway places in popular culture. Latin American music, film and literature, and the adaptation of Latin American themes by Soviet artists, represented a significant share of the new international element in Soviet culture from the mid 1950s. Unlike in their relations with other 'exotic' world regions that now loomed on the Soviet horizon, black Africa and South East Asia, Latin America played a prominent role for Soviet artists and intellectuals because they could build on contacts and an imagery of the Hispanic world that had already existed in the 1920s and 1930s. In many ways, however, Soviet culture during the Thaw, with its longing for the exotic outland, was also in tune with global developments of the 1950s and 1960s.

Exoticism and folklorism in East and West in the 1950s and 1960s

In Europe and the United States, too, exotic 'other' worlds in popular arts enjoyed great popularity. After the sufferings of the Second World

---

[9] Artemy Troitsky, *Back in the USSR: The True Story of Rock in Russia* (London: Music Sales, 1987).
[10] Holthusen, *Russische Literatur im 20. Jahrhundert*, p. 248.   [11] *Ibid.*, p. 289.
[12] E.g. Grigorij Aleksandrov's *Russkij suvenir* (The Russian Souvenir, 1960) and Georgij Danelija's *Ja šagaju po Moskve* (I Stroll around Moscow, 1963).

War and the hardships of the immediate post-war era, people found sanctuary in the idyllic worlds of modern entertainment. Tropical islands and Mediterranean beaches in songs and films took their audience, if only for short imaginary moments, to distant places that were still, for most people, unreachable in reality. Exotic entertainment distracted from the traumatic past and the monotony of everyday life, and promised cosiness, happiness and a dash of eroticism.

The exoticism of the 1950s and 1960s, in the East as in the West, was not an entirely new phenomenon, but dated back to the early days of European colonialism. Humble living conditions and restrictive morals at home made people project their spiritual and sensual fantasies on to spheres at the edge of the known world. These distant places were experienced directly by only a few travellers and sailors, but those back home shared the thrill of the new worlds sitting in armchairs and reading their travelogues and adventure stories. Like Tahiti for the French from the eighteenth century, Oceania and Brazil were for Germans in the nineteenth not only colonial possessions or areas of settlement, but lands that spurred fantasies of a harmonic and innocent existence unspoiled by the vices of modern life. Around the same time, tsarist Russia saw a similar literary mythologisation of the recently conquered Caucasus and Turkestan by Pushkin, Lermontov, Dostoyevsky and Tolstoy. While these views of the empire (as well as the 'exoticising' view of Russia itself by the West) have been studied thoroughly, scholars have not yet used this category for an analysis of the Soviet 'orientalist' view of the world after 1917.[13]

For westerners and Soviets alike, a mythological Latin America was, around 1960, something comparable to what Tahiti or the Caucasian Mountains had been a century before. Cultural theories have usually defined this exoticism strictly politically, as Eurocentric epistemological imperialism, as a strategy of legitimisation of political and economic dominance and as a derogatory representation of the other that shaped and privileged the European identity. Marxists such as Adorno or Barthes saw exoticism, and popular entertainment in general, as only an escapist pseudo-solution, a flight of the petty bourgeois from the repressive living conditions of (late) capitalism. While it is certainly

---

[13] A small selection of many more includes David van der Schimmelpenninck Oye, *Russian Orientalism: Asia in the Russian Mind from Peter the Great to the Emigration* (New Haven: Yale University Press, 2010); Michael David-Fox, *Orientalism and Empire in Russia* (Bloomington: Slavica, 2006); Martin Malia, *Russia under Western Eyes: From the Bronze Horseman to the Lenin Mausoleum* (Cambridge, MA: Belknap Press of Harvard University Press, 1999); Kalpana Sahni, *Crucifying the Orient: Russian Orientalism and the Colonization of Caucasus and Central Asia* (Bangkok: White Orchid Press, 1997).

correct to say that 'exoticism is an expression of power relations',[14] it also contains a dimension that has nothing to do with power and politics. The depiction of the Third World in the folklore of post-war Europe (including the Soviet Union) was not free of a certain sense of superiority. Yet the positive stereotypes of the 'exotic' expressed a somewhat naive curiosity and an escapist, and for that matter very apolitical, yearning for distant places – and not so much cultural imperialism.

Cultural echoes from the 1920s and 1930s

While Latin America as a theme of Soviet arts was part of the worldwide escapist exoticism of the 1950s, it had also roots in the leftist culture of socialist internationalism of the 1920s and 1930s.[15] The Russian avant-garde poet Vladimir Mayakovsky had described his experiences in Cuba, Mexico and Spain in several poems and a travel diary.[16] Sergei Eisenstein had directed the Proletkult theatre production *The Mexican*, based on a tale by Jack London, in Moscow in 1921, starring Ivan Pyr'ev, and developed a fascination for Mexico. Later, in 1930–1, Eisenstein spent almost an entire year there, together with the camera operators Edvard Tisse and Grigorij Aleksandrov. Their epos *¡Qué Viva Mexico!*, never officially completed, which they had shot on this occasion, was an anthological portrayal of Mexican history from the arrival of the *conquistadores* to the Mexican Revolution.[17]

Intellectuals, mostly from Leningrad, had run an Ispano-Amerikanskoe Obščestvo (Hispanic-American Society) from 1929. It was disbanded after only four years during a nationwide restructuring of scientific organisations in the mid 1930s, but its many members stayed in unofficial contact; many fought as volunteers in the Spanish Civil War.[18] Other members, including the consecutive presidents Boris Krževskij and David Vygodskij, translated works by many of the big

---

[14] Thomas Koebner and Gerhart Pickerodt (eds.), *Die andere Welt: Studien zum Exotismus* (Frankfurt am Main: Athenäum, 1987), p. 7; see also Institut für Auslandsbeziehungen (IfA) Stuttgart (ed.), *Exotische Welten, europäische Phantasien: Ausstellungskatalog* (Stuttgart: Edition Cantz, 1987), p. 10.

[15] Tobias Rupprecht, 'Die Liebe der Linken zu Lateinamerika: Vom Radical Chic zur Nikaragua-Solidarität', *Le Monde Diplomatique* 11 (2010), 16–17.

[16] Vladimir Majakovskij, *Meksika: pervye očerki* (Moscow: Biblioteka Ogonek, 1933); Vladimir Majakovskij, *Ispanija. Okean. Gavana. Meksika. Amerika: stichi* (Moscow: Gosizdat, 1926); Vladimir Majakovskij, *Moe otkrytie Ameriki* (Moscow: Gosizdat, 1926).

[17] Masha Salazkina, *In Excess: Sergei Eisenstein's Mexico* (Chicago: University of Chicago Press, 2009); Kutejščikova, *Moskva-Meksiko-Moskva*, p. 91.

[18] Boris Lukin, 'La sociedad hispanoamericana en el Leningrado de la preguerra', *América Latina* 3 (1979), 174–82.

names of Spanish and Latin American literature into Russian for the first time and discovered, among others, the young communist Brazilian author Jorge Amado for the Soviet readership. The young Ilya Ehrenburg, a frequent guest at Vygodskij's literary salons, had used the perspective of a Mexican on post-revolutionary Russia in his 1922 satire *Neobyčajnye pochoždenija Chulio Churenito* (The Unusual Adventures of Julio Jurenito). In his Paris exile, Ehrenburg had learnt Spanish and had made friends with the Mexican painter Diego Rivera, who stirred Ehrenburg's interest in Mexico and inspired him to create the character of Julio.

Rivera also introduced Ehrenburg to several Latin American intellectuals during his time as a war reporter in Spain. In the International Brigades, he met the Cuban poet Nicolás Guillén, the Chilean Pablo Neruda and the Mexican painter David Siqueiros, all of whose work Ehrenburg would later introduce to the Soviet Union. Just as among leftists from all over the Americas and Europe, the Spanish Civil War had stirred a revolutionary romanticism with many Soviet intellectuals. Many fought in Spain, and many – most notably the journalist Michail Kol'cov – fell victim not to Franco's Falange but to Stalinist purges in Spain and back in the Soviet Union. Ehrenburg dedicated more than 200 exuberant pages in his 1960s memoirs to his experiences in Spain.[19] Andrei Sakharov, later a human rights activist, recalled from his childhood: 'The paramount issue of the 1930s was the Spanish Civil War. That tragic conflict was treated by Soviet media as yet another diversion. How strange it is that fifty years later, the anxieties and bitterness of the Spanish war are still alive in people of my generation. There was some spellbinding force at work, a sense of romance, heroism, challenge – and possibly, a premonition of the evil fascism would bring.'[20] Thousands of communist refugees from the civil war and their families formed small Spanish-speaking communities in several Soviet cities, which would prevail until the 1970s, when they were allowed to return to Spain after the end of Franco's rule – many, however, had long assimilated into their Russian environment and decided to stay.

With the isolation of high Stalinism and the early Cold War years, Spain and Latin America all but disappeared from the Soviet cultural horizon. The Hispanic-American Society was closed by the suspicious authorities as early as 1933. Ehrenburg miraculously survived Stalinism, but Vygodskij was arrested in 1938 for anti-Party agitation and died in the Gulag in 1943. Ivan Lichačev, another prominent translator, was

[19] Ehrenburg, *Menschen, Jahre, Leben*, pp. ii, 198, 349–502.
[20] Andrei Sakharov, *Memoirs* (New York: Alfred A. Knopf, 1990), p. 30.

accused of espionage and fascist propaganda through the *obščestvo*, and was sentenced to forced labour and exile in Central Asia; he was rehabilitated only in 1957.[21] While Spain remained sealed-off territory for the Soviets until well into the 1970s, Latin America experienced a comeback with the official reappraisal of internationalism from the mid 1950s.

Internationalist culture and Soviet society after Stalin

Two strands of ideas defined the image of Latin America in Soviet arts from the mid 1950s: firstly a revolutionary romanticism that dated back to early Soviet perceptions of the Mexican Revolution, to Spanish-language leftist songs and to the struggle of the internationalist brigades in the Spanish Civil War; and, secondly, the worldwide rage for a mythical-exotic Latin America. This chapter will trace the dissemination of cultural products from and about Latin America in the USSR from the mid 1950s. It looks both at Soviet artists, who produced them, and at the Soviet public, which consumed them. That encounter with Latin America and its cultural representations was part of what Soviet society experienced as rekindled Soviet internationalism. Also in the realm of Soviet culture, internationalism after Stalin combined ideas of socialist internationalism of the 1920s and 1930s with elements of a global cultural internationalism of the 1950s and 1960s.

As a credo of Soviet self-representation to the world abroad, Soviet internationalism after 1953 has been analysed in Chapter 1. Here, internationalism is defined beyond that as also a mindset and a functional principle *within* the Soviet Union. During the Cold War, internationalism was not only about winning the world public over, but also directed inwards, advocated by intellectuals, embraced by artists and carried over to the Soviet population.[22] Even in the most remote areas, Soviet citizens were confronted with a flood of signs, demands, rituals and symbols of internationalism. This internationalist discourse has often been downplayed as empty rhetoric, compelled from above and ignored or ridiculed from below. This perception of internationalism is part of a long-lasting mono-directional understanding of the relationship between the Soviet state and its citizens. It was believed that Soviet power was based on passive loyalty to, and sullen acceptance of, the political system.

---

[21] Kutejščikova, *Moskva-Meksiko-Moskva*, p. 86; www.sakharov-center.ru/asfcd/auth/?t=author&i=396 (last accessed 22 Nov. 2011).

[22] Klaus Gestwa, *Die Stalinschen Großbauten des Kommunismus: Sowjetische Technik-und Umweltgeschichte, 1948–1967* (Munich: Oldenbourg, 2010), p. 329.

Integrative moments, which convinced not only the political and intellectual elite, but also ordinary citizens of the superiority of their state and societal model, have long been underestimated, Only lately have the victory in the Second World War and the successes of the space programme been interpreted in this sense.

The concept of *egemonia culturale* that Gramsci coined for capitalist societies can be applied just as well to the Soviet Union after Stalin: no longer did the state hold sway over its subjects through terror and physical violence. The consent of the political and intellectual elite and of the majority of the population was now based on shared cultural and ideological conceptions. To preserve this *status quo* of public compliance, the state – besides supplying basic material needs – needed only to make sure that certain cultural forms predominated over others. Western modernist art and rock-and-roll music were considered dangerous, for they seemed to promote anti-authoritarian individualism, uncontrolled emotions and sexual libertinism. They were banned and could not reach a mass audience in the USSR until the 1970s. Most Latin American cultural products, however, were considered, instead, to support the Soviet view of the world in content and form.

This chapter will show that rekindled internationalism, and the world-view Latin American art helped to create and sustain, added to the ideational cohesion of Soviet society from the mid 1950s: it provided a coherent world-view that reassured intellectuals and ordinary citizens of the superiority of their own political and societal model. Two sections will analyse the impact of the topos 'Latin America' in Soviet cinema and music, of both Soviet and Latin American origin. They prove that internationalism found its expression not only in state-directed pure propaganda, but also in branches of cultural production that found a receptive mass audience. It was through this mass culture that the majority of ordinary Soviet citizens developed their idea of the outside world. Based on the positive stereotypes of post-war exoticism, many of them not only learned to dance the mambo, but also at the same time incorporated their own interpretation of the ideals of international solidarity. Looking at cultural products by Soviet artists who included themes of the world abroad into their artistic repertoire also gives us an idea of how these artists perceived their role in the propagation and implementation of the renewed Soviet internationalism and their stance towards the new regime.

The third section will look at a privileged class of intellectual elites who were allowed to travel abroad again from the 1950s. The travelogues they wrote about their trips to many countries of the Americas give insights into their conception of themselves within the new global order of the

Cold War, their conception of Latin America and their conception of internationalism after Stalin. The infatuation with Latin America reached its peak after Fidel Castro's revolution. The last section will show the huge impact Cuba had on the Soviet Union not only politically but also in the realm of culture. At least for some time in the early 1960s and not least thanks to the Cuban Revolution, internationalism, embraced by all, while interpreted differently by political elites, intellectuals and ordinary people, had become an integral part of Soviet identity.

A window on the world: Latin America in Soviet cinemas and concert halls

The average Soviet citizen got his first glimpse of Latin America most likely during a night out at the movies, through an imported film or through a Soviet production that dealt with the area. Among modern media, cinema was cutting-edge in the 1950s. And film-makers were, after long years of international isolation, the first Soviets to travel to Latin America and give an account to their compatriots of what was happening there. Soviet film theatres had a tradition of showing opening programme pictures, usually news, cartoons or short documentaries. With the end of Stalinism, the latter enjoyed increasing popularity as they served a demand for new authenticity in the arts during the Thaw. The Moscow cinema Novosti Dnja (News of the Day) drew huge crowds screening solely these openers and documentaries.

For just such a short feature, Igor' Bessarabov and Sergej Gusev filmed the Soviet exhibition in Buenos Aires in 1955 and subsequently toured the country and shot their *Putešestvie po Argentine* (Journey through Argentina). It documented Argentine cities, monuments and architecture, the everyday life of townspeople, inhabitants of the Pampas and native tribes, and ended with performances of the song-and-dance company Chucaro and an audience with the Argentine actress Lolita Torres.[23] In the following year, their colleague Ilja Kopalin repeated their trip – and shot another film of the same name.[24] Violinist Igor' Bezrodnyj was also a hobby film-maker and, while touring Latin America as one of the first artists of the renewed Soviet cultural diplomacy, captured his travel impressions on celluloid.[25] In the years to come, numerous films were made by Soviets all across Central and South America. Guram Asatiani and Melor Sturua depicted their impressions of Colombia, Cuba, Mexico and Venezuela in a film called

---

[23] *Putešestvie po Argentine* (1955), RGAKFD #9811.   [24] *Pravda*, 25 Mar. 1956.
[25] Undated, GARF f.5283 op.14 d.672 l.7.

Raznoetažnaja Amerika (Multi-storeyed or Multi-layered America). The title alluded to Ilja Ilf's and Evgenij Petrov's famous 1936 United States travel report *Odnoetažnaja Amerika* (One-storeyed America). What Asatiani and Sturua found multi-layered in the neighbouring southern countries, was not simply the architecture, but above all the enormous social imbalances in both Americas – and as the sole culprit responsible for this misery they picked the United States. In the tradition of Sergei Eisenstein, Georgij Kublinskij declared his love for Mexico in another documentary (*Meksika, kotoruju my ljubim*, The Mexico We Love), which he later abandoned for new affairs with Cuba (*Divo Kuby*, The Miracle of Cuba) and Peru (*Peru: tysjača i tri goda*, Peru: One Thousand and Three Years), all before 1962. The Azeri El'beka Rzakuliev added more pictures to the Soviet perception of Mexico on a trip in 1960.[26] Lev Danilov was allegedly the first Soviet citizen ever to visit Ecuador, where he shot the movie *Den' v Ekvadore* (One Day in Ecuador), later followed by a documentary on Brazilian cities (*Po gorodam Brazilii*).[27]

The mental picture of Latin America that these films gave the Soviet audience was characterised by a fascination with exotic landscapes and peoples on the one hand – and the depiction of underdevelopment, poverty and US-backed exploitation on the other. Also in the field of cinema, experience with Central Asia and the Caucasus shaped the Soviet view of the global South: between 1945 and 1953, Soviet filmmakers had shot documentaries on every Soviet republic. Having surveyed cinematographically the traditions and histories of their inner periphery, the Soviets now incorporated the Third World into their cultural horizon.

To some extent, these first views abroad carried on old Soviet cinematic and literary traditions. Their style was declamatory and, in content, they essentialised national cultures and blamed all of the Americas' hardships on US imperialism. Prime examples were the ideologically overloaded historical re-enactments by Roman Karmen, the Soviet Leni Riefenstahl. With the same pathos and manichaeism that had characterised his earlier works from Turkmenistan and Kazakhstan, he now shot a series of films on the Hispanic world. The writers Konstantin Simonov and Genrich Borovik assisted in the production of films of the Cuban Revolution (*Kuba segodnia*, Cuba Today, 1960), the invasion in the Bay of Pigs, *Pylajuščij ostrov* (The Blazing Island, 1961) and later also the Spanish Civil War: *Grenada, Grenada, Grenada moja* (My Granada,

---

[26] I. Karetnikova, 'Po Meksike', *Tvorčestvo* 10 (1960), 17.
[27] Petr Tur, 'S kameroj po Latinskoj Amerike', *Iskusstvo Kino* 11 (1962), 16–19.

1967) was inspired by the 1959 song of the same name by Viktor Berkov-skij (who himself took the lyrics from a 1920s poem by Michail Svetlov).[28] Karmen also made films on Chile (*Čili: vremja bor'by, vremja trevog*, Chile: A Time of Struggle, a Time of Alarm, 1974), and *Serce Korvalana* (Corvalán's Heart, 1975), and the whole of South America, *Kamaradas: tovarišči* (Camaradas: Comrades, 1974), *Pylajuščij kontinent* (The Blazing Continent, 1972). Karmen's films are full of revolutionary pathos, very well shot technically and very convincing emotionally. But they were highly ideological propaganda in best Stalinist tradition. In the Hispanic world, he found inspiration and emotional fuel for his revolutionary fervour, which many of his contemporaries of the 1950s and 1960s had already lost or replaced with a less radical revolutionary romanticism.

By the same token, these new films from the 1950s offered a new window on faraway countries to all Soviet cinema-goers and captured their imagination. Soviet citizens got an image of the broad expanses of a hitherto hardly known outer world, an image which was full of both appealing exotic otherness and sympathy for the wretched of the earth. In this sense, these 'realist' films stood not only in the old Soviet inter-nationalist tradition, but also in an international context of the 1950s: feature films in the style of documentaries, usually with historical and socio-critical topics, *neorealismo* in Italy and *cinéma vérité* in France, were popular throughout Europe at the time.

Just as in the West, these dramatic and realist films lost favour with the public by the end of the decade to the benefit of more entertaining and easily enjoyable productions. In October 1957, Sergej Michalkov, long-time chairman of the Union of Russian Writers (famous for having written the Stalinist, the post-Stalinist and the post-Soviet Russian anthem) for the first time staged his play *Sombrero*. In it, Moscow young-sters develop a fascination for Mexico when one of their brothers returns from a diplomatic post in Mexico City and teaches them the Spanish language and local folk tunes. With its many Hispanic songs and colourful costumes, *Sombrero* became one of the most successful children's plays, popular throughout the history of the Soviet Union, with dozens of reprints and more than 800 performances in Moscow alone up to 1972. The cinema co-operative Progress filmed *Sombrero* in 1959, just two years after the first stage production, under the direction of Tamara Lisician at the Gorky Film Studios.[29] Just as popular with adults was the science fiction

[28] Telegramm Romana Karmena Fidel'ju Castro, 25 Mar. 1974, RGALI f. 2989 op.1 d.325 l.2.

[29] Anon., 'Sombrero', *Kultur und Leben* 8 (1960), cover; Sergej Michalkov, *Sombrero: komedija v 3 dejstvijach, 5 kartinach* (Moscow: Iskusstvo, 1957).

film *Čelovek-amfibija* (The Amphibian Man), directed by Gennadij Kazanskij and Vladimir Čebotarev. More than 65 million Soviet citizens saw it in 1962, which made it the most successful production of the Thaw period. They were thrilled by the story of a supposed sea monster falling in love with a beautiful girl to the backdrop of a mythical exotic Latin American country. Based on a 1928 novel by Aleksandr Beljaev, who had set the story in Buenos Aires, the film adaptation is somewhat more careless with geography and culture. It mixes a Caribbean-type landscape with Mexican dresses and Spanish dances and songs, which are played throughout the film. The film was shot before the Cuban Revolution had made its full cultural impact on the Soviets; hence Mexico still shaped the perception of Latin America. Artists had to base their work on a limited number of images of the subcontinent, and they used and combined what they knew from Mayakovsky, Eisenstein and the Spanish Civil War. The exotic setting and the Spanish-style (but Russian-language) music in *The Amphibian Man* contributed to the lasting popularity of the film. That the exotic elements were a mismatch did no harm to its success whatsoever.

Latin American film productions found their way into the Soviet Union, too. The Argentine actress Lolita Torres was a celebrity throughout the 1950s and 1960s. Soviet journals featured articles about her glamorous life, Soviet television interviewed her personally, and she received countless fan letters from all over the USSR. Torres's films, always guaranteed success in the Soviet Union, were usually simple love stories with a lot of dancing and jolly music. She sang herself and, knowing of the Soviets' enthusiasm for Latin American music, she toured the Soviet Union as a singer in 1963 with huge success – and Lolita became a popular name for a generation of Soviet girls.[30]

Two particularly popular films of the 1950s also came from Argentina: *Mi pobre madre querida* (My Poor Beloved Mother) and *Las aguas bajan turbias* (released in the United States as The Rivers Run Red), both directed by Hugo del Carril. The latter film is a South American classic about a workers' revolution in the Argentine–Paraguayan border region, based on a novel by Alfredo Varela. The topic of the movie and the political stance of the author superficially complied with Soviet preferences. Officials in Moscow probably did not know that Varela, a socialist but passionate anti-Stalinist, had served time in an Argentine prison for

---

[30] Donald Raleigh, *Russia's Sputnik Generation: Soviet Baby Boomers Talk about Their Lives* (Bloomington: Indiana University Press, 2006), p. 167; Jorge Greco, '"Moe serdce s vami" pišet Lolita Torres čitateljam Smeny', *Smena* 4 (1957), 22–3; Juan Gelman, 'U Lolity Torres', *Ogonek* 48 (1957), 28.

urinating on the Soviet embassy. The Soviet audience loved the film for its catchy Paraguayan folklore music: in a letter to the Latin American Friendship Society, a group of librarians from Novosibirsk expounded upon how much they adored the film and that they would be grateful for the lyrics and the sheet music.[31] In remarkable responsiveness to their petitioning citizens, the officials organised a visit of Hugo del Carril to the Soviet Union.[32] Varela, friends with Ehrenburg, organised the contact with del Carril, who, in 1961, took part in the Moscow film festival with his *Esta tierra es mía* (This Land Is Mine).[33]

Millions of Soviet citizens saw the films by the directors Gabriel Figueroa and Emilio Fernández (known as 'El Indio').[34] Deeply influenced by their collaboration with Eisenstein and cameraman Edvard Tisse in the 1930s, they reinvented Mexican cinema in the 1950s. Their films glorified the Mexican Revolution and the beautiful Mexican landscapes, and often featured stories reminiscent of Wild West movies in the United States – and they were blockbusters all across the Wild East. The 1971 Mexican melodrama *Yesenia*, finally, directed by German-born Alfredo Crevenna, found its way to Soviet cinemas in 1975 – and became the most successful film ever shown in Soviet cinemas. No fewer than 91 million Soviet cinema-goers suffered, cried and laughed through this turgid story of a militia man who falls in love with a racy gypsy woman, despite their differences and social prejudices. Soviet film critics and the intelligentsia wrinkled their noses – but analysed the film's wild success and prompted the production of more home-produced melodramatic films as a result.[35]

Latin American films met two crucial criteria for films to be successful in the Soviet Union: with their settings in faraway countries and their adventurous stories, they were different from the everyday and thus good escapist entertainment. 'These films were melodramatic, naive and exotic and there was always a beautiful heroine,' Vera Kutejščikova, *grande dame* of Soviet Latin Americanists remembered; 'this opened the audience's hearts and explains their success.'[36] By the same token, the socio-critical and often anti-US message underlying such films complied perfectly with the expectations of Soviet cultural officials. Continuing both the folkloristic depiction of the other and the revolutionary romanticism, El Indio, del Carril and the like have remained popular ever since. 'The Soviets love all these Mexican and Argentine films', a Brazilian

[31] 22 Jul. 1958, GARF f.9576 op.8 d.6 ll.141–142.
[32] Undated, GARF f.9576 op.8 d.7 ll.42/43.
[33] Pis'mo Varely Erenburgu, 5 Jul. 1961, RGALI f.1204 op.2 d.1354 l.11.
[34] Vera Kuteishchikova, 'Mexican Art Popular in USSR', *Moscow News* 74 (1960), 7.
[35] Stites, *Russian Popular Culture*, p. 170.
[36] Kutejščikova, *Moskva-Meksiko-Moskva*, p. 19.

visitor had already noted in 1955. It was probably more a sign of his own chauvinism than a valid assessment of Soviet cultural preferences that he added: 'that is not a sign of good taste'.[37]

Sombrero, moustache, guitar: folklorism and Latin American music

When, in 1957, tens of thousands of young people from all over the world flocked into the Soviet capital for the Sixth World Youth Festival (see Chapter 1), things turned out rather differently from how officials had planned. Youngsters from western countries brought jeans, short skirts and jazz records, and some Soviet girls apparently took the rapprochement of the peoples too literally. Much less disturbing for Soviet authorities and parents than pregnant *komsomolci* and western consumer goods was another, almost forgotten influence: dozens of Latin American folkloristic bands played hundreds of shows – and enjoyed enormous success among the Soviet audience. The pseudo-folklore of Soviet nationalities, in particular of the Caucasian and Central Asian ones, had been a common phenomenon during Stalinism.[38] Foreign popular musicians, however, were a rare sight in the Soviet Union until the festival.

The first Latino combos, among them one by the name of Los Mexicanos, had played concerts in Leningrad and Moscow in the mid 1950s. Their appearance corresponded to that of many other bands to come: three or four men of stereotypical appearance – big hats, moustaches, revolver belts and guitars – sang songs about love and other yearnings and combined their music with some comedy elements.[39] A very similar group, the trio Los Caballeros from Paraguay, went for the Moscow festival, played fourteen shows and was invited at least twice more to the Soviet Union.[40] The Argentine group Los Trobadores del Norte and Brazilian singer Silvio Caldas added a somewhat more sophisticated variant of Latin American folklore music. Many other groups followed during the festival and thereafter.[41] 'Guantanamera' and 'La Paloma' were soon tunes that most Soviet citizens could hum along with.

---

[37] José Guilherme Mendes, *Moscou, Varsóvia, Berlim: o povo nas ruas* (Rio de Janeiro: Editôra Civilização Brasileira, 1956), p. 53.

[38] Frank Miller, *Folklore to Stalin: Russian Folklore and Pseudofolklore of the Stalin Era* (London: Sharpe, 1990).

[39] Anon., 'Trio "Los Mechikanos"', *Sovetskaja Muzyka* 21/8 (1957), 126; Fyodor Yarikov, 'Moscow Likes Latin American Music', *Moscow News* 30/6 (1956), 7.

[40] O sostave i pribyvanii delegacij Latinskoj Ameriki na Vsemirnom festivale molodeži, undated, RGASPI f.3M op.15 d.204 ll.52–142.

[41] Anon., 'Melodie Mexikos und Gedichte Perus', *Kultur und Leben* 8 (1958), 55–6; Oskar Fel'cman, 'Gosti iz Brazilij', *Muzykal'naja Žizn'* 14 (1958), 21; O podgotovke Vsemirnogo festivalja molodeži, undated, RGASPI f.3M op.15 d.27 l.25.

It made little difference where the Latino bands came from exactly, be it Brazil or Cuba or Chile or Argentina. What they played was usually not authentic music 'of the folk', but a combination of elements of all kinds of traditions from all Latin American regions. Los de Ramón, yet another folklore group to play in the USSR, in their response to an invitation from the Soviet embassy in Chile, boasted they would play tunes from twenty Latin American countries.[42]

The common Soviet citizens seem to have been a grateful audience that ignored the advice of professional music critics. The specialist journal *Muzykal'naja Žižn'* (Musical Life) may have found fault with the groups' boorish behaviour and their overly emotional and technically bad singing.[43] Yet people flocked to their concerts and liked what they saw and heard. By the mid 1960s, these concerts would take place every other week. The Brazilian singer Victor Simón toured several times, once with twenty men and women from a dance company. They played fifty shows all over the Soviet Union in summer 1966, and combined folklore music with historic re-enactments of the history of Latin America. In their show, indigenous people fought against the *conquistadores*, descendants of Africans against slavery, and coffee planters against evil landlords. Honouring the repeated enthusiasm and hospitality of his Soviet audience, Simón added an extra surprise in the final scene: Brazilian dancers in costumes of Soviet cosmonauts sang Rio de Janeiro's samba anthem 'A cidade maravilhosa' (The Wonderful City) and celebrated a 'Carnival on the Moon'.[44]

In addition to the previously mentioned actress and singer Lolita Torres, another female artist also enjoyed huge success in the Soviet Union: the Peruvian singer Yma Sumac with her Inca Taky Trio. Sumac, too, played a fashionable mix of Peruvian folk music with elements of different Latin American styles, and especially Cuban mambo. In 1960, the group planned to come for two weeks to the Soviet Union, but proved so popular that, in the end, they stayed for six months and performed in forty cities. Even before her tour across the Soviet Union, Yma had enjoyed certain popularity there. Stories of her life as a person of mixed race in the United States and of her exotic music sung in Quechua were recurring topics in Soviet journals.[45] A film shot during her lengthy visit assembled all the stereotypes the Soviets had gathered

[42] Posol'stvo SSSR v Čili GKKS, 8 Feb. 1966, GARF f.9518 op.1 d.1017 l.40.
[43] Pavel Pičugin, 'Ansambl' iz Paragvaja', *Muzykal'naja Žizn'* 12 (1964), 23.
[44] Posol'stvo SSSR v Rio de Žanejro Ministerstvo Kultury, 30 Nov. 1965, GARF f.9518 op.1 d.324 ll.225–229.
[45] Vadim Birjukov, 'Doč' solnca', *Ogonek* 47 (1960), 29.

about Peru and exotic Yma, the 'soul of a faraway people'. It combined clips from her Moscow concert in the Tchaikovsky Theatre with images from her home country. Spooky stone gods and ruins alternated with wild animals, crocodiles, peacocks, snakes, parrots and indefinable creatures – and the Soviet viewers learned some facts about Peruvians and their country, about their lives and about their language, Quechua. Sumac's career was described with a somewhat overdone depiction of her as a talented but completely unsuccessful and impoverished artist in the United States – in fact she was a world star (albeit with monetary difficulties) before she went to the Soviet Union. Her concerts in the USSR, in any case, were a complete success; the enthusiasm shown by the Moscow crowd at the end of the film appears very authentic.[46]

All these concerts were organised by official Soviet organs, VOKS until 1957, and later the GKKS and the SSOD in collaboration with Goskoncert, the state concert organiser. From the official point of view, they were propaganda measures to promote internationalism, in the tradition of the depoliticising folklorisation of the peoples of Central Asia and the Caucasus. Yuri Slezkine once called these folklore evenings 'one of the most visible and apparently least popular aspects of Soviet official culture'.[47] This may have been true of the Azeri dances and Armenian poetry that Slezkine mentions. The Latinos, however, struck a chord with audiences. Soviet citizens did not much care about the political heritage, but appreciated the new, fresh, rhythmic, corporeal, earthy and exotic entertainment. Internal evaluations by the GKKS reveal that 'ensembles such as Los Lanchos, Los Mexicanos and Los Gallos enjoyed great success'.[48] In 1958, the Soviet audience saw concerts by twenty-nine Latin American folkloristic artists, a number that rose to fifty-nine the following year.[49] Latino folklore became part of the soundtrack of the Thaw: Georgij Danelija's film classic *Ja šagaju po Moskve* (I Walk around Moscow, 1963) portrayed Moscow as a sunny and romantic capital with a happy population – the boy-meets-girl story happens in Gorky Park to the backdrop of a big concert of Latin American musicians. In the same vein, in a late 1950s scene from the Oscar-winning Soviet drama, *Moskva slezam ne verit* (Moscow Doesn't Believe in Tears, 1980), the first of the

[46] *Pesnja Imy Sumak* (1961), RGAKFD #20083; A. Medvedev, 'Poet Ima Sumak', *Muzykal'naja Žizn'* 4/2 (1961), 12.

[47] Yuri Slezkine, 'The USSR as a Communal Apartment, or How a Socialist State Promoted Ethnic Particularism', *Slavic Review* 2 (1994), 448.

[48] Spravka o sostojanii i perspektivach razvitija kul'turnich i naučnich svjazej meždu SSSR i Meksikoj, 28 Nov. 1963, GARF f.9518 op.1 d.344 ll.139–141.

[49] Otčety o pribyvanii artistov, undated, RGANI f.5 op.35 d.85 ll.1–57 as well as f.5 op.36 d.56.

couples portrayed gets physical – and young Katerina pregnant – while Lucho Gatica sings his entire *Bésame mucho* (Kiss Me Lots).

The enthusiasm for erotic-exotic Latin America was not limited to the big cities of the Union. Reports from the provincial towns of Sochi, Kazan, Čeboksary, Joškar-Ola and Odessa describe the 'enormous success' of groups such as Los Bravos.[50] Neither did the craze for Latin American folklore pass unnoticed with foreign visitors: the Peruvian philosopher Francisco Miró Quesada, touring the Soviet Union in the summer of 1959, was surprised to see that 'everyone preferred Latin American music . . . to European music' and that 'many girls were able to sing tunes in Spanish'.[51] The visiting Colombian politician Alberto Dangond remembered that his young guide Ljudmila was very 'aficionada a los ritmos latinoamericanos'.[52] The Brazilian communist Eneida de Moraes was pleasantly surprised that the band in her Moscow hotel played Brazilian music.[53] And her compatriot journalist Nestor de Holanda was overwhelmed to hear rumba and samba in a restaurant in the Black Sea resort town of Sochi.[54] In the mid 1960s, the Soviet embassy staff in Brazil reported to the minister of culture, Ekaterina Furceva, that they had difficulties finding enough appropriate folklore bands for Soviet demands. Most professional artists had by this time been influenced too strongly by western music, as Ambassador Sergej Michajlov complained personally – and he recommended paying artists to design programmes specially tailored to fit more conservative Soviet tastes.[55]

Many more guest performances of Latin American groups took place in the Soviet Union throughout the 1960s. Some could be considered high culture, such as the concerts by the Argentine classical guitar player María Luisa Anido, who appeared at least five times on Moscow stages. But the overwhelming majority, in response to Soviet public request, were folkloristic bands, which presented – or were asked to present – a stereotypical view of Latin America. On the grounds that it would not interest the Soviet audience, officials occasionally declined offers to play

---

[50] Adelina Zundejas, 'Der kulturelle Austausch erweitert sich', *Kultur und Leben* 10 (1973), 28.

[51] Francisco Miró Quesada, *La otra mitad del mundo: treinta años despues* (Lima: Editorial Perla-Perú, 1989), p. 115.

[52] Dangond, *Mi diario en la Unión Soviética*, p. 21.

[53] Eneida de Moraes, *Caminhos da terra: URSS, Tchecoslováquia, China* (Rio de Janeiro: Antunes, 1959), p. 12.

[54] Nestor de Holanda, *O mundo vermelho: notas de um repórter na URSS* (Rio de Janeiro: Editora Pongetti, 1962), p. 135.

[55] 21 Feb. 1966, GARF f.9518 op.1 d.997 l.23.

by interpreters of classical music from Latin America.[56] It was entertainment the audience wanted and it was entertainment it got.

Folklorism, folklore, folk music

At the time, folkloristic tunes were a very modern phenomenon. 'Folkloristic music' – as opposed to 'folklore' or 'folk music' – is a type of mass-
produced modern entertainment that syncretically draws on elements of
traditional cultures and creates certain national or regional clichés. Not
necessarily pure invention, misleading or 'wrong', as Adorno or Barthes
would have called it, the 'folkloristic' is the use of a tradition outside the
cultural context in which it was created. This reference to folklorism in
popular music, in the East as in the West, reflected a yearning for exotic
outlands in the 1950s and 1960s. This happened most notably in West
Germany's *Schlager* music, where Latin America (along with the more
approachable Italy) became a projection screen for exoticist dreams of sun
and insouciance. While the Soviet Ivan Ivanovič learnt to dance the
mambo with Los Amigos and Eduardo Saborit ('Cuba, qué linda es
Cuba', Cuba, How Lovely Is Cuba), the German Heinz celebrated 'Fiesta
Mexicana', and ordinary Joes in the United States swayed to 'Quizás,
quizás, quizás' (Perhaps, Perhaps, Perhaps). Marxists on both sides of
the Iron Curtain criticised the escapist entertainment, but average citizens
could not care less: they appreciated the Latin American music as a
window on exotic countries that they would never be able to visit. These
tunes boasted catchy African-inflected rhythms and physicality that was
still commonly acceptable; but they were still quite close to European
listening habits, which may explain why it was precisely groups and
melodies from the Americas that became popular, not African or Indian
ones. They were exotic, but not too much so.[57]

Exoticist entertainment in general became widely popular at the time
because it served a demand for escapism; eventually, from the mid
1950s, it could be found everywhere in the northern hemisphere, which
had overcome the worst hardships of war, the post-war era and Stalinism.
The contrast with the Soviets' own cultural self-representation towards
Latin Americans, however, reveals another, very European, aspect of this
folklorisation: in its attempt to appear modern, civilised and cultivated,
the USSR mostly sent high-brow artists abroad. By doing this, they
constructed a cultural gradient between Soviet representatives of

[56] Letter from Goskoncert to the GKKS, 26 Dec. 1963, GARF f.9518 op.1 d.223 l.345.
[57] Christoph Marek, *Pop/Schlager: Eine Analyse der Entstehungsprozesse populärer Musik im US-amerikanischen und deutschsprachigen Raum* (Vienna: LitVerlag, 2006), pp. 59–60.

classical European high culture and the – selectively invited – folkloristic groups from Latin America. This practice shows a sense of cultural superiority Europeans maintained towards the rest of the world, be they from the East or the West of the old continent.

The escapist, and by definition conservative, folklore mingled in the following years with a different branch of Latin American popular music. Again both in western Europe and in the Soviet Union, the success of Los Bravos and the like paved the way for the reception of the more political, leftish folk music of the 1960s. Similar to the 'folkloristic' music, the Música Popular Brasileira, the Movimiento de Música Popular Argentina and, especially renowned, the Nueva Canción Chilena put together elements from Latin American and Spanish folk music traditions, but combined them with political lyrics on the living conditions of the poor and the impact of imperialism. Most Europeans who sang along to the refrain of 'Guantanamera' (a popular melody also in the 1960s Soviet Union) most probably did not know that it was originally written by the Cuban national hero José Martí and served as an anthem for many leftist movements worldwide. The latter had had a preference for Spanish-language songs ever since the days of the Spanish Civil War, when composers such as Ernst Busch or Hanns Eisler wrote their catchy tunes for the International Music Bureau at the Comintern.

When Víctor Jara, later a martyr of Chilean socialism and a global left-wing icon, went to Moscow in 1961, he was only an actor in a theatre company. Standing in for a colleague who had fallen ill, he found himself singing and playing the guitar. The audience's reaction to their beloved Latin American music was so overwhelming that he decided to become a singer and, that same night, wrote his first song in a Moscow hotel room. Together with Dean Reed, a US actor who also interpreted many Spanish-language protest songs, Jara was widely listened to in the Soviet Union – with the censors' benevolence and the audience's sympathy. After his assassination in Chile in 1973, the Soviets named a recently discovered asteroid after him, and some years later, an opera on the events surrounding his death was staged in Moscow.

By that time, Soviet musicians had long begun to include Latin American songs and topics into their own repertoire. Not only had the Latin American groups performed at concerts, but they had brought records and sheet music, too. The Soviets began to reproduce them, and they proved so popular that publishing houses constantly had to increase the number of copies.[58] Soviet publishers proved to be no

---

[58] E.g. Pavel Pičugin, *Narodnaja muzyka Argentiny* (Moscow: Izdatel'stvo Muzyka, 1971); Anon., 'Lateinamerikanische Literatur', *Kultur und Leben* 12 (1961), 16–18.

sticklers for details of copyright law: several Latin American companies complained about this behaviour, as did an Argentine record label in an angry letter in 1958.[59] Copyrighted or not, Soviet musicians now used both elements, the exoticist-folklorising view and the political message. The bard Viktor Berkovskij put Michail Svetlov's poem 'Grenada' to music in 1959. The – of course highly political – song on the Spanish Civil War became a classic in the repertoire of many other contemporary musicians. But even today, Berkovskij is most famous for his 1968 romantic hit *Na dalekoj Amazonke* (On the Far-Off Amazon). Together with Moris Sinel'nikov he had set to music a poem by Rudyard Kipling (notorious for his 'White Man's Burden' poem), 'The Beginning of the Armadilloes'. Its lyrics repeat the narrator's longing to see Brazil once in his lifetime, while he watches ships leaving the harbour: 'and I wonder, will I see Brazil, Brazil, Brazil, will I see Brazil before I get old?'

Jurij Vizbor, one of the most famous Soviet bards of the 1960s, wrote some of his songs on Latin American topics, too. Like his fellow bards Vladimir Vysockij and Bulat Okudžava, Vizbor became famous via *samizdat* home tapes; the music he wrote by no means represented official policies – yet still expressed sympathy and internationalist solidarity with the heroic feats of Soviet submariners in the Caribbean ('Karibskaja pesnja', The Caribbean Song, 1963), admired Latin America culture ('Bossanova', 1965) and celebrated its socialist martyrs ('Ballada o Viktore Chara', The Ballad of Víctor Jara, 1973). Jara's songs were covered, too, by the Soviet ensemble *Grenada*, founded in 1973 by Sergej Vladimirskij, who toured all around the socialist countries. At Moscow State University, the International Concert Brigade Venceremos played Spanish revolutionary songs – and Yevgeny Yevtushenko recorded an album, 'A los poetas soviéticos' (For the Soviet Poets), with the Chilean singer Rolando Alarcón in 1971.

Foreign influence on Soviet culture thus was no longer necessarily in conflict with the authorities or involved an act of resistance. Some internationalist songs were indeed produced with propagandistic intention – which again does not mean that they were necessarily unpopular. Yet many others were written independently and played by ordinary musicians. Internationalist solidarity was not just an empty political phrase from Soviet apparatchiks. It was embraced by many Soviet artists and citizens – even more so if there was no price to pay in return and if it could be expressed by singing or listening to a nice Latino tune.

---

[59] Undated, GARF f.9576 op.8 d.7 l.138.

Soviet intelligentsia abroad: exoticism and revolutionary romanticism in travelogues

Soviet intellectuals had maintained few personal contacts with Latin Americans through Stalinist isolationism. Ilya Ehrenburg was among the small number of Soviets who could travel abroad at all throughout the 1940s and 1950s. Being the most prominent, cosmopolitan and internationally recognised intellectual with much experience of the western world, he served a purpose that may have saved his life during Stalinism: he was sent around eastern Europe to convey a cultured image of the Soviet Union to the new Soviet satellite states. When, after Stalin's death, Latin America loomed on the Soviet horizon, it was again Ehrenburg who (re-)established contacts and signalled that the Soviet Union was willing to join the global intellectual discourse. In 1954, he was sent to Chile to award the Chilean poet Pablo Neruda a Soviet peace medal; later he met old acquaintances, the Brazilian novelist Jorge Amado and the exiled Spanish poets Rafael Alberti and María Teresa León, in neighbouring Argentina. Ehrenburg remembered great relief and excitement at the same time about this first trip of a Soviet intellectual to Latin America in many years. He felt that 'the Cold War was drawing to close' while 'the world had broadened up' for him personally, he who had so far known only Europe and the United States.[60]

With the cautious opening of the Soviet Union from the mid 1950s, Soviet writers, little by little, reconnected to the world abroad. Some ten years later, they were again recognised as intellectuals rather than as political agents and could travel rather easily all around the world. Yevgeny Yevtushenko spent long periods in Chile and was invited to Brazil under military rule.[61] In the mid 1950s, however, the first attempts to overcome their isolation were still confronted with serious difficulties and had to break down barriers built up from all sides. Ehrenburg had erred: the Cold War was still far from over in 1954 and his visit to Santiago de Chile was accompanied by angry anti-Soviet manifestations. The widespread fear of communism all over the world made it difficult for the Soviets to obtain entry visas, and some airlines simply refused to take them on board. Soviet authorities, too, remained highly suspicious and restrictive. Every Soviet person who wished to travel abroad needed

---

[60] Iosif Grigulevich, 'Ilya Ehrenburg y América Latina', *América Latina* 2 (1976), 181–96; Ehrenburg, *Menschen, Jahre, Leben*, pp. 476–80, 566.
[61] Jewgeni Jewtuschenko, *Der Wolfspass: Abenteuer eines Dichterlebens* (Berlin: Volk und Welt, 2000), p. 187; 23 Jun. 1967, GARF f.9518 op.1 d.998 l.75; 4 Jan. 1966, GARF f.9518 op.1 d.997 l.14.

to navigate a long, complicated procedure to get their exit visa; employers, the Party and the KGB had to give their approval to every applicant.[62]

In addition to such bureaucratic hindrances, there were mental barriers and cultural hurdles to surpass. A lack of qualified translators made communication difficult (later the Soviets would ask the Spanish refugees to help out). And in a more encompassing sense, it was not only linguistic knowledge of the world abroad that was lacking after the long isolation. The Soviets had gained their notion of Latin America exclusively from books – moreover, from books with a certain political leaning. The travellers embarked for Latin America with a somewhat naive cultural bias that, in a different context, Said has called a 'textual attitude'.[63] Being intellectuals, all the early Soviet travellers to Latin America wrote about their experiences in travelogues or at least short articles. Their writings give an idea of the way they perceived not only the New World, but also their own role in new Soviet internationalism. Their reports and books were churned out in millions of copies and read by many Soviet citizens and therefore shaped the way common Soviet citizens thought of both Latin America and the role of Soviet internationalism.

Vera Kutejščikova, back then one of the few Spanish-speaking employees at VOKS, went to Mexico in 1956 and – among others – met with the poet Alfonso Reyes.[64] The Ukrainian author Ljubomir Dmiterko, accompanied by a member of the Academy of Sciences, followed in late summer that year. They spent three weeks in Argentina, also in order to (re-)establish contacts with local intellectuals and scientists.[65] Their travel report, a small cheap paperback with many drawings and photos, published in both Ukrainian and Russian, set the standard in format and layout for many more travel reports to come.[66] They forewent the harsh ideological rhetoric of former publications of the kind – including Dmiterko's own writing during late Stalinism, when he himself had vociferously supported the anti-cosmopolitanism campaign. Instead, the new travel reports devoted more space to emphatic descriptions of the countries they covered, their history, geography, culture and people – albeit not without blaming imperialism for any shortcomings.

Konstantin Simonov made a similar trip to Argentina, Chile and Uruguay a year later. Just as for Dmiterko and Ehrenburg before him,

[62] Zubok, *Zhivago's Children*, pp. 88–120.   [63] Said, *Orientalism*, pp. 92–3.
[64] Kutejščikova, *Moskva-Meksiko-Moskva*, p. 265.
[65] Spravka, undated, RGANI f.5 op.28 d.463 ll.136–139.
[66] Ljubomir Dmiterko, *Pod južnym krestom* (Moscow: Sovetskij Pisatel', 1958).

his task was to establish contacts, and he was asked to report on the situation in the Latin American Soviet friendship societies. Simonov, a highly decorated war poet during Stalinism, initially had his problems adjusting to his new duty of courting non-communist intellectuals. Among the many writers he met were Jesualdo Sosa and his wife, the translator Susanna Sosa. For Simonov, they and the entire Uruguayan Writers' Committee were annoying 'rich leftist bourgeois', and he angrily recommended they should never again be invited to the Soviet Union. Other artists, however, and various public figures found Simonov's approval, and he laid the foundation for many subsequent visits to the Soviet Union (see Chapter 3).[67]

In 1958, Aleksej Adžubej, chief editor of the Komsomol's newspaper *Komsomolskaja Pravda* covered the inauguration of Arturo Frondizi as the new president of Argentina.[68] Afterwards, together with Nikolaj Gribačev, chief editor of the journal *Sovetskij Sojuz*, Anatolij Sofronov, head of the most important weekly journal *Ogonek*, and two other journalists, they started a long trip through four countries and wrote about their experiences in several books and many contributions to journals.[69] Most of the time, the group was hosted and guided by local intellectuals. In Buenos Aires, the writer María Rosa Oliver fed them; Pablo Neruda put them up in Santiago de Chile; and in Uruguay the old communist historian Francisco Pintos took care of them; only in Panama did the Soviet group have to find their own way.[70] In his travelogue, Adžubej lionised the possibilities of Latin America, its wonderful peoples and impressive landscapes. Essentially, he liked everything he saw; he welcomed the election of Frondizi ('finally progress and independence for Argentina'), a left-liberal reformer, but certainly no communist. If only, he wrote, there were not the (US-) Americans: it was they who had brought poverty and social injustice and years of oppression and backwardness to Latin America. Adžubej told his readers how terrorist US puppet regimes in Guatemala and Cuba (the trip took place before the revolution) suppressed their people. In cultural terms, too, Adžubej, a jazz aficionado, deplored the influence of the United States. He loved the

---

[67] Pablo Neruda, *Confieso que he vivido* (Barcelona: Plaza & Janés, 2001), p. 300–3; Konstantin Simonov: Nekotorye soobščenja k otčetu o poezdke v Urugvaj, Čili i Argentinu, 29 Dec. 1957, GARF f.9518 op.1 d.320 ll.160–167.

[68] Aleksej Adžubej, *Na raznych širotach* (Moscow: Pravda, 1959), pp. 103–10.

[69] Anatolij Sofronov, 'Dobro požalovat' v Čili!', *Moskva* 5 (1963), 196–204; Aleksej Adžubej, *Kueka i modern-meščane* (Moscow: Pravda, 1959); Adžubej, *Na raznych širotach*; Nikolaj Gribačev, *Dym nad vulkanom: očerki o stranach Latinskoj Ameriki* (Moscow: Molodaja Gvardija, 1959); Anatolij Sofronov, 'Otkrytie Južnoj Ameriki', *Ogonek* 37 (1958), 9–12.

[70] Adshubej, *Gestürzte Hoffnung*, p. 217; Adžubej, *Kueka i modern-meščane*, pp. 36, 41.

Argentine national dance *cueca* and tried to learn it. When the US rock-and-roll star Bill Haley performed in his favourite *cueca* club, Adžubej was appalled that this 'fat psychopath' attracted a bigger crowd than his beloved folk dance. He warned of dangerous American cultural imperialism and denounced the young fans as petty bourgeois philistines. It is noteworthy that Adžubej considered this episode so central for his trip that he named his book *Kueka i modern-meščane* (Cueca and the Modern Petty Bourgeois). In the world-view of leading Soviet intellectuals such as Adžubej, being truly *kul'turnyj* ('cultivated') required savouring either high-brow culture or at least sticking to one's own, national traditions. US cultural influence, to him, meant despicable decadence, loss of national identity, egocentrism and sexual libertinage. In a conversation with Haley after the concert, Adžubej let him know of his stance and added dutifully that he did not like abstract art, either. He was probably right to assume that many elderly Argentines agreed with him in this respect.[71]

In Uruguay, their first impression was one of a peaceful and clean capital city of Montevideo: 'a deceitful silence', as Adžubej entitled this chapter. His trained gaze, however, soon found the expected social injustice, poverty and the 'almighty US monopolies'. In Uruguay, too, the Soviet group sought contact with local intellectuals: the senator and newspaper editor Luís Tróccoli, welcomed them for a scholarly debate, and they met several other journalists and artists. The graphic artist Angelo Hernandez agreed to do the artwork for Sofronov's first travel report in *Ogonek*.[72] On their tour through Chile, a US entrepreneur joined the group. Not surprisingly, they strongly disagreed on the impact of US enterprises in Chile, their exploitation of copper and the treatment of the workers.[73] Yet the very fact that they discussed these issues openly with a representative of the arch-enemy shows a major change in Soviet attitudes. Throughout their reports, both authors repeatedly underlined their open approach to non-communists and their respect for religious feelings – a respect that believers back in the Soviet Union were completely denied at the time.

On the whole, the undertone in their reports is very optimistic. Adžubej and Sofronov, the latter a conservative watchdog against perceived anti-socialist tendencies in Soviet literature with a past as a notorious 'cosmopolitan' hunter, led their readers to believe that Latin America

---

[71] Adžubej, *Kueka i modern-meščane*, pp. 23–4.
[72] Adžubej, *Na raznych širotach*, pp. 90–6; Sofronov, 'Otkrytie Južnoj Ameriki'.
[73] Sofronov, 'Dobro požalovat' v Čili!'; Adžubej, *Na raznych širotach*, pp. 96–103.

was about to break its chains of imperialism and would overcome its backwardness soon. In his final chapter, Adžubej summed up: the days of the imperialists are numbered, friendship with the Soviet Union is on the increase everywhere, and not even the US Army based in Cuba would be able to stop the insurgence of the Latin American peoples.[74]

A recurring topic in these, as in many other travelogues of the kind, is an encounter with unhappy Soviet émigrés. Stanislav Kalesnik, a member of a group of Soviet scientists who spent two months in Brazil, did not write much about his scientific endeavours, but instead described his travels through the country and his encounters with nature, history and people in Brazil. On several occasions he ran into different groups of people who had emigrated from the Soviet Union, a Ukrainian priest, a former general of the White Guards and many war refugees. All, according to Kalesnik, lived miserable lives and bitterly regretted having left the Soviet Union.[75] The Uzbek football team, too, wrote a book about their tour in South America for their fans back home. After a description of the countries visited – and their football tactics – the sportsmen reported how they met Armenians who 'cursed the day they had left the Soviet Union and followed the rumours of sweet life in the West'.[76]

Even more than the travels in the relatively developed and more Europeanised parts of South America, impressions from countries such as Honduras or Bolivia with their indigenous majorities and a living standard below the Soviet Union's were apt to reinforce with Russian travellers the textbook belief in Soviet superiority and western malice. Some months after Adžubej and Sofronov, another Soviet writer undertook a long journey across Latin America: Vasilij Čičkov, *Pravda* correspondent in Mexico, drove several thousand miles through Central America and the Andean countries in late 1958. Like his predecessors, he wrote articles for *Ogonek* and also published a series of books, starting with *Buntujuščaja zemlja* (A Rebellious Land), about his journeys in late 1958 and early 1959.[77] These countries, largely dependent on US capital and, in Central America, indeed in the grip of US companies, must have appeared to Soviet eyes as prime examples of imperialist exploitation and

[74] Jewtuschenko, *Der Wolfspass*, p. 187; Adžubej, *Kueka i modern-meščane*, p. 61.

[75] Stanislav Kalesnik, *Po Brazilij: putevye očerki* (Moscow: Gosizdat Geografičeskoj Literatury, 1958), quote p. 42.

[76] Krasnickij, *Ot Rio-de-Žanejro do Montevideo*.

[77] Vasilij Čičkov, *Buntujuščaja zemlja: putešestvija i vstreči* (Moscow: DetGiz, 1961); Vasilij Čičkov, *Pod sozvezdiem južnogo kresto* (Moscow: DetGiz, 1960); Vasilij Čičkov, *Zarja nad Kuboj* (Moscow: Izdatel'stvo Instituta Meždunarodnych Otnošenij, 1960); Vasilij Čičkov, 'V vysokich Andach', *Ogonek* 24 (1959), 14–16.

consequent underdevelopment. Čičkov saw and reported to his Soviet readers an illiteracy rate of 70 per cent in Bolivia, economic and human rights crimes of the United Fruit Company in Honduras and apartheid conditions in Panama, and showed pictures of *campesinos* in their primitive clothes and accommodation. He climbed down a shaft with local miners, who told him that at least since the nationalisations of 1952 things had become a bit more bearable.

Čičkov's depiction of Latin America, like that of the other Soviet writers, on the one hand underlined the beauty of the landscape and the dignity of the people – including positive racial stereotypes of the 'noble savage' and 'hot-blooded Latino' kind.[78] On the other hand, it deplored the underdevelopment and made harsh accusations of oppression by the United States. The US citizens in his writings were caricatures of capitalists with big cars, nice villas and a constantly insulting manner, including towards him personally. All the depicted misery and poverty notwithstanding, Čičkov's travelogues sparkled with optimism. He reported on uniting workers, on the development of a political consciousness and increasing strikes. The title itself is telling, as it ascribes a revolutionary spirit to the area even before the outbreak of the Cuban Revolution.

Another popular author of travel reports from South America was Oleg Ignat'ev, the former Sovinformbjuro head in Argentina and now correspondent in Brasília. Throughout his career, he wrote more than a dozen books and booklets about his journeys in Latin America and Portuguese Africa. Ignat'ev's work found a large readership. Not only did he publish many books and articles in the usual magazines, but his works were published in several editions and translated into many languages of the Union and of eastern Europe, too.[79] In 1961, he published a commissioned work for the Znanie publishing house, a very typical travelogue of the time about a journey from Argentina to Venezuela, colourful, with many drawings, relatively short, cheap and directed to a fairly broad audience.[80] The optimism shown in earlier works prevailed. The readers, who used to 'know nothing about Brazil but coffee and football', learnt about Brasília, the 'ultra-modern city', built by Oscar Niemeyer, a leading character of the Brazilian Communist Party. They were told how the nationalised oil industry had led to great progress and economic independence. It is telling for the Soviet world-view that Brazil's history was presented as resembling the USSR's: the situation in Brazil during

---

[78] Čičkov, *Buntujuščaja zemlja*, p. 46.
[79] Oleg Ignat'ev, 'Skripka barabanščika', *Vokrug Sveta* 9 (1960), 13–16.
[80] Oleg Ignat'ev, *Ot Argentiny do Venesuely* (Moscow: Pravda, 1961).

the left progressive government of President João Goulart, according to Ignat'ev, could be likened to the Soviet one after the Civil War. Step by step, Brazil now had to nationalise its economy, as the USSR had done; then they would also be able to build a metro, as Moscow had done. Brazil allegedly saw the development of the Soviet Union as providing a role model.[81]

Igant'ev's comparison is a telling example of Soviet internationalist thought at the time; the idea that the Third World would follow the Soviet path was paternalistic and somewhat naive at the same time and had not changed much from the 'textual attitude' of the first travellers some years before. Ignat'ev considered Argentina to be in the same schematic category as Brazil: it had nationalised its natural resources, but US monopolies still had too much influence – which in his view explained the poverty of many Argentines.[82] The neighbouring countries Paraguay, Peru and finally Venezuela under the former regime of dictator Marcos Pérez Jiménez served as the counter-example to Brazil. Ignat'ev described the many sick people in the streets, the ubiquitous poverty and the brutality of the US-backed military junta in Paraguay. While excoriating the political system, Ignat'ev did not forget to mention some of this country's nicer aspects and continued also the exoticising trajectory of Soviet writing on Latin America: it was a 'tropical paradise' with beautiful landscapes – and its folklore was popular all across Latin America as well as already in the Soviet Union.[83]

Many more of these small booklets of travel reports were available to the Soviet readership from the mid 1950s, and especially after the Cuban Revolution had increasingly captured the interest of many Soviet citizens. Renowned journalists and writers, but also members of political delegations and of scientific excursions shared their experiences abroad.[84] *Kurs na Gavanu* (Tack towards Havana) told the adventures of a steamer crew of oceanographers from Kaliningrad and their research between Argentina and Cuba. It combined the longing for the exotic outland with elements of adventure and science fiction.[85]

Like the craze for Latin American music, this fascination was not limited to the inhabitants of the big cities of the Soviet Union. Authors

[81] *Ibid.*, pp. 1–23.   [82] *Ibid.*, p. 57.   [83] *Ibid.*, pp. 79–85.

[84] Clissold (ed)., *Soviet Relations with Latin America, 1918–1968*, pp. 182–3; Riza and Quirk, 'Cultural Relations between the Soviet Union and Latin America', 34; Rodionov, *V strane Inkov*; Spravka o poezke v Brasiliju (1958), undated, GARF f.9518 op.1 d.322 ll.56–73; Poezdka M. P. Georgadze v strany Latinskoj Ameriki (1961), RGAKFD #22357; see also chapter one.

[85] Iurij Ivanov, *Kurs na Gavanu* (Kaliningrad: Kaliningradskoe Knižnoe Izdatel'stvo, 1964).

from Tajikistan and Lithuania wrote similar travelogues.[86] Some of the most popular ones actually came from two Czechoslovak travellers: the adventures of Jiri Hanzelka and Miroslav Zikmund on their voyages in a Czech Tatra car all over Latin America and Africa filled hundreds of hours of radio broadcasts and several books that were all translated into Russian. The most famous one, *From Argentina to Mexico*, was made into a film.[87] Several Soviet magazines of the time, namely *Vokrug Sveta* (Around the World), *Na Suše i na More* (Ashore and Afloat), *Novoe Vremja* (New Times) and the aforementioned *Ogonek* (Little Flame) served, from the late 1950s, their readership's growing desire for stories and pictures from exotic places. The layout of these journals was lively, they featured many colour photographs and they toned down the ideological fervour of former similar publications like *Za Rubežom* (Abroad) which had vitriolic, hyper-ideologised rhetoric. They modelled themselves on US magazines such as *Time*, *Life* and *Look* and were enormously popular. Compared to Africa and Asia, Latin America has a very prominent position in these magazines. From 1959, the year of the revolution, Cuba takes up the most space, but every single other Latin American country appears from time to time.

These journals were not always looked upon favourably by the Soviet leadership: as early as 1958, its focus on international stories earned the editorial staff of *Ogonek* an admonition from above.[88] But this should not lead to the assumption that these publications, nor probably their readership, were overly critical of the current Soviet system. On the contrary, as has already been shown, their editors and authors were convinced socialists, in many cases also in leading positions of the Soviet *nomenklatura*. Their first experiences in the Third World did more to affirm their beliefs than to topple them. The reports from the exotic Third World also assured Soviet readers back home that they were on the morally superior – and the safe – side of the conflict. In a veritably Proustian literary move, an author of *Ogonek* shared his impressions from a journey through Colombia in 1962: back home in the safe Russian haven, the flavour of a cup of coffee brought back to him the traumatic

---

[86] Justas Paleckis, *V Meksike: putevye zametki* (Vilnius: Vaga, 1964).

[87] Jiri Ganzelka and Miroslav Zikmund, *Ot Argentiny do Meksiki* (Moscow: Izdatel'stvo Detskoj Literatury, 1961).

[88] Postanovlenie CK KPSS: O ser'eznich nedosdatach v soderžanii žurnala Ogonek, 9 Sep. 1958, in V. Afiani and E. Afanas'eva: Ideologičeskie komissii CK KPSS 1958–1964. Dokumenty (Moscow, 1998), pp. 87–8, quoted in Susan Emily Reid, 'Cold War in the Kitchen: Gender and the De-Stalinization of Consumer Taste in the Soviet Union under Khrushchev', *Slavic Review* 61/2 (2002), 215.

experience with images of the poverty and the imperialist oppression of the Colombian people.[89]

All these travelogues around 1960 had a number of characteristics in common. They all described Latin America with an exoticising admiration for its landscapes and cultures. At the same time, they compassionately depicted the poverty, the social imbalance, squalor, underdevelopment and economic backwardness of Latin American societies. Not one writer failed to blame the United States for this misery, for widespread illiteracy, for the enormous gap between the wealthy and the poor and for cultural imperialism that destroyed national identities; one Soviet traveller to Brazil found fault with the Yankees for the publicly displayed 'sexual licentiousness'.[90]

Exploitation and backwardness notwithstanding, all authors are remarkably positive about future developments in Latin America. This optimism was not unfounded; several dictators were overthrown in Latin America at the end of the 1950s, the time when most travelogues were written. The reports local Latin American communists and leftists cabled to Moscow took the same optimistic line: social protests are on the increase, Latin America is bursting its bonds and the semi-colonial system is on the point of collapse.[91] Some Soviet authors also referred to the Latin American revolutionary tradition and felt a 'revolutionary spirit' across the continent already before Fidel Castro's march to Havana. A later section (pp. 110–23) will explore how the Cuban Revolution finally was celebrated as *the* beacon for the liberation of Latin America from its century-old oppression.

In the travelogues from continental Latin America, all authors contrasted an allegedly superior Soviet living standard and Soviet technological and infrastructural achievements as role models for the countries they visited. More or less explicitly, the message was always that the Soviet method of state-led industrialisation and hence gaining true national independence was the key to progress. The perceived backwardness, in particular that of the less industrialised countries of the Americas, endorsed the progressive character of the Soviet state according to their own indicators of technology, industry and science. While Soviet travellers to western countries tended to question the official depiction of the Soviet Union and the world, the experience gathered in the Third World rather became a source instead of moral self-confirmation and general

---

[89] Iurij Gvozdev, 'Gork'ij kofe Kolumbii', *Ogonek* 51 (1962), 28–9.
[90] Krasnickij, *Ot Rio-de-Žanejro do Montevideo.*
[91] So does, for instance, the CIA-toppled Guatemalan ex-premier Jacobo Arbenz in *Pravda*, 26 Oct. 1960.

high self-esteem throughout the 1950s and 1960s. Soviet travellers to France may have found that the USSR looked backward upon their return: to those who went to Bolivia, it looked like a successful modern industrial state with a very good living standard.

The authors of the travelogues were part of the Soviet intellectual elite: literary writers, journalists and often both. They were supporting elements of a new, de-Stalinised Soviet Union in times of peaceful coexistence, and they were convinced of the prospects of socialism. When these intellectuals, politically socialised in times of Stalinism, went to Latin America (or other parts of the world) for the first time, it was only to a limited extent that they gained new insights and broadened their horizons. Above all, they filled their already existing categories of thought with new images. A eulogy allegedly given by an elderly physician to Adžubej somewhere on his journey symbolises what the Soviets wanted to hear from their Third World friends: 'the first satellite in the sky – yours. Ob, Moiseev's dancing company – yours ... the best pavilion at the Brussels world exposition – yours, the victories at the Olympic games – yours as well, Ojstrach – yours, and no one ever staged the Quixote as humanly and emotionally as you did'.[92] One is tempted to dwell upon the reference to the Knight of the Sorrowful Countenance: the first Soviet travellers to Latin America in the late 1950s saw themselves as fighters for a better world. But Don Aleksej Adžubej and his Sancho Panza Anatolij Sofronov kept their ideological 'textual attitude' and perceived the world still in the schematic categories of their existing book-knowledge – just like Quixote with his chivalric novels. The Soviets' experience in Latin America only corroborated their belief in the superiority of their own ways. They returned to the USSR to encourage a stronger engagement in the Third World, and the travelogues they wrote were part of this propagation, to political decision makers as well as to the Soviet public.

The successful careers many of the travellers enjoyed after their return made them influential advocates for Soviet Third World activities: filmmaker Melor Sturua later became deputy foreign editor for the newspaper *Izvestija* and was an influential member of the 'brain-trust' of Soviet foreign policy and a speech-writer for Nikita Khrushchev. Konstantin Simonov was already chief editor of *Novij Mir* and secretary of the Union of Soviet Writers when he travelled to Latin America; he later became a member of the Central Committee of the CPSU. Journalist Aleksej Adžubej was at the time of his travels head of *Komsomolskaja Pravda* and – in informal Soviet power networks certainly just as important – married to Khrushchev's daughter. From 1959, he was chief

---

[92] Adžubej, *Kueka i modern-meščane*, p. 58.

editor of *Izvestija* and, as a member of the Central Committee and Khrushchev's personal counsellor, one of the most influential political figures of the Soviet Union. Adžubej's fellow traveller Nikolaj Gribačev was editor of the journal *Sovetskij Sojuz* for almost fifty years, secretary of the Union of Soviet Writers, candidate for the Central Committee and eventually head of the Supreme Soviet. Sofronov remained loyal to Latin America and became head of the newly founded Spanish-language radio station Progreso from 1964.[93]

For Soviet readers, the travelogues satisfied a growing curiosity about the world abroad and combined it with a political message. Colourful with many pictures, relatively short, cheap and published in large numbers, they reached a broad audience back home and carried their internationalist spirit and self-confirming attitude across to common Soviet citizens. Adžubej's books alone all had a six-figure circulation, and many travelogues were reprinted in second editions. Together with the documentary and feature films and the musical folklore, the travelogues established the view the broad Soviet population had of Latin America. Not only did these books entertain and inform their readers about the history and current cultural and political affairs of a hitherto little-known area of the world, their function was also to assure the Soviets they were on the right track themselves, to showcase the admiration they ostensibly got from the exploited peoples of the earth and condemn the evil intentions of US-backed imperialism.

The new Soviet internationalism allowed authors and readers alike to combine their fascination for the exotic outland with a political self-affirmation of their own superiority. In the late 1950s and early 1960s, events and developments in the Third World were monitored closely by many of the intellectual elites in the Soviet Union, and they shared their interpretations with millions of readers in their books and articles. The impressions they got on their travels and conveyed back home were ideologically determined, but the prevalence of poverty, social injustice, oppression and exploitation in many Latin American states was real enough to lend plausible credence to their world-view.

'Magic' ousting 'socialist' realism: Latin America in Soviet belles-lettres

Latino music, films and the first travelogues from the Americas rekindled a fascination for Latin America among fiction writers as well – just as, a

---

[93] *Izvestija*, 24 Jul. 1964.

generation earlier, Ilja Ilf and Evgenij Petrov had let their picaresque hero Ostap Bender dream of Rio de Janeiro. The Lithuanian poet Vytautas Sirijos-Gira was the first to revive this literary exoticism with his novel, *Buenos Airés*, in 1956. The Russian Jurij Slepuchin, who followed in his footsteps, already had some first-hand experience of the Americas: as a displaced person after his incarceration in a German prisoner-of-war camp, he emigrated to Argentina and wrote his first books in Spanish, but, in 1957, decided to move back to the Soviet Union, where he finally had some success with a series of novels on Latin American topics. *Džoanna Alarika* (Juana Alarica), a tragic tale of a young girl in Guatemala during the 1954 putsch, appeared in 1958. In his 1961 novel *U černy zakata* (At the Edge of Sunset), motifs of Slepuchin's own odyssey were mixed with descriptions of Argentina and most of all Buenos Aires. His alter-ego in the book, a talented French artist of the realist school, does not find recognition for his work in western Europe, where abstract art dominates. He decides to seek happiness and fulfilment in South America.[94] Julij Annenkov's 1962 *Šachterskij senator* (The Miners' Senator) is a novel featuring Pablo Neruda. It combines Neruda's poetry with photographs from Chile and invented stories of his encounters with ordinary people, who adore him – strikingly similar to Antonio Skármeta's *Ardiente Paciencia* twenty years later, which was adapted in the film *Il Postino*.[95] Poems, too, reflected the rediscovery of the Americas: the translator and lyricist Margarita Aliger, who went with a delegation to Latin America in 1963, put her Chilean experience into a poetry collection called *Čilijskoe leto* (A Summer in Chile) two years later.

Aside from this handful of novels and poetry collections, a considerable number of shorter tales on Latin America found their way into Soviet literary journals. Oleg Ignat'ev, the correspondent in Brasília, also had a vocation for belles-lettres. His *Skripka barabanščika* (The Drummer's Fiddle) is a novella about Venezuelan lovers Osvaldo and Katia and their struggle against the stooges of the dictator Jiménez.[96] In addition, Vladimir Kuz'miščev, a historian at the Moscow Institute of Latin America (see Chapter 5), wrote several historical novels on Latin American subjects. His *Tajny žrecov maja* (The Secrets of the Maya Priests), and *Carstvo synov Inkov* (The Realm of the Sons of the Incas) found an enthusiastic young readership from the end of the 1960s until long after the end of the Soviet Union. In their representation of Latin America, these fictional works followed the same pattern as the travelogues: they mixed a fascinated view

---

[94] Jurij Slepuchin, *U černy zakata* (Leningrad: Lenizdat, 1961).
[95] Julij Annenkov, *Šachterskij senator* (Moscow: GosIzDetLit, 1962).
[96] Ignat'ev, 'Skripka barabanščika'.

of exotic peoples and landscapes with a more politicised depiction of exploitation and revolutionary esprit.

The world abroad had an increasing impact on Soviet cultural production from the mid 1950s not just via Soviet writers. Works of foreign authors and artists were published and exhibited in ever larger numbers, too. Western modernist art and literature suffered as they were profoundly disliked by Soviet authorities and – probably just as in the West – by the majority of the population. African and Asian literary cultures were, mentally not spatially, much further away and therefore not easily accessible for a mass readership. Latin America filled the gap: as early as 1959, the number of works by Latin American authors translated into Russian exceeded 1,500.[97] Nevertheless, the Union of Soviet Writers demanded the publication of more Latin American works in the Soviet Union and put together a series of anthologies.[98]

Since the 1930s, two Latin American authors had been particularly influential on the Soviet literary scene. The Cuban author Nicolás Guillén combined the European literary tradition with Afro-Cuban elements in his *mestizaje* poetry. His work, translated by Ilya Ehrenburg, was widespread in the Soviet Union long before Castro's Revolution made him the Cuban national poet. Guillén enjoyed tremendous popularity not just among Russians, but all across the Union. By the mid 1960s, his poems had been translated into Armenian, Bashkir, Chuvash, Estonian, Georgian, Latvian, Lithuanian, Romanian (for the Moldavians), Tatar and Tajik.[99] Even more important for the Soviets was the godfather of Latin American poetry in the twentieth century: the Chilean Pablo Neruda not only saw all his works translated and distributed throughout the Soviet Union, including his memoirs of the Spanish Civil War, *España en el corazón* (Spain in the Heart), translated again by Ehrenburg in 1939. Neruda experienced worship close to a personality cult. He was highly celebrated on his several visits to the Soviet Union, and after his death a library and a Spanish-language high school in Moscow were named after him.[100] Even in the late 1970s, Neruda (just like Víctor

---

[97] Joseph Gregory Oswald, 'Contemporary Soviet Research on Latin America', *Latin American Research Review* 1/2 (1966), 77–96; Miguel Angel Asturias, 'Die russische Literatur in Lateinamerika', *Kultur und Leben* 3 (1958), 46–9.

[98] Ob izdanii knig latinoamerikanskich pisatelej v 1958–1960 gg., undated, RGALI f.631 op.26 d.4380 ll.1–2.

[99] Lev Okinsevic and Robert G. Carlton, *Latin America in Soviet Writings: A Bibliography* (Baltimore: Johns Hopkins University Press, 1966).

[100] A. Schpetny, 'Wir lernen Spanisch', *Kultur und Leben* 10 (1971), 39; the so-called *specškoly* were Soviet high schools in which some of the classes were conducted in a foreign language. They were especially popular among families of the urban intelligentsia, who were ambitious about their offspring's careers. The Spanish one in

Jara) was celebrated in a rock opera based on his libretto *Splendour and Death of Joaquin Murieta*, written by Pavel Gruško and Mark Zakharov, and made into a movie by Vladimir Grammatikov.[101]

Both Guillén and Neruda, however, were convinced party-line communists. Their celebration in the Soviet Union did therefore not come as a big surprise. Their work continued to be published – as were writings by other, much less gifted communist authors. From the mid 1950s, however, non-communist Latin American authors were also published and read widely in the USSR. To meet the growing demand, the Soviet publishing house for belles-lettres established its own Latin American department – as did the Union of Soviet Writers under the leadership of Elena Kolčina.[102] The boom in Latin American books began with belated translations of works written in the 1920s. *Doña Barbara*, a precursor work of magic realism by Rómulo Gallegos (president of Venezuela for a short time in 1948), was finally published in Moscow in 1959. The first print run of 150,000 copies sold out within a few days.[103] It was reviewed very positively in Soviet literary journals, which irritated a Venezuelan communist, who, in a letter to Moscow, felt the need to snipe that Gallegos was a staunch anti-communist.[104] The 1924 novel *La vorágine* (The Vortex), by Colombian writer José Eustasio Rivera, sold more than 300,000 copies in two weeks once it was finally translated by Boris Zagorskij and published in 1961; this made it the most successful work of fiction in the Soviet Union at the time. Magic realism found its way to the Soviet Union through Miguel Angel Asturias's *Señor presidente* (translated by Natalja Traubergy and Margarita Bilinkina), another tremendous success in the Soviet Union that won its author the Lenin Peace Prize in 1966.[105]

Bookshops and publishing houses were not able to supply the growing demand for Latin American literature with their translations and prints. The Latin American friendship societies helped to find

---

Moscow was Specškol No. 25: anon., *Čile–Rossija: 100 let diplomatičeskich otnošenij 1909–2009* (Moscow: [Embassy of Chile], 2009), p. 5.

[101] Archie Brown, *Seven Years That Changed the World: Perestroika in Perspective* (Oxford: Oxford University Press, 2007), pp. 213–37.

[102] Anon., 'Lateinamerikanische Literatur in der Sowjetunion', *Kultur und Leben* 3 (1958), 46; Valcárcel, *Reportaje al futuro*, p. 211.

[103] Vera Kuteishchikova, 'Latin American Literature in the Soviet Union', *Moscow News* 48 (1960), 7.

[104] Undated, RGALI f.631 op.26 d.4397 ll.1–3.

[105] Gabriel García Márquez, *De viaje por los países socialistas: 90 días en la 'Cortina de Hierro'* (Bogotá: La Oveja Negra, 1982), p. 162; Valeri Stolbov, 'Libros Latinoamericanos en la editorial Judozhestvennaya Literatura', *América Latina* 11 (1980), 112–18.

translators and to establish contacts with authors – and they gave Spanish classes, so Soviet readers could read the originals. Latin American literature was selling 'like hot cakes', as Kutejščikova put it.[106] Between 1959 and 1964, at least a further 425 books by contemporary authors followed.[107] The most important Soviet journal for international literature, *Inostrannaja Literatura* (Foreign Literature), acknowledged the trend and published a special issue on current developments in Latin American writing in 1960.[108] One of the most popular authors throughout the Soviet Union was the Brazilian Jorge Amado. Not only was his trilogy of novels *Os Subterrâneos da Liberdade* (The Freedom Underground) full of praise for Stalin and the USSR. It was also known to nearly everyone in the entire country, as the Soviet author Michail Apletin assured Amado in their correspondence, in which quoted at length from letters the Union of Soviet Writers had received from Soviet citizens expressing their admiration for Amado's work.[109]

By the end of the decade, the number of Latin American literary works distributed in the Soviet Union exceeded 5 million copies, even before the most influential Latin American novel of the time found its way to Soviet readership.[110] The publication of Gabriel García Márquez's *One Hundred Years of Solitude*, firstly in *Inostrannaja Literatura* in 1971, had an enormous impact on Soviet literary life. The Russian translation and commentary (not an easy task considering the numerous specific Colombian expressions and the poetic language of the novel) was undertaken by Valerij Stolbov and found widespread approval.[111] Socialist realism – already being questioned – came under severe attack from its magic counterpart, which presented Latin America as the 'Arcadia of revolutionary socialism'[112] – and fostered the image of Latin America as a very exotic place. More than 1 million copies of García Márquez's *magnum opus* were sold in the Soviet Union and, even though some passages were considered too erotic and fell victim to puritanical censors, Soviet readers were overwhelmed by what they read. Many times over the years, García Márquez repeated the anecdote of an elderly Russian woman who copied the whole novel word for word by hand, because she could not believe

[106] Kuteishchikova, 'Latin American Literature in the Soviet Union'.
[107] Okinsevic and Carlton, *Latin America in Soviet Writings*, pp. 198–220.
[108] *Inostrannaja Literatura* 12 (1960).
[109] Pis'mo Michaila Apletina Žoržy Amado, undated, RGALI f.631 op.26 d.4461 ll.3–4.
[110] Riza and Quirk, 'Cultural Relations between the Soviet Union and Latin America'.
[111] Undated comment by co-editor Tomaševskij, RGALI f.631 op.26 d.5324.
[112] Walter Bruno Berg and Michael Rössner, *Lateinamerikanische Literaturgeschichte* (Stuttgart and Weimar: Metzler, 2007), p. 529.

what she had just read. Her explanation: 'I needed to know who had gone crazy, the author or me.'[113]

The fascination with the Latin American novel continued throughout the 1970s, parallel with a similar boom in the West. Juan Rolfo's *Pedro Paramo* had a first print run of 100,000 copies in 1970. By the mid 1970s, sales of books by Mexican authors alone exceeded 2 million, the successful writings by Carlos Fuentes contributing most to this high volume.[114] By the late 1970s, the Latin American section of one Moscow publishing house, Chudožestvennaja Literatura, had published more than 14 million copies.[115] The reason for this popularity was similar to that for Mexican and Argentine films since the 1950s or for the visual art of muralists Diego Rivera and David Siqueiros: they all combined a realist form (even in 1961, the Latin American commission of the Union of Soviet Writers declared: 'the fight for realism is the fight for art as such!')[116] with a mix of social criticism and exoticism in the content – an aesthetic that suited both Soviet officials and audience. Readers loved the exotic worlds these novels and images revealed, while censors loved the fact that these foreign authors upheld the official Soviet view of the rest of the world as a place of oppression, exploitation and imminent revolution.

State-run publishing houses and political interference in the process of cultural production do not allow us to consider high numbers of editions alone as evidence of actual popular appreciation. Yet impressions of foreigners confirm the popularity of Latin American literature in the Soviet Union completely. Hardly any of the many visitors from the Americas fail to mention the deep and widespread knowledge Soviet citizens had about Latin American writers. When the Chilean author and politician Raúl Aldunate was shown around Moscow State University in 1959, his 17-year-old guide lectured him: 'the Yankees do not let you study under good conditions, because they do not want you to become too educated. It was very similar with us under the tsar: the gentry did everything they could to keep the peasants from studying.' Aldunate was ready to contradict her but was dumbstruck when the girl expounded further: 'it is true; I have read *El roto* and *La Pampa* [socio-critical novels from the 1920s and 1930s by the Chileans Joaquín Edwards Bello and Víctor

---

[113] Kutejščikova, *Moskva-Meksiko-Moskva*, p. 324; Gene Bell-Villada, *García Márquez: The Man and His Work* (Chapel Hill: University of North Carolina Press, 1990), p. 4.

[114] Kutejščikova, *Moskva-Meksiko-Moskva*, p. 328; Sapata and Kulidžanov, 'Luče znat' drug druga'.

[115] Stolbov, 'Libros Latinoamericanos en la editorial Judozhestvennaya Literatura'.

[116] Inostrannaja komissia Sojuza pisatelej SSSR, materialy po Latinskoj Amerike i Ispanii, 1 May 1961, RGALI f.631 op.26 d.4381 ll.1–12.

Domingo Silva]!'[117] Dominican students recalled that the Brazilian playwright Guilherme Figuereira enjoyed huge success in the Soviet Union and almost everyone knew the books of Jorge Amado and Gabriel García Márquez.[118] And García Márquez himself remembered being slack-jawed after a young Soviet, who had approached him during a visit on Moscow's Gorky Prospekt, recited long poems by the not particularly well known Colombian poet Rafael Combo over some glasses of beer they shared.[119]

Heroes of their time: Castro, Guevara and the Cuban Revolution in Soviet perception

The impacts of Latin America on Soviet cultural life were manifold, but they would have remained a side note in Soviet cultural history without one decisive event on New Year's Eve 1958. After several years of guerrilla struggle in the woods of eastern Cuba, the revolutionaries around Fidel Castro assumed power in Havana, and dictator Fulgencio Batista fled the country. Castro and his 26th of July movement had few if any personal contacts in the Soviet Union at that time and, while some members, including Ernesto 'Che' Guevara and Raúl Castro, considered themselves Marxists, there were only loose ties to the old established Cuban communist party Partido Socialista Popular (PSP). The violent struggle, after all, contradicted Moscow's orders to take a peaceful path. Their success, however, and their subsequent rapprochement with the USSR, albeit beginning only some eighteen months after the revolution with Mikojan's promise to buy sugar, caused many policy makers to reconsider their stance. For a short while, the Kremlin revelled in its possibilities on the 'blazing continent', as Latin America was often referred to in Soviet publications,

Based on their perceptions of Latin America as an exploited continent in upheaval, Soviet politicians and intellectuals saw the Cuban Revolution as proof that the world was successfully going the Soviet way of anti-imperialist struggle and overcoming economic backwardness. The numerous influences of the USSR on Cuba, and the 'Sovietisation' of the island have been subject to many historical assessments (see Introduction). This section will take a look in the other direction, on the impact of Cuba back in the Soviet Union, on its politicians, intellectuals

---

[117] Raúl Aldunate, *En Moscú* (Santiago de Chile: Ultramar, n.d.), p. 72.
[118] Ramón Alberto Ferreras, *¿Infierno? 1974–1980: vida estudantil en la URSS* (Santo Domingo: Editorial del Nordeste, 1981), p. 410.
[119] García Márquez, *De viaje por los países socialistas*, pp. 179–80.

and ordinary citizens. What they heard, saw and read of the events in the Caribbean triggered an enormous infatuation with Cuba at all levels of Soviet society and catalysed political and cultural enthusiasm for the whole of Latin America.

Situation reports by the Cuban Communist Party, visits by Cuban journalists in summer 1959 and translations of the *New York Times*'s coverage had kept Soviet officials informed about the activities of the Castro group.[120] But, initially, the Soviets kept a low profile, hesitant to provoke the near neighbour to the north, and sent only journalists. Short visits by *Pravda*'s Mexico correspondent Vasilij Čičkov and the KGB-affiliated TASS reporter in Mexico Aleksandr Alekseev in October and November were the only contacts until the new Cuban revolutionary government asked for the Soviet exhibition in Mexico to be held in Havana as well – official diplomatic relations would only be established almost a year later.[121]

These journalists wrote accounts of their trips to Cuba, and they took pictures: the bearded revolutionaries with their cigars and sunny beaches with bikini-clad beauties and palm trees suddenly appeared everywhere in the Soviet mass media. On the occasion of the exhibition, Genrich Borovik, reporter for *Ogonek* and part of Mikojan's entourage, inter-viewed Fidel Castro and wrote a – later famous – photo story about Cuba for his magazine. His photographs showed Che Guevara admiring scale models of Soviet accomplishments in the exhibition, but also everyday scenes of life on the island. Meeting Ernest Hemingway in his Havana exile, Borovik presented him with a model of Sputnik and told him how popular his books were among the young generation in the Soviet Union (what he did not tell him was that they had actually been banned from 1945 until 1955, when Ilya Ehrenburg finally pushed through the publi-cation of *The Old Man and the Sea* in *Inostrannaja Literatura*).[122] Borovik also wrote a booklet of episodes from his experiences on his first trip to Cuba.[123] That the first edition had a print run of 150,000 copies gives an idea of how popular the island and its tropical imagery had immediately become among Soviet citizens and intellectuals.

In the years until mid 1962, the elite of Soviet writers made pilgrim-ages to the revolutionary island, and most of them wrote about their

---

[120] E.g. US newspaper clippings collection, 8 Feb. 1957, RGANI f.5 op.28 d.498 l.29; O položenii v Kube, 27 Oct. 1956, RGANI f.5 op.28 d.440 ll.76–79.

[121] Mikojan, *Anatomija Karibskogo krizisa*, pp. 17–20; Jorge Castañeda, *Compañero: The Life and Death of Che Guevara* (New York: Vintage, 1997), pp. 173–4.

[122] Jewtuschenko, *Der Wolfspass*; Genrich Borovik, 'Pylajuščij ostrov', *Ogonek* 7 (1960), 4–5.

[123] Genrich Borovik, *Kak eto bylo na Kube* (Moscow: Pravda, 1961).

impressions for Soviet readers back home. Among the Soviet vanguard was a group of journalists led again by Aleksej Adžubej, who went to Cuba full of 'romantic notions of the Cuban events', as he later remembered.[124] Sergej Smirnov, former head of the literary journal *Literaturnaja Gazeta*, toured Cuba with the poet (and Neruda translator) Semen Kirsanov, the Ukrainian poet Dmitrij Pavlyčko, the Uzbek novelist Chamid Guljam and the literary critic Elena Klčina.[125] Dmitrij Gorjunov was one of the most influential journalists of his time, former head of *Komsomolskaja Pravda*, deputy editor of *Pravda* and now president of the news agency TASS. He wrote about his 1961 Cuban trip in a series of articles in *Ogonek*, which proved so successful that they were collected in a book, again with the impressive circulation of 150,000 copies in the first edition. Kutejščikova experienced the magnetic effect of Cuba and Castro when she went to the island in 1961.[126] As Cuba became the mecca of Soviet intelligentsia, writer Daniil Granin, famous for his novels about Soviet intellectuals, travelled there himself, met with Cuban artists and authors, and uncritically embraced everything he saw in his booklet *Ostrov molodych* (Island of the Young).[127]

All these early Soviet texts about the island displayed a great enthusiasm and optimism for the prospects of an independent and industrialised Cuba. It is also interesting to see that Soviet journalists, initially, saw the Cuban Revolution not as a surprising and exceptional case, but as the first (if somewhat coincidentally so) Latin American country to break the chains of imperialism – others would certainly follow soon: Gorjunov introduced his book with a quote by Neruda about the liberation of the Latin American peoples and explained how all the visitors from the Latin American continent would soon carry the revolution to their home countries.[128]

The revolution in the faraway Caribbean filled the imagination of a generation of Soviet writers, and Cuba left its mark on Soviet cultural life in the early 1960s. The journalist Borovik felt so inspired during his first stay in Cuba that, upon his return home, he ventured into literary writing. He wrote the script for Roman Karmen's historical epic film *Pylajuščij ostrov*; and, in his novel *Povest' o zelenoj jaščerice* (Novella about

[124] Adshubej, *Gestürzte Hoffnung*, p. 285.
[125] Sergej Smirnov, *Poezdka na Kubu* (Moscow: Sovetskij pisatel', 1962); Surkov, 'Interv'ju'.
[126] Kutejščikova, *Moskva-Meksiko-Moskva*, p. 208.
[127] Daniil Granin, *Ostrov molodych: rasskazy o Kube* (Leningrad: Lenizdat, 1962).
[128] Dmitri Gorjunov, *Zdrastvui, Kuba!* (Moscow: Pravda, 1961), p. 32; Soviet regional experts at the time shared this view: Lavričenko, *Ekonomičeskoe sotrudničestvo SSSR so stranami Azii, Afriki i Latinskoj Ameriki*, p. 97.

the Green Lizard, the poetic description of Cuba on a map, 1963), he combined short stories that romanticised episodes of recent Cuban history. It was brought out in a huge print run of 215,000 copies.[129]

Vasilij Čičkov, the *Pravda* correspondent in Mexico, made a similar journey from journalism to fiction. His 1961 children's book *Pepe, malen'kij kubinec* (Pepe, the Little Cuban) told the story of the Havana street child Pepe and his pals Negrito, Armando and Luis, with many detailed descriptions of Cuba and especially Havana. The boys cannot afford to go to school and try to make a living through odd jobs and by cleaning the shoes of tourists from the United States. Their lives change only when Castro assumes power. Pepe and the gang become partisans in the street fights of Havana. Having fought victoriously, they finally get what they apparently always wanted: they can go back to school or get decent jobs and live happily thereafter. In spite of the half-violent, half-didactic story, Soviet youngsters seem to have liked the book. Detizdat, the Soviet publishing house for children's literature, sold 265,000 copies in two editions by 1963.[130] It was also adapted into a play, *Mal'čiški iz Gavany* (The Boys from Havana), and Konstantin Listov set poems by Guillén to music, which were played during the enactment. The book edition featured a speech by Fidel Castro to the children of the world.[131]

Not only youngsters had the chance to see interpretations of the Cuban Revolution on Soviet stages. The Georgian playwright Georgij Mdivani had been in the crowd of Soviet pilgrims to Cuba. Overwhelmed like all the others, he wrote the three-act play *Den' roždenija Terezy* (Teresa's Birthday). It premiered in Moscow's distinguished Pushkin Theatre in early 1962 and came to be the most popular of several Soviet dramas about the Cuban Revolution. The story takes place in a village on southern Cuba's Playa Girón (Bay of Pigs) in April 1961. Teresa Fernandez is celebrating her 40th birthday with her children and the US artist Adlev Hamilton, a veteran of the Spanish Civil War. Music is playing, people dance, joke and praise the accomplishments of the revolution, when suddenly counter-revolutionaries land on the beach. The group flees to hide in the basement of a former US luxury hotel, but Hamilton is shot on the run by a traitor from within. Finally, Fidel and the Cuban Revolutionary Army defeat the invaders. Teresa enters with an impassionate final monologue, a desperate *'J'accuse'* to the reactionaries, who would not let the Cubans live in freedom. Ten times in a row she screams 'Why do you kill our children?' – and the curtain falls.

---

[129] Genrich Borovik, *Povest' o zelenoj jaščerice* (Moscow: Molodaja gvardija, 1963).
[130] Vasilij Čičkov, *Pepe, malen'kij Kubinec: povest'* (Moscow: DetGiz, 1961).
[131] Vasilij Čičkov, *Mal'čiški iz Gavany* (Moscow: DetGiz, 1963).

The play combined the elements the Soviets thought they knew about Latin America at the time. Happy, music- and dance-loving peoples are harassed by imperialists, as had been the case in the Spanish Civil War. Unlike their government, some US citizens actually supported the Cuban Revolution, as represented by Hemingway's alter-ego Hamilton. In Cuba, the imperialists have been expelled, the former luxury hotel is now a dwelling house. But people still have to be on the alert for counter-revolutionaries and traitors, as the real invasion of CIA-backed troops at the Bay of Pigs had shown. It was good that the Cubans had such a brave heroic leadership, but did not Teresa's screams also call for anti-imperialist help from the Soviet Union?

Mdivani and the officials of the GKKS were keen to know what their new Cuban friends thought of the play. They invited representatives of the Cuban ministry of education to see the première. The answer they got was a polite slamming: Paco Alonso, head of the theatre department in the Cuban ministry, wrote a letter to GKKS president Georgij Žukov. After some niceties, he criticised the play heavily: the music they used was not Cuban but meringue from the Dominican Republic; the revolutionaries were presented as pretentious rum-guzzling bouncers instead of the humble and restrained human beings they allegedly were; and the depiction of the Cubans was full of incorrect stereotypes, for example using 'Señor' and 'Señorita' in addressing acquaintances, which Cubans would not do. As in various clichéd depictions of the other in art (and not only Soviet art), these shortcomings did no harm to the play's popularity. It was considered a success and republished ten years later.[132]

On an even larger scale than the playwrights, Soviet poets caught fire in the Cuban Revolution. For a 1961 volume of verse, the editors Nikolaj Anciferov and Sergej Polikarpov put together forty-four of the most renowned lyricists they could get hold of. *Tebe Kuba! Stikhi* (To You, Cuba! Poems), they called their volume. More than a hundred poems celebrated the heroism of Fidel and Che, praised the beauty of Cuba and its *guajiras* (girls) and, full of pathos, pledged their solidarity. Older poets remembered their fascination with Spain in their own childhood. One day, Anisim Krongaus wrote in a poem to his son, 'Synu', the son might remember his 'first romance' just as his father had dreamt of the exotic places of Madrid and Catalonia. Aleksej Adžubej did not contribute pompous poems, but he, too, remembered the romanticism about Spain in his 1930s childhood, when children would wear Spanish berets and

---

[132] 27 Feb. 1962, GARF f.9518 d.334 l.101; Georgij Mdivani, *Den' roždenija Terezy* (Moscow: Izdatel'svo Iskusstvo, 1962).

play fascists and republicans – their variant of cops and robbers.[133] Lev Chalif, too, drew continuities from the Spanish Civil War to the Cuban Revolution and to the anti-imperial struggles in Africa. What had failed in the 1930s was now finally going the Soviet way. As Dmitrij Kovalev put it in his poem 'Echo': 'the echo of our Baltic *Aurora* goes around the world. Greetings Africa! Greetings far-off Cuba!'[134]

The topos of the spreading revolution was joined by the topos of love in the writings of many poetically inspired Soviet writers: Aleksandr Prokrovev's heart was set on fire by Cuba ('Ognennoe serdce', Flaming Heart); Marija Borisova was, after some doubts, ultimately convinced that she had fallen in love with Cuba ('Ja ljublju tebja, Kuba', I Love You, Cuba); for Gennadij Maslennikov, Cuba was 'all my love'. Yevtushenko asked Havana like a lover in bed: 'Gavana, mne ne spitsia, a tebe?' ('I can't sleep, can you?'). One of the comments US fair hosts and hostesses most often heard at their exhibitions in the Soviet Union was why they did not share this intimate compassion for Castro and Cuba.[135] The young representatives of the United States probably did not grasp that there was a dimension to the Soviet craze for Cuba that had little to do with communism. Cuba was not only a geo-strategic conquest, but the Soviets' very own island of love, an erotic utopia found in imaginations throughout European cultural history. Kythera, the Greek island of Aphrodite's temple, set the precedent for this convention: the Romans knew the legend of an *insula divina* somewhere beyond the Pillars of Hercules in the open Atlantic; Boccaccio and Torquato Tasso imagined mythical *isole felice*; Portuguese seafarers fought the austerity on board their ships with stories of the *ilha namorada*. Thomas More's Utopia was an island in the Atlantic; later his English countrymen would fantasise about exotic and erotic adventures on Caribbean islands. The French colonial name for the South Sea island Tahiti was 'Nouvelle Cythère'; even before Wilhelmine Germans finally got their own colonies, they dreamt about erotic libertinage on oceanic islands in pompous literature.[136] Russia, now a world power in its own right, found and cherished Cuba.

The translator Pavel Gruško, who spent two years on the Soviet island of love, joined the chorus of cheering lyricists in a series of his own and

[133] Adshubej, *Gestürzte Hoffnung*; for the perception of the Spanish Civil War, see also Karl Schlögel, *Terror und Traum: Moskau 1937* (Munich: Hanser, 2008), pp. 136–52.

[134] Nikolaj Anciferov and Sergej Polikarpov (eds.), *Tebe, Kuba! Stichi* (Moscow: Sovetskij Pisatel', 1961).

[135] Vajl' and Genis, *60-e*, p. 59; Sorensen, *The Word War*, p. 200; Gennadi Maslennikow, 'Kuba – meine ganze Liebe', *Kultur und Leben* 12 (1966), 36–7.

[136] Dieter Richter, *Der Süden: Geschichte einer Himmelsrichtung* (Berlin: Wagenbach, 2009); Koebner and Pickerodt (eds.), *Die andere Welt*, p. 241.

translated poems about Cuba.[137] But of all Soviet writers, no one was as enthusiastic and prolific as Yevtushenko, the poet of the Thaw period, celebrated as the voice of this generation. Full of scorn for the old cultural officials in Moscow, he adored Fidel Castro, 'who back then was young and full of charm', as he remembered later.[138] He travelled three times to Cuba in the early 1960s, learnt Spanish and contributed poems not just to Ancifero's anthology, but published dozens more in several journals. He hailed Castro and Guevara as 'Mozarts of the Revolution' and the revolution as 'Beauty Queen'.[139] When Castro gave a speech on the Placa de la Revolución in Havana on the occasion of the visit of Yuri Gagarin, Yevtushenko was in the crowd. A young Cuban mother next to him began to breastfeed her baby – an epiphanic moment for him, which resulted in the ponderous poem 'On a Rally in Havana'.[140] Yevtushenko's *magnum opus* on the Cuban Revolution was 'Ja – Kuba: poema v proze' ('I Am Cuba: A Poem in Prose'). For eighty-seven pages (!), he depicted the pre-revolutionary island, teased the decadent US tourists, portrayed the Cuban Carnival and celebrated its music and its beautiful women. In a monotonous staccato, Yevtushenko begins every verse with the subject; there are no conjunctions in the whole poem, breaks only every fifth verse, and now and then direct speech. The end sets a pathetic apogee:

> I am Cuba.
> You can kill a man
> Hundreds, Thousands
> 10,000 or 100,000
> But to kill a people
> That is impossible.
> Patria o muerte!
> Venceremos![141]

Yevtushenko's epic poem was used for a Soviet–Cuban film production also called *Ja Kuba/Soy Cuba*. Starring Cuban amateur actors, in four episodes it tells of the oppression and the liberation struggle of the Cuban people. Enormous technical efforts were made for the film that resulted in spectacular camera work with incredibly long tracking shots. In the end, the Soviet film team around director Michail Kalatozov and

---

[137] Pavel Gruško, 'Licom k Kube: stichi', *Družba Narodov* 1 (1965), 139–45.

[138] Jewtuschenko, *Der Wolfspass*, p. 227.

[139] Evtušenko, *Nežnost'*, pp. 127–87; one-third of this large volume of poems is dedicated to Cuba, the revolution and Fidel Castro.

[140] Evgenij Evtušenko, 'Stichi', *Sovetskaja Literatura* 10 (1962), 147–52.

[141] Evgenij Evtušenko, 'Ja – Kuba: poema v proze', *Znamja* 3 (1963), pp. 3–89. The final two lines may be translated: 'Fatherland or death! / We shall be victorious!'

cameraman Sergej Urusevskij spent almost two years in Cuba. Like most Soviet intellectuals, they had profound sympathy for the Cuban Revolution and they considered *Soy Cuba* to be their 'contribution to the anti-imperialist struggle' (Kalatozov). Camera operator Aleksandr Kal'catyj later remembered: 'we knew little of Cuba, its history, even where it was located. But we were enthusiastic about a revolution with a human face, ostensibly much less cruel … Later we came to know more and our opinion changed, but at this time we were completely overwhelmed.' The further history of the film and its crew is tragic. Kal'catyj, upon his return to Moscow after two years in Cuba, was unable to reintegrate into less exotic Soviet everyday life and finally fled to the West. The film itself was the most expensive flop in the history of the Soviet cinema. It was shown only once in Moscow in 1964, where the audience found it too arty, and officials disliked it for its display of a 'tropical eroticism' and libertine US lifestyle in pre-revolutionary Cuba. The Cubans did not like it for its cumbersome pathos. 'No Soy Cuba' headlined *Hoy*, the newspaper of the Cuban Communist Party – 'I Am Not Cuba'.[142] The film reels disappeared in Soviet archives and were rediscovered only in the 1990s by US film-maker Martin Scorsese. Today, the film is considered a classic of world cinema.

The next Soviet–Cuban co-production came only many years later and was less arty. The adaptation of Thomas Mayne Reid's novel 'The Headless Horseman' (*Vsadnik bez golovy*, 1972) was filmed by Vladimir Vajnštok in Cuba. The pathos of *Soy Cuba* gave way to suspense and romance in a Mexican setting – and Soviet youth loved it. While artistic cinema celebrating the Cuban Revolution did not appeal to a broad audience, music certainly did. On the occasion of Fidel Castro's first visit to the Soviet Union in 1963, the lyricists Sergej Grebennikov and Nikolaj Dobronravov and the musician Aleksandra Pachmutova composed the now classic Soviet tune 'Kuba – ljubov' moja' (Cuba Is My Love). The lyrics glorified both the heroism of the revolutionaries and the beauty of the 'island of the red sunset' (*ostrov zari bagrovoj*); the music is very catchy, albeit closer to a Russian wartime song than to Cuban mambo. The most famous Soviet crooners such as Iosif Kobzon and Muslim Magomaev included the song in their repertoires. Kobzon, who in terms of music, popularity and alleged connections to the mafia has often been compared to Frank Sinatra, starred in a musical of the same name written in 1963 by Pavel Pičugin and Rauf Gadžiev (both of whom had been to Cuba themselves). Russian ballet dancers slipped into

---

[142] Vicente Ferraz, *Soy Cuba, o mamute siberiano* (documentary film, Brazil/Italy 2005); Enrique Pineda Barnet, 'Ein sowjetisch-kubanischer Film', *Neue Zeit* 10 (1962), 16–17.

uniforms in the style of the Cuban revolutionaries, wore fake beards and carried machine guns. Another musical, the *Kubinskaja novella* (Cuban Novella) followed, and Viktor Vanslov composed an entire opera called *Patria o muerte* (Fatherland or Death).[143]

An opera on Cuban events was written by Konstantin Listov in 1962. *Doč revolucii* (Daughter of the Revolution) recounted the life of Angela Alonso, a Cuban housewife who became a fervent supporter of the revolution. The Cuban newspaper *Noticias de Hoy* had reported the real Angela's story: her husband, critical of the Batista regime, had been tortured in prison. After his release he continued his political activities, but asked his wife to keep a suicide pill and hand it over to him should he be arrested again. In what was later considered a heroic act she did so the next time police showed up. Her beloved husband died, and Angela, previously an ordinary Cuban mother, joined the rebel forces against the dictator. After the revolution, she joined the pantheon of Cuban heroes in the Soviet Union. She was painted by Russian artist Viktor Ivanov and became the heroine of Listov's opera.[144]

Finally, even the Russian circus followed the Cuban craze. The musician Pacho Alonso (no known relation to Angela and Paco) and his band, the Bocucos, joined the Moscow Circus for a show called the Cuban Carnival in October 1962. While the world was coming close to a nuclear war, when US intelligence discovered the Soviet missile base being built on Cuba, a clueless Moscow audience enjoyed an entertaining re-enactment of two years of shared Soviet–Cuban history.[145] On 'Black Saturday' itself, when at the height of the crisis a US destroyer launched grenades at a Soviet nuclear submarine and a US Air Force reconnaissance plane was shot down by a Soviet rocket on Cuba, *Moscow News* featured an article about 'the spectacle of the heroic island'.[146] A film was screened on stage, in which Yevtushenko declaimed his poems and 200 actors performed a mass pantomime about the downing of a US airplane over Cuba and the defeat of the counter-revolutionaries at Playa Girón. The audience was probably not aware that it was experiencing one of the most absurd and macabre performances ever seen on a stage.

---

[143] Pičugin, 'Ansambl'' iz Paragvaja'.

[144] A. Tišenko, *Konstantin Listov* (Moscow: Sovetskij Kompozitor, 1987), p. 115; I. Veršinina, 'Anchela Alonso: geroinia opery', *Ogonek* 15 (1962), 28; dozens more examples can be found at sovmusic.ru/list.php?gold=yes&idsection=12 (last accessed 30 Jun. 2010).

[145] N. Michajlova, 'Spektakl' o geroičeskom ostrove', *Sovetskij Cirk* 8 (1962), 1–3.

[146] E. Ivanova, 'Cuban Carnival', *Moscow News* 43 (1962), 12; Michajlova, 'Spektakl' o geroičeskom ostrove'.

Humankind survived the crisis and, while Soviet geo-strategists somewhat toned down their global aspirations, many ordinary Soviet citizens and certainly the intellectuals continued their admiration for the Caribbean island. In 1964, the publishing house Progress launched a monthly magazine appropriately called *Kuba*. In a layout strikingly similar to the US *Time* and *Life* magazines, its Cuban–Soviet editors informed their readership in the big cities of the Union of recent developments in the revolutionary process in Cuba and the rest of Latin America.[147] The first issue's title introduced a motif that became widespread in Soviet (and also US) depictions of Cuba: the revolutionary shotgun dame, who combined two points of interest in Cuba, revolutionary romanticism and tropical eroticism.[148]

In the early 1960s, Soviet readers could open any journal to see the iconography of the Cuban Revolution – and if they picked, as many did, *Ogonek* or *Novoe Vremja*, they could hardly avoid it. Fidel Castro and Che Guevara ranked equally with the Soviet cosmonauts as the heroes of their time. They were young, handsome and dynamic, and apparently honest characters, and thus a welcome replacement of boring clichés of late Stalinist propaganda images. When, in the wake of the Cuban Crisis, Castro was invited for a lengthy state visit all across the Soviet Union, he experienced a devotion probably never given to any foreign state representative in any country. During the forty days that Castro travelled to twelve cities of Uzbekistan, Siberia, the Urals, the Volga basin, Ukraine, Georgia and finally Leningrad and Moscow, Soviet media basically reported nothing but his visit. *Pravda* and *Izvestija* ran front-page reports for a month straight.[149] When he gave his final speech in front of 125,000 people in the Lenin Stadium, all the notables of the Soviet state gathered and listened reverently. The Soviet audience was deeply impressed by his improvised speech and his chummy behaviour to his translator – something they had never seen on such official occasions.[150] After his first visit, an elaborate coffee-table book collected exciting pictures and rather boring speeches of his journey, and propaganda films were shot and

---

[147] Oleg Dal'nev, '"Kuba" – novyj žurnal', *Sovetskaja Pečat'* 9 (1964), 56; Illustrirovannyj žurnal 'Kuba', Razdely žurnala, undated, around October 1963, GARF f.9518 op.1 d.335 ll.131–134.

[148] *Kuba* 1 (1964); compare also A. Geršber, 'Kubinskaja revoliucija v fotografijach', *Sovetskaja Fotografija* 23/2 (1963), 5; Ivan Suščenko, 'Patria o muerte!', *Ogonek* 47 (1962), 14–15; anon., *Živopis' Kuby: katalog vystavki* (Moscow: Sovetskij Chudožnik, 1962); anon., *Grafika Kuby: katalog vystavki* (Moscow: Sovetskij Chudožnik, 1960).

[149] Leonov, *Licholet'e*, p. 85; Genrich Borovik, 'Pervye šagi po Sovetskoj zemle', *Ogonek* 19 (1963), 28–9, as well as the following issues; *Pravda* and *Izvestija*, 28 Apr. 1963 to 24 May 1963.

[150] Joaquin Gutiérrez, *La URSS tal cual* (Santiago de Chile: Nascimento, 1967), p. 75.

screened to the Soviet audience.[151] Castro had become an eminently important propaganda figure and, at the same time, a source of self-affirmation for Soviet officials. But he was also kind of a pop star for Soviet citizens. The enthusiasm people displayed in photographs taken whenever he went to the Soviet Union goes visibly beyond the usual *mise-en-scène* of putative friendship of the peoples.

Che Guevara's case is more complicated. In the early 1960s and before his career as revolutionary icon in the West, he was an officially celebrated socialist superhero in the East. On his first visit to Moscow, he was placed next to Khrushchev on Lenin's mausoleum during the military parade of Revolution Day – in the symbolic politics of Soviet rituals an extraordinary honour, which he was the first foreigner to receive after Stalin's death.[152] His later visits to the USSR were shown live on Soviet television and radio, together with fellow superhero Gagarin.[153] Off stage, Guevara repeatedly mocked his Soviet hosts for their petty bourgeois tastes, such as their ties and the porcelain tableware during a dinner at Aleksandr Alekseev's house.[154] Yet what really lost him Soviet benevolence were his political allegations and endeavours. From the mid 1960s, Guevara came under attack as a 'leftist adventurer'. His on-going attempts to spread the revolution in Latin America and Africa became a thorn in the side of Soviet foreign politicians in times of peaceful coexistence and even more so in the context of the rivalry that erupted with Maoist China. That Guevara continuously denounced the Soviets for having betrayed the revolution, and the fact that he sought closer contacts with China did not win him many friends in the Kremlin. He was no longer mentioned in Soviet media.

Meanwhile, Guevara was developing into a global symbol of socialism and romantic rebellion. Alberto Korda's famous picture turned into an icon of the worldwide student movement and, after his assassination in the Bolivian jungle in 1967, more than 50,000 young people gathered in front of Washington's Lincoln Memorial to denounce US imperialism. Foreign students in all big cities of the USSR gathered as well and held memorials; in Moscow, Lumumba University students spontaneously rallied in front of the US embassy.[155] The leading representative of Soviet counter-culture, Artemij Troickij, remembered being deeply shocked by

---

[151] *Fidel' Kastro v Sovetskom Sojuze* (1964), RGAKFD #22485; *Gost' s ostrova Svobody* (1963), RGAKFD #22437; anon., *Viva Kuba! Vizit Fidelia Kastro Rus v Sovetskij Sojuz* (Moscow: Pravda, 1963).

[152] Jacobo Machover and Hainer Kober, *Che Guevara – die andere Seite* (Berlin, Potsdam: Wolbern, 2008), p. 83.

[153] 11 Nov. 1964, GARF f.9576 op.2 d.187a.   [154] Leonov, *Licholet'e*, pp. 60–6.

[155] Andrew and Mitrokhin, *The World Was Going Our Way*, p. 96; undated Komsomol report, RGASPI f.1M op.39 d.231 ll.40–45.

the news of Guevara's death; in his memoirs, he is portrayed sitting at his desk below a huge Che Guevara poster.[156] The KGB's leading Latin America expert, Nikolaj Leonov, usually a rather sober intellectual, remembered being profoundly shocked by the news of Guevara's death. Eulogising him as a 'pure, fearless and to a gigantic extent a human apostle', whose murder was 'not less significant than Jesus' crucifixion', Leonov recalled that his own 'grief and chagrin were infinite'.[157]

For a long time, the Kremlin had failed completely to recognise Che Guevara's symbolic capital. It took officials 'two or three days of intense consideration on how to react to the death of Che Guevara ... as if it was an issue of complex international character',[158] Leonov recalled. Finally, the Party leadership paid their tribute to Che's merits in somewhat lackadaisical obituaries.[159] But since a dead foreign 'left-adventurist' could himself do no more harm, and with a certain experience in personality cults, Soviet officials resumed the apotheosis of the hero some years later. The Party-line poets Evgenij Dolmatovskij, with 'Ruki Gevary' (Guevara's Hands) in 1972, and Dmitrij Pavlyčko and Jaroslav Smeljakov worshipped Che's martyrdom in poems. The Latin Americanist Iosif Grigulevič published his biography of Che in the book series 'Žizn' zamečatel'nych ljudej' (Lives of Remarkable People).[160] A series established in the 1930s by Maxim Gorky, these biographies represented the pantheon of Soviet heroes and role models. On the tenth anniversary of the execution in Bolivia, another Latin Americanist, Kiva Majdanik, published a euphoric eulogy on Che in the scholarly journal *Latinskaja Amerika*.[161]

Official and established Soviet entertainment music, the so-called *estradnaja muzyka* of the likes of Kobzon, ostentatiously celebrated the icon of the New Left, too. Former ideological disagreements were now blanked out entirely. With the onset of the guerrilla wars in Central America in the late 1970s, finally, also Guevara's theoretical work was rehabilitated and translated into Russian. In fact, next to Gagarin, Che Guevara proved to be the most successful socialist icon in the Soviet Union and an example of the successful incorporation of a broad public into the discourse of internationalism.

---

[156] Troitsky, *Back to the USSR*, p. 34.   [157] Leonov, *Licholet'e*, pp. 99–100.
[158] Nikolai Leonov, 'La inteligencia soviética en América Latina durante la Guerra Fría', *Estudios Públicos* 73 (1999), 35.
[159] *Pravda* and *Izvestija*, 18 Oct. 1967.
[160] Grigulevič published under a pseudonym: Iosif Lavreckij, *Ernesto Če Gevara* (Moscow: Molodaja gvardija, 1972).
[161] Kiva Majdanik, 'Revoljucioner', *Latinskaja Amerika* 6 (1977).

The inspiration the Cuban Revolution gave to Soviet writers and artists was not subject to these political ambiguities. Besides the relatively well-known authors presented so far, many other, lesser-known people from the provinces of the Soviet Union and also eastern Europe wrote about their fascination for Cuba in novels, short stories, poems, performances and music. Soviet technicians sent abroad wrote travelogues, as did a group of Komsomol members from Stavropol. The Bashkir journalist and novelist Anver Bikčentaev wrote adventurous short stories set during the Cuban Revolution, *Trudno čeloveku bez borody* (It Is Difficult for a Man without a Beard) in 1960 and *Ad'jutanti ne umirajut* (Adjutants Don't Die) in 1963. The Uzbek Chamid Guljam travelled to Cuba and wrote a book about the Third World's awakening. Ukrainian and Belorussian poems and even a Mordvinian ditty by folk poet Nikul Erkaj were dedicated to the Cuban heroes. In Tbilisi, a Georgian drama about the revolution was staged. Eulogies from China were translated into Russian, and attempts were made to encourage the Polish to join the antiimperialist struggle as well with the poem *Kogda poliaki srazhalis'za svobodu Kuby* (When the Poles Fought for Cuba's Liberty).[162]

Some of the Soviet writing on Cuba was pure propaganda. Some was commissioned work; other authors jumped on the bandwagon on their own initiative, as they had a sense of what the authorities wanted. Yet this cannot explain the extensive appeal Cuba had among the Soviet audience. Besides, many writers themselves, as members of the Soviet *nomenklatura*, were among those who gave the orders. Their enthusiasm was real and it was political: the events in Cuba generated a revolutionary romanticism among the Soviet elite. In their famous account of the *šestidesjatniki*, the young Soviet generation of the 1960s, Petr Vajl' and Aleksandr Genis dedicated a long chapter to Cuba as their 'metaphor of revolution' within the Soviet Union. 'The Cuban Revolution', they recalled from their 1980s United States exile, 'was a striking event for the Soviet person of the 1960s, a powerful, creative social revolution combined with an exotic distant sea.'[163]

More than others, the Cuban craze encompassed a relatively young generation of future leaders in politics, media, arts and architecture.

---

[162] Anver Bikčentaev, 'Ad'jutanti ne umirajut', *Oktjabr'* 5 (1963), 7–34; Amiran Servašidze, *Devuška iz Sant'iago: viva Kuba!* (Moscow: Sovetskaja Rossija, 1963); G. Ivanov, 'Na pylajuščem ostrove: pisma s Kuby', *Stavropol'e* 3 (1962); Dmytro Pavlyčko, *Pal'mova vit'* (Kiev, 1962); Anciferov and Polikarpov (eds.), *Tebe, Kuba!*; Chamid Guljam, *Kontinenty ne spjat* (Moscow: Sovetskij Pisatel', 1961); Anver Bikčentaev, 'Trudno čeloveku bez borody', *Družba Narodov* 5 (1960), 105–8; anon., 'Kogda poliaki srazhalis'za svobodu Kuby', *Inostrannaja Literatura* 12 (1960), 260.

[163] Vajl' and Genis, *60-e*, pp. 52–64.

Moscow's Kalinin Prospekt was modelled after a modern quarter of Havana; Michail Posochin's huge mosaics on the facade of the Oktjabr' cinema were clearly inspired by the Mexican muralists. Yet in the early 1960s, Cuba and its revolution were, for once, a case where indeed the entire political, intellectual and artistic elite took the same line and all embraced this ostensible feat of Soviet internationalism. For very many ordinary Soviets, Cuba was a welcome enrichment and expansion of their cultural horizon, which had an ineradicable political dimension. The case of Che Guevara made clear that this harmony was not to prevail long. But at least in the aftermath of the revolution, the older, high-ranking Party members also cherished Cuba, because it reminded them of their own revolutionary past. To quote Anastas Mikojan after his first visit to Cuba: 'yes, this is a real revolution. Just like ours. It feels like I have returned to my youth!' Or the long-term Soviet ambassador to Mexico, Vladimir Vinogradov, after his first Cuban voyage: 'I felt as if I were twenty again.' Foreign minister Andrej Gromyko, the fierce 'Mr Nyet' and later opponent of Soviet Third World adventures, finds only the warmest words for the Cubans in his memoirs. And Khrushchev himself told US reporters after his first meeting with Castro in his Harlem hotel: 'if he is a Marxist, I do not know. But I sure can tell that I am a Fidelist!'[164]

Exoticism and internationalism: Latin America in Soviet arts and public reception

In contrast to the extreme isolationism of late Stalinism, Soviet cultural life in the mid 1950s opened up to the world. After years of destructive in-breeding, Soviet artists and intellectuals rejoined global discourses, and ordinary people could develop a sense of the world abroad that had ceased to be irrevocably hostile. Texts, photographs and films provided elements to create a notion of parts of the world, about which the Soviet population had previously had only the vaguest ideas. This was true for the entire emerging Third World and had the most remarkable reper-cussions in the case of Latin America.

Selected members of the intellectual elite were allowed to travel to all parts of Latin America from the mid 1950s. In their political world-view, the global South was a place full of poverty, backwardness, social injust-ice, oppression and exploitation; what they saw on the ground during

---

[164] Vladimir Vinogradov, *Diplomatičeskie memuary* (Moscow: Rossijskaja Političeskaja Enciklopedija, 1998), p. 144; Leonov, *Licholet'e*, p. 55; Andrej Gromyko and Hermann Kusterer, *Erinnerungen* (Düsseldorf: Econ, 1989), pp. 256–9.

their trips – and the regular news of US interventions – only confirmed their already existing textbook knowledge. Yet all travellers sensed a spirit of optimism and a revolutionary spirit among the Latin American peoples, who would soon burst their imperialist chains. In opposition to US materialism and individualism, Soviet intellectuals styled themselves as the same humanist idealists as their Latin American colleagues. In their travelogues, they conveyed this world-view to a broad readership back home. All of them contrast the enhancement of Soviet living standards, infrastructure and technological development compared to the countries visited – and at least in the case of the poorer Andean and Central American states not entirely wrongly.

Enthusiasm about the prospects of a worldwide de-Stalinised socialism had seized not only the members of a rather political intelligentsia, but also many Soviet artists and writers. They shared the fascination with a Latin America that they, too, saw as a half-underdeveloped, half-revolutionary and, added to that, an excitingly exotic place. In a large array of fiction, feature and documentary films, and songs, in form and content pleasing to both cultural officials and the mass audience, they spread this image all over the Soviet Union. This politicised view, with its imperialist villains and admiration for the Soviets all around, could build on an originally apolitical fascination for exotic and adventurous outlands and found immediate acceptance among many Soviet citizens. They quickly internalised Latin American revolutionary catchphrases, many of which derived from the Spanish Civil War: *¡no pasarán!* ('They shall not pass!'), *¡venceremos!* ('We shall be victorious!) or *¡que viva ...!* ('long live ...') soon no longer needed a translation for the Soviet audience; even today, everyone in Russia knows what *¡Patria o muerte!* means and refers to the Cuban revolutionaries as the *barbudos* (the bearded ones). It is characteristic of this post-Stalinist internationalism as a mindset of the Soviet population that it successfully incorporated non-communist elements into its discourse and gave them an ideological edge that a well-entertained audience readily and happily accepted. Selectively imported Latin American productions, Latino folklore, socio-critical films and revolutionary-romanticising novels again confirmed the Soviet internationalist view of the world – and were all the rage. Many reports by foreigners who visited the Soviet Union, letters by Soviet citizens to the authorities, and the adaptation of Latino motifs by unofficial artists endorse the assumption that Latin American popular culture was not politically imposed, but indeed highly popular.

The Cuban Revolution catalysed the exoticist fancy for Latin America and gave very convincing evidence that the world was going the way Soviets had perceived it. The political and intellectual elite, artists, writers and large parts of the Soviet public literally fell in love with the island. The set of revolutionary symbols it provided, images of charismatic leaders and martyrs, armed women, heroic children, catchy songs and slogans, were spread to the most distant nooks of the Soviet empire – and stood in a remarkable contrast to the harmonious and idyllic image of doves of peace and shaking hands in Soviet self-representation towards the world abroad (as presented in Chapter 1).

Soviet internationalism after Stalin was not a mere political credo, but an ideal embraced by many Soviet intellectuals and artists. During de-Stalinisation, most of them saw themselves as 'vanguard of a fair and egalitarian society', and many believed in the necessity of joining the CPSU to improve it from within. Demonising Stalin, they glorified the leftist culture of the 1920s and with it socialist internationalism. From the mid 1960s, their enthusiasm waned remarkably. Khrushchev's boorish attitude towards the arts, new show trials against writers and, finally, the invasion of reformist Czechoslovakia in 1968 destroyed much of the socialist and internationalist idealism of this generation's artistic and literary intelligentsia.[165] They retreated to private life, emigrated to Israel or became Russian nationalists. While the next two chapters will change perspectives and tell the story of Soviet internationalism from Latin American points of view, this book's fifth and last chapter will show how academic intellectuals stuck much longer to the internationalist spirit that the artistic intelligentsia had lost.

To some extent, Allende's presidency in Chile from 1970 to 1973 and the victory of the Sandinistas in the Nicaraguan Civil War rekindled the infatuation with Latin America; there was little in the way of substantial political or financial Soviet help for the Frente Popular, but at least there was a lot of public rhetorical support. Latin American songs were sung again and, after the 1973 putsch in Chile, a minor martyr cult was celebrated around Allende and Víctor Jara. Yet the political circumstances had changed during Stagnation, and artists and the public did not display the same inexperienced optimism as around 1960, when internationalism had just been rekindled successfully. That said, Latin American motifs remained popular in Soviet music. From the 1970s, many officially endorsed artists sang about Cuba or Chile, but the key changed from revolutionary major to melodramatic minor: the 'Ballada o Če Gevary' (Ballad of Che Guevara), written by the Belorussian composers Gennadij Buravkin and Igor' Lučenok, is a sad goodbye to the former revolutionary idol. And in 'Pamjati Če Gevary' (In Memory to Che Guevara, 1981), composer Vladimir Migulja and poet

---

[165] Zubok, *Zhivago's Children*, pp. 34–6, 79–84.

Nikolaj Zinov'ev dramatically mourn the melting down of a bronze memorial of Che Guevara in Santiago de Chile.[166] Other artists deprived their Latin music completely of a political message: 'Eto govorim my' (Here's What We Say) was a huge hit in 1978. The vocal ensemble Plamja sang the famous chorus 'Kuba daleka, Kuba rjadom ...' (Cuba Is Far, Cuba Is Nigh ...), written by Georgij Movsejan and Lev Ošanin. The tune sounded very much like the contemporaneous western style of disco – and shared its apolitical jollity just as much as Brazilian *lambada*, a popular dance in the crumbling Soviet Union of the late 1980s.

This chapter has presented Soviet internationalism after Stalin as a functioning principle within Soviet society. As in the outward sense examined in Chapter 1, it was a combination of socialist internationalism of the 1920s and cultural internationalism of the 1950s and 1960s. The perception of the Hispanic world in the early Soviet Union had been framed by a revolutionary romanticism for the Mexican Revolution and the Spanish Civil War and their songs, tales and heroes. After the end of Stalinist isolation, Soviet artists firstly bolted on these elements when describing Latin America, before some of them had the chance to go there themselves. The folklorisation of Latin Americans echoed similar attitudes towards 'backward' minorities within the USSR earlier. But in many ways, the Soviet Union, after 1953, was in tune again with developments in the rest of the world and, in particular, the West. Soviet cinema reflected a longing for authenticity, as did western art-house cinema at the time; Latin American music – or local music with a dash of 'Latin American' flair – was an important element of popular entertainment everywhere in the northern hemisphere in the 1950s. A decade later, both in the USSR and in the West, socio-critical Latin American folk music and the leftist literature of the Latin American boom fostered the enthusiasm for the romantic revolution. Rebellious youngsters on both sides of the Iron Curtain cherished Cuba and the modern Jesus, Che Guevara. In the Soviet Union, popular culture, by Soviet and imported artists, spread a certain imagery of the world abroad in Soviet society and in doing so helped entrench the ideal of internationalism to ordinary Soviet citizens. Internationalism, for them, came in an appealing wrapper of exciting and exotic entertainment and, initially, in the form of the apparent global success of their home country as a new and widely respected world power. The Cuban revolutionaries caused a serious setback for the admirers of the United States, Artemij Troitskij remembered, 'Soviet youth erupted in euphoric enthusiasm.'[167]

---

[166] See sovmusic.ru/download.php?fname=ball_che (last accessed 1 Aug. 2013).
[167] Troitsky, *Back to the USSR*, p. 19.

Members of this generation recall being convinced of living in the strongest country on earth at the time: 'Seriously, I really believed this back then!', remembered one interviewee in 2006 and added, on the subject of Fidel Castro: 'well, we used to sing such wonderful songs, I can't recall them today, but we basically loved him ... And we were even fonder of Che Guevara. He was, as they say now, even cooler than Castro.'[168] 'I'm very favourably disposed toward Cuba both now and back then. I have a deep admiration for these people, who, despite their small numbers, solved such large problems',[169] added another. 'Cuba! What brotherhood!',[170] exclaimed a third. Images of Fidel Castro and Che Guevara hung in many private flats, and 'everyone knew how to sing "Kuba – liubov moja"'.[171]

Cuba ranked prominently in Soviet revolutionary romanticism, but the phenomenon extended over the entire 'blazing continent': 'It was a melodic revolution, a musical one', remembered Aleksandr Snitko, a Belorussian worker, who later founded of a small museum of Latin American artefacts in Minsk, 'Latin America did even its revolutions with songs. While others dug the Beatles, I dug the records of Víctor Jara, this singer of the revolutionary Chilean people.'[172] Events in Latin America, as they were presented in the Soviet Union, seemed to prove that the world was going the Soviet way – at least to the domestic audience. What Soviet internationalism after Stalin meant for the foreign target groups of Soviet advances is the subject of the following two chapters, which look at Latin American intellectuals and students respectively.

---

[168] Raleigh, *Russia's Sputnik Generation*, pp. 234–5.   [169] *Ibid.*, p. 260.
[170] *Ibid.*, p. 129.   [171] Vajl' and Genis, *60-e*, p. 55.
[172] See belarus.indymedia.org/7387 (last accessed 25 Nov. 2013).

3 Paradise lost and found: Latin American intellectuals in and on the Soviet Union

Cando se mira el Oriente desde el Occidente y viceversa, ocurre, casi invariablemente, una distorsión similar a la que produce un espejo cóncavo.

Pedro Gómez Valderrama[1]

Pablo. Efraín.
Hay una hora cuando cae el día,
una semilla de oro al pie de Gorki,
la primera advertencia de ceniza,
la adorada palabra al pie de Pushkin,
la luz sacude su cola de pez
...
Vallejo, Rivera, Gide, Bréton,
Rilke, Neruda, Siqueiros.
Moscú es una caja de emociones B caben
la luz + la luz + el hombre.

Roberto López Moreno. *Poema a la Unión Soviética*[2]

Raised expectations: Latin America in the 1950s and 1960s

During the period when Nikita Khrushchev was struggling to implement his de-Stalinisation programme, and reviving Soviet internationalism, the Colombian novelist Gabriel García Márquez was living and working as a newspaper correspondent in Paris. Most states in Latin America, including his native Colombia, were ruled at the time by military dictatorships. García Márquez recalled that his Paris neighbourhood was full of intellectuals from the Latin American diaspora, who were desperately waiting for political change and reform back home. One early morning,

---

[1] 'If you look from the West to the East, and vice versa, there is, almost inevitably, a distortion like the one a concave mirror creates': Pedro Gómez Valderrama, *Los ojos del burgués: un año en la Unión Soviética* (Bogotá: Oveja Negra, 1971), p. 197.

[2] Part of a 25-page Dadaist poem about the Soviet Union by a Mexican poet: Roberto López Moreno, *Poema a la Unión Soviética: la tierra y la palabra* (Mexico City: Claves Latinoamericanas, 1986), p. 2.

the Cuban poet Nicolás Guillén excitedly ran up and down the alley, shouting in Spanish: 'He is down, he is down! They toppled him!' His shouting caused great turmoil in the drowsy street, which soon filled with curious Latin Americans. The exiled fellow Cubans thought Guillén meant the Cuban strongman Fulgencio Batista. Paraguayan intellectuals hoped it might be their dictator Alfredo Stroessner; the Guatemalans crossed their fingers it was Carlos Castillo Armas. The Peruvians thought of General Manuel Odría, the Venezuelans of Marcos Pérez Jiménez and the Dominicans of their psychopathic president Rafael Trujillo. García Márquez would have liked to hear of the ousting of Colombia's general-president Gustavo Rojas Pinilla, while the Nicaraguans hoped it was the end of the Somoza dynasty. As it soon turned out, the toppled dictator was Juan Perón. The Argentines celebrated, while the others – happy for Argentina, but disappointed about their own country – went back to have breakfast in a Paris café and discuss the future of Latin America.[3]

García Márquez's story is most likely invented or at least lavishly filigreed. But even if Guillén did not run yelling through the Paris streets that morning, the scene nicely encapsulates some characteristics of the political and intellectual landscape of early Cold War Latin America. When the Organisation of American States (OAS) was refounded in 1948, most of its members were military dictatorships, and anti-communism was to justify their autocratic rule all over the subcontinent. In 1954, representatives from seventeen of these countries met in Mexico City to form the Comisión Permanente del Congreso Contra la Intervención Soviética en América Latina. Even in a broad definition, only Chile, Costa Rica and Uruguay could be considered democracies at that time. Cold War violence exploded occasionally, especially cruelly in Colombia. Yet from the mid 1950s, a remarkable wave of democratisations hit the whole of Latin America. Year after year, the dictators in Brazil (1954), Argentina (1955), Peru (1956), García Márquez's home country Colombia (1957), Venezuela (1958) and Cuba (1959) were overthrown – to the delight of the exiled intelligentsia.[4]

The following years of economic growth engendered a cultural and intellectual renaissance as well as considerable hopes for a quick modernisation of all Latin American states. Serious attempts were made to drive back the illiteracy that had hitherto predominated. Many

---

[3] Harald Irnberger, *Gabriel García Márquez: Die Magie der Wirklichkeit* (Frankfurt am Main: Fischer, 2005), p. 171.

[4] Bethell and Roxborough, 'The Impact of the Cold War on Latin America'; Bethell, *Latin America*.

governments still restricted suffrage to those who could read and write – urbanisation, expanded education and a heritage of populist rule led to greater political participation of the masses. At the same time, improvements in medicine and hygiene had helped the population to increase to an extent the continent had never before seen. This demographic development, however, hampered and dampened the positive effects of a booming economy on most people's living standards. While in many societies the poorer strata of the population also profited from years of economic growth, the richer did so disproportionately, which further widened what was already the world's largest gap in distribution of income and living standards. Political exclusion and social inequality lingered on.

In a parallel development, the 1950s and 1960s saw a communication revolution that changed the way Latin Americans perceived themselves in the world. While television remained a privilege for a few, millions of cheap Japanese radios flooded the continent.[5] More urbanised and literate populations learned what was happening on the rest of the planet. Most importantly, they heard about living conditions in the booming countries of North America and western Europe. Even in 1966, however, the average Latin American went to school for as little as two years; 40 per cent of the adult population were illiterate. Infant mortality was four times as high as in the United States. Malnutrition, inadequate housing and hygiene limited life expectancy to 46 years.[6] This combination of raised and often disappointed expectations led to widespread discontent and an increasing sense of backwardness.[7]

Social mobilisation came as a result of this frustration. Student and union protest activities were the order of the day from the mid 1960s. Many Catholic clerics sought earthly solutions for pressing problems in what came to be known as 'liberation theology'. Disappointed with the failed modernisation models, intellectuals found an explanation for Latin America's backwardness in 'dependency theory'. A good chunk of its attraction lay in the fact that it put the blame on the outside world and especially the United States. These tensions with their northern neighbour dated from long before, but culminated in the Cold War era with the experience of US intervention in Guatemala and the Cuban Bay of

---

[5] Stephen G. Rabe, *The Most Dangerous Area in the World: John F. Kennedy Confronts Communist Revolution in Latin America* (Chapel Hill: University of North Carolina Press, 1999), p. 23.

[6] Brands, *Latin America's Cold War*, p. 71; Hernando Agudelo Villa, *La Revolución del desarrollo: origen y evolución de la Alianza para el Progreso* (Mexico City: Roble, 1966), pp. 42–3.

[7] Goldenberg, *Kommunismus in Lateinamerika*.

Pigs, their quasi-colonial presence in Guantánamo Bay, in Panama and Puerto Rico, and in particular with the unscrupulous support for the anti-communist dictators, who had grabbed power again all over Latin America from the mid 1960s. By the end of that decade, Argentina, Bolivia, Brazil, the Dominican Republic, Ecuador, El Salvador, Guatemala, Honduras, Panama and Paraguay were again under the tight grip of military dictators. In all other states, the generals had significant influence on politics.

García Márquez's episode from a decade earlier illuminates not only a hopeful moment in Latin American political history, but also a characteristic of Latin American intellectuals at that time. Similar languages, Catholicism, and a shared history had been the basis for a common Latin American identity since independence from Europe in the early nineteenth century. But it was the alienation of many of the Latin American leftist intelligentsia from their respective governments, and the émigré situation in the European or intra-Latin American exile during the Cold War that made this sense of a continental togetherness stronger than ever before or afterward in Latin American intellectual history.

Military rulers in their home countries, before and after the democratic decade around 1960, wished them and their reformist or revolutionary ideals good riddance. Backed by local oligarchies and the wary United States, the dictators fostered strong anti-imperialist sentiments in the mostly oppositional intellectual milieu. While the Latin American intellectuals thought about alternative paths for their homeland, be it over red wine in a Paris café or in a Guatemalan prison cell, they all agreed that the United States bore a great deal of responsibility for their situation. During the peak of the Cold War, they, as a consequence, also considered what advantages the enemy of their enemy had to offer.

Some communist authors were able to see their motherland of socialism even before Stalin's death; many more writers and intellectuals from different political backgrounds flocked to the Soviet Union from the mid 1950s. The generous invitation of these foreign intellectuals was an integral part of Soviet internationalism after Stalin. Many of them travelled to all parts of the Soviet Union, and they wrote travelogues and reports about their impressions from a country that some still revelled as a socialist utopia, and others instead as a state that had managed to modernise a 'backward' agrarian society into a global superpower that had ostensibly managed to keep up with the United States in geo-politics and technological development.

This third chapter looks at Latin American intellectual travellers and their official and unofficial trips to the Soviet Union. The attempts of the Soviets to create a sympathetic stance towards themselves in the global

South, as scrutinised in Chapter 1, were targeted especially at writers and scholars. With precursors during the last years of Stalinism, the USSR aimed at reform-minded Latin American university professors, journalists, novelists and poets. The Soviet organisers did not discriminate strictly between intellectual members of the communist parties and travellers from other political backgrounds, and, for that matter, neither does this chapter. Both groups were unhappy with their own societies and saw inspiration in the Soviet model to overcome deficiencies in their own countries.

The invitation programme was intensified after Stalin's death, and increasingly got a Third World spin. Ever more writers from fairly underdeveloped and smaller countries of the Americas were invited to visit the Soviet Union. Some got their travel expenses paid; some went for more personal reasons and on their own budget. They met with Soviet cultural figures, and they went on tour programmes that often led them through the entire USSR, to cities, schools, universities, ministries, sanatoria, hydroelectric power plants, or whatever they asked to be shown and did not fall under Soviet access restrictions for foreigners. Professional guides from VOKS, the GKKS and the SSOD took care of them. Some 3,000 Spaniards, refugees of the Spanish Civil War, still lived in Moscow in the 1950s and provided a great source of native speakers. But an increasing number of staff in the internationalist organisations spoke fluent Portuguese or Castilian – and enthusiastically took over the task of showing their Latin American guests around the Soviet Union.[8]

Wittingly or unwittingly, the Latin American visitors belonged to a tradition that had started with the October Revolution and had been interrupted with the outbreak of the Second World War. In the 1920s and 1930s, it had been mostly European intellectuals who paid visits to the great political experiment happening to their east. These 'fellow travellers' from France, Germany and Great Britain have been the subject of some scholarly research – and heavy criticism for their 'myopic romanticism' towards the Soviet state, its large-scale reform programmes and its exorbitant violence and repression.[9]

---

[8] Kutejščikova, *Moskva-Meksiko-Moskva*, pp. 260–4.

[9] David Caute, *The Fellow Travellers: Intellectual Friends of Communism* (New Haven: Yale University Press, 1988), p. 16. The scorn for communist sympathisers, 'useful idiots' according to an unsubstantiated Lenin quote, left an even bigger mark on Paul Hollander's study of political pilgrims, which culminates in an awkward bashing of conscientious objectors in the United States: Paul Hollander, *Political Pilgrims: Western Intellectuals in Search of the Good Society* (Piscataway, NJ: Transaction, 1997). A much more balanced study was done recently by Michael David-Fox, who draws extensively on

The western leftists' view of the Soviet Union is usually told as a tale of a paradise lost. Communist unanimity, chipped away already by several Trotskyist and other anti-Stalinist leftists from the 1930s, finally ended with Stalin's death in 1953 and the revelations of some of his crimes by Khrushchev at the 20th Party Congress in 1956. The invasion of Hungary the same year dealt a blow to those who still nourished hopes of a de-Stalinised socialism. The Cuban Crisis put other apologists off. With the invasion of Czechoslovakia to end the alternative socialist path of Alexander Dubček in 1968, the USSR finally forfeited any serious support from west European leftists even in the communist strongholds of France and Italy.

Visits of intellectuals from the global South to the Cold War Soviet Union have not been much studied – and they complicate this picture of a utopia withering away.[10] Accounts of the intellectual history of postwar Latin America have put the Soviet Union aside a bit too readily. Claudia Gilman is wrong to state that 'Latin American intellectuals had lost all interest in the Soviet Union by the early 1960s.'[11] And while Carlos Castañeda is correct to say that 'much of the Latin American left of the sixties and seventies was rabidly pro-Cuba, though sharply critical of and disenchanted with the Soviet Union', he only speaks of the *left*, not of the entire intelligentsia, and he skips the decade of the 1950s.[12]

During the early Cold War, western leftists' hopes in the USSR gradually eroded at the same time as the Soviets were augmenting – rather successfully – their attempts to present their country in a positive light to the Third World. The Latin American visitors, this chapter will demonstrate, are particularly apposite for illustrating these contrary developments: the most renowned of them were actually part of a western discourse community. They usually came from white upper-class backgrounds and had spent much time of their lives in western Europe. But many other, less publicised writers from humbler, often indigenous, family backgrounds identified themselves more strongly with the Third World. They were brought up not in European-style urban environments, but with the experience of essential needs: many did not see

---

archival material from both sides, the hosts and the visitors: David-Fox, *Showcasing the Great Experiment*.

[10] The only book about Latin American travellers to the Soviet Union after the Second World War is a collection of original travelogues from the Soviet Union, China and Cuba, with some brief commentary: Sylvia Saítta, *Hacia la revolución: viajeros argentinos de izquierda* (Buenos Aires: Fondo de Cultura Económica, 2007).

[11] Claudia Gilman, *Entre la pluma y el fusil: debates y dilemas del escritor revolucionario en América Latina* (Buenos Aires: Siglo Veintiuno, 2003), p. 68.

[12] Castañeda, *Utopia Unarmed*, p. 177.

running water, higher education or a visit to a doctor as a matter of course. Some of them were the first in their families who could actually read and write. From the mid 1950s, representatives of both groups went to Moscow, and their judgements of the Soviet Union differed clearly from those of the European visitors.

'Latin American' 'intellectuals' and their discourse on socialism and the Soviet Union

An analysis of the travels of Latin American intellectuals to the Soviet Union requires, to begin with, a clarification of the terms 'Latin America' and 'intellectual'. Their semantic and historical contextualisation connects this story of East–South encounters and perceptions during the Cold War to older intellectual trajectories, especially the history of socialism in Latin America, which shaped the later perception of the USSR. The idea of a 'Latin' America dates back to the end of Spanish rule in the Americas, when Napoleon tried to forge an anti-Anglo-American coalition that was to justify his rule over Mexico. 'Latin' replaced 'Hispanic' to construct common Romance roots of the Spanish, Portuguese and French-speaking inhabitants. This idea, which included Louisiana and Québec in Latin America, soon disappeared again. The name, however, remained, and while the competing terms 'Ibero-America' and 'Indo-America' prevailed until well into the twentieth century, a common non-Anglo-Saxon American identity has existed ever since among Spanish and Portuguese speakers, who both refer to this realm as 'América Latina'. The overwhelming majority of its inhabitants indeed share the same history and the same religion; they speak the same or a similar language, live in similarly structured societies and have a similar conception of themselves against their northern neighbour.

All iconic historical figures and intellectuals of the nineteenth century carried on their idea of *Nuestra América* (Our America). 'Para nosotros, la patria es América!' ('For us, the homeland is America'), declared the liberation hero Simón Bolívar at the beginning of the nineteenth century. The Cuban poet José Martí, and the Nicaraguan liberation fighter Augusto Sandino, a generation later, even envisioned a Latin American nation. In 1920, Mexican philosopher José Vasconcelos countered European racism with his idea of a *raza cosmica* (cosmic race) that had come into being in the melting pot of Latin America. Also in Mexico, and roughly at the same time, the Peruvian socialist Víctor Haya de la Torre founded the Alianza Popular Revolucionario de América

(APRA) as an originally pan-Latin American and anti-US political movement.[13]

Latin America was thus never only a simplifying category from the perspective of outsiders, but a weighty idea throughout the intellectual history of the subcontinent. At times, Latin American thinkers themselves levelled the disparities between different parts of the hemisphere 'by analysing the identity of their own countries and extending their affirmations to the rest of Latin America'.[14] The relevance of this pan-Latin Americanism, however, fluctuated over time, and its popularity was always to do with the political orientation of the intellectuals who represented and advocated it.

The modern, secular idea of an 'intellectual' had its origins precisely where the Latin American émigrés settled down in the 1950s: the Paris-based *philosophes* of the Enlightenment were the archetype for a stratum of men and women of letters, which came into being throughout the Americas in the late nineteenth century. Just like their heirs who are presented in this chapter, they were public writers in a 'continental European' sense, as in the French *homme de lettres* or the German *Intellektueller*. They were novelists, poets, playwrights, academics in humanities or visual artists, who – through their intellectual and artistic work, or simply based on their popularity – participated in public political and societal debates. In this sense, they differed from 'intelligentsia' in the broader Russian/Soviet definition, which usually includes the technocratic elite and academic civil servants – a concept that is often shared in the Anglo-Saxon world.[15]

Just as in Europe, this Latin American milieu of intellectuals was radicalised through the Mexican and Russian Revolutions between 1910 and 1920. The Argentine philosopher José Ingenerios wrote the key text *Los tiempos nuevos* (New Times) that heralded the Bolshevik Revolution in Russia as a 'spirit of renewal'. Manuel Maples Arce, founder of the Mexican avant-garde movement Estridentismo, praised the apparent workers' paradise in his 'Urbe: superpoema bolchevique en cinco cantos' (Bolshevik Super-Poem in Five Cantos). But socialism in

---

[13] Gerd Koenen, *Traumpfade der Weltrevolution: Das Guevara-Projekt* (Cologne: Kiepenheuer & Witsch, 2008), pp. 45–56; Arturo Ardao, *Génesis de la idea y el nombre de América Latina* (Caracas: Centro de Estudios Latinoamericanos Rómulo Gallegos, 1980); Eduardo Galeano, *Las venas abiertas de América Latina* (Montevideo: Editorial Universidad de la República, 1971), p. 432.

[14] Jorge Larraín Ibáñez, *Identity and Modernity in Latin America* (Cambridge: Polity Press, 2000), p. 1.

[15] Dietrich Beyrau, *Intelligenz und Dissens: Die russischen Bildungsschichten in der Sowjetunion 1917–1985* (Göttingen: Vandenhoeck & Ruprecht, 1993).

Latin America was, from its beginning, not limited to the Leninist variant. Two lines of Marxist thought, brought in by German, Italian and Spanish immigrants, had already evolved in the early twentieth century: the Peruvian writer José Carlos Mariátegui conceptualised a Maoism *avant la lettre*, a countryside- and indigenous-based socialism similar to the one propagated by the Russian social revolutionaries. Workers and intellectuals in the industrial, and rather European, urban centres, however, stuck to traditional Marxism. After the October Revolution in 1917, they founded communist parties all over the continent and integrated into the evolving Comintern.

The success of Marxism among Latin American intellectuals from early on had to do with a widespread feeling of alienation among them, for their position towards the state had changed to their disadvantage. The nineteenth-century tradition of the poet-president or the *caudillo*-thinker that Simón Bolívar represented was – with some notable exceptions – interrupted; intellectuals were downgraded to 'ideologues, either as co-opted supporters or as ritual opponents' of the state.[16] They were systematically excluded from participating in high-level politics and demoted into the lower levels of state bureaucracy. That so many internationally renowned Latin American intellectuals served as diplomats only masked this exclusion. Sending Pablo Neruda, Carlos Fuentes, Alfonso Reyes or Miguel Angel Asturias abroad was an elegant way of getting rid of an unwanted critic. Unlike in Europe, however, the main source of status for intellectuals in Latin America had always been the state, not a particular class or social sector, simply because, until the 1960s, there was no mass reading public on much of the subcontinent.[17] Fuentes therefore described the role of the Latin American intellectual as one of 'a tribune, a member of parliament, a labour leader, a journalist and a redeemer of his society' all at the same time, and therefore a substitute for a civil society that barely existed.

Leninism in particular caught on with many Latin American writers and poets as it provided not only a possible solution to their societies' problems, but also promised to give an important role in overcoming these problems to intellectuals as the vanguard of the revolutionary process. Many of those who stayed in their countries became members of communist parties and made their living in universities. In these

---

[16] Nicola Miller, *In the Shadow of the State: Intellectuals and the Quest for National Identity in Twentieth-Century Spanish America* (London and New York: Verso, 1999), p. 95; the most important exception was the novelist Rómulo Gallegos, president of Venezuela in 1948 as well as a widely read author in the Soviet Union from the 1950s.

[17] *Ibid.*, p. 95.

exclusive and excluded areas, the *intelectual comprometido*, the Latin American *littérateur engagé*, developed. Under the influence of Leninist Marxism, they were 'more preoccupied with power than with knowledge', as Nicola Miller has reproached them, and they never managed to 'establish independent critical communities that could have provided leadership to a civil society capable of challenging the legitimacy of the state'.[18]

Instead, some put down the pen and took up the gun. In the 1930s, several Latin American intellectuals fought in the Republican Brigades of the Spanish Civil War, which was to become a key experience for the worldwide left. Miguel Angel Asturias, David Siqueiros, César Vallejo, Eudocio Ravines and many more not only organised and struggled in the Comité Iberoamericano para la Defensa de la República Española (Ibero-American Committee for the Defence of the Spanish Republic), but they also came into contact with the European leftist voluntary fighters, including those from the Soviet Union. The civil war laid the foundation for contacts with Moscow, and it was in Spain that Ilya Ehrenburg, who knew some Spanish, deepened his friendship with Latin American cultural figures such as Diego Rivera and Pablo Neruda.

It was also in Spain that the first prominent leftist Latin American intellectual was cured of socialist dogmatism: Octavio Paz, an early admirer of the USSR, went to Valencia for the anti-fascist second International Congress of Writers in Defence of Culture in 1937 – and was appalled by Soviet-inspired and sometimes Soviet-led purges and killings within the ranks of the republicans. After the Hitler–Stalin pact, and even more so after he learned of Stalin's crimes in Paris around 1950, Paz turned into an ardent critic of the Soviet Union, an attitude that met with the hostility of many of his Latin American colleagues.[19] Similarly, Víctor Haya de la Torre, founder of ARPA (which was then socialist) had shown an early fascination with the USSR which faded after a 1931 visit to Moscow. He rejected the Soviet Union as a role model and advocated an independently socialist 'Indio-America' instead, '¡ni con Moscú, ni con Washington!' ('neither with Moscow, nor with Washington!'). Few other Latin Americans went to see the Soviet Union in person during this time. Rivera and Siqueiros had made a quick visit in 1927, as had the Brazilian historian Caio Prado Junior. Others, mostly Mexicans, went in the course of the 1930s. The small Latin American sections of the

[18] *Ibid.*, p. 93.
[19] Kutejščikova, *Moskva-Meksiko-Moskva*, pp. 359–63; Nicola Miller, *Soviet Relations with Latin America, 1959–1987.*

Comintern and and its trades union association, the Profintern, sent some delegations. Communists who, like the Colombian Ignacio Torres Giraldo, settled down in Moscow remained an exception.[20]

The international image of the Soviet Union improved tremendously through the victory in the Second World War, in which (at least on paper) most Latin American states fought alongside the Red Army against Germany. But, except for a short period of relative popularity between 1943 and 1947, Latin American communism did not profit much from the good reputation of the socialist motherland. With the exception of the Cuban and Chilean parties, it remained a salon phenomenon that attracted urban intellectuals and artists but still not many factory workers. More than for toilers, Soviet-style Marxism was attractive for intellectuals in the Americas. It gave reputation, status and an important task to their profession; it claimed to have a solution to the prevailing social injustice in an area of the world with the highest income inequalities; and it offered an example of progress and modernity that did not refer directly to the United States or western Europe, Latin America's unattainable role models for a century. Marxism also provided an anti-imperialist theory that shifted the blame for this underdevelopment on to others.[21] Latin America was much more Europeanised than Asia or Africa. Nonetheless, there was a gulf between their living conditions and those of the Western world. On the one hand, reformers and intellectuals suffered from this gap, which they had tried to overcome since independence in the early nineteenth century. On the other hand, many of the world's angry and alienated intellectuals blamed poverty and underdevelopment precisely on the apparently all-powerful, but deeply resented West.

Based on these anti-western sentiments, pan-Latin Americanism experienced possibly its greatest heyday among writers and activists from the 1950s through the 1970s, at a time when – with the exception of Jorge Luis Borges – all notable Latin American intellectuals were committed leftists. Pablo Neruda's 'Canto General' (General Song, 1950) told the history of all Latin America, his *patria grande*, in rhyme.[22] After the Cuban Revolution, which initially catalysed pan-Latin American intellectual sentiment, the Havana-based journal of the Casa de las Américas became a platform (and an important financer) for leftwing writers from

[20] L. Chejfec, "'Čtoby rasskazat' pravdu o SSSR": pervye latinoamerikanskie delegacii v Sovetskom Sojuze', *Latinskaja Amerika* 12 (1982), 73–83.

[21] Andreas Boeckh, 'La modernización importada: experiencias históricas con importaciones de conceptos de desarrollo en América Latina', *Diálogo Científico* 14/1–2 (2005), 51.

[22] Nicola Miller, *In the Shadow of the State*, p. 128.

Mexico to Argentina.[23] The Mexican pan-Latin Americanist philosopher Leopoldo Zea, a frequent commentator in Soviet journals, was among the most influential thinkers in post-war Latin America. Brazilian writers of the left, long more interested in French intellectual life than in the surrounding Hispanic world, joined the *latinoamericanismo* wholeheartedly after many of them were expelled from their country in the wake of the 1964 military putsch. They found sanctuary and joined intellectual discourses in the Spanish-speaking countries around.

The boom in Latin American literature in the 1960s and 1970s was the quintessence of this pan-Latin Americanism. José Revueltas, Alejo Carpentier, Carlos Fuentes and Julio Cortázar made Latin American (and not 'Mexican', 'Cuban' or 'Argentine') literature hugely popular in Europe and the United States for the first time. All of them were politically left-leaning, and they were proponents of Latin American solidarity. Macondo, the setting of *A Hundred Years of Solitude*, is a mythical Latin American town, not a Colombian one – just as most readers identified its author Gabriel García Márquez not so much with Colombia (or with Mexico, where he spent the greater part of his life), but as the archetype of the Latin American leftist activist novelist. The politically more libertarian Mexican poets Octavio Paz, Gabriel Zaid and Enrique Krauze published the literary journal *Plural* from 1971 (renamed *Vuelta* from 1976), in which authors from all over Latin America found a common platform. The Peruvian Mario Vargas Llosa, the Mexican Carlos Fuentes and the Argentines Jorge Luis Borges and Adolfo Bioy Casares wrote for it, as did the Cubans Guillermo Cabrera Infante and Reinaldo Arenas.[24]

Political activists of the left shared the intellectuals' pan-Latin Americanism. Che Guevara, in a position he disliked as Cuban minister of industry, announced: 'we see the events in Cuba as a reflection of those qualitative changes that take place on the entire American continent ... in our epoch of transition to socialism'.[25] The iconography of leftist guerrilla movements, even if they called for *national* liberation, always carried the silhouette of the whole of Latin America on their flags and emblems, not of their respective nation states. And, in the early 1970s, proponents of dependency theory pleaded for the economic integration

[23] Oscar Terán, Gerardo Caetano, Sofia Correa Sutil and Adolfo Garcé García y Santos, *Ideas en el siglo: intelectuales y cultura en el siglo XX latinoamericano* (Buenos Aires: Siglo Veintiuno, 2004), p. 75; Nicola Miller, *In the Shadow of the State*, p. 125.
[24] Larraín Ibáñez, *Identity and Modernity in Latin America*, pp. 107–46.
[25] Ernesto Guevara, 'Kuba und der Kennedy-Plan', *Probleme des Friedens und des Sozialismus* 2 (1962), 119–20.

of Latin America to overcome foreign exploitation and the resulting backwardness.[26]

The Soviets, too, saw Latin America as one spatial category, 'Latinskaja Amerika'. When they sent intellectuals and delegations across the ocean, they always went to several states; the groups they received in Moscow were usually cobbled together with travellers from many different Latin American states, and they generally debated the political situation of the entire region. Just like Guevara, initially the Soviets saw the fact that the Cuban Revolution had been the first Latin American country to take steps to the historically necessary next level as somewhat arbitrary – the others would follow soon. In sum, for all contemporary agents in the scope of this study, southerners, easterners and westerners alike, the concept of 'Latin America' was a meaningful category.

Cold War and *tercermundismo*

The geo-political constellation of the Cold War from 1947 was reflected in both Latin American politics and intellectual debates as an all-encompassing 'struggle over political and social arrangements'.[27] Most elites continued to perceive world communism as a serious threat not only to the political, but also to the ethical and cultural foundations of their societies. For many intellectuals, however, Marxism still seemed an increasingly attractive solution to the continent's problems. But, in the 1950s, Latin American leftist intellectuals could choose from several socialist trajectories other than Soviet-style communism: there were Trotskyist splinter groups, there was homemade socialism with its focus on indigenous togetherness and there were populist mass movements. For the more radical-spirited, the Chinese Revolution offered a model of revolution based on agrarian societies, and, most importantly, the Cuban example proved that revolution was actually viable in Latin America, too.

While the Soviets, during de-Stalinisation, proposed peaceful coexistence with the West and a peaceful path to socialism for Latin America, the model of violent struggle actually sounded more appealing to many impatient intellectuals. From the 1960s, the market of alternative social and political models became even more abundant, as the proponents of 'dependency theory' used the Leninist model of centre–periphery relations to explain Latin American 'backwardness' (in Moscow, they were

---

[26] Galeano, *Las venas abiertas de América Latina*, pp. 431–2.
[27] Brands, *Latin America's Cold War*, p. 9.

long ignored completely; only in the 1970s did Soviet expert journals review their work – often very critically; see Chapter 5).[28]

The increasing feeling of insurmountable backwardness, and old resentments against the 'Yankees' in the North, led many Latin Americans to develop an anti-imperialist identification with the colonial and post-colonial states and peoples of Asia and Africa. The 1960s came to be the decade of *tercermundismo* (Third Worldism). The struggle of nationalists in Algeria and Indochina fascinated the radical left. But reformist Latin American statesmen, too, looked increasingly not only to the North, but also to their fellows of the global South, who had formed a loose Non-Aligned Movement (NAM) in the wake of the 1955 Afro-Asian conference in Bandung. Much debated was a visit by Indonesian president and Third World icon Sukarno to Bolivia in 1961.[29] The Brazilian president Jânio Quadros was said to have photographs of Nasser, Nehru and Tito on his desk and supported – rhetorically – the liberation movements in Angola, Mozambique and Guinea Bissau, all at the time still under Portuguese colonial rule. Quadros decorated Che Guevara with a Brazilian state medal and touted membership in the Non-Aligned Movement among Latin American statesmen. Emphasising a 'common ethnic and cultural heritage . . . as well as current underdevelopment', he founded an Afro-Asian Institute, which gathered prominent left-wing intellectuals and became an influential voice in a new, independent Brazilian foreign policy.[30] His successor Goulart invited Tito to Brazil and, during his visit as the first western statesman to communist China, drank a toast with Mao Zedong to Afro-Asian-Latin American friendship. Imperialism, they agreed, was the culprit for their countries' backwardness: earlier in history, it had been Portugal, the Dutch or the British; now it was US monopolies that aimed at keeping Brazil merely a supplier of raw materials.

Latin America still differed from the rest of the Third World in that most of its states had long gained independence and that its elites were broadly European or Europeanised. But by the mid 1960s, Latin

---

[28] I. Bekopitov, 'Raul' Prebiš: v poiskach al'ternativ', *Latinskaja Amerika* 5 (1976), 200–5.

[29] Anon., 'El presidente A. Sukarno afirmó que existe similtud de espíritu entre los pueblos de Bolivia e Indonesia: cordial bienvenida tributo la población paceña al mandatorio visitante', *Presencia*, 8 May 1961. Several of the books on which this chapter is based were actually edited by a Bogotá publishing house called Ediciones Tercer Mundo (Third World Editions).

[30] James Hershberg, '"High Spirited Confusion": Brazil, the 1961 Belgrade Non-Aligned Conference, and the Limits of an "Independent Foreign Policy" during the High Cold War', *Cold War History* 7/3 (2007), 373–88; Jorge Amado, *Navegação de cabotagem: apontamentos para um livro de memórias que jamais escreverei* (Lisbon: Editora Record, 1992), pp. 93, 285; Prizel, *Latin America through Soviet Eyes*, pp. 47–52.

America had become an 'integral part of the Third World'.[31] Apart from Argentina, all Latin American states finally joined the Non-Aligned Movement. To be sure, membership also served as leverage for economic support from the United States. And changing regimes and different states showed varying degrees of enthusiasm about *tercermundismo*. Not all went as far as Peru under Juan Velasco and Mexico under Luis Echeverría, who actually sought leading roles in the NAM, a tendency that always aroused suspicion among conservatives all over the Americas. With the exception of Cuba and Salvador Allende's Chile, all states remained aligned politically to the United States, and at least their European-rooted elites considered themselves as fully part of the Western world.[32] Yet, at the same time, many Latin Americans identified with the underdeveloped part of the planet. Latin America hung somewhere between the South and the West, and its intellectuals were keen on getting to know the East.

First contacts during the Cold War: Latin American travelogues from the Soviet Union

This chapter will analyse some two dozen travelogues by writers from all over Latin America, from Mexico to Argentina and from Chile to Nicaragua, who went to see the Soviet Union with their own eyes between 1949 and 1973. It is probably fair to say that, until the 1970s, every public intellectual in Latin America still had an opinion on the Soviet Union but, with many other inspirations for the left, it was more important for some than for others. The judgements of those who visited depended on the political-historical context in his or her specific home country. They depended even more on the authors' regional, social and indeed ethnic origin. The influence of these factors will be considered in every example. However, this was the high point of *latinoamericanismo*, and all Latin American authors referred in their writing to other travellers from all over the subcontinent; they agreed or disagreed with or even insulted those who had gone before them and gave their opinion on issues that concerned the whole of Latin America – regardless of their nationality. Beyond their national, regional and social idiosyncrasies, all travellers also felt themselves to be part of a pan-Latin American community of travellers, based in no small measure on the anti-imperialist

---

[31] Jorge Volpi, *El insomnio de Bolívar: cuatro consideraciónes intempestivas sobre América Latina en el siglo XXI* (Buenos Aires: Debate, 2009), p. 18.

[32] Marcello Carmagnani, *L'altro Occidente: l'America Latina dall'invasione europea al nuovo millennio* (Turin: Einaudi, 2003).

sense of a common revolutionary heritage, formerly against the Spanish and now against the United States. The Dominican Ramón Alberto Ferreras based his book on a criticism of the travelogue by the Colombian Gabriel García Márquez. The Bolivian Fausto Reinaga travelled with other Latinos through the Soviet Union and was excited about the pan-Latin American spirit. The Cuban Nicolás Guillén often visited together with the Brazilian Jorge Amado, who in turn inspired the Paraguayan poet Elvio Romero to travel; the Argentine Alfredo Varela was a close friend and discussion partner of the Chilean Pablo Neruda; and so on.[33] This interwovenness allows us to speak of a shared Latin American intellectual discourse on the Soviet Union.

For those Latin American intellectuals who travelled to the Soviet Union during the Cold War, not only had the number of alternative social and political models increased, but there was also considerably more information on the USSR available in Latin America than ever before. Many Spanish exiles had written about their experiences in the USSR – generally very critically – and published them in Mexico. West European debates about Stalinism were, in theory, accessible. Most Latin American intellectuals at the time read French, English and German, and the standard volumes of the genre had been translated. The classic travelogues by Klaus Mehnert, Arthur Miller, André Gide, Bertrand Russell and John Steinbeck were available in Spanish translations in Latin American libraries, as was much of the contemporary expert literature on the USSR by Merle Fainsod, Boris Meissner and Wolfgang Leonhard. In the 1960s, writings on Soviet communism by New Left authors from Herbert Marcuse to the Cohn-Bendit brothers were immediately translated. Debates within the Soviet Union, from de-Stalinisation and the treatment of Pasternak, Brodski and Solzhenitsyn, to the trial against Andrej Sinjavskij and Julij Daniel' were also followed by Latin American scholars.[34] If travellers from Latin America still got duped by the Soviet feel-good programme, it was certainly no longer due to a lack of available information on the Soviet Union.

The travelogues usually reveal the author's stance on their first pages, when they describe the border controls. The era when Clara Zetkin had

---

[33] Amado, *Navegação de cabotagem*, p. 229; Fausto Reinaga, *El sentimiento mesiánico del pueblo ruso* (La Paz: Ediciones SER, 1960), p. 60; Pis'mo Žorži Amadu o poezdke v SSSR paragvajskogo poeta El'vio Romero, 27 Oct. 1957, RGALI f.631 op.26 d.4466 l.1.

[34] Max Hayward, *Proceso a los escritores: el estado soviético contra Siniavski y Daniel* (Buenos Aires: Editorial Americana, 1967); Victor Flores Olea, 'La crisis del stalinismo', *Cuadernos Americanos* 5–6 (1962), 80–108; Douglas Prince, 'Los intelectuales soviéticos atacan el conformismo en la literatura impuesto por el estado', *Ultima Hora*, 24 Apr. 1961.

demanded that visitors take off their shoes upon entering the holy ground of Soviet territory was over.[35] Anyone who has ever crossed a border in eastern Europe is bound to become suspicious if visitors portray their first encounter with Soviet officials as a pleasant experience. Such travelogues always turn out to be blind eulogies. The same goes for the whitewashing of negative first impressions: there were no seat belts on the airplane, one visitor noted, but 'Soviet planes are so safe, they do not need them.' When the plane arrived in Moscow after a long delay, he took that as a sign that the Soviets never risked a human life for commercial interests.[36] On the other hand, negative comments on first experiences were not necessarily a sign of a renegade view. García Márquez was sure that the GDR was 'a hideous country' after his border procedure (the East–West border had been moved significantly to the West since Zetkin's days). Yet his description of the USSR was quite balanced all the same.[37]

After sporadic visits from communist Latin American intellectuals during late Stalinism, several Soviet intellectuals, from 1954, were sent to countries all over the Americas to reconnect to other colleagues across the Atlantic (see Chapter 2) – and to take them to the USSR. When Ehrenburg, Dmiterko or Simonov returned from their trips, they always brought recommendations to Moscow on whom to invite next.[38] The more famous or influential writers were usually received at least once by Ehrenburg himself for discussions in his cottage in Peredelkino or dinners in his apartment on Gorky Prospekt. The visiting intellectuals were often asked to give recommendations on whom to invite next – and whom better not.[39] Meetings of the Soviet-controlled World Peace Council, which took place all over the world with many left-leaning authors, were used to find new potential guests, too. The 1957 World Youth Festival, as well, was an occasion to cement contacts with Third World intellectuals. The *haute volée* of Latin American leftist intelligentsia met for this event in Moscow – even though for many of them, like the Peruvians and the Brazilians, travel to the Soviet Union was still explicitly marked as illegal in their passports. García Márquez was not yet well

---

[35] Michail Ryklin, *Kommunismus als Religion: Die Intellektuellen und die Oktoberrevolution* (Frankfurt am Main: Verlag der Weltreligionen, 2008).

[36] Jesualdo Sosa, *Mi viaje a la URSS* (Montevideo: Ediciones Pueblos Unidos, 1952).

[37] García Márquez, *De viaje por los países socialistas*, p. 9.

[38] Konstantin Simonov: Nekotorye soobščenja k otčetu o poezdke v Urugvaj, Čili i Argentinu, 29 Dec. 1957, GARF f.9518 op.1 d.320 ll.160–167.

[39] E.g. Zapis' besedy s zam. general'nogo sekretarija ZK KP Ekvadora, ekvadorskim pisatelem Enrike Chilem Chil'bertom [Enrique Gil Gilbert] v Inokomissii SP SSSR, 30 Jan. 1967, GARF f.9518 op.1 d.1018 ll.105–109; Gilbert, secretary of the Ecuadorian CP, had a long list of Ecuadorian writers showing who was recommended and who not.

known at the time and had to sneak in as an accordion player. But Nicolás Guillén, the novelist Carlos Augusto León and the poet Pedro Dona from Venezuela were invited officially, as were the playwright Saulo Benavente, the composer Gilardo Gilardi and the puppeteer and poet Javier Villafañe, as well as the authors Juan Gelman and María Rosa Oliver from Argentina. The Brazilian novelist Jorge Amado was there, as was his Guatemalan friend Miguel Angel Asturias. From Mexico came the playwright Emilio Carballido, from Chile the poet Praxedes Urrutia, from Bolivia Jorge Calvimontes.[40]

This enormous influx of dozens of Latin American intellectuals to the Soviet Union at the same time for the festival remained an exception, but many more attended, officially invited or on their own initiative, throughout the 1950s, 1960s and 1970s. In addition, twenty-three Latin Americans were awarded the Stalin/Lenin Peace Prize between 1950 and 1985 and usually received it during a ceremony in Moscow.[41] The Latin American intelligentsia obviously had not yet lost all contact with or interest in the Soviet Union.

A very important part of all these guided tours through the Soviet Union, something that a critical reader of these travelogues must consider, was a technique of hospitality that Paul Hollander has called 'ego massage'. Visitors in official tours were always and everywhere the centre of the attention: 'I felt like the most important man in the entire Caucasus', remembered a Brazilian visitor after his trip.[42] The guides were instructed to avoid controversial political topics and focus on achievements of the Soviet Union instead – and to butter the guests up: 'lavish banquets are addressed both to the stomach and the ego', Hollander put it.[43] For the stomach, cheerful – and often boozy – gala dinners were organised. 'They even paid for my cigarettes', remembered Graciliano Ramos, who ironically died of lung cancer immediately after his return.[44] For the ego, many foreign writers were published in large

[40] Memorandum o kul'turnych svjazjach, undated, GARF f.9518 op.1. d.339 ll.7–19; anon., 'Prekrasnaja vosmožnost': beseda s kubinskim poetom Gil'enom', *Molodež' mira* 4 (1957), 15; RGASPI f.3M op.15 d.263 l.395.
[41] Heriberto Jara Corona (1950), Jorge Amado (1951), Eliza Branco (1952), Pablo Neruda (1953), Baldomero Sanin Cano (1954), Nicolás Guillén (1954), Lázaro Cárdenas (1955), María Rosa Oliver (1957), Fidel Castro (1961), Olga Poblete de Espinosa (1962), Oscar Niemeyer (1963), Miguel Ángel Asturias (1965), David Alfaro Siqueiros (1966), Jorge Zalamea (1967), Alfredo Varela (1970–1), Salvador Allende (1972), Enrique Pastorino (1972), Luis Corvalán (1973–4), Hortensia Bussi de Allende (1975–6), Vilma Espín Guillois (1977–8), Miguel Otero Silva (1979–80), Líber Seregni (1980–2), Luis Vidales (1983–4), Miguel d'Escoto (1985–6).
[42] Holanda, *O mundo vermelho*, p. 123.   [43] Hollander, *Political Pilgrims*, p. 355.
[44] Graciliano Ramos, *Viagem: Tcheco-Eslováquia–URSS* (São Paulo: Martins, 1970), p. 62.

numbers of copies, and they were paid commission (albeit in non-convertible rubles only) for smaller publications in Soviet journals and interviews on Soviet radio (which were first recorded, then broadcast).[45] Konstantin Simonov, after all a writer himself, had recommended using this feature more often in foreign propaganda especially in order to win the favour of non-communist authors.[46] And it worked well: rather critical visitors, too, recalled how flattered they felt during the trip: 'the kindness was excessive, the expenses enormous, the attention constant', remembered one, 'I made many rubles writing for journals and magazines about Brazilian literature', another, and a third 'had the immense satisfaction of receiving copies of the Russian edition of [his] book'.[47]

One central feature of these guided tours was to present the positive awareness and appreciation of literature and the status of intellectuals in the Soviet Union – which, for reasons propounded above, was particularly appealing to Latin American intellectuals. Countless libraries and publishing houses, as well as museums, ballets and conservatories, existed all over the USSR and needed no presentation in the style of Potemkin villages. The privileged treatment of intellectuals was not an invention of Soviet officials either: when the Portuguese communist Francisco Ferreira first went to the Soviet Union as political refugee, he worked in a Kharkov factory. He managed to get a job at the Moscow radio station that produced programmes for Brazil – and noted that the directors earned ten times as much as the skilled workers back in Ukraine and received free vacation houses. He himself earned 400 rubles as a worker and 1,200 as a radio speaker. Some of his Spanish colleagues made up to 5,000 rubles.[48] Like many other visitors, a Brazilian noted the enormous privileges Ehrenburg enjoyed, including his private cook, a car with a driver and a *dacha*.[49] Another mentioned that intellectuals had the same status in this society as politicians: 'Has the work of a writer seen that much appreciation in any capitalist country?'[50] When the Chilean poet Nicanor Parra, the lifelong poetic antipode to Neruda, saw a huge crowd of Soviet women lining up on a square in downtown Moscow during his visit, he first thought they might be selling fresh

[45] Genival Rabelo, *No outro lado do mundo: a vida na URSS* (Rio de Janeiro: Editôra Civilização Brasileira, 1967), p. 31; Asturias, 'Die russische Literatur in Lateinamerika'.

[46] Konstantin Simonov: Nekotorye soobščenja k otčetu o poezdke v Urugvaj, Čili i Argentinu, 29 Dec. 1957, GARF f.9518 op.1 d.320 ll.160–167.

[47] Pedro Jorge Vera, *Gracias a la vida: memorias* (Quito: Editorial Voluntad, 1993); Ramos, *Viagem*, p. 18; Aldunate, *En Moscú*, p. 104; Moraes, *Caminhos da Terra*, p. 34.

[48] Francisco Ferreira, *26 años na União Soviética: notas de exílio do Chico da CUF* (Lisbon: Edições Afrodite, 1975), pp. 105–6.

[49] Mendes, *Moscou, Varsóvia, Berlim*, p. 64.   [50] Saítta, *Hacia la revolución*, p. 20.

pastry. It was, however, a stall with books by Chilean authors. Parra, who unlike Neruda had no communist leanings at all, was deeply touched and dedicated a poem called 'Pan caliente' (Hot Bread) to the Soviet Union.[51]

The privileges of intellectual work also met with the disapproval of some visitors, who found it unjust that writers received 'twice the salary and twice the vacation days of an ordinary worker'.[52] What found unconditional approval, however, was the status of literature and the arts. One visitor came to unfavourable conclusions about his native Brazil when comparing the illiteracy rates and the publication of hundreds of thousands of copies per book – in Brazil, in the 1950s still with the majority of the population illiterate, the average novel came out in some 1,000 copies.[53]

VOKS, and later the GKKS and the SSOD, knew very well the of impression that the erudition of the average Soviet citizen had on intellectual visitors, even more so if they came from lesser developed countries with illiterate masses. Sometimes, they may have 'helped' this effect to happen: when the Irish playwright George Bernard Shaw, back in the 1930s, boarded a train at the Soviet border, the first thing the very young and very pretty female conductors told him was how much they liked his writing. Shaw, a naive fellow traveller if ever there was one, was probably once more hoodwinked by his Soviet hosts. But even much more critical visitors recall similar occurrences: García Márquez's encounter on Gorky Prospekt with the young Russian admirer of Colombian poetry is a case in point.[54] Considering that García Márquez was not on an official visit, it is unlikely that this meeting was staged. Latin American literature was very popular indeed in the USSR (see Chapter 2), and the young man probably had just happened to have read a lot of Latin American poems. The Soviet host organisations profited from such encounters, but they also did an extremely good job of pointing out to visitors the positive aspects – real as much as beautified ones – of the Soviet Union compared to the states their guests came from.

Committed and compromised: Latin American left intellectuals and de-Stalinisation

The Spanish term for the *littérateur engagé* has a double meaning that is telling for many left-wing Latin Americans and their attitudes towards

---

[51] Nicanor Parra, *Canciones rusas* (Santiago de Chile: Editorial Universitaria, 1967).
[52] Mendes, *Moscou, Varsóvia, Berlim*, pp. 58–9.   [53] Ramos, *Viagem*, p. 180.
[54] García Márquez, *De viaje por los países socialistas*, pp. 179–80.

the Soviet Union before 1953: *intelectual comprometido* translates as both 'politically committed public intellectual' and 'compromised intellectual'. No small number of – mostly Mexican – writers had admired the Soviet Union during the worst time of Stalinist terror in the 1930s. The novelist José Revueltas had gone, at an early age, to Moscow for a 1935 Comintern congress and proclaimed, 'I adore Stalin more than anything else on earth.' His compatriots Vicente Toledano, Víctor Manuel Villaseñor, José Muños Cota and José Mancisidor wrote about their pilgrimages to Stalinist Moscow as 'travels to the future of the world'; Octavio Paz, later an ardent critic of totalitarianism, wrote letters full of admiration for the Soviet project as late as 1937; and Siqueiros was even involved in the murder of Stalin's arch-enemy Leon Trotsky in Mexico City in 1940.[55]

During late Stalinism and the early Cold War, many Latin American left intellectuals continued this admiration for the dictator and his realm. Those who had acquired their political socialisation in the 1920s and 1930s revelled even more in Stalin after the victory in the Second World War, as he seemed to have freed the world from fascism. Others now made their first pilgrimages to the socialist mecca: one of the first Latin Americans to visit the USSR after the war was the Argentine novelist and journalist Alfredo Varela (1914–84). From late 1948 to March 1949, VOKS officials showed him around Moscow, Leningrad, Odessa and Kiev. Varela was completely taken in by the programme and indeed so enthralled that, upon return, he wrote a 400-page eulogy on the Soviet Union. *Un periodista argentino en la Unión Soviética* (An Argentine Journalist in the Soviet Union) drew parallels between the liberation struggle of the Latin Americans and the Soviets against their constant attacks from the West.[56] But his enthusiasm was not limited to Soviet fighting spirit. He glorified the USSR as an earthly paradise, where all people were happy, healthy and positive, where workers were always sober and masters of their fate and where health care and education were free. Varela perceived Soviet politics as deeply democratic and the USSR as the well-spring of mankind – for these accomplishments, he hailed Stalin as 'the greatest man of our epoch'.[57]

---

[55] Kutejščikova, *Moskva-Meksiko-Moskva*, pp. 89–90, 115, 134; David Siqueiros, *Me llamaban el Coronelazo: memorias* (Mexico City: Grijalbo, 1977), p. 369; José Mancisidor, *Ciento veinte días* (Mexico City: Editorial México Nuevo, 1937); Vicente Lombardo Toledano and Victor Manuel Villaseñor, *Un viaje al mundo del porvenir* (Mexico City: Publicaciones de la Universidad obrera de México, 1936).

[56] Alfredo Varela, *Un periodista argentino en la Unión Soviética* (Buenos Aires: Ediciones Viento, 1950).

[57] *Ibid.*, p. 167.

Varela's good friend Pablo Neruda (1904–73) would certainly have agreed. The poet had become politicised by the Spanish Civil War, had been a member of the Chilean Communist Party since 1945 and made his first trip to the Soviet Union in 1949. Neruda, 'the greatest poet of the twentieth century in any language', according to his admirer Gabriel García Márquez, did not draft a prose travelogue. He was, however, inspired to many poems during his trip ('Pushkin, you were the angel / Of the Central Committee')[58] and, in his 1973 memoirs, he still recalled in very poetic language the startling impressions he experienced during his stay: 'I loved the Soviet earth at first sight, and I understood that not only did it exude a moral lesson to all corners of the human existence, an equalisation of the possibilities and a growing progress in creating and distributing. But I also inferred that from this steppe continent, with all its natural purity, was going to be produced something with great meaning for the world. All mankind knows that the gigantic truth was manufactured here, and there is, in our world, an intense and stunned waiting for what is going to happen.' When VOKS organised a reading of Pushkin's poems to peasants in their traditional garb, Neruda had his final awakening experience: 'nature seemed to finally form a victorious unity with the human being'.[59]

The Uruguayan Jesualdo Sosa (1905–82), a writer of children's books, widely read pedagogue and head of the Uruguayan–Soviet Friendship Association, joined the cheering crowd of Latin American admirers of Stalin. His detailed travel account *Mi viaje a la URSS* (My Voyage to the USSR) celebrated in depth the completely new world he had encountered during his trip in 1951.[60] Shown around by VOKS guides on self-chosen itineraries, he was overwhelmed by the programme: the Metro, the university, the Volga canal, the libraries, the theatres and especially the production of children's books left him awestruck. The workers to him seemed to work self-determinedly, good-humouredly and effectively; their salary was fair, the jobs secure, the unions strong.[61] There was state insurance, a fantastic health care system and free education. Museums, theatres and cultural palaces were all around. A strong sense

---

[58] Pablo Neruda, 'En la Unión Soviética', *Cuadernos de la Fundación Pablo Neruda* 37 (1999), 29–37.

[59] 'Amé a primera vista la tierra soviética y comprendí que de ella salía no sólo una lección moral para todos los rincones de la existencia humana, una equiparación de las posibilidades y un avance cresciente en el hacer y el repartir, sino que también interpreté que desde aquel continente estepario, con tanta pureza natural, iba a producirse un gran vuelo. La humanidad entera sabe que allí está elaborando la gigantesca verdad y hay en el mundo una intesidad atónita esperando lo que va a suceder': Neruda, *Confieso que he vivido*, p. 237.

[60] Sosa, *Mi viaje a la URSS*.   [61] *Ibid.*, p. 91.

of responsibility that all Soviet citizens shared prevented problems with discipline, Sosa believed he had discovered.[62] During the obligatory excursion to the Caucasus, he admired kolkhozes, universities and sanatoria.

After his Soviet trip, Sosa met up with a large group of Latin American intellectuals in Czechoslovakia. The Ecuadorian author Enrique Gil Gilbert, the Cuban poet Nicolás Guillén, the Brazilian Jorge Amado, the Puerto Rican-Mexican novelist José Luis Gonzales and the Uruguayan Jesualdo Sosa sat in a restaurant in downtown Prague and, in pan-Latin American solidarity, agreed on the higher significance of what was happening in the Soviet Union. The new Soviet man, they concluded, was ascetic and creative, brave, educated and immune to the cheap temptations of life. Perhaps after several rounds of smooth Czech beer, Sosa emphatically contrasted free life in the Soviet Union to the sad serfdom in their home countries: 'all America was for a moment with us, with its dreams and its realities ... imprisoned by tyrants and their lackeys and scum'.[63]

Two of the other guests in the Prague restaurant that night completed the group of the most notorious Latin American admirers of Stalin: before he became Brazil's most famous and cherished author of the twentieth century, the Brazilian novelist Jorge Amado (1912–2001) was already a staunch believer in Soviet communism. After years of commitment to the Brazilian Communist Party, he finally went to the USSR for the first time in 1951, where he was awarded the Stalin Peace Prize. His extensive travelogue *O mundo do paz* (The World of Peace) was yet another eulogy on every aspect of the Soviet system and even justified the east European show trials.[64] Many years later, in his memoirs, Amado showed deep regret and remembered with shame how they actually knew of the persecutions and the anti-Semitism of late Stalinism – but accepted it tacitly.[65] Amado had been so convinced by the world he was presented that, only a year later, he went again, this time with some friends: the writers Graciliano Ramos (1892–1953) and Dalcídio Jurandir (1909–79), like Amado, were communist party militants. Ramos, a renowned novelist and head of the Brazilian authors' association, collected his impressions in a long travelogue called *Viagem* (Voyage). Very benevolently and in poetic language he praised the Soviet Union to the skies and mocked western panic-mongering: 'yes,

---

[62] *Ibid.*, p. 111.   [63] *Ibid.*, pp. 285–7.

[64] Jorge Amado, *O mundo da paz: União Soviética e democracias populares* (Rio de Janeiro: Editorial Vitória, 1951).

[65] Amado, *Navegação de cabotagem*, pp. 31, 67.

they have a cruel dictatorship there, one that steals the worker's sleep and excessively educates him'. After the trip to Moscow, Leningrad and Georgia, which he found overwhelming, Ramos developed doubts as to whether his pessimistic literature about poverty, misery and disease in north-eastern Brazil was still appropriate for this fantastic and happy new world. Ramos did notice the excesses of Stalin's personality cult, but believed that 'westerners were simply not able to comprehend this, this unconditional devotion to the leading politician'. And after all, this was certainly just a passing phase, necessary to involve all these Siberians and Kyrgyz people in the grand project of building the new society.[66]

The Cuban poet Nicolás Guillén (1902–89), finally, had come to the USSR in 1952. He had already met his intimate friend Amado in Moscow before they went together to the Prague dinner. Shortly after this trip, his second time in the Soviet Union after a first stay in 1948, Guillén summed up his impressions in a short prose text that he later added as a chapter to his memoirs. He recalled being amazed by Moscow, by the architecture, by the large selection in grocery shops (!) and by the advances in technology he saw at a 3D screening in a Moscow cinema. His summary: the Soviets were full of childlike elation as one allegedly often finds in young nations, just like the United States. In 1954, Guillén was awarded the Stalin Peace Prize and, from that point onwards, was going to be one of the most faithful and loyal Latin American visitors to the Soviet Union – he went back at least ten more times.[67]

Until the mid 1950s, Latin American travellers to the Soviet Union went to see the utopia they expected to find. Their ideas and expectations were very similar to those of their west European and Mexican colleagues in the 1930s: they took the world that was staged for them as real and hailed the Soviet Union as a utopian place. Yet hardly any of them went as far as Ignacio Torres Giraldo and the Honduran writer Ramón Amaya Amador and actually stayed to live in the eastern bloc. Even Guillén, who at the time was not allowed to return to his native Cuba, preferred his Paris exile between his many short visits to Moscow. Yet in their writing, they all hailed Stalin's dictatorship and his apparent achievements for the Soviet Union and the world.

---

[66] Ramos, *Viagem*, pp. 53, 58; the first edition came out in 1954, a good dozen more appeared until the late 1980s.

[67] Nicolás Guillén, *Páginas vueltas: memorias* (Havana: Unión de Escritores y Artistas de Cuba, 1982).

The Stalinists' crossroads: Khrushchev's secret speech

It was not until the death of the dictator in 1953 and the cautious condemnation of his crimes by Khrushchev during the 20th Party Congress in 1956 that a serious rethinking about the Soviet Union happened among most of these Latin American leftists. Neruda recalled that he had learned about the extent of Stalin's crimes only through Khrushchev's speech: 'it was a harrowing occurrence which opened our eyes'. Yet Neruda did not lose faith in the Soviet Union, and instead harboured 'a feeling that we were new born ... and we continued with the truth in our hands!'[68] In consequence, he did not question his own blind faith or the Soviet project as such, but made a break with *maoestalinismo* and vowed complete dedication to the 'new' Soviet Union under Khrushchev's leadership. Instead of an abstract utopia, he now turned to the more concrete achievements of the post-Stalinist Soviet Union: he poetically celebrated hydroelectric power plants as 'temples by the lake'[69] and became an ardent supporter of the space programme. During his subsequent visits, he met the cosmonauts Gagarin and Titov and praised Sputnik in poems. Until the end of his life, Neruda remained a faithful friend of the Soviet Union, whatever new directions its leaders would take. Even in 1968, he refused to comment on the invasion of Czechoslovakia and did not stand up for Alexander Solzhenitsyn when he was threatened. He excused himself by explaining that he did not want to create anti-Soviet propaganda and pointed at the allegedly worse situation for intellectuals in the Western world.[70]

Jorge Amado remembered learning of Stalin's death at a communist party meeting in Rio de Janeiro: 'I was paralysed, desolate, lost. My eyes were dry, my heart convulsed.' He rushed to meet Neruda and the Chilean communist Volodia Teitelboim in Buenos Aires to cope with the grief. Unlike his comrades, however, Amado soon developed a critical stance towards Khrushchev's USSR, after the revelations of the Party Congress made him reconsider his political stance. On the one hand, he still felt 'linked to the Soviet Union as through an umbilical cord'. He struggled and tried not to lose faith: 'days of fear, damned, unholy, which become dark weeks and months. The doubts mount up, we may not doubt, we want no doubts, we want to continue in unscathed faith, in certitude, want to follow the ideal. In sleepless nights we look at each other, with lumps in our throats and a wish to cry.' In the same year, Amado left the Brazilian Communist Party. He protested against the

---

[68] Neruda, *Confieso que he vivido*, p. 250.   [69] *Ibid.*, pp. 282, 291.
[70] Hollander, *Political Pilgrims*, p. 72.

treatment of Pasternak in 1960 ('even though I did not like the novel') and, later in his memoirs, showed deep regret for his *O mundo do paz*. Nevertheless, Amado went back many times to the Soviet Union, 'cured of Stalinism, immune against the virus of radicalism'.[71] No longer attracted to Soviet-style communism, he was a loyal friend and pen-pal of many Soviet intellectuals including Ilya Ehrenburg, Oleg Ignat'ev and Vera Kutejščikova, his 'Soviet family'.[72] Politically, Amado looked for new horizons: he supported Fidel Castro's Cuba, if at times critically, and campaigned for Third World interests.

José Revueltas (1914–76) passed through a similar gradual, complex and painful process of apostasy. A member of the Mexican Communist Party from 1928 (when he was 14 years old), he had been expelled in 1943 for a lack of party discipline. Yet, while Amado abandoned the party after the revelations about Stalin's crimes, Revueltas initially was inspired by the opportunity of a new and just socialism. 'With the death of Stalin in 1953, socialism took on new dimensions of hope', he remembered; 'there was a newly recaptured glamour of international communism as a political strategy.' Revueltas was allowed back into the Mexican Communist Party, dutifully backed the Soviet invasion of Hungary and made a second trip to the motherland of socialism in 1957. Revueltas's political careening was reflected nicely in his literary work: his 1949 novel *Los días terrenales* (The Terrestrial Days) was a sharp repudiation of left dogmatism, heavily criticised by Pablo Neruda at a World Peace Council meeting in Mexico. In the year of Khrushchev's speech, and readmitted to the party, Revueltas again wrote two rather conventional socialist realist criticisms of capitalism. *En algún valle de lagrimas* (translated into English as 'Valley of Tears') in 1956 and *Los motivos de Cain* (Cain's Motives) were completely conversant with Soviet aesthetics and morals. On his way to Moscow in spring 1957, he wrote his 'letter from Budapest to the communist writers', blaming them for having been silent on Stalin's crimes – while being very silent himself about the recent Soviet violence during the Hungarian uprising.[73] Yet Revueltas's pro-Khrushchev phase was short-lived. His 1958 *Ensayo sobre un proletariado sin cabeza* (Essay about a Headless Proletariat) was consequently again a criticism of the entire left and, somewhat pharisaically, of reformism and opportunism. In 1960, he was expelled once more from the Mexican Communist Party 'for revisionist tendencies'. With his 1964 novel *Los*

---

[71] Amado, *Navegação de cabotagem*, pp. 79, 145, 148, 156, 268.

[72] *Ibid.*, p. 244; Korrespondencija Erenburg–Amado, RGALI f.1204 op.2 d.1206.

[73] Kutejščikova, *Moskva-Meksiko-Moskva*, p. 123; Sam L. Slick, *José Revueltas* (Boston: Twayne, 1983), p. 169.

errores (The Mistakes), he, finally and for good, renounced Soviet-style communism. Dedicated to the memory of the executed Hungarian reform communist Imre Nagy, the novel contraposed idealistic militants to party dogmatists in 1930s and 1940s Mexico and described the mirror images of the Moscow purges in the ranks of the Mexican party. The positive protagonist is an idealistic left professor who, in the 1950s, tries to trace his 'disappeared' comrades. The party communists, depicted as a bunch of violent criminals, try to silence him.[74] Revueltas, now excluded permanently from the circle of friends of the Soviet Union, repeatedly dealt with questions of loyalty and dogmatism in his work for the rest of his life. In 1966, he wrote a passionate defence of the Soviet writers Andrej Sinjavskij and Julij Daniel' called 'A Soviet "Freeze" on Free Expression of Thought'.[75] Having lost his admiration for the USSR, Revueltas still remained an active advocate of socialism and travelled many times to Castro's Cuba. In 1968, he became one of the intellectual initiators of the student movement in Mexico, an activity for which he spent several years in prison.

Just like Revueltas, Diego Rivera (1886–1957) saw the revelations of the 20th Party Congress as a chance to be readmitted to the party from which he had been excluded in 1929 under the somewhat obscure reproach of being a 'Trotskyite'. His memoirs, written shortly after his readmission in 1954, accordingly included all-encompassing praise of the Soviet Union.[76] From late 1955 to early 1956, Rivera went again to Moscow to get treatment for his cancer but died in Mexico the following year. His perennial rival David Siqueiros (1896–1974), who had visited Rivera's sickbed during a Soviet trip that year, had been a Stalinist from the very beginning and a lifelong member of the Mexican Communist Party (albeit excluded and readmitted three times). Siqueiros wrote his memoirs at a time when Stalin was already partially rehabilitated by the Kremlin and did not comment directly on the Party Congress. But in a speech he gave during the Thaw at the Soviet Academy of Arts, he criticised what he saw as a drift towards formalism and 'another form of cosmopolitanism' in Soviet culture. This was such an obvious call for a return to Stalinist aesthetics that even Aleksandr Gerasimov, president of the Academy and notorious for both his Stalin portraits and his political conservatism, left the hall. Yet Siqueiros's general depiction of the USSR remained very positive, both from this

---

[74] José Revueltas, *Los errores* (Mexico City: Fondo De Cultura Economica, 1964).
[75] Slick, *José Revueltas*, p. 173.
[76] Diego Rivera and Gladys March, *My Art, My Life: An Autobiography* (New York: Citadel, [1960]).

trip ('I saw a sea of luxury ... and the most immense optimism on earth') and from another one in 1967. He was elected an honorary member of the Soviet Academy of Arts and won the Lenin Peace Prize (donating the 25,000 rubles to Ho Chi Minh). Like Neruda, he stayed a loyal friend of the Soviet Union until the end of his life: 'I reiterate, for what remains of my life, my intention of fidelity to the Party and to proletarian internationalism.'[77]

More intellectuals of this generation remained loyal to the Soviet Union and simply avoided commenting on the revelations about Stalinism: the Argentine feminist writer and political activist María Rosa Oliver (1898–1977) received the Lenin Peace Prize in 1958. 'I love your land for what it is and for the fact that it gives us hope for a better future', she declared. 'In Moscow, I felt something important was happening, something decisive for all mankind and that its citizens knew.' Stalin's crimes and Khrushchev's speech she did not mention at all. For events such as the Hungarian uprising, some leftist intellectuals like Oliver reiterated the flimsy Soviet explanations of a fascist counter-revolution supported by the capitalists through Radio Free Europe.[78]

For the writer Pedro Jorge Vera (1914–99), Moscow was still 'the symbol of our ideals of justice'[79] when he went to the USSR in the early 1960s, where was received by Khrushchev personally: 'to feel the reality of this new world strengthened our convictions'. He expressed a certain relief that Stalinism had been overcome, was very positive about the prospects for Soviet communism and sent his son to study at Lumumba University. After these allegations and another journey to the USSR, Vera could not return to his native Ecuador and sought refuge in Chile. His close friend Joaquín Gutiérrez (1918–2001), the best-known novelist from Costa Rica, opted for a four-year exile in Moscow. Both Vera and Gutiérrez had the same take on the USSR even during de-Stalinisation: not completely uncritical, but definitely benevolent. Gutiérrez summed up his experiences in a 1967 book called *La URSS tal cual* (The USSR as Such).[80] He tried to explain both extreme adulation and the damnation of the Soviet Union in terms of a lack of knowledge and gave a lot of factual information in his book. He commended the rise in living standards, the successes in agriculture, the technological achievements and the development of public opinion. Convinced of the effectiveness of Soviet

---

[77] Philip Stein, *Siqueiros: His Life and Works* (New York: International, 1994), pp. 322, 373; Siqueiros, *Me llamaban el Coronelazo*, p. 458.

[78] Hebe Clementi, *María Rosa Oliver* (Buenos Aires: Planeta, 1992); Korrespondencija M. R. Oliver–Boris Polevoj, 21 Dec. 1958, RGALI f.631 op.26 d.4413 l.1.

[79] Vera, *Gracias a la vida*; Jan. 1961, GARF f.9518 op.1 d.339 l.62.

[80] Gutiérrez, *La URSS tal cual*.

medical care, he had his good friend Carlos Luis Fallas (himself a renowned Costa Rican writer who used the pseudonym Calufa) travel to Moscow for treatment in 1965. Gutiérrez was rather benign on Stalin ('30 per cent bad, 70 per cent good')[81] and saw Brezhnev as the man to solve some of the problems that Khrushchev had been unable to. Gutiérrez's depiction of Soviet society no longer emphasised its utopian character, but instead underlined its normality: people lived like everywhere else on earth, had families and worked for money. 'The state [was] puritan, the population [was] not', education was very important, religion tolerated but not encouraged.[82] His bottom line, not just after a superficial guided visit, but after four years living among Soviet citizens as one of them: 'the best qualities of all peoples have condensed in the Soviet Union. A sense of solidarity, not only towards the family but the entire society ... There is more honesty, less prejudice, more sensibility and less pride.'[83]

The official revelation and acknowledgement of Stalin's crimes shocked a generation of Latin American leftists, but it did not altogether destroy their fascination for the Soviet Union. Vera Kutejščikova, the official VOKS guide for Latin American visitors, noted in late 1956 that 'most of my Mexican friends are glowing with socialist ideas; in me, they saw the representative of a state that had implemented these ideas. Soviet society was in their eyes a paradise, and I was their guide to this paradise.'[84] But, before long, this utopian view of the USSR disappeared. The metaphysical dimension of the admiration, the rhapsodising of a political system that was to redeem the rest of the wretched world, gave way to a more sober assessment of concrete achievements and advantages of the Soviet state. Sooner than others, Jorge Amado rescinded his utopian idealising of Soviet realities altogether, but he stayed in contact with many Soviet intellectuals. Alfredo Varela, the most enthusiastic of all fellow travellers during late Stalinism, also lost his blind idealism during Khrushchev's de-Stalinisation campaign. No one in the Soviet Union seems to have registered his change of mind (or, for that matter, his urinating against the Soviet embassy in Buenos Aires): he remained a popular and officially supported author and film-maker. Like Amado, Varela was now occasionally critical of the Soviet Union, but stayed in contact.[85] For other Latin American leftists, de-Stalinisation temporarily rekindled their hopes for socialism: José Revueltas struggled and wavered

[81] *Ibid.*, p. 17.   [82] *Ibid.*, p. 72.   [83] *Ibid.*, p. 144.
[84] Kutejščikova, *Moskva-Meksiko-Moskva*, pp. 29–30.
[85] Korrespondencija Varela–Erenburg, Letter by Varela to Erenburg, 19 Oct. 1953, RGALI f.1204 op.2 d.1354 ll.1–6.

for a long time. Initially, he saw, just like Diego Rivera, his chance to be readmitted to a communist world movement that seemed back on track again. Revueltas's friend, the poet Eduardo Lizalde (1929–) passed through a similar development: 'after visiting the Soviet Union, you feel confident that a new world can be built', he said after his first trip. It was the anti-Stalinist socialist spirit in the Soviet Union that made him join the ranks of the Mexican Communist Party in 1955. But, like Revueltas, he, too, was soon disappointed with Khrushchev's USSR. Both were excluded from the ranks of the Mexican Communist Party in 1960 and began their common quest for new socialist horizons.

¡Cuba sí, Soviet no! A new generation of leftists

Some Latin American left intellectuals without a Stalinist past, *intelectuales comprometidos* without the Spanish double meaning, from the beginning saw the Soviet Union with less empathy. The godfathers of magic realism, the Guatemalan Miguel Asturias (1899–1974) and the Franco-Cuban Alejo Carpentier (1904–80) showed no particular interest in the Soviet utopia.[86] Although both travelled several times to the USSR in the 1960s (Asturias even won the Lenin Peace Prize), they never wrote much about it. The Mexican novelist and essayist Carlos Fuentes (1928–2012) had great hopes for Khrushchev's Thaw as he perceived it during a 1963 visit. But he claimed to be more useful to the left cause as a writer than as an activist and did not bother much with inspirations the Soviet Union could potentially give to Latin America. He gave up his optimism anyway, when the USSR invaded Czechoslovakia in 1968. Fuentes travelled to Prague the same year, together with Julio Cortázar and Gabriel García Márquez, to show their support for the reform socialists.

A younger generation of rebellious intellectuals looked primarily to Cuban socialism and perceived the Soviet model as a rather distant and strange phenomenon. The Peruvian Mario Vargas Llosa (1936–) belonged to this group in his younger years. Better than anyone else, however, Gabriel García Márquez (1926–2014) represents this generation. Affiliated with the Colombian Communist Party from 1955, he nonetheless held a very critical stance towards the Soviet Union from the

---

[86] 'Magic(al) realism' was coined in Europe, and and it was later applied to Latin American literature, including in North America. Latin American authors themselves actually sought their own version of socialist realism. See Volpi, *El insomnio de Bolívar*, p. 69; Arturo Taracena, 'El camino política de Miguel Angel Asturias', *Mesoamerica* 38 (1999), 86–101.

beginning of his political activism. In 1957, after some failed attempts to obtain a visa, he finally managed to get to Moscow under the pretext of being an accordion player in a Colombian folklore band. His collection of essays about his trip, *90 días en la 'Cortina de hierro'* ('90 Days in [*sic*] the Iron Curtain') was first published in the journal *Cromos*.[87] The book edition came out only after a year-long struggle with the publishing house, but later became a best-seller, making it to at least seven editions by the 1980s.[88] Much debate accompanied the publication: while, for conservative readers, García Márquez showed too much empathy with Soviet realities, many leftists reacted indignantly, as he was very critical of many aspects of Soviet life.[89] Overall, García Márquez's account might be the most balanced and insightful account of Soviet life by a foreign intellectual in the 1950s. In the company of a French journalist and his Colombian friend Plinio Mendoza (to whom he referred in the book merely as an Italian journalist, to protect his anonymity), he travelled for three months through communist Europe. One of the first aspects he noticed was how many people on his trip spoke his mother tongue: on the train to Moscow, he shared a compartment with Spaniards who had come as refugee children from the Spanish Civil War. And in Moscow he believed Spanish to be the 'most widely spoken foreign language'. García Márquez described the dangerous naivety of the many Latinos he met on his trip and tried to contrast their view with a blunt picture of the USSR ('Like women you have to get to know countries in the early morning, without the makeup . . .'). People looked very much alike to him at first glance, and it always took him longer in conversation to actually note the differences. In an interesting contrast to the paternalistic stance many Soviets held towards the Third World, García Márquez felt that most of them suffered from an inferiority complex. He was struck by the megalomania of Moscow's architecture, which he felt was suffocating and gloomy, and described the capital as a huge, somewhat backward village, fettered by slow bureaucracy and completely dead at night. While he did note, like most travellers, an impressive knowledge and education in the world's languages and geography ('[my translator] knew more about South America than most South Americans'), García Márquez also described an ignorance about current world affairs: 'no Soviet I talked to knew of Marilyn Monroe!' Asking about political change, García Márquez noted that most people knew the details of Khrushchev's secret speech from the year before, but hardly anyone spoke out against Stalin openly. Only one elderly lady, a

---

[87] García Márquez, *De viaje por los países socialistas*.
[88] Saldívar, *García Márquez*, pp. 354–8.   [89] Irnberger, *Gabriel García Márquez*, p. 179.

decorator at the Gorky Theatre who offered herself as guide and translator, criticised Stalin for hours and described him as the biggest criminal in Russian history.

García Márquez made no attempt to object to her view, but he did try to do justice to the Soviet system: 'with the same belief with which we see the negative sides, we also have to discern that no one suffers from hunger and no one is unemployed'. He liked the well-functioning infrastructure and the punctual trains. Most people in the street, including soldiers, he found very friendly, helpful, curious and generous – and very anxious to draw a positive picture of their state: 'it is clear that they back their political system'. He was also, half-ironically, happy not to see a Coca-Cola advert across 22,400,000 km^2. Knowing of the dangers of short visits to the Soviet Union, García Márquez reflected on several occasions during his visit upon staged worlds and the realities behind them. He noted the contrast between the impressive scientific and technological achievements and the relative poverty most people had to live in. Somewhat surprising, therefore, is his cautious assessment of the Hungarian revolt. He was allowed to visit Budapest as one of the first foreign observers. While he did criticise the brutal methods of the Soviet Army, he also stated that 'without Soviet troops there would be no more Communist Party and nothing similar to a democracy' and, towards the end of his travel report, was rather positive about János Kádár.[90]

There were very different reactions and attitudes to Stalin's death and Khrushchev's de-Stalinising Soviet Union within the Latin American left intelligentsia. The old Stalinist guard remained, by and large, faithful unto death to the Soviet Union despite all revelations and changes, as did Neruda, Rivera, Siqueiros, Rosa Oliver, Guillén, Vera and Gutiérrez. Others, such as Revueltas and Lizalde, initially hailed the spirit of the Thaw as a new chance for real socialism, while Varela and Amado were disenchanted with the Soviet Union and turned to Cuba instead. All of them, however, including the most obedient friends of the Soviet Union, gave up the chiliastic view of the country as a red utopia. The metaphysical rhetoric of socialist paradise and communist redemption did not stand up to the realities and gave way to a more sober view of the – often still idealised – accomplishments of the Soviet state.

As the first generation of Latin American admirers of the Soviet Union, born between 1890 and 1920, gradually lost its influence, most of the younger leftists, born in the 1920s and later, no longer took much inspiration from the red empire. The Soviets did try to stay in contact

---

[90] García Márquez, *De viaje por los países socialistas*, pp. 25, 115–29, 133, 138, 152, 176.

with the Latin American left, but now their own conservatism stood in the way of the more revolutionarily spirited Latinos: when, in 1966, Luis Pedro Bonavita, head of the Uruguayan Frente Izquierda de Liberación (Left Liberation Front) was, just as many Third World intellectuals before him, shown around the Caucasus, his translator and guide reported to his GKKS bosses: 'They are nice people, but their political education is weak. They really believe in a speedy continuation of the revolution in Uruguay.'[91] The lack of support by the Soviets for Third World revolution disappointed many a Latin American leftist. Abraham Guillén, intellectual godfather of the Uruguayan city guerrilla Tupamaros, called the Soviet Union itself an imperialist state.[92] A similarly radical renunciation of the Soviet model of development by a leftist came from Eduardo Galeano (1940–). In his 1971 manifesto *Las venas abiertas de América Latina* (Open Veins of Latin America), the young literary hero of dependency theory put western and Soviet reformism in the same sack.[93]

This seems like the final word about Latin American intellectual interest in the USSR. In the long run, most Latin American leftists were indeed completely disenchanted with the Soviet Union as socialist utopia. This section, however, like many accounts of Latin American intellectual history, has considered only a certain type of writer: all of them were from their country's upper or upper middle class; all felt linked to the intellectual traditions of the West; all had spent much time in Europe or the United States; all were leftists. With the exception of Nicolás Guillén they were all white, and with the exception of María Rosa Oliver all male. In the course of the 1950s and 1960s, this classic type of the Latin American intellectual lost interest in the Soviet Union. Others did not.

The Soviets' new friends: indigenous authors, conservatives and Catholics

It was midnight when the Peruvian poet and novelist Gustavo Valcárcel (1921–92) arrived in his Moscow hotel room in October 1963. Moved to tears, he listened to the 'Internationale' played over the hotel intercom system, stepped on to the balcony, overwhelmed by his feelings, and

---

[91] Otčet o pribyvanii v SSSR prezidenta Levogo fronta osvoboždenija Urugvaja (FIDEL) Luisa Pedro Bonavity s suprugoj, 9 Mar. 1966, GARF f.9518 op.1 d.1014 ll.28–31.

[92] Abraham Guillén, *El capitalismo soviético: última etapa del imperialismo* (Madrid: Queimada Ediciones, 1979).

[93] Galeano, *Las venas abiertas de América Latina*, p. 235.

looked upon 'the capital of world socialism, illuminated by lights and the future … I took one of the many hammer-and-sickles from the firmament and I engraved with them a letter: Violeta, we have not fought in vain! I have seen the accomplished reality of all our dreams!'[94] Back in his room, Valcárcel wrote – on paper – a series of emphatic poems about the Soviet Union and the future of a socialist America.

It was his second trip to Moscow. In 1960, he had written a travelogue that unconditionally celebrated the new Soviet Union under Khrushchev. *Reportaje al futuro: crónicas de un viaje a la URSS* (Report to the Future: Chronicles of a Trip to the USSR) objected to a recent and rather balanced account by his liberal compatriot Francisco Miró Quesada (see next section, pp. 177–8).[95] Following contemporary Soviet Party doctrine 100 per cent, Valcárcel denounced the excesses of Stalin's personality cult but, beyond that, drew an over-optimistic picture of the Soviet model as the future of mankind. For almost 400 pages, Valcárcel extolled the superiority of efficient Soviet industry, agriculture and education with a barrage of statistics. Rents were low, incomes high, the women emancipated and children happy. Schools and universities and health care and sanatoria were free. Soviet youth, though free to dance to rock-and-roll as much as they liked, still patriotically loved their national cultures. Amazed by the spirit in Soviet art that continued to fight against decadent formalism, Valcárcel welcomed the treatment of Pasternak. He denounced the Hungarian insurgents as fascists and celebrated the Soviet Third World solidarity he felt during a visit to Lumumba University. At a parade for the cosmonauts Gagarin and Titov on Red Square, Valcárcel got an honorary seat next to his Latin American colleagues Pablo Neruda, Joaquín Gutiérrez, the Chilean feminist activist Olga Poblete de Espinosa and the Haitian writer René Depestre. Valcárcel summed up this first Soviet trip as 'one of the most intense emotional experiences of my life'.

In 1965, Valcárcel went to Moscow again, in order to see his son, whom he had sent to study at Lumumba University. After his epiphany and all the eulogies to Khrushchev's accomplishments during the first and second trip, Valcárcel, upon return, was initially a bit sceptical about the Party leader's ousting. But he quickly accepted the official explanation that Khrushchev had stepped back for health reasons. He sighed with relief and wrote yet another book, *Medio siglo de revolución invencible: segunda parte de 'Reportaje al futuro'* (Half a Century of Invincible

---

[94] See gustavoyvioletavalcarcel.blogspot.com/2009/02/biografia-y-obra-de-gustavo-valcarcel. html (last accessed 16 Nov. 2010).
[95] Valcárcel, *Reportaje al futuro*.

Revolution: Second Part of the 'Report to the Future'). For another 320 pages, Valcárcel harped on about the usual feats of his socialist utopia, the architecture, the education and health care system, the women's rights, the family values, the overall progress. One part of the book was hinted at already in Chapter 1: the section 'Kasajstan: un ejemplo para América Latina' (Kazakhstan: A Role Model for Latin America) drew parallels between the Soviet republic and his native Peru. Both had around 11 million inhabitants, among them 'large masses of indigenous people' who had lived in misery. Thanks to the Soviet modernisation of the 1930s, Valcárcel continued, all the backwardness of the Kazakhs, their lack of industry and their illiteracy rate of 98 per cent had been overcome, without the painful phase of capitalism. Some 10,000 schools and 38 universities now provided free education in several languages. The virgin lands campaign, according to Valcárcel, was much more successful than the western press had depicted it. Agricultural output, the exploitation of minerals and industrial production had increased a hundredfold. Art and culture were allegedly blossoming in the modern cities. Unlike Peru, Kazakhstan had made huge progress from the same starting level. In this unfavourable comparison, Valcárcel saw the reason why Peruvians were actually prohibited by their government from travelling to the Soviet Union.[96]

Gustavo Valcárcel came from a very humble family background and thought of himself as a *poeta del pueblo* (poet of the people). Other writers who, like him, did not identify themselves so much with the European tradition of the mostly white, urban intellectuals, but with their indigenous ancestry were invited to the USSR in the 1950s and 1960s. While García Márquez or Fuentes no longer maintained an idealised perception of the Soviet Union, some of these indigenous poets still continued – for a while – the metaphysical celebration of the Soviet Union as anti-western socialist utopia.

The Bolivian novelist, poet and indigenous activist Jesús Lara (1898–1980) belonged to this group of writers: considering himself an '*Indio puro* ... with only a few drops of Spanish blood', he wrote most of his literary work in his native language Quechua – much of which was also translated and spread in eastern Europe and the Soviet Union. A member of the Bolivian Communist Party from 1952, he travelled to the Soviet Union a year later and hailed the 'land of the new man' in his travelogue *La tierra del hombre nuevo: experiencias de viaje a la Unión Soviética* (Experiences from a Trip to the Soviet Union).[97] Lara's

---

[96] Valcárcel, *Medio siglo de revolución invencible*, pp. 17, 50–64, 182–7, 217.
[97] Mario Lara, 'Jesús Lara (1898–1980): homenaje', *Marxismo Militante* 24 (1998), 79–83.

compatriot, the writer Fausto Reinaga (1906–94) reported from the red utopia in a similar vein. From a poor *campesino* family, he had learned to read and write only at the age of 16, but later became Bolivia's most widely read and influential indigenous intellectual. On the brink of losing his faith in Marxism due to the boundless sectarianism of the Bolivian workers' movement, he had long felt the need to see the Soviet Union in order to restore his ideals. A desired trip to Moscow for the World Youth Festival failed in summer 1957, as he could not afford the travel costs. In autumn, he could not wait any longer: 'and if I die on the way, I have to get to Russia!' Luckily for him, Bolivia was governed by the Movimiento Nacionalista Revolucionario (MNR) at the time. No less a figure than the Bolivian president himself, Hernán Siles Zuazo, agreed to contribute to his trip.

On his odyssey to Moscow, Reinaga experienced both the remnants of colonialism and the pan-Latin American and anti-imperialist sentiments prevailing at the time: in Brazil, he was appalled by the racist attitudes he perceived against the black population. Stuck without money after his next leg in Buenos Aires, he was supported by Argentine intellectuals for weeks, and they finally bought him a ticket to Europe. He crossed the Atlantic and on his way saw the 'French imperial system' during a stop in Senegal and 'fascism in power' in Spain. 'It caused nausea and I was completely disillusioned with Europe', Reinaga recalled.[98] From Spain, he took a ship to Genoa, a train to Stuttgart, another one to Leipzig (from where he admired Sputnik), and, after a weeklong journey, he finally arrived in Moscow. The title of his book on the Soviet Union, *El sentimiento mesiánco del pueblo ruso* (The Messianic Demeanour of the Russian People) may sound like a condemnation of red imperialism. But, in fact, Reinaga embraced every aspect of Soviet life. He was deeply impressed by the technological feats, the atomic energy, the factories, the health care and education systems and the ubiquitous rhetoric of peace on earth. Like his hosts, Reinaga excoriated the United States on every occasion – and returned to Bolivia reassured of his Marxist ideals: 'I went with some petty bourgeois doubts, but I left enthusiastically with an assignment and a clear world-view.'[99]

Around the same time as Reinaga, in 1957, a young Nicaraguan by the name of Carlos Fonseca (1936–76) went to Moscow. Born and raised under the poorest conditions as an illegitimate child, he could afford to study law only thanks to financial benefits from his well-off father, and had become the head of a Marxist university group in Managua. In this capacity, he was – unlike Reinaga – awarded one of the few travel grants

---

[98] Reinaga, *El sentimiento mesiánico del pueblo ruso*, p. 38.   [99] *Ibid.*, p. 29.

to the World Youth Festival in Moscow and to a meeting of the World Federation of the Democratic Youth in Kiev. Many years later, already as founder and leader of the Frente Sandinista de Liberación Nacional (FSLN), full of nostalgia, Fonseca remembered his first stay in the Soviet Union in a book called *Un Nicaragüense en Moscú* (A Nicaraguan in Moscow).[100] He recalled his sentiments upon standing in the centre of Moscow, 'I thought I was dreaming.' He contrasted the allegedly 'massive counter-propaganda against the USSR in Nicaragua' with his positive impressions. During forty years of communism, the Soviets had had to spend eighteen years in defensive warfare, Fonseca explained somewhat cryptically. If he took into consideration the destructive forces of war, the progress of this society seemed fantastic. All the Soviets he met were highly educated and well dressed, students were paid and no one was unemployed. Religion and the press were completely free, Fonseca claimed, and, even in villages, libraries were better than the biggest one in Managua. Defending Stalin against international reproaches, the Nicaraguan explained the perception of Khrushchev's speech with a false translation: 'criticism', he lectured his readers, actually meant critical acknowledgement in Russian. The events in Hungary he explained, just as in the official Soviet depiction, as attempts at a fascist putsch.[101] Upon return to Nicaragua, Fonseca was arrested, interrogated for three days and finally went to Cuba, but remained an ardent supporter of the Soviet Union.

This lingering idealistic view of the USSR under Khrushchev as a flawless utopian society was typical for a group of intellectuals who shared certain features: they all came from poor backgrounds, mostly from the least developed countries of the Americas, as did the Bolivians Lara and Reinaga and the Nicaraguan Fonseca. They also identified strongly with the indigenous people of their home countries, as did the Peruvian Valcárcel and the socialist writer and journalist Fernando Benítez (1912–2000), who, from 1954, travelled many times to the Soviet Union, where he shared his knowledge as a renowned expert on the indigenous tribes in his native Mexico.[102] These writers were impressed longer by Soviet self-representation due to the circumstances they grew up in: Soviet living standards around 1960 were indeed higher than for the average person in their home countries. And the fact that Latin American critics of the Soviet system were usually white upper-middle-class men made their allegations unreliable to some of the *mestizo*

---

[100] Fonseca, *Un nicaragüense en Moscú.*   [101] *Ibid.*, pp. 20, 40, 48, 60.
[102] Otčet o rabote s meksikanskim pisatelem Fernando Benitesom, 29 Nov. 1966, GARF f.9518 op.1 d.1021 ll.27–32.

authors, who explicitly wrote their eulogies of the Soviet Union against García Márquez's or Miró Quesada's assessments of Soviet life.

This ethnic factor in the perception of the USSR could have offered an advantage to Soviet attempts at spreading a positive image of their country in the Third World. However, the documentation of the GKKS does not reveal a policy or an order to specifically target non-white intellectuals in their invitations. A reason for this self-restraint may have been that not all *indigenistas* shared this uncritical admiration for the Soviet Union. Rosario Castellanos and José María Arguedas, both from upper-class white families but famous for their espousal of *indigenismo*, never showed particular interest in Russia. And the admiration of the Sovietophiles did not last for too long, either: like Haya de la Torre in the 1930s, many drifted away from Soviet-style communism with its focus on industrialisation and rational progress to a specific kind of Latin American indigenous socialism. Lara abandoned the Communist Party in 1969 because it – upon orders from Moscow – propagated only a non-violent path to socialism and for that reason had deserted Che Guevara in his fights in the Bolivian jungle. Reinaga was arrested directly after his return to Bolivia, where the local communists made no move to help him. After his release, he made a pilgrimage to Machu Picchu, site of an ancient Inca town, and established the first indigenous party Partido de Indios Aymaras y Keswas (PIAK), later renamed Partido Indio de Bolivia (PIB). From the 1970s, Benítez and many other indigenous writers, just like many urban white leftists, included the Soviet Union in what they considered the camp of European imperialists. Manuel Scorza, guerrilla fighter in Chile and Peru and *indigenista* writer, dedicated a chapter of his last novel, *La danza inmóvil* (The Immobile Dance, 1983), to the disillusion of Peruvian communists with the Soviet Union, in which he complained 'Moscú ya no es Moscú' (Moscow Is No Longer Moscow).

Conservatives and Catholics

Fausto Reinaga was not only a militant *indigenista* Marxist. He was also an anti-clerical but pious Christian, who hailed Moscow as 'the new Jerusalem' and felt 'like Lazarus after Jesus' healing' when he saw Lenin in his mausoleum.[103] The young Salvadoran poet Roque Dalton (1935–75), too, was a devout Christian when he went to Moscow for the 1957 World Youth Festival (which did not keep him from writing

---

[103] Reinaga, *El sentimiento mesiánico del pueblo ruso*, p. 29.

kitschy poems about Lenin). Dalton was later radicalised, participated in the guerrilla struggle in El Salvador and was finally shot by his own comrades, who wrongly suspected him of being a CIA agent. During his stay in Moscow, however, the Catholic Dalton was still attracted to the Soviet Union for its redemptive promise of a just society. The messianic demeanour of the Soviet Union, as Reinaga put it in his book title, indeed appealed to more than just socialists. Most authors from the entire political spectrum dedicated parts of their travelogues from the Soviet Union to the question of religion. Almost all of them reported that freedom of faith prevailed at least on paper and that persecutions of believers were long over, yet still noted that few people went to church.

The GKKS tour guides adapted to the interest and concerns of their Christian visitors. When the Brazilian journalist Nestor de Holanda and a Catholic travel companion went to the Georgian capital Tbilisi, they were presented to an Orthodox priest, who confirmed to them: 'the communists and we Christians actually fight for the same goal: to humanise human life. The socialist regime is, above all, humanitarian. We Christians and communists belong together.'[104] As a matter of fact, many Catholics were actually not so interested in the Russian or Georgian Orthodox Church, but in the ideology of the state itself, an ideology in which many perceived Christian elements. André Gide, as early as the 1930s, had believed many Catholic ideals had been realised in the USSR.[105] Many Latin Americans continued this spiritual view of the Soviet Union during the Thaw.

The Colombian pedagogue Agustín Nieto Caballero (1889–1975) was a member of best circles of his native Bogotá, founder of an alternative school system comparable to Maria Montessori's in Europe, and a practising Catholic. Impressed like many by the successful Sputnik flight, he travelled to the Soviet Union in 1959. His intention was to get to know the education system that could produce enough knowledge to lead to the 'historic leap of the Russian people'.[106] His report *El secreto de Rusia* (Russia's Secret) was published as a series of articles in the newspaper *El Tiempo* and, in several editions, as a book. The Soviet deputy minister of education and the general secretary of the Academy of Pedagogy explained the educational system to Nieto Caballero, showed him schools, universities and libraries and organised visits to research institutes. Nieto Caballero was deeply impressed. He considered education in the Soviet Union 'excellent' – and found interesting

---

[104] Holanda, *O mundo vermelho*, p. 26.   [105] Ryklin, *Kommunismus als Religion*, p. 134.
[106] Nieto Caballero, *El secreto de Rusia*, p. 16.

reasons for its success: Soviet students were so bright, Nieto Caballero claimed, because they were not confronted with sexual lures as everything vaguely erotic was prohibited. Taverns, bars and restaurants hardly existed, he noted delightedly, and newspapers did not feature gossip and scandal. As a Catholic, Nieto Caballero believed he had found 'a new religion [in the Soviet Union], the religion of work' and concluded: 'the materialist ideology of the Soviet man is intimately impregnated by the bourgeois Christian morality'.[107]

Nieto Caballero, the conservative Catholic, did not return a communist, but he found plenty of parallels between his *ora et labora* attitude and Soviet policies: 'Soviet ideals and goals are like our Christian ones; this is something capitalism is lacking', he felt and agreed with certain limitations on freedom of expression in the USSR: 'ugly degenerations of modern art should not be tolerated!'[108] Nieto Caballero's summary was accordingly positive: 'this Russian people, which we find so distant from us physically and spiritually, is nevertheless, even if we would never have believed that this could happen, giving lessons to us, lessons of purity, of honesty, of love of our studies, of tenaciousness in our most difficult endeavours, of humble conduct'.[109] The book edition of Nieto Caballero's pro-Soviet account was allowed to be published in Colombia only if it contained an afterword by the editors. They did not deny Soviet feats and successes, but felt the need to comment: Nieto Caballero, an otherwise unblemished and renowned thinker, they said, unfortunately had fallen in with western fellow travellers to the Soviet Union. The USSR, they warned, was very attractive at first glance, but a useless and possibly dangerous example for Colombia.[110]

Nieto Caballero was not the only conservative Latin American Catholic who developed particular sympathies for the Soviet Union. Ironically, while many leftists turned their back on the USSR in the 1960s, conservatives increasingly took an interest in what some of them perceived as a genuinely conservative state. Alberto Dangond (1933–) was a man of many vocations, a trained lawyer and a producer of television programmes. He was also a practising Catholic and sat in the Colombian parliament for the Partido Conservador (Conservative Party) – and he liked travelling: in early 1967, he toured the Soviet Union and, being also a writer, wrote a book about his experience. *Mi diario en la Unión Soviética: un conservador en la URSS* (My Diary in the Soviet Union: A Conservative in the USSR)[111] is perhaps the most surprising account of Soviet life ever written: a staunch Catholic conservative Latino

---

[107] *Ibid.*, p. 32.   [108] *Ibid.*, pp. 58–64.   [109] *Ibid.*, pp. 64–5.   [110] *Ibid.*, pp. 95–9.
[111] Dangond, *Mi diario en la Unión Soviética.*

praising the motherland of atheist socialism to the skies. The president of the Partido Conservador, Alváro Hurtado, contributed one of the forewords. No less surprisingly, he claimed that 'we conservatives need the Revolution, the challenge. We have domesticated Marxism and we lack intellectual incentive!' It was the late 1960s, and the conservatives agreed that the western alternative with its youth in destructive rebellion was much worse than what was happening in the East: 'you cannot live without ideals!'

Dangond got the standard tour programme through the Soviet Union and, like many others before him, was impressed by hydroelectric power plants, the electrification of Siberia and the result of the literacy campaigns. A true Latin American intellectual, he found the quality and variety of cultural life in Leningrad fantastic ('I am ashamed of Bogotá compared to it'). What makes his report particular is how he paralleled Soviet communism to his own political and moral ideals, and discovered more similarities than with his liberal compatriots. In Minsk, Dangond was invited to debate population policies and birth control – and found only like-minded persons: 'I am radically anti-communist, this is the truth, but I, Catholic and patriotic Colombian, conservative, from a small underdeveloped and tropical nation, met here, in the capital of communist Belorussia, a government official, who says exactly the same words and thinks the same ideas that I would have said, with the same human warmth!' He had always thought that Marxism wanted to destroy the family, Dangond explained, the basis of his conservative values and traditions, but now in the USSR he saw precisely the opposite: 'the application of Marxism in this Soviet Union has produced, at least as I perceived it with my eyes and in good faith, a practice of morals, of a social life and of a development of the human being which are easily identifiable with our best and most valued Christian, Catholic ideals.' At first glance, this was a great conservative system, Dangond wrote, 'there is no lack of order, no anarchy, no lack of discipline! ... Everyone respects the authorities, discipline, order!'; furthermore: 'these hierarchies in the Soviet Union correspond perfectly with the nature of man; it is authoritarian and at the same time wonderfully dynamic and vital within a jurisdictional order and the consent of everyone'.[112] The conservative Catholic Dangond saw all his own ideals realised, social stability and an apparently high standard of private morals of Soviet citizens, seemingly Christian elements in the Soviet constitution, family policy, sexual habits, the ubiquitous patriotic rhetoric of national unity and a messianic

---

[112] *Ibid.*, pp. 41, 139, 156, 179.

spirit: 'the Soviet Union is the best example of how the impetus of revolution and conservative philosophy can be harmonised'.[113]

Dangond's position was extreme, but not an exception. Many intellectuals from his political and religious background shared his views of the Soviet Union – in Brezhnev's USSR, some Latin Americans saw a modern successful conservative state. The Argentine traveller Joaquín Torres, while impressed with their accomplishments, felt that the socialist countries would become increasingly conservative and nationalistic.[114] After his trip to Moscow, the journalist Pedro Clavijo reasoned: 'there is no more traditional society than the Soviet one!'[115] Gonzalo Canal Ramírez (1916–94), a Colombian novelist, professor of sociology and Christian politician, wrote a rather similar, if more differentiating account of a 1968 trip to Moscow, where he was received as a guest of the press agency APN. In *La Unión Soviética: reto moral* (The Soviet Union: A Moral Challenge), Canal Ramírez demanded a fair assessment of the USSR and communism as such. One has to understand the conditions under which it developed, he claimed, and instead of rejecting it per se, one should have a close look at the positive values it contained. Canal Ramírez conceded that religion was oppressed in the early days of the revolution, but defended these measures as an anticipation – only a little overzealous – of the Second Vatican Council. Now in the late 1960s, while religion was completely tolerated, the real faith of the people was the belief in the Soviet state and its ideology. Art was considered a religion now, and the Russians prayed in countless museums, orchestra halls and cinemas and on the radio. Canal Ramírez saw close parallels between the Christian catechism and the values of Soviet society: a strong belief in an idea and a high esteem for work, collectivism, appreciation of the family and intolerance towards enemies of the faith and towards parasitical conduct characterised both Soviet communism and Latin American Catholicism. Lenin in this view appeared as another redeemer, and Canal Ramírez indeed compared each of his April Theses to the Gospels. Thanks to this conception of the world, all Russians were cheerful and optimistic, and in addition highly educated and yet still modest. 'What impressed me most', Canal Ramírez summed up, 'were not the technological achievements, the hydropower, the spaceships, but the new man as Lenin created him ... This new man, his cultural and

[113] *Ibid.*, p. 161.

[114] Joaquín Torres, *Viaje a Rusia y a otros países socialistas* (Buenos Aires: Edición del Autor, 1962), p. 281.

[115] Carta de Moscú: El Año Nuevo Socialista, clipping from an unknown newspaper, 27 Dec. 1974, Archive of the Instituto Cultural Colombo-Soviético.

moral values, is the great strength of the Soviet Union.'[116] A Soviet reviewer of the book could 'of course not agree' with Canal Ramírez's Christian idealism instead of historic materialism, but commended the contribution it delivered for a better understanding of the Soviet Union among Latin Americans.[117]

Not all Latin American Catholics felt a spiritual kinship with a conservative USSR. The closer they were to the official church, the likelier people were first of all to condemn the atheist state and its deputies in the Americas. The Chilean Raúl Aldunate (see next section, pp. 176–7) was harsh in his criticism of the anti-religious stance of the Soviet government.[118] Many religious visitors, among them the Peruvian philosopher Francisco Miró Quesada and the Venezuelan writer Miguel Otero Silva, were appalled by the museum of atheism in Leningrad's Kazan Cathedral.[119]

Catholic *guerrilleros* such as the Colombian priest Camilo Torres (1929–66), by the same token, hardly cared about the old Soviet Union. Some of them, like Torres's *compañero* priest Gustavo Pérez, had been to the USSR in the late 1950s, but eventually found the Chinese model of armed struggle much more useful for their aims. Similarly, the more pacific arm of liberation theology was not inspired or supported directly by the Soviets. The Nicaraguan poet and excommunicated socialist priest Ernesto Cardenal (1925–) did pay a visit to Moscow at some point in the late 1970s. But for him as well the role models now lay elsewhere.

Complaints about the loss of spiritualism in an increasingly materialist world dominated by economic interests gained weight from the late 1960s.[120] The uncritical celebration of the USSR in the style of Nieto Caballero, Dangond and Canal Ramírez was not representative of Colombian or Latin American Christians. Mystical Catholicism and the widespread hope of redemption, however, led some conservative Catholics to believe that the Soviet Union was perhaps not a perfect place, but at least better than the materialist, soulless West. In all the travelogues presented in this section a deep contempt resonated for the decadent and immoral western Europe and North America, its

---

[116] Gonzalo Canal Ramírez, *La Unión Soviética: reto moral* (Bogotá: Imprenta y Rotograbado, 1969), pp. 11, 38, 69, 76–7, 140, 175.

[117] V. Vanin, 'Review of "Gonzalo Canal Ramírez; La Unión Soviética: reto moral"', *América Latina* 1 (1973), 182–5.

[118] Aldunate, *En Moscú*, p. 90.

[119] Miró Quesada, *La otra mitad del mundo*, p. 60; Miguel Otero Silva, *México y la revolución mexicana: un escritor venezolano en la Unión Soviética* (Caracas: Universidad Central de Venezuela, 1966), p. 33.

[120] E.g. Angel Rama, *Los poetas modernistas en el mercado económico* (Montevideo: Universidad de la República, 1967).

incomprehensible modern art and music, its increasing sexual libertarianism and even tolerance towards homosexuality, drugs, its confused and disoriented youth and their excesses and superficial amusements.[121] That Canal Ramírez usually referred to 'Russia' rather than to 'the Soviet Union' in itself points at a new, or rather very old, mystifying perception of eastern Europe that resurfaced in the course of the 1970s.

The liberal flirtation with illiberalism

Some conservatives and Catholics, who deplored the loss of tradition and spirituality through western influence on their own societies, displayed sympathy for the traditional elements of Soviet society. Another group of Latin American intellectuals, more in line with worldwide progressive-optimistic sentiments of the 1950s and 1960s, still hailed modernisation. They, too, found that the Soviet Union offered something they were missing at home. Left liberal thinkers, writers and politicians sought national progress and reform of their political systems, their constitutions and their societies. Liberal more in the American than the European sense, they came mostly from the rather developed and comparatively rich countries of the hemisphere, and they had no particular interest in communism, but were reform-oriented with somewhat social-democratic ideals. Dictatorships had ended all over the Americas, which lead to a general optimism among many of the countries' intellectual elites and a widespread sense of raised expectations. A communications revolution spread information on the higher living standards in the western world, and a demographic boom and the introduction of universal suffrage drew masses of peasants to the big cities all over Latin America, where they sought better lives and demanded political participation. Latin American cities had to cope with an influx of mostly illiterate new citizens and their immediate need for modernised infrastructure.

The Latin American liberals were, just like the leftists, usually white males from a long-established upper middle class. And they, equally, acknowledged that the Soviet Union had made tremendous progress in fields they wanted to see improved within their own countries, most notably the expansion of the education system and state health care. Some of these liberals went to the USSR to see for themselves and wrote about their impressions for an audience back home. José Guilherme Mendes was a young journalist for several Brazilian newspapers when

[121] Canal, *La Unión Soviética*.

he went to Moscow in 1955. The populist dictator Getúlio Vargas had just committed suicide and Brazil had started its decade of development-alism with huge state campaigns for the modernisation of the country. Mendes wrote a series of essays on all aspects of life in the USSR and eastern Europe, which were published in Brazil as *Moscou, Varsóvia, Berlim: o povo nas ruas* (Moscow, Warsaw, Berlin: The People in the Streets).[122]

The industrial and agricultural development in the USSR palpably impressed the Brazilian visitor. After a tour through Stalingrad, Mendes commended the quick and effective reconstruction after the Second World War. In Armenia and Azerbaijan, he marvelled at the electrification programme and the education and health care systems. Illiteracy – in 1920 still at the same low level as in contemporary Brazil – had been erased here, he was told, and people flocked to museums and libraries that had been built in every little town of the formerly agrarian and 'backward' Transcaucasian republics. Like many other visitors, Mendes had never come across such deep knowledge about his native country abroad, and every single person he met knew at least Jorge Amado and the Brazilian Communist Party boss Luis Carlos Prestes.

During his two-and-a-half-month trip, Mendes analysed not only the political system and the administration. With a great deal of empathy, he also described people's habits, lifestyles and opinions of their country as he, knowing some Russian, perceived them in numerous personal con-tacts and conversations. The Soviets were 'indeed a new type of man' for Mendes, all obvious shortcomings notwithstanding, they – while in great fear of a new war – appeared proud and patriotic: 'no power in this world will be able to topple this Soviet system. It has become inherent to this country as parliamentarism has to the West.' People seemed very friendly and open whenever he talked to them. Yet they tended to avoid a second meeting out of fear of being seen regularly with a potentially hostile foreigner – a phenomenon many other travellers to Soviet Union described throughout its existence. Mendes did note several negative aspects of life in the USSR. He found the controlled media terrible, the television boring and the much-praised Soviet cinema mediocre at best. In contrast to Soviet perceptions of the Third World as entirely under-developed, the Brazilian considered many aspects of the Soviet Union – the average living standards or the way people dressed – as 'backwards' or 'uncivilised'. In a debate with Ilya Ehrenburg, both agreed that much of Soviet architecture was simply ugly. Compared to many leftist – or

---

[122] Mendes, *Moscou, Varsóvia, Berlim*.

Catholic – visitors, he neither expected nor described a metaphysically superior society, but criticised many other repressive or appalling aspects of the Soviet state. Yet the quick state-led modernisation of the country and its recuperation after the devastating war, the expansion of the health care system and an education system that eradicated illiteracy not only among the urban masses but also in formerly underdeveloped regions of the country's periphery impressed the liberal journalist, whose home country was confronted with rather similar challenges. Mendes accordingly concluded after his trip: the Soviet Union 'is neither hell nor paradise'.[123]

His compatriot, the journalist Nestor de Holanda (1921–70), visited Moscow, Leningrad, Kiev, Tashkent and Tbilisi in 1959. Aleksandr Alekseev, official GKKS guide and later ambassador to Cuba, was initially very sceptical about his protégé. 'He has very vague ideas about the Soviet Union ... and asked a lot of provocative questions that I refused to answer', he wrote in the obligatory report to his superiors.[124] But Alekseev's concerns were unfounded. More than any other liberal Latin American visitor to the USSR, de Holanda was taken in by the official programme staged for him. His suspicious, critical stance in the beginning gave way to one of the most enthusiastic reports on the USSR ever written by a non-communist. De Holanda's travelogue *O mundo vermelho: notas de um Repórter na URSS* (The Red World: Notes of a Reporter in the USSR) became a multi-edition best-seller that uncritically celebrated the USSR for its readers in developmentalist Brazil, shortly before the left populist presidents Quadros and Goulart established diplomatic relations with countries of the eastern bloc and sought to modernise their country with state-led campaigns. De Holanda's descriptions of life in the Soviet Union began as rather objective and distant in the first half of the book, as they repeated only standard facts on the history, geography, climate and infrastructure of the Soviet Union. De Holanda, too, was palpably pleased at how well informed Soviet citizens were about the rest of the world and Brazil in particular; everyone in the Soviet Union appeared to love Brazilian football and Amado, and everyone knew the current Brazilian president Kubitschek and his project to build a new capital in the highlands of inner Brazil. A poignant moment for de Holanda occurred in an Uzbek library: he found, in the midst of Central Asia, all volumes of his beloved Brazilian author Antônio Frederico de Castro Alves on the book shelf. All these references to his home country plus several well-paid offers to publish in Soviet

---

[123] *Ibid.*, pp. 9, 18, 20, 40–4, 51, 80.   [124] Jul. 1959, GARF f.9518 op.1 d.322 l.143.

newspapers were very flattering, and his guide Alekseev seems to have done a good job, too. More and more, de Holanda absorbed many clichés of Soviet self-representation. Prostitution had been eradicated, he claimed, and alcoholism and crime were well on the way to becoming extinct. Women were free, productive and still chaste, truthful and kind. Soviet cultural life was colourful and as international as in the West. Transport and hotels were cheap, and Soviet citizens travelled a lot. This progress of the Soviet Union, compared in a flood of statistics with the predominantly agrarian tsarist Russia of fifty years before, truly left an impression on the Brazilian visitor.[125]

In order to share his experience with even more Brazilian readers, de Holanda wrote another book, *Diálogo Brasil–URSS* (Dialogue Brazil–USSR).[126] He had collected questions by anti-communists and politically indifferent Brazilians before his departure to Moscow and forwarded them to Soviet citizens he met during his trip – 'without any interference of the state', de Holanda claimed, but of course always with an official translator present. One hundred of these questions and answers were collected in the book. Soviet housewives explained to Brazilian housewives how they did their shopping and how they raised their children. A Catholic priest in Moscow assured his Brazilian colleague that he was absolutely free to practise his religion. Factory workers responded likewise to factory workers, politicians to politicians, judges to judges and children to children in their best Soviet speech. Soviet journalists assured their Brazilian counterparts that complete freedom of the press prevailed and they themselves decided what to print and what not ('I have never seen a censor in my life!'). Artists defended the Soviet state's hostile position towards abstractionism. One of the most obvious untruths de Holanda believed and forwarded was an answer to the question as to why Soviet people could not travel abroad: 'I am very surprised indeed at this question', a random man in the street allegedly had responded to de Holanda; 'We all are free to travel anywhere we want to. Whoever does not acknowledge that has no idea about the Soviet Union.'

De Holanda managed to remain a respected journalist in Brazil for all his blind following of the Soviet Union. While other benevolent observers also pointed out repressive or ineffective elements of the Soviet model, de Holanda, in 1963, wrote yet another book, *Como seria o Brasil socialista?* (What Would a Socialist Brazil Look Like?), which suggested

---

[125] Holanda, *O mundo vermelho*, pp. 80–1, 118, 135, 207–8.
[126] Nestor de Holanda, *Diálogo Brasil–URSS* (Rio de Janeiro: Editôra Civilização Brasileira, 1962).

reforms for all parts of Brazilian society and politics along Soviet lines. De Holanda incorporated not only political ideas but also Soviet language into his work, and he, still claiming not to be a communist, worked with the Brazilian Communist Party on several book projects for Soviet publishing houses.[127]

The Brazilian fascination with Soviet modernisation programmes lasted even when, in 1964, a putsch ended Goulart's presidency and the subsequent military government persecuted communists and leftists throughout the country. Genival Rabelo, originally a left liberal journalist, now collaborated with the new regime in the field of development politics, and travelled to the Soviet Union in 1967. In his travelogue *No outro lado do mundo: a vida na URSS* (In the Other Part of the World: Life in the Soviet Union), he boasted: 'I have visited 17 towns, big and small, starting with Moscow which has a population of about 7 million and ending with Neftyane Kamny, an oil town of only 5,000 . . . I have been to different republics, seen factories and mills, schools, dwellings, homes for the aged, sanatoria and health resorts, power stations, sports clubs, research institutes, and churches. I have spoken freely to people holding responsible posts in that country, and with workers, peasants, students and clergymen.' Visiting construction sites, oil derricks in Baku, airports and giant dams in Siberia, he revelled in the progress in gender roles, health and child care and the highest proportion of students on earth. He stressed the tempestuous growth of culture in Transcaucasia, noting that Azerbaijan had more than twenty higher educational institutions, an Academy of Sciences, and one hundred plus newspapers. Due to his origins in the huge country of Brazil, Rabelo was enthusiastic about the civilisation that came with Soviet power to the former backwoods and unexplored areas of Siberia: 'as late as the thirties, Siberia was a neglected land, a predominantly agrarian area, like Brazil. Now that it is being electrified, its heavy industry is growing rapidly. It is producing steel. Many labour processes are being mechanised. It will not be long before Siberia really becomes one of the richest places in the world. Even today it provides 90 per cent of the Soviet Union's hydropower resources and 80 per cent of its timber wealth.' Soviet people seemed very hospitable to Rabelo: 'they are very much interested in the Brazilian people', and they appeared eager to learn about life in other countries and displayed a feeling of internationalism and fraternal concern for the working people of the world.

---

[127] Nestor de Holanda, *Como seria o Brasil socialista?* (Rio de Janeiro: Editôra Civilização Brasileira, 1963).

Rabelo's account, like de Holanda's, was very benevolent, but it was not overly ideologised. He did see and describe the mediocre living standards, the small number of private cars and the prevalence of prostitution. But he welcomed the ostensible irreversibility of socialist development, 'not only due to the strength of the state, but because Soviet citizens want it'. Rabelo perceived the Soviet people as happy and free to travel, work, love and enjoy the amenities of life. Rabelo's take on the Soviet Union was a mix of a western revisionism and a typical Third World view. He believed the Soviet Union to be a generic industrial state with impressive achievements that were much more recognisable from a southern than a western perspective. His overall take is remarkable: 'twenty more years, and the Soviet Union will be the most progressive and happiest country on earth'.[128] With this conclusion, Rabelo's colleague and Sovietophile de Holanda could easily agree, and he wrote the introduction to the book. The Iron Curtain did exist, de Holanda believed, but the curtain rail was on the western side.

While de Holanda's uncritical embrace of the Soviet Union remained an exception among Latin American liberal intellectuals, several other observers from the liberal political consensus wrote accounts of their trips to the Soviet Union. Like Mendes or Rabelo, they were usually critical of many aspects, but made no secret of their fascination for successes in the modernisation of the infrastructure of a formerly predominantly underdeveloped country. Raúl Aldunate (1906–79) was a member of the Chilean authors' association and a parliamentarian for the liberal party in the National Congress in Santiago. A former career in the military had taken him all around the world; in 1959, he spent some time in the Soviet Union and wrote a travelogue, *En Moscú* (In Moscow), based on his impressions. Explicitly distancing himself from both communist eulogies and demonisations of the USSR, he described his experience in extensive detail. He went as a private man to the Soviet Union, which made obtaining a visa a difficult and protracted procedure – very different from the invited friends of the Soviet Union, who were supplied and supported from the very beginning. Once in Moscow, Aldunate claimed, he was free to go wherever he wanted, albeit only in the company of his guide and translator. He noted the enormous efforts the Soviets kept expending to portray themselves as positively as possible towards foreigners. This pride was not limited to officials. Ordinary people also reacted very sensitively when he – always in the presence of the official translator – questioned some of the Soviet feats he was

---

[128] Rabelo, *No outro lado do mundo*, pp. 2, 5, 91, 193, 238.

presented. Aldunate, however, was not overly critical in any case. People to him seemed to live better lives than fifty years before. At least in part due to their biased opinion about the outside world, Soviet citizens appeared to him proud and content. Walking through the poorer Moscow neighbourhoods, Aldunate was pleased not to see any beggars and the misery he knew from Latin America's big cities. His negative impressions included the masculinised appearance of Soviet women and the precocious lectures by Soviet students he met at the Latin American department of the Moscow State University. And in a conversation where no translator was necessary, he learned more of the downsides of life in the Soviet Union: he met Argentine and Chilean communists, who had given up their citizenship in order to live in the socialist utopia with a Soviet passport. They had long lost their revolutionary idealism, but now were stuck in the USSR.

Aldunate had never shared their utopian idealist view of the Soviet Union but summed up his impressions from the USSR in a very positive light anyway: the Chilean liberal was very enthusiastic about the progress the Soviets had made in their educational and scientific systems. He described Soviet political decision makers as intelligent, well meaning and capable. The Soviet Union, according to Aldunate, had contributed positively to peace on earth and suffered only from a biased and ignorant perception by the rest of the world.[129]

The Peruvian Francisco Miró Quesada (1918–), who also went to the Soviet Union in 1959, was more critical of Soviet realities in his best-selling travelogue *La otra mitad del mundo: la Unión Soviética* (The Other Half of the World: The Soviet Union), whose title already made clear to which part of the planet he felt he belonged. Life especially in the Soviet countryside, Miró Quesada felt, was very monotonous and over-regimented. In a conversation with *Izvestija* editor Aleksej Adžubej ('actually a very smart guy') he criticised heavily the lack of freedom in Soviet media ('the press was the worst thing I saw in Russia'). Adžubej tried to defend and explain the Soviet idea of freedom of the press as something genuinely different from what it meant in the West, something that meant true freedom. In front of the entire chief editorship of *Izvestija*, Miró Quesada asked why, in this case, the Soviet press, even though allegedly always representing the interest of the people, had never criticised Stalin. There was palpable turmoil in the office, he recalled, and no one dared to answer his question. While the Peruvian communists in Miró Quesada's group ('actually intelligent and affable people') found

---

[129] Aldunate, *En Moscú*, pp. 41, 50, 98, 110.

everything they saw in the USSR 'maravilloso', Miró Quesada also insistently criticised the treatment of Pasternak and the occupation of eastern Europe.

Yet in several editions of his book up until the 1980s (The Other Half of the World: Thirty Years Later),[130] Miró Quesada explained why he, like many other Latin American liberal intellectuals, found the Soviet Union an interesting place anyway: 'the enormous technical achievements of the Soviet Union greatly interested the Latin American public. We should not believe that this has to do with communist leanings. On the contrary, most of us are not communists, but people who are fed up being swathed in the confusing fog of systematic campaigns of distortion, campaigns that are run in order to keep our country in its miserable situation.' The at least decent living standards of even the poorest and the apparent gender equality was to Miró Quesada's liking, as was the 'existence of a collective spirit that leads the masses to a defined goal'. His hopes for Peru lay in an organisation that would end the exploitation of men by men in a similar way. All his detailed criticism of Soviet realities notwithstanding, Miró Quesada drew a surprisingly positive conclusion about the achievements of the Soviet state.[131]

In his *Viaje a Rusia y a otros países socialistas* (Voyage to Russia and Other Socialist Countries), the Spanish-born Argentine liberal Joaquín Torres, too, initially reported rather critically about his Soviet experience.[132] The first parts of the book contain constant complaints about bad food, terrible service in shops and restaurants, the climate, the way people are dressed, the boring media, the lack of entertainment and the absurdity of different classes in trains and airplanes in an ostensibly classless society. Just like Miró Quesada's, however, his description showed ever more sympathy as he proceeded. After some days in the Soviet Union, and probably after having overcome a serious cultural shock, he increasingly acquired a liking for many aspects of life in the USSR. Illiteracy had been eradicated, he noted, and the mostly very well-educated Soviet citizens spoke many languages, often including Spanish. His guides explained without hesitation that this had been the result of a Soviet education policy in which free training in more than a hundred languages was given to more than 1.8 million students in schools and at universities. The Soviet Union, Torres learnt, printed more than 278 million books a year and produced 7,246 journals. More numbers rained down on him, on agriculture, industrial output, ethnicities, some number more doctors and engineers than in the United States – and

---

[130] Miró Quesada, *La otra mitad del mundo.*   [131] *Ibid.*, pp. 10, 45, 49, 68, 86, 108.
[132] Torres, *Viaje a Rusia y a otros países socialistas.*

Torres conveyed them to his readers. Like many other non-communist liberal observers, Torres was impressed by the education system, the free health care and the well-functioning public transport system in the Soviet Union.

Another traveller in this spirit was was Miguel Otero Silva (1908–85), an author, journalist, editor and humourist, whose work was translated and distributed in the Soviet Union. He had been a member of the Venezuelan Communist Party, but had left its ranks in 1949, appalled by its dogmatism during late Stalinism. As the left liberal he developed into, he maintained an interest in the Soviet Union and travelled there shortly after Khrushchev's dismissal. Like many other writers, Otero Silva began his *Un escritor venezolano en la Unión Soviética* (A Venezuelan Writer in the Soviet Union)[133] by dissociating himself from all other travellers before him: 'observers usually to go to the Soviet Union in two different ways, both prejudiced. Some come to find everything despicable, discover starving masses and gagged people ... The others are like Muslim pilgrims to Mecca, prostrating before each and every smokestack that rises in front of their steps, poor sinners returned to the terrestrial paradise.' Otero Siva himself claimed to give a completely objective account instead. He declined the offer of special treatment by the Union of Soviet Writers and instead travelled on the usual tourist routes through the USSR. He found Moscow a terribly ugly city and believed he felt the legacies of Stalinism in many aspects of Soviet life, from art policies to people's behaviour in public.

While some Latin American Catholics had found the messianic spirit in Russia attractive, the ex-communist Otero Silva found fault with the quasi-religious worship of Lenin. 'People actually venerate him with a devotion comparable to the Christians who go to Jerusalem ... like the enlightened apostle of universal communism.' But in this prevailing spirit, he also saw parallels with the United States. Compared to the latter, Otero Silva pointed out, the general living standard was much lower, but there were no slums and 'ghettos like those of the negroes in Los Angeles'. There was no hunger and no misery, and, considering where this country had stood fifty years before, this was great progress. The experience of the Civil War and the Second World War, an observation many other travellers to the Soviet Union made around that time, had resulted in a great desire for peace in the population.[134] This cautious praise of the USSR, far from the eulogies of de Holanda or some Catholics, was enough to win Otero Silva the Lenin Peace Prize in 1979.

---

[133] Otero Silva, *México y la revolución mexicana.*   [134] *Ibid.*, pp. 33, 37, 54.

The Colombian Mario Laserna Pinzón (1923–2013), finally, combined many characteristics of a Latin American *intelectual*: he was a widely travelled writer and a university professor, founder of Bogotá's Universidad de los Andes, the first independent private university in Latin America – and he was also a politician and a diplomat. In 1966, he embarked on a trip to Moscow, Leningrad, Kiev and Tbilisi. In a verbose essay before his trip, Laserna Pinzón had explored his and the world's interest in the Soviet Union and put it in the context of other exemplary theories or utopian societies in the European history of ideas from Christianity to the Enlightenment and the French Revolution. 'We are interested in the USSR', was one of his philosophical conclusions, 'because it is an experiment, a particular example of a general theory that men with political power must implement ... be they Marxist-Leninist communists or not, under threat of disappearing from the course of history, or even from mankind.' His initial concern about how he would be treated in the USSR was soothed by a friend: 'no need to worry, as soon as they learn that you are South American, they will associate you with Cuba, and you will be very popular!'[135] Laserna Pinzón seems to have been treated very hospitably during his trip, since he returned to Colombia 'with a huge sense of admiration for the positive moral and human qualities of the inhabitants of the Soviet Union ... Independently of my political opinion, I have to say: it was impressive what the government has done for the benefit of their people. What I saw there is meaningful for the problems of today's Colombia.'[136]

Laserna Pinzón's judgement focuses on an important factor that shaped the perception of the Soviet Union by Latin American liberal intellectuals. None of them, not even de Holanda – whose uncritical embrace remained an exception anyway – cared much about the communist character of the Soviet regime. They were interested in Moscow's success in the modernisation of the country, because they sought inspiration on how to cope with concrete problems in their own states. The Brazilians, with large-scale urbanisation and industrialisation programmes at home, looked at the Soviet Union not as a communist paradise or hell, but as a state that had only just – within not more than a few decades – crossed the threshold to becoming a modern society. Laserna Pinzón was merely one of many liberal Colombians who were deeply impressed by the progress of the Soviet state against the

---

[135] Mario Laserna Pinzón, 'Formas de viajar a la Unión Soviética', *Razón y Fábula* 4 (1967), 57–66.
[136] Mario Laserna Pinzón, 'El Doctor Laserna en la URSS', *Boletín del Instituto Cultural Colombo Soviético* 1 (1966), 9.

dominance of the church in politics and society. And with a long tradition of classical European education, first of all in Bogotá, the 'Athens of South America', the Colombians were deeply impressed especially by the education of the masses in the Soviet Union, a fascination that lasted until the 1970s and crossed all political boundaries. Most Latin American liberals at that time had a highly nuanced view of the Soviet Union. They did not repudiate it nor did they uncritically embrace it; instead they displayed an interest in certain aspects they considered relevant for their own countries. In a similar way to his compatriot Aldunate and to many other visitors from all over Latin America, the Chilean minister of health told his guides during a 1966 visit to Moscow: 'I have a special interest in the Soviet Union due to its continuous experience of almost half a century in maintaining functioning social systems.'[137]

Exoticism in reverse

Latin American liberals continued to travel to and write about the Soviet Union throughout the 1970s, yet gradually the fascination with certain achievements of the Soviet state faded in favour of a completely depoliticised view – a view that ironically mirrored the way the Soviets had looked upon Latin America a decade before, as it exoticised a distant and strange area of the world. Pedro Gómez Valderrama, a novelist, later a liberal state councillor and Colombian minister of education, was sent to represent his country as ambassador to Moscow in the late 1960s. After his return, he summed up his experiences in *Los ojos del burgués: un año en la Unión Soviética* (The Eyes of the Bourgeois: One Year in the Soviet Union).[138] Gómez Valderrama considered his stay in the USSR 'a fascinating experience from an intellectual and human point of view' and was in general quite positive about life in the Soviet Union and about its founding father Lenin, 'the most important man of the twentieth century'. Soviet citizens appeared to him content and proud of their country. On the one hand, Gómez Valderrama compared, as many had before him, Latin America's problems and challenges to those of prerevolutionary Russia, namely social imbalance, poverty and illiteracy, and acknowledged Soviet success in overcoming these problems: 'I see this country, at this moment, not like a country of extreme revolution, but as the country of a very vigorous realisation of the propositions that initiated the socialist revolution. I see this happening with respect and admiration.'

---

[137] 3 May 1966, GARF f.9518 op.1 d.1017 l.141.
[138] Gómez Valderrama, *Los ojos del burgués*.

Now in the early 1970s, however, the liberal flirtation with Soviet methods of state-induced modernisation had given way to a cooler, more distant analysis. Instead of suggesting the implementation of some Soviet policies in the Americas, Gómez Valerrama merely came to the Soviets' defence against exaggerated hostility from the West: 'much of what is being criticised is simply incomprehensible from a bourgeois point of view ... the western world believes that, under communist serfdom, 200 million starving people crave the downfall of socialism and a western lifestyle. The reality is different. We should not confuse de-Stalinisation with westernisation.' The Soviet model was no longer considered particularly inspiring for Latin American needs, but seen as a fascinating, yet completely different world: 'this is one of the most stable countries on this globe', Gómez Valderrama explained, 'with major economic, political and social possibilities ... Next to a disoriented western Europe, the giant Russian bear has simply, after 1,000 years of sleep on the right side, turned around and will now continue to sleep unwaveringly on the left side.' In addition to the reference to the 'Russian bear', Gómez dedicated many more pages of his memoirs not to political issues or possible inspirations from the Soviet Union, but to topoi of Old Mother Russia, as he pondered Russian literature, described Orthodox churches in the countryside or winter life in Moscow.[139]

Against the geo-political backdrop of *détente*, the perception of the Soviet Union lost some of its ideological edge. Most major Latin American states had built up diplomatic relations with the USSR and, in 1973, the Mexican president Luis Echeverría went for the first official visit of a non-socialist Latin American head of state to the Soviet Union. He got the usual tour for friends of the Soviet Union, which took him to Moscow, Leningrad, Irkutsk and the hydroelectric power plant near Bratsk. During a meeting with Nikolaj Podgorny (chairman of the Supreme Soviet) and Brezhnev, the latter appeared very interested in Mexican model of one-party rule with the co-optation of potential adversaries into the Partido Revolucionario Institucional (PRI). First arrangements were made that led to economic co-operation agreements between Mexico and the socialist Council for Mutual Economic Assistance (Comecon) two years later.

Two Mexican journalists were included in Echeverría's entourage and wrote books about their trip that, like Gómez Valderrama with his Russian bear, showed less fascination for the political system of the Soviet Union than for the exoticism of the country they were visiting.

---

[139] *Ibid.*, pp. 10, 25, 52, 191, 195.

The journalist and novelist Luis Spota (1925–85) described, in his travelogue *El viaje* (The Voyage), his long-standing dream of finally seeing
the USSR. With some sympathy, he noted reasonable living standards,
especially the absence of slums and *favelas*. There was freedom of religion, he believed, and a very anti-*machismo* attitude towards women.
Some years after the 1968 student protests in Mexico (as former minister
of the interior, Echeverría had actually been responsible for the massacre
of Tlatelolco), Spota noted that students in the Soviet Union were very
quiet and unsuspicious. Ordinary Soviet citizens he saw as no different
from those anywhere else in the world. On the negative side, Spota felt
confronted by very offensive prostitution and constant surveillance by
secret agents.[140] An episode with his guide and translator Sergej illustrates how little the Latin American visitors still saw the Soviet Union as a
role model – and just how little the Soviets realised that: during a wine-
tasting, the young Russian explained that Soviet champagne was the best
in the world. One of the Mexicans interposed ironically that in France
they made a decent copy of it. 'This is possible', answered Sergej; 'the
entire world imitates us. They make vodka in Poland, they make caviar in
Iran – and now socialism in Cuba and Chile.'[141]

In the same entourage as Spota travelled another renowned Mexican
left liberal journalist, María Luisa Mendoza (1930–). She, too, was very
excited about her trip: '¡Dios mío, estoy en Rusia!' ('Oh my God, I am in
Russia!'), was her first awestruck thought at the airport. More than any
other book, her travelogue allows us to comprehend how much the
perception of the USSR by most Latin American intellectuals had
changed. Mendoza dropped reflections on socialism and Soviet modernisation altogether, and wrote a colourful booklet full of stereotypical
depictions of Russia with matrioshka dolls and onion-domed towers.
The title alone speaks volumes: *Raaa reee riii rooo Rusia: la URSS* needs
no translation and went a long way from de Holanda's fantasies about the
Sovietisation of Brazil. Mendoza was now in line with old European
exoticising assessments of Mother Russia: 'trying to explain it is non-
sense; it is made for novels'. Like the Catholic visitor Gonzalo Canal
Ramírez, Mendoza hardly used the term 'Soviet Union' and described
'Russia' as some fairy-tale place without commercials, criminality, traffic
jams, beggars and drugs. The population, including the youngsters in the
streets, appeared to her like anywhere else on the planet. But what the
West liked to criticise so much about Russia was, according to Mendoza,

---

[140] Luis Spota, *El viaje* (Mexico City: Joaquin Moritz, 1973), pp. 121–210.
[141] *Ibid.*, p. 208.

precisely what made it idiosyncratic.[142] The novelist Sergio Pitol (1933–), who lived in Moscow in the 1970s as Mexico's cultural attaché, shared these apolitical sentiments towards the Soviet Union: he felt as if he were in a novel by Tolstoy and adored 'this incredibly exotic atmosphere: snow, sledges, family life in Moscow and in the countryside … tea and cakes'; Russian literature became 'a very important part of his life'.[143] By the end of the 1970s, Latin American reformist liberals still found literary inspiration and exotic adventures in the Soviet Union. As an alternative political model, however, the USSR had served its time.

From the mid 1950s on, many visitors who belonged to Latin America's liberal political spectrum had come to the Soviet Union, some officially invited, some on self-financed trips, with much curiosity about the developmentalist policies of the Soviet state. Most found a lot to criticise about life in real existing socialism; they noted the lack of freedom, a clichéd conception of the world abroad and a grey and sad atmosphere in the streets. Yet none of the reports is confrontational, and many observers throughout the 1950s and 1960s were impressed by certain accomplishments of the Soviet Union, which they saw from the background of specific problems in their own countries. Literacy rates and the omnipresence of free education and affordable high culture was a feat all visitors esteemed highly. A typical observation from Latin American visitors concerned the absence of *favelas*, of slums as they knew them from their home countries, with their serious poverty and misery.

As a matter of course, the judgement of the Soviet Union depended always on the national, social and ethnic background of the visitor. The liberal intellectuals presented in this section were all from relatively developed countries of the Americas, from Argentina, Brazil, Chile, Mexico and Venezuela. Their conception of the Soviet Union differed clearly from reports by visitors from Bolivia or Nicaragua also presented above. There is hardly a trace in the liberals' reports of the utopian idealisation that *indigenista* leftists still displayed towards Khrushchev's Soviet Union. In addition, the metaphysical, spiritual, anti-western, anti-pluralist, anti-materialist dimension that some conservatives and Catholics found appealing in the Soviet Union is absent in the writings of the liberals. They were interested, throughout the 1960s, in concepts that might help them tackle concrete problems in their own countries. The most enthusiastic reports about the Soviet Union were written in Brazil

---

[142] María Luisa Mendoza, *Raaa reee riii rooo Rusia: la URSS* (Mexico City: Fondo de Cultura Económica, 1974), p. 30.
[143] Kutejščikova, *Moskva-Meksiko-Moskva*, pp. 336–7.

with its many geographic and demographic commonalities – and with both left reformers and military dictators using Soviet methods of enforced development. The typical assessment of the Soviet Union by Latin American liberals commended the feats and the positive spirit of a peace-loving population and the – at least in theory – human spirit of the state ideology, but even more the concrete accomplishments in the fields of education, health care and infrastructure.

Towards the end of the 1960s, most of the visitors still drew rather positive conclusions about the present and future of the USSR, yet they also made it clear that they considered the Soviet model good for the Soviet Union, but not for Latin America. Hundreds of thousands of Latin Americans read these travelogues and subscribed to this respectful view of the Soviet state. Moscow Party and state archives are full of letters written by ordinary Latinos who felt the need to share their admiration of Sputnik and Gagarin, or of the free health and education systems. Many liberal newspapers all over the continent reported, not uncritically, but very favourably about Soviet endeavours and achievements. This respectful view lasted well into the 1970s, but, increasingly, a depoliticised view of Russia gained the upper hand, a view that stood in continuity with an old European tradition of exoticising the East as an irrational, non-western realm of the anti-modern. Soviet leaders still praised their progressive state, but few cared to listen.

A complex disenchantment: Soviet internationalism, intellectuals and new socialist horizons

In the larger picture, the history of Latin American intellectuals and their perception of the Soviet Union after Stalin is a history of a loss of utopia. In detail, things are much more complicated, and Soviet efforts to win people's support for their state were not all in vain. The almost metaphysical view of the USSR as a communist mecca or a redeeming utopia, however, came to an end during the Thaw. Many leftists, including some explicitly anti-Stalinist Marxists, still – temporarily – had great hopes in the future of de-Stalinised communism. Yet peaceful coexistence was, on the one hand, too conservative a concept for Latin American intellectuals with socialist revolution on their mind. On the other hand, the invasions of Hungary in 1956 and, more so, Czechoslovakia in 1968 ended the remaining idealist illusions about the character of the Soviet state for most Latin Americans as much as for the west Europeans.

But with the paradise lost, the interest changed from socialist romanticism to a more pragmatic view. Latin American intellectuals during the Cold War were still very interested in certain achievements and features of the Soviet state. Three main lines of argument have crystallised out of the analysed travelogues and memoirs: firstly, an interest in the Soviet development concept that promised a path to industrial modernity that was not based on the unattainable model of western Europe and the United States. Liberal middle-class Latin Americans saw some inspiration in the Soviet Union until well into the 1970s: travellers were impressed by Soviet industrial output, by Soviet technology, by the modernisation of the 'backward' periphery, electrification programmes and hydroelectric power plants. They also commended the ostensible gender equality and the progressive family law (while, at the same time, conservatives were glad to see traditional family values and laws intact in the same country). More than anything else, however, liberal observers were interested in the Soviet education system, its successful literacy campaigns, schools and universities. This fascination prevailed throughout the history of the USSR, though, from the 1970s, an exoticising view of the Soviet Union gained popularity among many travellers, who perceived the Soviet state in continuity with the irrational and mystical Mother Russia. The second line of interest was directed against the West as well, but was the very opposite of trust in modernisation: increasingly from the 1960s, Latin American Catholic, conservative and indigenous authors identified with what they perceived as an anti-materialist spirit in the Soviet Union. Thirdly, with their interpretations of the distant Soviet Union, Latin American intellectuals also debated their own role within their societies, as they all admired the high status of intellectual work in the USSR.

An important factor in the perception of the Soviet Union was the author's origin. Latin America with its position in between South and West demonstrates clearly the different perceptions of the USSR in the respective world areas. The absence of misery and starvation, and the provision of running water in all buildings, for example, impressed hardly any western visitors in the 1960s. For Third World observers, in contrast, these achievements were of immediate relevance. More than western visitors, who usually went to see the Soviet Union as an end in itself, the Latin Americans always drew parallels with their home countries: David Siqueiros thought Georgia looked like Mexico and the women like those from the Caribbean. Gabriel García Márquez, who visited the Soviet Union many more times in the 1970s and 1980s, thought rural Russia looked like Colombia. Fausto Reinaga equated the Russian *mužik* and the Bolivian *campesino*. According to José Mendes, the Armenian capital Erevan and its inhabitants looked like a Brazilian city; the Argentine Joaquín Torres felt that all Armenians were like Latinos; and Genival Rabelo saw northern Brazilians in the Georgians.[144]

For Latin Americans with an indigenous background, the Soviet periphery with its own 'indigenous' majorities was particularly interesting. Some paralleled the Caucasus with its ancient high cultures that fell victim to 'imperialist aggression' with the history of Central American and Andean countries. Interestingly, no one ever said a critical word about Soviet modernisation of the periphery, after all an act of imperialism in its own right. Most western fellow travellers went to the Soviet Union to celebrate the modernisation of Russia, not for inspiration for their own societies. For Third World visitors after Stalinism, this is certainly not the case. They went to get inspiration for the improvement of the situation in the countries they came from. The Colombian traveller María Mercedes Carranza called this *El discreto encanto del socialismo* (The Secret Appeal of Socialism).[145] She knew very well of the many downsides of life in the Soviet Union, but argued in a conversation with a French diplomat, who complained bitterly about the sad and grim country: 'I see all this with very different eyes – the eyes of an underdeveloped country that rotates in an orbit of influence which determines it economically. Ours is a very different case from the European one ... I recommend that you always write two letters back to Paris, one from your perspective, and one that corresponds to our point of view. We do not care about the spies and the grain trade. Our problems are very far away from that and do not belong to this dimension ... In the Soviet Union, at least, no one suffers from hunger, they have enough doctors and they have eradicated illiteracy and prostitution.'

The guides from Soviet internationalist organisations did a good job in creating a pro-Soviet stance among the visitors; the tenor of most travelogues is predominantly positive. As part of renewed Soviet internationalism after Stalin, the guided tours for Latin American intellectuals, like Soviet self-representation abroad and like the representation of the world abroad in the arts, drew on elements of socialist internationalism of the 1920s and 1930s, when – mostly western – visitors were invited by VOKS for organised visits to the young communist state. With their emphasis on technological and infrastructure achievements, however, both the Soviet organisers and the curious Latin American visitors (with the

---

[144] Stein, *Siqueiros*, p. 350; Rabelo, *No outro lado do mundo*, p. 90; Reinaga, *El sentimiento mesiánico del pueblo ruso*, p. 80; Mendes, *Moscou, Varsóvia, Berlim*, p. 213.

[145] María Mercedes Carranza, 'El discreto encanto del socialismo', *Nueva Frontera* 127 (1977), 23–4.

exception of the Catholics) operated in the context of a worldwide craze about progress and industrial development in the 1950s and 1960s. Travelling to the other side of the planet in order to learn about Soviet achievements, the Latin American intellectual travellers were part of the expanded cultural internationalism of the time.

Those visitors who lost their faith in the USSR usually did not do so during their trip but in reaction to Soviet higher politics or quarrels within their own communist parties. Meanwhile, many who went with neutral views returned home with a rather positive stance towards the USSR. Conflicts and problems did occur, of course, during the guided visits. Translators reported arrogant and bumptious behaviour of their protégés as well as embarrassing situations when terrible service in restaurants and hotels threatened to destroy the positive impressions carefully built up.[146] But, as a rule, the Soviet internationalist organisations were quite successful. It was not until the 1980s that really negative reports were written by Latin Americans about the Soviet Union. The only travelogue by a Latin American which actually describes a trip as a reason for apostasy was written by a young Mexican communist in 1980. Christopher Domínguez lost his faith entirely when his guides refused to respond to any conversation on Stalinism and the many flaws he saw during his trip: 'Ford-style exploitation of the workers', utterly unemancipated women, revolting anti-Semitism, alcoholism and finally 'Latvian communists who looked and behaved like the SS in their black uniforms'.[147] Domínguez became a social democrat after his Soviet trip.

Some Latin Americans kept their pro-Soviet stance until the very end. The Uruguayan communist writer Rodney Arismendi (1913–89) spent eight years in exile in the Soviet Union from the late 1970s to the early 1980s. He died just in time to avoid seeing his paradise fall apart. Pablo Neruda and David Siqueiros, too, maintained their enthusiasm for the Soviet Union until the day they died. Many other notable Latin American communists such as Luis Corvalán (1916–2010) or Volodia Teitelboim (1916–2008, in Moscow during Augusto Pinochet's reign, where he worked for Spanish-language radio) stayed faithful until death tore them from Moscow, and they were buried to the sounds of the 'Internationale'. Luís Carlos Prestes, head of the Brazilian Communist Party, spent ten years in a cherished Moscow exile with his family from 1970.

---

[146] E.g. Otčet o rabote s čilijskim pisatelem Manuelem Rochas v period s 5 do 27 maja 1966 goda, 7 Jul. 1966, GARF f.9518 op.1 d.1018 ll.2–14; O rabote s čilijskom poetom Chuvensio Val'e, 29 Nov. 1966, GARF f.9518 op.1 d.1021 ll.33–39.

[147] Christopher Domínguez Michael: Recuerdos del Partido Comunista (1999), www.letraslibres.com/index.php?art=6086 (last accessed 3 Nov. 2010).

But in the 1960s, many other leftists turned to Cuba as new socialist utopia. Unlike the grey Soviet Union, Cuba had many assets that made it a lot more appealing to a younger generation: it was much closer culturally, there was a romantic spirit, heroism in the mountains, young and good-looking leaders, a cheering people to the backdrop of a tropical paradise and sexy rhythms. Intellectuals all over continental Latin America were happy to see themselves celebrated and supported by Havana's Casa de las Américas publishing house. The enthusiasm was dampened palpably when Fidel Castro publicly approved of the invasion of Czechoslovakia in 1968. For many, the craze came to an end in 1971: the Cuban revolutionary leaders had the poet Heberto Padilla (1932–2000, himself in the Soviet Union from 1962 to 1964) arrested and forced him to an embarrassing Soviet-style *autocrítica*. It was the culmination of an ever more repressive atmosphere against critical artists in Cuba and caused many left intellectuals on the continent, most notably Mario Vargas Llosa, to lose faith also in ostensibly the last socialist utopia. Staunch anti-Soviet communists turned to China (especially in Peru) or Albania – the Brazilian Partido Comunista do Brasil (PCdoB) was to be the last remaining international friend of an otherwise completely isolated Albania in the 1980s. Yet contacts were never particularly intense and involved only a tiny minority of the Latin American left.

Some indigenous intellectuals idealised the Soviet Union in the utopian style of the 'westerners' before them as late as the 1960s. From the end of the decade, however, they turned to an explicitly anti-modern 'indigenous exceptionalism'. The fascination of conservatives and Catholics for the anti-modern, spiritual element they perceived in the Soviet Union cut in two directions. Some conservatives, like the Brazilian military rulers from the mid 1960s, developed a rather unspiritual interest in enforced modernisation through the state and the repressive techniques of power developed in Moscow.[148] Many Catholics, on the other hand, gave up conservatism and fought for not only spiritual, but also national and economic liberation. Catholic *guerrilleros*, however, were hardly interested in the stagnating old Soviet Union and found the Chinese model of armed struggle much more useful for their aims.

The Soviet Union gradually lost its position as a role model from the 1960s, if not as fast and directly as sometimes suggested. In the 1970s, few Latin American intellectuals outside the communist parties still cheered the socialist paradise. The Soviet Union remained, however,

---

[148] Tobias Rupprecht, 'Socialist High Modernity and Global Stagnation: A Shared History of Brazil and the Soviet Union during the Cold War', *Journal of Global History* 3 (2011), 505–28.

an object of fascination for many. Throughout its existence it inspired Latin American writers not only as a political alternative, but also in a literary way. Spanish and Portuguese poems by Pablo Neruda, Jorge Amado, Eduardo Lizalde, Roberto Cruz, Roque Dalton, Nicanor Parra and many more celebrating Lenin, Stalin, the USSR, the cosmonauts and Soviet internationalism are legion and filled Soviet literary journals. As late as 1986, the Mexican poet Roberto López Moreno wrote his 25-page 'Poema a la Unión Soviética' (Poem to the Soviet Union).[149] Though no longer a eulogy to Soviet feats, this Dadaist text juggled with names and motifs from sixty years of Soviet history. The short segment that introduced this chapter can be read as a mocking of the early fellow travellers and their adulation of Moscow, their *caja de emociones* (box of emotions). With 'Pablo. Efraín. / Hay una hora cuando cae el día' ('Pablo [Neruda]. Efraín [Morel]. / There is a time when the day draws to a close'), Moreno turned Neruda's verses against their own 'compromised' author. Irony or harsh criticisms of the 1980s, however, should not be projected back too straightforwardly on the perceptions and experiences of the decades before. This caveat goes just as much for one crucial element of Soviet internationalism after Stalin that comes under scrutiny in the next chapter. Just like the offspring of Pedro Jorge Vera and Gustavo Valcárcel, several thousand young Latin Americans received, throughout the Cold War, their higher education from Soviet universities. And, just like the grown-up intellectuals, these young Latin Americans, too, developed a different opinion of the Soviet Union from that of their western compatriots.

[149] López Moreno, *Poema a la Unión Soviética.*

From Russia with a diploma: Latin American
      students in the Soviet Union

If you want to produce a communist, send him to Paris; if a capitalist, send him to Moscow.

US Sovietologist Alvin Rubinstein[1]

It was definitely the best time of my life.

Luis Soto, Chilean student in Moscow, 1964–69[2]

Soviet higher education for foreigners, western fears and global reactions

In January 1965, the *New York Times* published a review of a book by Jan Carew, an Afro-Guyanese writer and activist alongside W. E. B. DuBois and Malcolm X in the global black civil rights movement. Carew had combined his experience from studying in Czechoslovakia in the late 1940s with reports he had heard in London from foreign students returning from Moscow, and had poured these impressions into the semi-autobiographical novel *Green Winter*, which portrayed the life of Third World students in the Soviet Union. According to the *New York Times* review, this life must have been hell. Students were daily confronted with massive 'racialism', and the Russians were 'just as prejudiced as the whites in Alabama'. The young Africans, Asians and Latin Americans were treated like 'caricatures to illustrate communist slogans and not as human beings in their own right'. At university, they were either ignored or spied upon, and they had tremendous problems with Soviet bureaucracy.[3]

The review, however, gave simply an incorrect impression of Carew's book. In no way was it a 'short and angry novel', as the reviewer called it,

---

[1] Rubinstein, 'Lumumba University', 68.   [2] Soto, 'Un verano en Siberia', p. 4.
[3] *New York Times* book review, 28 Mar. 1965, p. BR42; Jan Carew, *Moscow Is Not My Mecca* (London: Secker & Warburg, 1964), pp. 56, 110; for a similar devastating western account of Third World students in the Soviet Union, see Victor Lasky, *The Ugly Russian* (New York: Trident, 1965), pp. 60–91.

but actually a rather nuanced and balanced assessment of student life in the USSR. In the style of a collective biography, the book told the story of a fictional South American called Josef, who represents the perspective of Third World youth in Moscow. He had struggled to make ends meet in early 1960s London, until he was awarded a grant to study and live in the Soviet Union he admired. His somewhat naive enthusiasm and high expectations are dampened by a series of disappointments, the cold winter, the lack of entertainment and indeed Soviet bureaucracy and, occasionally, discriminatory incidents. He discovered that 'Moscow is not my mecca' – the title of another edition of Carew's book. After a failed love affair with a Russian woman, Josef decides to continue his studies back in London. What the *New York Times* reviewer decided to ignore completely is the fact that the book is also full of positive remarks about the Soviet Union, about great teachers and acquaintances and about the hospitality and solidarity towards people from Third World countries he experienced. 'The Russians', Josef observed, 'because they have lived through the same experience, understand that this is an age in which people from the under-developed countries are in a hurry.' Most Soviet people he met did not know Guyana but, whenever he explained that it was in South America, they were enthralled that he came from where Fidel Castro lived. Josef was overwhelmed by some aspects of the Soviet Union, in particular in Central Asia, where he – like most visitors from Third World countries – was shown around. 'The Revolution had brought fantastic benefits to Uzbekistan', he noted; 'if the other colonial and ex-colonial powers had shown the same enlightened self-interest when they controlled such large areas of the world, the gap between the haves and the have-nots would not have been as wide as it is today.'

Josef was disappointed because he, as a black man, expected finally a place free of racism – which the Soviet Union was not, just as Britain was not – and Guyana was not. In fact, he experienced the worst ethnically motivated exclusion in Moscow from his own white and *mestizo* compatriots. All in all, the book was just as critical about the West as it was about the Soviet Union. Before leaving Moscow, Josef summed up his experience: 'I am grateful to the Soviet Union for the free scholarship ... [but] I learned there is no paradise on earth.'[4]

Carew's book, and its distorting review in the *New York Times*, is a telling example of the perceptions and realities of higher education for foreigners from the global South in the Soviet Union during the Cold War. From the mid 1950s, Soviet organisations invited ever more

---

[4] Carew, *Moscow Is Not My Mecca*, pp. 42, 95, 174, 194.

students from the emerging Third World for free education at universities all over their country. Between 1957 and 1970, their number rose by a factor of 100.[5] The Soviets made this lavish offer as part of their post-Stalin image campaigns, in order to present their country as a modern and advanced society, free of racism and full of altruistic international solidarity. There was no intention to incite students to revolutions, but it was reckoned that the students, upon return, would spread a positive stance towards the USSR from their positions in the administration, politics and education of their home country. Thousands of youngsters from all countries of the Third World went to study in the Soviet Union, and were confronted with a sometimes harsh reality that did not always adhere to Soviet self-representation. Nonetheless, many deeply appreciated the generous Soviet offer of free higher education.

Western misjudgements, or even fears, had their roots in historic experience: the Soviet Union was already giving free education to foreigners from the 1920s. During the early days of the USSR, and lingering through the Stalinist period, the intention was explicitly to spread worldwide communism. A University of the Toilers of the East was founded 1921 in Moscow and transferred to Tashkent in 1930. Throughout its existence until 1952, a large proportion of the future communist leaders of Soviet Central Asia and South East Asia got at least part of their higher education there. The Tatar Bolshevik Mirza Sultan-Galiev, who propagated a specific Muslim national communism, and the founder of both the Indian and the Mexican Communist Parties, Manabendra Nath Roy, were among the teaching staff. Alumni included internationally known political and cultural figures of the global left such as Vietnam's Ho Chi Minh and the Turkish communist poet Nazım Hikmet.[6] From 1925, Sun Yat Sen University in Moscow, headed by Karl Radek, instructed primarily Chinese students. Many of them later became influential party functionaries, most notably perhaps the future party leader Deng Xiaoping. Western communists studied primarily at the Comintern's International Lenin School and at a Komsomol university in Moscow, where East Germany's Erich Honecker, Yugoslavia's Josip Tito and thousands of other young communists acquired their ideological formation.[7] Several other political leaders from what, from a Western perspective, was now the Cold War enemy camp, North Korea's Kim Il-Sung to

---

[5] V. Ilchenco, *A la URSS por los conocimientos* (Moscow: Progreso, 1971), p. 70.

[6] Dirnecker, 'Die "Patrice Lumumba-Universität für Völkerfreundschaft"', 213.

[7] Julia Köstenberger, 'Die Internationale Leninschule 1926–1938', in Buckmiller and Meschkat (eds.), *Biographisches Handbuch zur Geschichte der Kommunistischen Internationale*, pp. 287–309.

name but one more example, had attended Soviet military schools for ideological education and practical training.[8]

When the Soviets restructured and expanded their offer of free education to students from all over the world starting in the mid 1950s, western observers believed they were seeing a continuation of this Soviet tradition. While the official goal of Soviet education during the Cold War was now indeed to educate, and not to influence students, the West expected more communist indoctrination. But in fact, no longer were Third World students in the Soviet Union taught to be communists. In the times of great conflict with the West, the Soviets had humbler hopes. Students should see the progress made in the Soviet Union and develop sympathy for this advanced and altruistic friend of the Third World. Their anti-western and anti-imperialist sentiments should be fostered, and, upon return, they were to convey this stance to their compatriots.

One of the greatest efforts in the field of education of foreigners in the USSR was the foundation of Moscow's Patrice Lumumba University of the Friendship of the Peoples. This university, established exclusively for students from Africa, Asia and Latin America, will be discussed in detail in the first section of this chapter. Its first rector, the former deputy minister of education Sergej Rumjancev, admitted the inspiration they took from the West, where students from the colonies had been trained since the end of the First World War, in his opening speech: 'our experience is based on the accomplishments of Soviet science, but we have also considered the experience of other national systems of education and the accomplishments of international science'.[9] After years of Soviet international isolation and very russocentric interpretations of scientific history, this was quite a remarkable statement. Yet not only were the Soviets inspired by the West, but influence also flowed in the other direction: the new Soviet advance towards the 'developing countries' caused worldwide curiosity, debates and concrete reactions. Within the socialist world, ministries of education copied Soviet concepts. Bulgaria, Czechoslovakia and China founded their own universities for foreigners, and all socialist states developed programmes that provided scholarships for international students at existing universities.[10]

The West felt challenged. The US Department of Education hired experts for an 'Office of Education in the Eastern Bloc', which closely

---

[8] Joel Kotek, *Students and the Cold War* (Oxford: Macmillan, 1996).

[9] *Izvestija*, 27 Jun. 1966.

[10] Paul Jostock, 'Die Lumumba-Universität in Moskau', *Die neue Ordnung in Kirche, Staat, Gesellschaft, Kultur* 1 (1962), 62–5; Dirnecker, 'Die "Patrice Lumumba-Universität für Völkerfreundschaft"', 221; Alvin Rubinstein, 'Friendship University', *Survey* 34 (1960), 8–10.

monitored what was happening at Soviet universities.[11] The US embassy in Moscow tried time and again to contact foreign students. Probably precisely to that end, Norris Garnett, the only African-American in the Foreign Service at the time, was redeployed to the Soviet Union as cultural attaché in 1964 – but was expelled by the Soviets shortly thereafter, because, allegedly, he repeatedly tried to recruit Third World students as informants, offering cigarettes, cognac and jazz records in exchange.[12] In western Europe, reactions focused more on internal reform and the expansion of scholarship programmes for foreigners. Vatican officials decided to invite Africans to study at their own university, and in the long debates on the creation of the European University Institute in Florence there were – explicitly referring to Lumumba University in Moscow – proposals to include students from the Third World.[13]

Gradually, western observers became more relaxed in their view of Soviet education of foreigners. In 1971, the *New York Times* asked jovially 'What they do at Old Lumumba U' and discounted rumours about Soviet alumni in a recently failed *coup d'état* in Mexico (ironically, their participation was later actually confirmed).[14] While the experience of communist cadre training had initially shaped the western perception of Soviet education of foreigners, there was soon acknowledgement that attitudes towards international students in the USSR had actually changed. Another reassuring factor was the small number of students. By the mid 1960s, about 10,000 Third World students were attending universities in the USSR, along with roughly 2 million Soviet students.[15] West Germany alone, even without West Berlin, boasted almost the same number, with a total of only 150,000 students, the United States more than twice as many.[16] The Soviets, especially after the end of their great optimistic phase

---

[11] Seymour Rosen, *The Development of the People's Friendship University in Moscow* (Washington, DC: US Department of Health, 1973).

[12] Henry Tanner, 'Soviet Ousts US Cultural Aide as Inciter of African Students', *New York Times*, 12 May 1965.

[13] Jean-Marie Palayret, *Un'università per l'Europa: le origini dell'Istituto Universitario Europeo di Firenze (1948–1976)* (Rome: Presidenza del Consiglio dei Ministri, 1996), p. 155.

[14] Theodore Shabat, 'What They Do At Old Lumumba U', *New York Times*, 18 Apr. 1971.

[15] UNESCO, 'Statistics of Students Abroad, 1962–1968: Where They Go, Where They Come from, What They Study / Statistiques des étudiants à l'étranger 1962–1968: où vont-ils? D'où viennent-ils? Qu'étudient-ils? (Paris: UNESCO, 1971); anon., '21,000 Foreign Youth Attending Universities in Soviet Union', *New York Times*, 13 Jan. 1965; Soviet documents reveal about the same numbers: Naučnyj i meždunarodnyj otdel CK KPSS – CK KPSS: Predloženija po ispravleniu Universiteta Družby Narodov im. Patrisa Lumumby za lučego social'nogo sostava i za sniženii raschodov, 10 Dec. 1965, RGANI f.5 op.35 d.221 ll.160–161.

[16] Dirnecker, 'Die "Patrice Lumumba-Universität für Völkerfreundschaft"', 224.

around 1960, could afford to accept only a fraction of Third World students applying for their programme of free higher education.

This chapter will take a close look at the life of Latin American students in the Soviet Union, an essential element of both Soviet internationalism and post-war cultural internationalism. Two sections analyse the official stance towards students; organisational and institutional aspects and a short history of the Patrice Lumumba University of the Friendship of the Peoples shed light on this particular branch of Soviet internationalism after Stalin. The second half of the chapter is dedicated to the students themselves. The introductory episode of Carew's book made it clear: so far, their story has usually been told from either a distorted Soviet or a distorted western perspective. Here they will have their own say. Their perspectives, subjective and often nostalgically glorifying as some of them are, are crucial to an understanding of the effectiveness of education as a means of Soviet advances towards Latin America. It will become obvious that Soviet efforts, as long as exclusively western standards are not imposed, were actually rather successful.

Latin American students at Soviet universities: facts and figures

The first Latin American students went to the Soviet Union in the late 1950s. Moscow State University gave scholarships to a very small group of Latinos, for the first time not for ideological but proper academic training. From 25 students in 1959, their number rose to a more or less constant community of 3,000 Latin American students during the 1960s and 1970s (not including the high number of Cubans) in the entire Soviet Union, from Lvov to Novosibirsk. Statistical data for later periods includes the Cubans again: in 1980, there were 11,390 Latin American students enrolled at Soviet universities. Excepting Cubans, the largest constant contingents came from Mexico and Colombia. Others varied over time and depended on the political situation in the countries of their origins: more Chileans, for example, went during the Allende presidency. During the left-wing military rule in Lima from 1968, there was an enormous influx of Peruvians, who after some years represented the second-largest group. And when the Sandinistas took power in Nicaragua in 1979, the eastern bloc welcomed them with 2,000 scholarships for their students from 1979 to 1983 alone.[17]

---

[17] Konstantin Katsakioris, 'Soviet Lessons for Arab Modernization: Soviet Educational Aid to Arab Countries after 1956', *Journal of Modern European History* 1 (2010), 96; Sofinskij, 'Pomošč v podgotovke kadrov'.

Like their fellow students from other foreign countries, the Latinos had to organise within structures that were established by the Soviet state; a Seminario Permanente de Estudiantes Latinoamericanos (Permanent Seminar of Latin American Students) offered support from its office on Moscow's Gorky Prospekt and was responsible for collaboration with embassies and Soviet officials and academics. The Seminario also co-ordinated the work of the umbrella organisation of Latin American territorial associations of students in the USSR. Branches existed at every university; usually all Latin American students were lumped together in one group. At Lumumba University additional groups existed for each single country. These territorial groups served different purposes: on the one hand, they were indeed forums of interaction among students, where they discussed problems that required the involvement of the university administration. They also organised the students' leisure activities, sports, folklore concerts they were expected to give occasionally, seminars, travels and summer work. On the other hand, the heads of these student councils were always appointed by the university – which ensured that they were reliable members of their respective communist parties. The territorial associations hence existed to help students, but also to keep control of them.[18]

While universities were more interested in their students' academic results and their behaviour in private life, the Komsomol took care of their political leanings. Komsomol members regularly wrote reports on their foreign fellow students and assessed them according to their political allegiances and assertions. Documents reveal that Latin American students, due to a selection procedure that involved the relatively well-established communist parties and networks of friendship societies in the Americas, tended to be more political and left-leaning ('progressive') than their fellow students from Asia and Africa.

In the student groups from the more developed countries, Argentina, Brazil, Chile, Mexico, Uruguay and Chile, a significant share, roughly one-third, were party communists. The Komsomol reports sometimes also recommended certain groups for 'propaganda activities' (such as their participation in the Spanish-language radio programme) – and usually referred to students from these countries as particularly reliable. Students from Bolivia, Ecuador, Peru, the Caribbean and Central

---

[18] Položenie v zemljačestvach studentov iz stran Latinskoj Ameriki i o sostojanii raboty s etim kontingentom inostrannych učaščichsja v SSSR, 13 May 1969, RGASPI f.1M op.39 d.231 ll.53–79; for 1971: d.232 ll.7–10; Sobre el Seminario Permanente de Estudiantes Latinoamericanos en la URRS, undated, RGASPI f.1M op.39 d.399 ll.17–143.

America, places where higher education was a privilege for a tiny elite, were either less political and went only to study – or they exhibited much-feared Maoist tendencies. 'Ultra-leftist' views were found especially among youngsters from Guatemala, Nicaragua and Peru; their Komsomol fellow students disclosed that some had contacts with the Chinese embassy.

The bulk of these reports, however, were rather benevolent. Along with political stances, moral behaviour was reported as well as academic performance and social commitment. Direct attempts to influence students ideologically happened only when they showed Maoist leanings. In these cases, and only in these cases, the Komsomol recommended talking the respective students out of their ideological stance. Beyond that there was no attempt to influence students politically other than the constant praise of Soviet greatness and criticism of western imperialism.[19]

The flagship of Soviet internationalism: Patrice Lumumba University in Moscow

Until well into the 1960s, Latin Americans, unlike Africans and Asians who were spread all over the Union, primarily attended Patrice Lumumba University of the Friendship of the Peoples in Moscow. Established in 1960 for Third World students, its representative character distinguished it from all other Soviet institutions of higher learning: it was to convey a certain image of the post-Stalinist Soviet Union, not as an ideology-exporting cradle of world revolution, but as a modern European state that was altruistically helping developing countries to follow its own path. These symbolic dimensions of Lumumba University have already been analysed in Chapter 1. This section will take a closer look at the history of the institution, at the selection of students, at their daily life on and off campus and at interactions and frictions with the Soviet state and population.

Students from Latin American countries, just like those from Asia and Africa, could apply for programmes in seven departments. Most popular were vocational careers such as engineering, agriculture, medicine and pharmacy. Economics and law were offered too but, due to the different socio-economic systems and jurisdictional traditions in their home countries, fewer students signed up. A department of natural sciences offered chemistry, biology, physics and mathematics. Humanities were limited

---

[19] O situacii studentov iz Latinskoj Ameriki v SSSR, 13 May 1969, RGASPI f.1M op.39 d.231 ll.60–79; 13 May 1966, RGASPI f.1M op.39 d.30 ll.1–14.

to history, anthropology and philology, which trained translators. Lumumba University was the only institution of higher learning in the Soviet Union which, initially, eschewed the usually obligatory ideological classes in Marxism-Leninism. The first year was spent in a preparatory faculty, which first and foremost tried to teach students the Russian language. Studies took five or six years, or up to seven for those in medical school. Classes were given in a former military academy in the neighbourhood of Moscow State University, until a new campus was built in the late 1960s. The criteria for the selection of students were simple: they had to have attended a higher school, be no older than thirty-five and come from Asia, Africa or Latin America. Gender, ethnicity and religion did not matter. Quotas for countries did not exist officially, but the number of students from the three continents was always roughly the same.

Prospective students could apply through different channels for Lumumba University. In countries with which the USSR had diplomatic relations (not many in the early days of the university), the Soviet embassies accepted applications. The worldwide network of Soviet friendship societies also advertised the chance to study in Moscow and distributed scholarships for Lumumba. So did the Komsomol-controlled International Federation of Students, the local communist parties and some trade unions. In addition, students could also apply directly to the university's selection committee in Moscow, an assembly of professors and official representatives of Komsomol and the World Federation of Democratic Youth. Criteria were performance in high school and recommendation letters; those who had no chance to get higher education elsewhere got preferred treatment.[20]

The foundation of Lumumba University made a huge impact in the media worldwide. The number of applicants was accordingly huge. Of 43,500, the admission committee invited 1,200 to Moscow for selection talks, and half were sent home at Soviet cost. Finally 120 young Latin Americans, 142 Asians, 193 Africans and 46 Middle Easterners began their classes in autumn 1960.[21] In Moscow, students received full scholarships that covered travel expenses, their studies, medical care, warm

---

[20] Ob organizacija Universiteta Družby Narodov, rešenie Soveta ministrov, 5 Feb. 1960, GARF f.5446 op.1 d.698 l.698; Rupprecht, 'Die Liebe der Linken zu Lateinamerika'; Dirnecker, 'Die "Patrice Lumumba-Universität für Völkerfreundschaft"', 218; Alexander Ustanov, 'The First Ball at the Friendship University', *Moscow News* 79 (1960), 2.

[21] S. Rumjancev, 'Pervyj god universiteta', *Vestnik vysšej školy* 5 (1961), 108–10; Dirnecker, 'Die "Patrice Lumumba-Universität für Völkerfreundschaft"', 224.

winter clothes and a monthly allowance of 90 rubles.[22] By Soviet standards, and also considering the living standard most students had been
used to before they went to the Soviet Union, these were very lavish
sums. Soviet students got an average of 30 rubles, and even the highly
coveted Lenin scholarship for talented young Soviets stood at only 80
rubles – reason for some envy towards the foreigners. Nonetheless, the
numbers of applicants had already dwindled by the second year and
remained at between 7,000 and 8,000 annually throughout the 1960s,
of which 500 to 600 were accepted.

Besides Third World youngsters, 225 Soviet students enrolled annually.[23] Their presence had several purposes: for one thing, they were to
help the foreigners with the hardships of the Russian language – a major
problem for most students throughout the history of the university. For
another, after years of international isolation during Stalinism, there was
a blatant lack of knowledge and expertise on the world abroad. Chapter 5
will further examine how the Soviets tried to overcome this ignorance –
one method was to send future regional experts to Lumumba University,
where they were to pick up linguistic and cultural knowledge from their
foreign fellow students. The ideological tolerance shown by the university towards Third World youth did not extend to the Soviet students:
they had to be either CPSU or Komsomol members and undergo a harsh
testing procedure, in which the Soviet Army had a word to say.[24] After
all, Soviet students at Lumumba University had a third task, which was
an open secret to everyone on campus: they were to report on the
academic, political and private behaviour of their foreign fellow students.[25] But, again, there were no systematic attempts to influence the
foreign students ideologically.

These reports to the Komsomol were in most cases not on individuals,
but on national groups, which were classified according to Cold War
categories. Anti-Soviet sentiment was hardly ever encountered. To be
sure, students were not all free to say and act as they pleased without
getting into conflict with the suspicious Soviet authorities. Since the
times of peaceful coexistence and the subsequent schism with China,

---

[22] *Pravda*, 27 Jun. 1962.
[23] O situacii studentov iz Latinskoj Ameriki v SSSR, 13 May 1966, RGASPI f.1M op.39
d.30 ll.1–14.
[24] O rabote Komsomola v Universitete Družby Narodov im. Patrisa Lumumby, 17
Jun. 1970, RGASPI f.1M op.39 d.286 ll.15–22; 21 Mar. 1967, RGASPI f.1M op.39
d.143 ll.35–36.
[25] O situacii studentov iz Latinskoj Ameriki v SSSR, 13 May 1966, RGASPI f.1M op.39
d.30 ll.1–14; Položenie v zemljačestvach studentov iz stran Latinskoj Ameriki i o
sostojanii raboty s etim kontingentom inostrannych učaščichsja v SSSR, 13 May 1969,
RGASPI f.1M op.39 d.231 ll.53–79.

however, the ideological front lines had changed. The greatest concern
now was Maoist sentiments among the students, which meant that they
would have supported a violent revolutionary path for their home countries. As a Novosti reporter told the Mexican journalist Luis Spota during
his visit in Moscow: 'look, those Latin Americans who come to study ...
they are very political, have subversive ideas. "You have to strike for this
and that!", they say, "you have to scream in the street against this and
that!"... This is all they know. They do not know the value of discipline,
and criticise everything!'[26] Soviet fears were actually often quite the same
as those of western observers.

Just as for the Soviet students, strict criteria were applied to the
teaching staff of Lumumba University. Only renowned internationalists
and communists were shortlisted for positions. The first professors
included Ivan Potechin, president of the Africa Institute of the Academy
of Sciences, and Anatolij Sofronov, chief editor of the weekly *Ogonek*,
who had a reputation as a conservative hard-liner in cultural debates
during the Thaw.[27]

In the run-up to the foundation of the University of the Friendship of
the Peoples, Soviet officials had underlined that only 'societal groups'
had proposed and would run the university. During the implementation
phase, however, the Soviet state and the CPSU did interfere on several
levels. The ministry of education allocated professors and curricula, and
the Council of Ministers defined the organisational structures of the
university, including hierarchies and working hours. The financing ran
initially on a state reserve fund, as the decision to build the university was
most likely one of Khrushchev's impetuous solo projects and no
resources on that scale were actually to hand. Figures from the late
1970s indicate that the university had a budget of more than 16 million
rubles yearly.[28]

The most urgent problems the university faced with its students were
their lack of knowledge of Russian classroom language and their very low
average level of education when they arrived in Moscow. Highly qualified
students and those who could afford it still went to study in the West.
The ones who went to Moscow had either a fascination for the Soviet
Union or had found it difficult to get education elsewhere. Their educational level was at times 'catastrophic', as a member of the Colombian–

[26] Spota, *El viaje*, p. 183.
[27] Dirnecker, 'Die "Patrice Lumumba-Universität für Völkerfreundschaft"', 220.
[28] Craig Whitney, 'Lumumba U: Is It a Soviet Tool?', *New York Times*, 6 Jan. 1980;
Rešenie Soveta ministrov, 14 Jun. 1960, GARF f.5446 op.1 d.702 l.604; Ob
organizacija Universiteta Družby Narodov, rešenie Soveta ministrov, 5 Feb. 1960,
GARF f.5446 op.1 d.698 l.698.

Soviet Cultural Institute reported from his trip to Moscow. Students could not even recognise the Soviet Union or Moscow on a world map and had never heard of their compatriot writer Gabriel García Márquez.[29] By 1963, as many as 61 students had already been expelled due to weak academic performance or 'inappropriate behaviour', and 109 more had given up voluntarily.[30] Up to 1968, altogether 465 students dropped out and 225 were dismissed. Considering that the university had only 1,236 graduates by that time, this was quite a large number.[31]

In order not to endanger the political task of the university, the general academic level had to be lowered. In the long run, however, this led to problems with the recognition of Lumumba diplomas in some countries and to a bad reputation among Soviet academics. Those in charge of Lumumba University were aware of these deficiencies. As early as 1962, special preparatory classes in Leningrad and Tashkent were introduced for those who still needed very basic training.[32] Where possible, students had to take Russian classes in their home countries before they were conceded a grant.[33] The Scientific and International Departments of the Central Committee of the CPSU compiled an entire catalogue of suggestions to improve the situation in 1965. The number of foreign students per year was cut back to 500; instead, it was proposed that more Soviet students should be admitted and the length of study should be reduced. The ministry of education recommended curtailing 50 per cent of the scholarships to students with bad academic results, a measure that put more pressure on the students and saved money. Interviews in Moscow were abolished, and an increasing number of bilateral state contracts put the responsibility for the selection of the future students in the hands of their home countries.

On the inside, the university tightened strings with regards to its students, while at the same time scaling down expectations: 'first and foremost this is an institution for young people who cannot get an education either in their home countries or in the West', Rector Rumjancev now declared. And indeed, more than half of the students at Lumumba University in the late 1960s came from a peasant or

---

[29] Letter from Moscow to the Soviet–Colombian Friendship Association, 9 Sep. 1970, Archive of the Instituto Cultural Colombo-Soviético.

[30] Shabat, 'What They Do At Old Lumumba U'.

[31] Komsomol – Ministerstvo Obrazovanija: O meropriatach dal'nejšego ispravlenija kačestva podgatovka kadrov v Universitete Družby Narodov, 4 Jun. 1968, RGASPI f.1M op.39 d. 143 l.10.

[32] *Pravda*, 10 Sep. 1962.

[33] Anon., 'Reglamento para la adjudicación de becas en la Universidad de la amistad de los pueblos "Patricio Lumumba" de Moscú en 1967', *Boletín del Instituto Cultural Colombo Soviético* 1 (1966), 4–5.

working-class background. No longer did it consider itself a competitor with the West for the education of Third World elites.[34]

While the university administration increasingly sought to save money and avoid trouble, the influential Komsomol retained a much less pragmatic stance. In 1968, its own Central Committee handed over a list of claims to the ministry of education. They brought up the problem of low-quality classes, but insisted even more on a stronger ideological penetration of the university. Students of economy should be much more directed towards the advantages of a planned economy, there should be 'anti-religious campaigns' on campus, and obligatory classes in Marxism-Leninism should be introduced also at Lumumba. Soviet history – in fact the history of the CPSU – now became a compulsory subject for all foreign students in the preparatory classes, but the standard classes in Marxism-Leninism were limited to Soviet students.[35]

The university sometimes put up some resistance against the brisk Komsomol activists. In a letter to the Central Committee of the Komsomol in a letter, the rector reminded the overzealous young communists that 'the university's task is to teach these students not to become communists, but to become friends of the Soviet Union!'[36] And in the speech that Aleksej Kosygin gave to the first class of graduates in the Kremlin Palace in 1966, the new Soviet prime minister repeated the old ideal of ideological neutrality of the university. 'The foreign students can observe how the economy and the culture of our country develop, how Soviet society advances ... We do not impose our opinions on others, including foreign students at our universities.' Both university administration and the highest political elite had a more moderate approach than the communist youth activists, who were still glowing with ideological fervour. Concerning the West, however, Kosygin's rhetoric remained as usual: 'the western imperialists present themselves as the only carrier of world civilisation. They suggest to the freed peoples that their spiritual renaissance and their development are possible only on the basis of western thought.' Those graduates who gave speeches at the same occasion were in accordance: 'while imperialism slaughters in Vietnam, the

[34] Naučnyj i meždunarodnyj otdel CK KPSS – CK KPSS: Predloženija po ispravleniu Universiteta Družby Narodov im. Patrisa Lumumby za lučego social'nogo sostava i za sniženii raschodov, 10 Dec. 1965, RGANI f.5 op.35 d.221 ll.160–161; Ministerstvo Obrazovanija – CK KPSS, 3 Dec. 1965, RGANI f.5 op.35 d.221 l.130.

[35] V. Kerov, '30 let Universitet Družby Narodov im. Patrisa Lumumby', *Novaja i Novejšaja Istorija* 5 (1990), 227–9; Komsomol – Ministerstvo Obrazovanija: O meropriatach dal'nejšego ispravlenija kačestva podgatovka kadrov v Universitete Družby Narodov, 4 Jun. 1968, RGASPI f.1M op.39 d.143. ll.1–21.

[36] RGASPI f.1M op.46 d.356 ll.98–102.

Dominican Republic and Congo, the peace-loving Soviet Union sends excellently trained specialists back to their Third World home countries', a Venezuelan trumpeted. As 1 of only 187 graduates (of 539 who had started their studies 6 years before) he now returned to his home country with a Lumumba degree.[37] In all, 2,375 graduates from 23 Latin American countries (excluding Cuba) followed his example until 1971 and returned to the Americas with a Soviet diploma; the most popular fields continued to be engineering and medicine.[38]

In 1970, Vladimir Stanis, like his predecessor a former deputy minister of education, followed Rumjancev as rector and remained in post until the 1990s. When he took office, 4,061 students were enrolled, 969 Soviets, 964 Latin Americans, 770 Middle Easterners, 834 Africans and 524 Asians.[39] Cubans, now considered inhabitants of the Soviet hemisphere and not of the Third World, no longer studied at Lumumba; neither did Chinese students, who, after the Sino-Soviet split, were no longer allowed to study in the USSR at all. Female students were in the minority with a lopsided ratio of 1:8.[40] In a stagnating Soviet Union, these numbers remained roughly the same.

Throughout the 1970s, Lumumba University remained a showpiece of Soviet internationalism. Just as in the more turbulent early 1960s, the programme for Third World delegations in Moscow usually included a tour around the campus. The agitations and quarrels were now over; ever more non-communist countries collaborated with Soviet authorities in the selection process.[41] The university simply allocated a certain number of scholarships to one country. National student grant distributing institutions, the Instituto Columbiano de Crédito Educativo y Estudios en el Exterior (ICETEX) in Colombia and the Instituto Nacional de Becas y Crédito Educativo (INABEC) in Peru, to give two examples from Latin America, selected students and sent them to the Soviet Union, just as they sent others to the United States.

The students' point of view

A 1963 promotional film for Lumumba University neatly shows the idealised official Soviet perception of their foreign students. The film begins in an Indian village, where the postman delivers a letter from

[37] *Pravda*, 30 Jun. 1966; www.rudn.ru/index.php?pagec=2022 (last accessed 3 Sep. 2009); figures do not include Soviet students and graduates.
[38] Stanis, 'Kuznica kadrov dlja razvivajuiščichsja stran', 118.   [39] *Pravda*, 7 Feb. 1970.
[40] Rosen, *The Development of the People's Friendship University*, p. 8.
[41] Rubinstein, 'Lumumba University', 65.

distant Moscow. An elderly man wearing a turban proudly announces to the village community that his son has been accepted to the University of the Friendship of the Peoples. The camera follows the young Indian and his new friends from all over the world through their everyday life in Moscow. It shows an idyllic and happy world full of stereotypical depictions, where black Africans frolic in snow, Asian girls attentively do their coursework and rakish Latinos never put down their guitars. With much emotion, several students confirm that they would never have had the chance to get education in their home countries, that classes were outstanding, and how grateful they were to the Soviet Union.[42]

This staged harmonious everyday life is in stark contrast to the picture given by contemporary western observers. According to them, students had to endure repression, racism and dreariness in order to get a rather poor education. But how did the students themselves actually perceive their lives in Moscow? Contemporary sources reveal only the Soviet and western perspectives. This section is based on information gained from memoirs, questionnaires and interviews with alumni from Soviet universities. A total of fifteen of these former students are quoted here; they began their studies at Lumumba University, Moscow State University and the universities of Astrakhan, Kharkov and Odessa between 1964 and 1979. While some were members of trade unions or leftist parties, either before or after their studies in the USSR, none of them were enrolled in communist parties or considered themselves communists. Two of them are female, which approximately corresponds with the average gender ratio of 1:8 for foreign students in the Soviet Union. Their countries of origin are Bolivia, Brazil, Chile, Colombia, the Dominican Republic, Ecuador, Panama, Uruguay and Venezuela.

While interviewees have been selected representatively, the aim of this survey is not so much to give an elaborate quantitative analysis of foreign students in the USSR. It seeks much more to give a voice to Latin American alumni, their motivations, experiences and memories. That said, certain tendencies in the evaluation of their stays and studies depending on their social and national origins have become obvious and will be summarised.

Motivation, selection, arrival

Two factors motivated young Latin Americans to study in the USSR. A political fascination for the Soviet Union and a vaguely leftist, but not

[42] Z. Tusova: *Universitet Družby* (1963), RGAKFD #19274.

necessarily communist stance was a reason on the one hand. On the other hand, there was a pragmatic interest in the free higher education that was offered, which was expensive and difficult to obtain for many in their own countries. Both aspects played a role for most students, but with a clear tendency: the richer the country they came from and the higher the social background, the more important the political reasons were. Youngsters from Brazil, Chile, Mexico and Uruguay and those from academic families were in the main either affiliated with parties or youth organisations of the left. Many of them also went from a mixture of curiosity and vague sympathies for the left. A Chilean student, who received his scholarship through the Komsomol-coordinated World Federation of Students, remembered: 'for a youngster of twenty years, getting to know Moscow was something very exciting; it symbolised a lot and was very exotic. I could have gone to Prague, but chose Moscow.'[43] Another middle-class alumnus put it like this: 'I was no communist at all, but had sympathies for the left and I found it very exciting to meet Yasser Arafat, Schafik Jorge Handal and these communist leaders like Luis Corvalán from Chile, Rodney Arismendi from Uruguay and Luis Carlos Prestes from Brazil.'[44] Others recalled their identification with the Third World and a global counter-movement of the 1960s that fought for more justice on earth, and with the anti-colonial struggle in Africa and the youth and civil rights movements in Europe and the United States.[45]

While many students from poorer areas and countries (at least in retrospect) considered themselves leftists, too, they remembered a different main motivation to study in the USSR: 'I was invited by the authorities of my university', a Bolivian explained; 'scholarships for the Soviet Union were given to the best students. I had my first degree, but my parents could not afford to pay for further studies, nor did they even exist in my country. I was offered a scholarship from the United States, too, but I needed to pay for the trip myself, which I could not afford at the time. So I went to Russia.'[46] Quite similar were the memories of an alumnus from the Dominican Republic: 'I wanted to study in the United States, but I did not get a grant.' He learned from a friend that the local

---

[43] Interview with a male Chilean alumnus, middle-class background, student at Lumumba University 1976–82, history, university professor, no political affiliation.
[44] Interview with a male Colombian alumnus, middle-class background, student at Lumumba University 1979–85, history, journalist, no political affiliation.
[45] Soto, 'Un verano en Siberia'.
[46] Interview with a male Bolivian alumnus, working-class background, Quechua, student at Lumumba University 1965–70, mathematics, university professor, no political affiliation.

communist party, albeit illegal in the country, gave scholarships to study in the Soviet Union. Although he was apolitical at the time, he successfully applied and went to study engineering in Ukraine.

'Many people in the Dominican Republic and the whole of Latin America at the time admired the Soviet Union', the Dominican recalled. The victory in the Second World War and Russian classical literature and music were the only two things he knew of the USSR before he went.[47] Admiration for the Soviet state, which existed despite much fervent anti-communism all over Latin America, was based on very rudimentary knowledge: 'I knew what a Chilean *campesino* would know about the Soviet Union, which was very little', remembered another alumnus; 'Upon recommendation of my professors at the night school I attended, I applied to the Soviet–Chilean Friendship Society in Santiago – and was accepted. I could not have afforded to study in Chile.' A compatriot of this Chilean recalled similarly: 'my friends either did not know anything about the USSR or had a vaguely positive opinion. There was this Sputnik we knew of, and more recently the Soviet team at the World Cup [the football world championships 1962 in Chile, where the hosts won 2–1 over the Soviets in the quarter-final].'[48]

Some years later, students would be aware of what was written about them in international media concerning racism and ideological infiltration. One alumnus remembered a rude prank the older students at Lumumba would play on the newly arriving Latin American students. 'Some of us borrowed uniforms from the campus police, they took the new ones to an empty room at the university and staged a fake interrogation with a lamp directed on their face and a deodorant stick placed on the desk as microphone. 'What's your political affiliation?' they would ask harshly; 'those who are not communists we send to Siberia immediately to convert them … And if you dare to get bad grades, you'll be sentenced to forced labour', the alumnus recalls; 'any child would have recognised how absurd the interrogations were, but these youngsters bought it because this was what they knew about the Soviet Union from Hollywood films. It was a joke that should have cleared the minds of the new students of Cold War thinking and show them the dimensions of their prejudices.'[49]

---

[47] Interview with a male Dominican alumnus, peasant background, student in Kharkov and Odessa 1973–9, engineering, engineer and civil servant, trade union activist.

[48] Interview with a male Chilean alumnus, peasant background, student at Lumumba University 1967–73, engineering, engineer and civil servant, member of Partido Socialista Unido de Venezuela; Soto, 'Un verano en Siberia', p. 30.

[49] Soto, 'Un verano en Siberia', pp. 32–4.

Education

Almost all alumni agreed that the level of education in the Soviet Union was very high compared to what they knew from back home. One former student recalled: 'from the first day, everything was very different from what I was used to in Bolivia, but in a positive sense. Teachers took care of each of us personally, they were excellent academically, we got any help and assistance we needed. The academic level was very high, indeed difficult to follow for many. But it was okay for me, I studied hard and I had learnt some Russian already before coming to Moscow.'[50] Most others considered the academic level 'excellent'. However, many experienced problems or at least observed them with their fellow students due to insufficient preparation in their home countries: 'I had serious difficulties in mathematics; back in Chile we never studied maths at this level.' Teachers were perceived by all students as very good and extremely helpful. 'They were always approachable and even ate with us in the canteen. This would never ever have happened where I come from', is a representative memory.[51] In the perception of the educational level, there is again a divide among alumni according to their origin. Students from peasant families and from Bolivia, the Dominican Republic and Ecuador, for example, unanimously described classes as very taxing. Several Colombian middle-class students agreed that the quality of education was usually very good. It was too good for many students, though. 'The academic level was very good, but many students would not understand a word', a philologist remembered from his classes in the mid 1960s.[52] Another Colombian, a student of history, described the same problem from the late 1970s: 'some of our professors were really outstanding. For them it was sometimes frustrating, more than half of the students would basically not participate at all in class. They simply did not understand what the man up front was talking about ... Also there was excellent literature available in the Lumumba library, also on recent debates in western historiography, which was not used in class, but was freely accessible ... In classical areas the teaching programme was still really excellent; in contemporary history [it was], however, a

[50] Interview with a male Bolivian alumnus, working-class background, Quechua, student at Lumumba University 1965–70, mathematics, university professor, no political affiliation.
[51] Interview with a male Chilean alumnus, peasant background, student at Lumumba University 1967–73, engineering, engineer and civil servant, member of Partido Socialista Unido de Venezuela.
[52] Interview with a male Colombian alumnus, petty bourgeois background, student at Lumumba University 1966–73, philology, university professor, no political affiliation.

catastrophe.'[53] While in the early days Lumumba University completely forewent any ideological treatment of its students, they introduced obligatory classes about the history of the USSR and the CPSU from the late 1960s. In all other Soviet universities, foreigners would not attend the Marxism-Leninism lessons, as their Soviet fellow students had to, but were given the same classes in history of the USSR. These were quite unpopular. One of the Chilean alumni, from an intellectual middle-class background, portrayed these classes: 'we had very good professors, except those that taught history of the USSR. They were really doctrinaire, and indeed expected us to repeat their ideological views.'[54] However, with the exception of economics, where capitalist economy was taught but questioned at the same time, ideology was limited to these classes in history. All students, including the most critical, reflective and nuanced ones agree upon that in their memories. 'Upon my honour, never, never were there any attempts to influence me politically. The only influence was living in a socialist society without unemployment; everyone had their chance to study, medical assistance, and – if at times difficult and not with western luxuries – housing', a Bolivian answered emphatically.[55] In a letter to the Colombian newspaper *El Tiempo* in 1970, alumni complained about the negative depiction of studies in the USSR, underlining that they had never been under any ideological influence, as the paper had put it.[56]

Spare time

One of the aspects of life in the Soviet Union that all students recalled wistfully was the range of opportunities they had in their spare time. Especially those from poorer backgrounds enjoyed many amenities they were not used to back home. For westerners, or in general youngsters from middle-class families anywhere, running hot water any time of the day and free sports facilities on campus were hardly spectacular. For many Third World students, however, the Soviet Union was not grey and boring, but a revelation of possibilities they never had before. With their

[53] Interview with a male Colombian alumnus, middle-class background, student at Lumumba University 1979–85, history, journalist, no political affiliation.

[54] Interview with a male Chilean alumnus, middle-class background, student at Lumumba University 1976–82, history, university professor, no political affiliation.

[55] Interview with a male Bolivian alumnus, working-class background, Quechua, student at Lumumba University 1965–70, mathematics, university professor, no political affiliation.

[56] Letter by Colombian alumni of Lumumba University to *El Tiempo*, 20 Jan. 1970, archive of the Instituto Cultural Colombo-Soviético.

scholarships, they could easily afford the inexpensive tickets for cinemas and sports stadiums. Theatres, operas, ballets and museums, affordable only for the upper classes in their home countries, were cheap, too. Thanks to low-priced transport they could travel all around the Soviet Union, one-sixth of the earth as the Soviets kept telling them, and all across eastern Europe. 'The university did not care about what we did in our spare time' explained an ex-student, 'I travelled to all parts of the Soviet Union.'[57] Officially, the students were given visas only for their city of residence. For travel, they needed the authorisation of their university, but these permits were usually given easily. However, leverage remained in the hands of university officials: if someone did not behave according to the rules or got poor grades, the issue of visas could be denied as a 'pedagogical measure'. At least from the late 1970s, this rule hardly seems to have been enforced: 'I travelled from one end of the USSR to the other; I never asked for a visa and nobody cared', a Colombian alumnus explained.[58] This freedom of movement in the strictly controlled Soviet Union may sound implausible and might indeed be exaggerated through the interviewee's nostalgia. However, similar accounts by East Germans who travelled for long periods of time illegally through the USSR suggest that, with the right combination of courage, chutzpah and bribes, and thanks to the hospitality of many Soviet citizens, unrestricted travel was indeed possible.[59]

During their summer holidays, many students went to western Europe, usually to Sweden and to a lesser extent to Finland and northern Germany. Manual labour was still sought after and well paid in these countries. The students arrived, worked for some weeks and returned with hard currency and western consumer goods to their Soviet cities, where their popularity increased accordingly. Especially on the campus of Lumumba University, a busy black market for jeans and records blossomed. To break up a cartel of students who dealt on a grand scale, the university even called in the KGB in 1965.[60] As a reaction, the university council tried to forbid its students to go to capitalist states during summer holidays. As the bulk of students, throughout the 1960s

[57] Interview with a male Chilean alumnus, peasant background, student at Lumumba University 1967–73, engineering, engineer and civil servant, member of Partido Socialista Unido de Venezuela.
[58] Interview with a male Colombian alumnus, middle-class background, student at Lumumba University 1979–85, history, journalist, no political affiliation.
[59] Cornelia Klauß and Frank Böttcher (eds.), *Unerkannt durch Freundesland: Illegale Reisen durch das Sowjetreich* (Berlin: Lukas Verlag, 2011).
[60] Undated and untitled KGB document, RGANI f.5 op.35 d.221 l.65.

and 1970s, reported that they worked in western Europe, this ban was either never enforced or lifted again shortly afterwards.

For students who did not spend the summer in their home countries or in Swedish factories, the universities organised large holiday programmes. On shorter trips, they could get to know the cities of the Soviet Union and eastern Europe. At summer camps with agricultural internships in the Caucasus, with the grape harvest in Moldova or on kolkhozes at the Black Sea, students could earn some money in the mornings and enjoy a programme of sports, excursions and cultural events in the afternoon. Upon request by leftist students, Lumumba University organised theoretical seminars during these summer camps. During the 'Week of Latin America', for instance, held in Sochi in 1965, the Latin Americans, all voluntarily, met students from the GDR and Iraq to discuss the socio-economic situation in the Third World, and to debate these points with ambassadors from Latin American countries. At night, Latin American films were shown and folklore bands played.[61]

While many Lumumba students contributed to the building of the new campus on the outskirts of Moscow, others even volunteered for work camps in Siberia. What may sound to many like *Crime and Punishment* or the Gulag was, for some students, indeed a convenient change from academic work and a chance to earn some money while returning their Soviet hosts' hospitality. Luis Soto, a Chilean student at Lumumba, had come as a leftist without political affiliations to Moscow and spent 'the best time of his life' in the 1960s Soviet Union. In 1967, he joined working brigades in Železnogorsk-Ilimskij. Some 1,200 km northeast of Irkutsk, he took part in the preliminary works for the Baikal–Amur Mainline in a group of Third World students. In his memoirs, written forty years later, he remembered, full of nostalgia, the idealism and the solidarity among the workers during his two months in the Siberian taiga. 'We learnt human values that made us better citizens of the world, we learnt dignity, pride in our heritage and solidarity with our fellow have-nots, dedication to social justice and respect for the human being.'[62] Explicitly distancing himself from empty official discourse ('on the last day they gave a speech that no one listened to'), he portrayed the enthusiasm and the feeling of having accomplished something for the community, which he shared with all his fellow workers. As in most

---

[61] O meroprijatach po letnemu otdychu studentov Universiteta Družby Narodov im. Patrisa Lumumby 1968g., RGASPI f.1M op.39 d.143 ll.50–52; 17 May 1968, RGASPI f.1M op.39 d.138.

[62] Soto, 'Un verano en Siberia', p. 210.

reminiscences of older people about their youth, there is certainly a nostalgic moment of idealisation, but there is no reason to doubt that most students also considered this part of their stay in the USSR as positive and fulfilling.

Contacts with Soviet realities

Western Sovietologists sometimes called Lumumba University 'Apartheid University', as they believed it was built to keep foreigners away from Soviet students and the Soviet population. While most foreigners on the Lumumba campus did indeed spend most of their day-to-day life within the university facilities on the outskirts of Moscow, contacts with Soviets off campus were not under official restriction. Those interested, be they Lumumba students or foreigners at other universities, could interact freely with whomever they wanted (at least as long as they were not westerners). Alumni memories give a sense of what ordinary Soviet citizens thought of foreigners, about the world abroad – and of Soviet internationalism.

One aspect most students (like many other foreigners) noticed was how well informed their Soviet acquaintances were concerning international issues and the cultural production of their home countries.[63] And there was a great curiosity among Russians about the foreigners – many of the students back then palpably enjoyed this chance to stand in the limelight. 'I was always and everywhere very welcome!', a Panamanian remembered, 'soy Latino!'[64] – being a Latin American obviously was an asset in a society where people loved Latin tunes and Fidel Castro. 'I had many Soviet friends, and relations were excellent. My two Soviet roommates were like brothers to me; I was the best man at both of their weddings!' another alumnus answered in the same vein.[65] Even the most critical students, such as a Colombian one from the late 1970s, confirmed that contacts with the Soviet population were no problem at all: 'ah, this was very relaxed! I had many Russian friends, many of them children of higher functionaries. They were highly educated and knew very much about Latin America, especially about literature . . . And they were quite critical of the system

[63] *Ibid.*, p. 87.
[64] Interview with a male Panamanian alumnus, petty bourgeois background, student at Moscow State University 1970–7, engineering, engineer and civil servant, member of non-specified political party.
[65] Interview with a male Bolivian alumnus, working-class background, Quechua, student at Lumumba University 1965–70, mathematics, university professor, no political affiliation.

they lived in … I also had contact with people from the embassies and with western journalists.'[66] Some remembered having cordial relations with Soviet fellow students, but no friendships, while others complained about the surliness in public. Yet dominating alumni memories is the great curiosity about and high respect towards foreigners they experienced. 'Actually, some of us students often exploited that', one of them conceded in hindsight.[67]

The fact that Soviet students at Lumumba University had to report on their international fellow students did not affect the relations among them much, as they did not talk the foreigners into their own political views. 'I had my Soviet friends and cordial relations with many locals … There was never any attempt to influence me; there were some Spanish communists we knew and they talked about politics to us, but I was a convinced socialist anyway … I heard of some guys snitching, but these were isolated cases, certain people were known for that and we simply avoided them, but these were exceptions', said an alumnus, playing down the issue.[68]

Some students did come into very close contact with Soviet authorities: from the arrival of the first Third World students in the mid 1950s, several internationalist organs tried to recruit students as contributors. After the isolation of the Stalin years, there was a great lack of knowledge and, simply, of people who spoke the languages of those countries the Soviets were targeting with their grand charm offensive. Foreign students, usually after consultation with the communist party in their home country, now assisted at the news agency TASS, on several journals, film productions and radio stations as translators, narrators, actors or writers. Radio Moscow introduced a weekly broadcast: in 'Letter to the Homeland', foreign students would tell their compatriots back home about their everyday life in the Soviet Union in their native languages.[69]

It is difficult to estimate whether students were involved with the secret services beyond that. The interviewees denied that this ever happened to them or anyone else they knew. The accessible archive material gives no hints at all in this direction – which does not exclude its happening. After

[66] Interview with a male Colombian alumnus, middle-class background, student at Lumumba University 1979–85, history, journalist, no political affiliation.
[67] Interview with a male Ecuadorian alumnus, petty bourgeois background, student in Astrakhan 1973–9, biology, businessman, no political affiliation.
[68] Interview with a male Chilean alumnus, peasant background, student at Lumumba University 1967–73, engineering, engineer and civil servant, member of Partido Socialista Unido de Venezuela.
[69] O situacii studentov iz Latinskoj Ameriki v SSSR, 13 May 1966, RGASPI f.1M op.39 d.30 ll.1–14; Head Sergej Rumjancev to the Central Committee of the CPSU, 8 Jun. 1965, RGANI f.5 op.35 d.221 ll.51–55, 56.

all, the first vice president of Lumumba University was Pavel Erzin, a major general in the KGB. But it was certainly not a common practice.

The Third World students did not live in apartheid in the Soviet Union. They were free to interact with their Soviet fellow students as well as with the Soviet population – if they chose to do so. In contrast to the stance towards some visitors and students from the West, there was no general suspicion against them. 'I had contacts with people from everywhere … Relations with Soviet students were excellent, full of solidarity, I never had the impression they would spy on us; why should they? What danger did we represent?', an alumnus summed it up.[70] Western youngsters potentially brought officially despised western customs, music or subversive political ideas. The Latinos brought folklore music, and Mexican students introduced baseball to the Soviet Union – as long as they did not take political action, this was no problem for Soviet authorities.

Sex and the Cold War

An integral part of the general feeling of contentment can be ascribed to another phenomenon: 'the majority of us had Soviet girlfriends!'[71] Indeed most male interviewees got married to Russian or Ukrainian women at some point during their time in Moscow – or to women from the Latin American group. Most female students, outnumbered by 1:8, got pregnant while in Moscow, related one Lumumba alumnus.[72] 'Then I got pregnant from this other Latin American guy', a female Uruguayan ex-student at Lumumba confirmed.[73] Very few foreign women sought partners outside their compatriot community, while Latin American men usually found women outside the student community rather than in other national communities on campus (which had the same problematic gender ratio).

The stance of the university towards sexual relations is not quite clear. Some alumni claimed to know that relations with Soviets were

[70] Interview with a male Dominican alumnus, peasant background, student in Kharkov and Odessa 1973–9, engineering, engineer and civil servant, trade union activist.
[71] Interview with a male Dominican alumnus, peasant background, student in Kharkov and Odessa 1973–9, engineering, engineer and civil servant, trade union activist.
[72] Interview with a male Chilean alumnus, peasant background, student at Lumumba University 1967–73, engineering, engineer and civil servant, member of Partido Socialista Unido de Venezuela.
[73] Interview with a female Uruguayan alumnus, peasant background, student at Lumumba University 1964–70, chemistry, university professor, member of non-specified political party.

technically prohibited, 'but of course they happened anyway',[74] or that 'they were not allowed on campus, but outside the university there was no problem at all'.[75] Others explicitly denied that limitations ever existed; university regulations never mentioned the issue. Especially difficult was the situation for one Colombian student at Lumumba. His girlfriend lived in one of the many closed neighbourhoods in the Soviet Union. He, like all other friends of the girl's family, could not enter – and she could officially not get into his place on the Lumumba campus. The couple still managed to have three children. Rules and difficulties aside, there were relationships in abundance and many Soviet–Latin American babies. About half the relationships broke up in the end when the student-fathers returned to the Americas. Some Soviet women made the effort to undergo complicated bureaucratic applications, risk harassment and the denial of an exit visa.[76] Some finally managed to emigrate with their new families to various parts of Latin America, as did the girl from the closed city.[77] Today associations of 'Russian Wives of Lumumba University Alumni' and similar groups exist all over the continent.

Race and the Cold War

In the review of Carew's book as in many other early western accounts of student life in the Soviet Union, there is always reference to blatant xenophobia in the Soviet public and bureaucracy. As early as March 1960, African students wrote a public letter to Khrushchev in western newspapers complaining about racist treatment. They felt constantly threatened and insulted. One of them was even beaten up for dancing with a Russian girl.[78] The first drop-outs returned to their home countries and readily gave accounts of their traumatic experience.[79]

---

[74] Interview with a female Chilean alumnus, working-class background, student at Lumumba University 1971–7, economics, unknown occupation, former member of communist party.

[75] Interview with a male Colombian alumnus, petty bourgeois background, student at Lumumba University 1966–73, philology, university professor, no political affiliation.

[76] Interview with the ex-wife of a Colombian student in Leningrad, who after a year-long bureaucratic struggle with and many insults from the authorities was given an exit visa in the late 1970s.

[77] Interview with a male Colombian alumnus, middle-class background, student at Lumumba University 1972–8, economics, businessman, no political affiliation.

[78] Maxim Matusevich, 'Journeys of Hope: African Diaspora and the Soviet Society', *African Diaspora* 1 (2008), 53–85.

[79] E.g. Andrew Richard Amar, *Als Student in Moskau* (Stuttgart: Seewald, 1961).

No doubt, racism, or at least ignorance of the 'exotic' foreigners that some perceived as racist, certainly prevailed in Russian-Soviet society. The great majority of students, however, never encountered any problems of the kind at all. Some explicitly disavow that racism existed at all in those days. 'In the 1960s, during the peak of the Cold War, the absence of racist and class prejudice within the population was a success story of this society', believed a Chilean alumnus, who had an African girlfriend himself.[80] 'In fact, I was treated just like another Soviet guy, just with a different colour and different accent', the Bolivian alumnus, who came from a Quechua family, remembered.[81] One of the Colombian alumni, while very critical of many aspects of Soviet reality, claimed: 'no, never ever have I experienced or heard of anything like that! On the contrary, we as foreigners were highly popular and there was great curiosity about us!'[82]

It was not only in (possibly glorified) memories that alumni by and large denied that racist prejudice was a common phenomenon for Third World students in the Soviet Union. Contemporary documents, too, confirm this view: in a 1968 interview with a group of Latin American students they all said that they 'encountered no racial or political discrimination and that freedom of belief prevailed'.[83] Visitors from the West in the early 1970s also reported, perhaps too optimistically, that relationships between black Africans and Russians in public no longer caused great stir.[84] Many Africans, too, speak nostalgically about their youth in the USSR. To be sure, many accusations certainly had some foundation. But racist incidents were the exception rather than the rule. They provided a welcome target for western media though. In winter 1963, a medical student from Ghana was found dead in a Moscow suburb a day before he was due to get married to his Russian fiancée. As a result, indignant African students demonstrated on Red Square, and western newspapers made serious allegations against the treatment of foreigners in the Soviet Union. Later it turned out that the young Ghanaian had drunk too much alcohol at his stag party and had tragically

---

[80] Soto, 'Un verano en Siberia', p. 106. The tenor is the same in interviews with other Chilean alumni, in Daniela Derostas, María Jesús Poch and Carmen Winter, *Un crisol de experiencias: Chilenos en la Universidad de Amistad de los Pueblos Patricia Lumumba* (documentary film, Chile, 2008).

[81] Interview with a male Bolivian alumnus, working-class background, Quechua, student at Lumumba University 1965–70, mathematics, university professor, no political affiliation.

[82] Interview with a male Colombian alumnus, middle-class background, student at Lumumba University 1979–85, history, journalist, no political affiliation.

[83] Riza and Quirk, 'Cultural Relations between the Soviet Union and Latin America', 37.

[84] Rubinstein, 'Lumumba University'.

frozen to death.[85] That the foreign students immediately suspected a racist murder is not proof, but hints at bad experiences with Soviet citizens – or perhaps rather with white people in general, which made them perceive the rude Soviet public attitudes as racist. The one and only memory of an incident in interviews and memoirs in this direction came from a Colombian student: 'I remember a scene lining up at a store. I heard negative comments by a drunk about African students, something like "This is a white country" ... But a woman immediately came up and said something like "You know it's forbidden to touch the foreigners." They knew they would get into trouble if they harmed strangers.'[86]

Lumumba University reacted and published glossy brochures that addressed the constant reproaches of racism. What students related in these booklets sounds like stereotypical Soviet propaganda – but coincides astonishingly with the students' own memories.[87] Quarrels kept on happening but, as two other alumni recalled, mainly between the different ethnic groups on campus. 'There was a bit of trouble with some Africans and Arabs; there were some cases but not many.'[88] 'There were many reasons for these fights ... Sometimes one guy just made a joke that someone took the wrong way ... Or something about girls ... Usually there was alcohol in the case.'[89]

While xenophobic violence did become a huge problem from the 1980s, it was not a day-to-day issue for foreign students in the 1960s and 1970s. These memories, to be sure, cannot form the basis of an examination of racist thought in the Soviet Union. They only recount the experience of Third World students, who in their overwhelming majority encountered no problems of the kind. In the Cold War battle for the sympathies of the Third World, anti-racism was indeed an asset for Soviet self-representation: while black people in the southern United States were heavily discriminated against, the Soviet Union gave Africans free education. The Soviet state enforced this anti-racist stance within its own population as well. As for the hardships of Soviet everyday life which some misunderstood as racism, a quote by a Caribbean Marxist is telling.

---

[85] Julie Hessler, 'Death of an African Student in Moscow: Race, Politics, and the Cold War', *Cahiers du Monde Russe* 47/1–2 (2006), 33–63.

[86] Interview with a male Colombian alumnus, middle-class background, student at Lumumba University 1979–85, history, journalist, no political affiliation.

[87] E.g. Fradkine (ed.), *Le monde sous un même toit.*

[88] Interview with a male Dominican alumnus, peasant background, student in Kharkov and Odessa 1973–9, engineering, engineer and civil servant, trade union activist.

[89] Interview with a male Chilean alumnus, middle-class background, student at Lumumba University 1976–82, history, university professor, no political affiliation.

He had come as the only black man in a group of US technicians in 1933 and decided to stay in the country that promised him an end of all discrimination. 'I seldom had problems as a negro in this land', he told a Chilean student in Moscow in the 1960s, 'but as an individual, the problems were plentiful ... I enjoyed full equality as a Russian citizen during Stalin's regime' – like many native Russians, he had to spend seven years in Siberian labour camps.[90]

Frictions

Almost all alumni remembered their studies in the USSR with great nostalgia. Asked explicitly about problems they encountered, most referred to very private issues. 'Of course there were problems, requited love, unreached goals, problems you would have in any life in any place.'[91] Borscht and solianka seem to have been the major concern for most Latinos. 'In the beginning, we didn't like the food, but I got used to it and eventually liked it. Other problems I can't recall.'[92] 'The food was terrible! Besides that, well, some got homesick and the climate was harsh.'[93] The Panamanian concluded: 'the only thing I could never accept in the Soviet Union was cold soups!'[94]

The story by another Colombian shows that life in the Soviet Union could potentially still offer much nastier aspects than an unwonted diet. While most of his compatriots came from poor families or out of a political conviction, he was an apolitical youngster from a Bogotá middle-class family. It was the late 1960s and, like many of his contemporaries of the same social background in Europe and the United States, he rebelled against the boring philistine lifestyle of the older generation. He grew long hair, listened to rock music and sought to leave his bourgeois parental home. Paris was his first choice, but the Soviet offer of free transport, living and studies sounded tempting and adventurous at the same time. He became a student at Lumumba University. In

---

[90] Carew, *Moscow Is Not My Mecca*, p. 142.

[91] Interview with a male Bolivian alumnus, working-class background, Quechua, student at Lumumba University 1965–70, mathematics, university professor, no political affiliation.

[92] Interview with a male Dominican alumnus, peasant background, student in Kharkov and Odessa 1973–9, engineering, engineer and civil servant, trade union activist.

[93] Interview with a male Chilean alumnus, peasant background, student at Lumumba University 1967–73, engineering, engineer and civil servant, member of Partido Socialista Unido de Venezuela.

[94] Interview with a male Panamanian alumnus, petty bourgeois background, student at Moscow State University 1970–7, engineering, engineer and civil servant, member of non-specified political party.

Moscow, he befriended a young Bolivian of the same age who, although the son of a high-ranking communist, had the same interests in music, drugs and women. Both got into trouble constantly for a demeanour they considered normal, and the university officials considered vile. It was enough to publicly read a copy of *Time* magazine brought in from the US embassy or a book by Solzhenitsyn on campus to irritate their Soviet hosts. They also got something more than they bargained for when they invited two US girls to their dormitory. Their guests worked as secretaries and nannies for the US embassy. Shortly after they – as required by all visitors – handed in their (in this case diplomatic) passports to the university guard, the military police showed up and they all were invited to the deputy rector. The head of the Latin American territorial association confronted them as well some days later: 'we cannot understand why you invite people who kill babies in Vietnam'.

The pair thus already had a reputation at Lumumba, when they did something that could have got them into trouble in the West also, but had terrible consequences in the Soviet Union. 'We had made quite a bit of money selling jeans and records I had brought from my last European trip,' the Colombian remembers; 'it was the day Allende visited Moscow; the city was packed, traffic jams everywhere, when we got an offer from this Uzbek guy we met in the street. We bought a huge piece of hashish from him.' When the university learned that the young Colombian and Bolivian had smoked joints in their dormitory, the students got to know the uglier side of life in the Soviet Union. Unsuspectingly, they welcomed a new Russian roommate, who ostensibly became a good friend. Shortly afterward, their third roommate, also a Colombian, was stopped by the police while taking a taxi in Moscow. He was arrested and forced to undress while being interrogated. The police took a photograph of him naked and blackmailed him into becoming an informant on campus. He agreed, but told his friends that he had to meet a KGB agent every two weeks and give reports. The new Russian roommate, who was probably sent to spy on them, disappeared. Finally, the young Colombian was kicked out of the Soviet Union, but not before the rector of Lumumba University personally warned him that he was not to mention his story in the West, or he would give away details of his private life. When the university realised that he had not, as he was told to, gone directly to Colombia, but to Sweden, Komsomol activists spread the rumour on campus that he and his Bolivian friend were homosexuals.[95]

The story, while an exceptional case, exemplifies the limits of liberalisation and freedom in the late Soviet Union. Foreign students usually

[95] Interview with a male Colombian alumnus, middle-class background, student at Lumumba University 1970–4, history, university professor, no political affiliation.

lived a happy and untroubled life. Should they violate the rules, and behaving like many normal western youths meant breaking the rules seriously, reactions were still terrible, for foreigners and Soviet citizens alike.

Students' judgements of the Soviet Union

Those students who did not yield to the temptations of sex, drugs and rock-and-roll experienced their stays in the Soviet Union as very positive. The Soviet goal in offering free higher education was to create a positive stance towards their state. The alumni's opinions about the USSR reveal to what extent these intentions were successful.

Most students were not completely uncritical of Soviet politics. Even those who mainly rave nostalgically of their stays did see negative aspects: 'I was the only one of my friends who saw the invasion of Czechoslovakia as a mistake', a Chilean alumnus wrote in his memoirs; 'I also did not agree with the argument that environmental problems arose only as a result of the western capitalist system . . . I saw that the living standards in the countryside were, while acceptable, still worse than in the cities.' 'It was an undemocratic state', conceded a Colombian, 'but on a personal level it was great!'[96] While higher politics often drew their disapproval, students still considered many aspects of the Soviet way of life very appealing. 'Socialism developed positively in the 1960s, there were more consumer goods and cultural products; it demanded much from people but gave a lot . . . There was no room for egoism and individualism . . . Necessities, not income, defined what a family could consume . . . Everyone in the Soviet Union lived the living standard of the middle class in my country [Chile]. There was a shortage of some products, but there was no poverty . . . They actually had the same ideals as Jesus; it does not make sense that the Catholics here are conservative and anti-socialist.' The Chilean's conclusion was clear: for him, unlike for Jan Carew's novel hero Josef, the USSR was still 'the mecca of leftist culture . . . a real and invigorating example of the values and principles we held'.[97] 'There were many problems, no doubt, but this system has in many respects many advantages compared to the capitalist system, from a humanist point of view!', the Venezuelan agreed.[98]

---

[96] Interview with a male Colombian alumnus, petty bourgeois background, student at Lumumba University 1966–73, philology, university professor, no political affiliation.

[97] Soto, 'Un verano en Siberia', pp. 45–63, 93.

[98] Interview with a male Chilean alumnus, peasant background, student at Lumumba University 1967–73, engineering, engineer and civil servant, member of Partido Socialista Unido de Venezuela.

In contrast, students from Latin American middle-class families recalled 'in some cases parlous living conditions'[99], and experiences 'that cured me of left radicalism, more towards a stance of social democracy.'[100] But the majority went home with a very positive image of Soviet realities and followed the disintegration of the USSR with a sense of regret: 'it was very sad what happened in 1990, they kept the bad things and abolished everything positive'.[101] 'I saw with sadness what happened with the USSR. Today's Russia is full of poverty, mafia and western values such as egoism and vanity instead of solidarity and well-being.'[102]

Returns, careers and memories

There is a convincing piece of evidence that most students did perceive their studies in the Soviet Union as very positive: 'I sent my son to study in Moscow, too', the Bolivian said; after all, 'those were the best years of my life and I miss them every day!' Just like him, many others recommended the studies to their friends and families. Even today, a common reason for Latin Americans to study in Russia is their fathers' nostalgic tales from the good old times. Associations of alumni have been founded all over Latin America where they commemorate their youth – often with a sense of gratitude to their Soviet hosts. The Colombian who married his girlfriend from the closed Soviet city, after a successful career as a merchant, felt nostalgic about his Soviet experience and later opened a Russian café in his native Bogotá. A Chilean alumnus, later a civil servant in the Venezuelan oil ministry under the Hugo Chávez administration, emphatically summed up: 'I remember my old man, a poor *campesino*, almost without education, working every day for a miserable salary, seeing sadly that his sons had to follow his steps, as there was no alternative. I remember my elder brothers who had to bury their dreams and struggled to survive … To me, the Soviet people, without knowing who I was, paid my long trip from Pudahuel to Carrasco to Sao Paulo to Rio de Janeiro to Madrid to Paris and finally Moscow. They paid for my education and required nothing from me but to study. I met people from

---

[99] Interview with a male Colombian alumnus, middle-class background, student at Lumumba University 1972–8, history, university professor, no political affiliation.

[100] Interview with a male Chilean alumnus, middle-class background, student at Lumumba University 1976–82, history, university professor, no political affiliation.

[101] Interview with a female Uruguayan alumnus, peasant background, student at Lumumba University 1964–70, chemistry, university professor, member of non-specified political party.

[102] Interview with a male Colombian alumnus, petty bourgeois background, student at Lumumba University 1966–73, philology, university professor, no political affiliation.

all over the world; I learned their languages and customs. This opened a path in my life, gave me the tools to live a better life. Many bad things were and are said about the socialist system, but the help they gave to us, who had no chances in our home country, is something no one can deny ... I would be a very ungrateful person if I said I was not very obliged to the Soviet Union.'[103] A Colombian female student wrote back to the Friendship Society in a letter of thanks: 'I became a new human being in the Soviet Union, a *nastaichi chilaviek* [broken Russian for "real person"]!'[104]

Upon return to their home countries, most students initially faced difficulties and aroused suspicion. 'To go to the Soviet Union for whatever reason was a subversive and unacceptable act for many people from the political right.'[105] A group of Bolivians had to travel to Chile first and then cross the border illegally – the Bolivian state had simply refused to let them back in.[106] A Colombian remembered being harassed by customs officials and arrested at the airport when he returned in 1973.[107]

There were some reasons for suspicion: Lumumba University – if involuntarily – did indeed bring forth a handful of aspiring revolutionaries. Ilich Ramírez Sanchez, later known as Carlos the Jackal, studied at Lumumba, but was dismissed after repeated drunken rampaging and molesting of female fellow students. In the years to come, he made a fortune as a contract terrorist for, among others, the Palestinian Liberation Organisation. The Soviet authorities had nothing to do with that, but he had made his first contacts with the Arabs on the Lumumba campus.[108] The Mexican author Salvador Castañeda and some of his fellow students from Lumumba caused some stir in 1972: they had formed the Movimiénto de Acción Revolucionaria (MRA), got in contact with North Koreans in Moscow and flew to Pyongyang to prepare a *coup d'état* in Mexico. The authorities arrested them all immediately at the airport in Mexico City. Finally, a number of guerrilla fighters in the

---

[103] Interview with a male Dominican alumnus, peasant background, student in Kharkov and Odessa 1973–9, engineering, engineer and civil servant, trade union activist.

[104] Letter from Moscow to the Soviet–Colombian Friendship Association, 23 Mar. 1970, Archive of the Instituto Cultural Colombo-Soviético.

[105] Soto, 'Un verano en Siberia', p. 25.

[106] Ministerstvo Obrazovannija – CK KPSS, 22 Jul. 1965, RGANI f.5 op.35 d.221 ll.30–31.

[107] Interview with a male Colombian alumnus, petty bourgeois background, student at Lumumba University 1966–73, philology, university professor, no political affiliation.

[108] Oliver Schröm, *Im Schatten des Schakals: Carlos und die Wegbereiter des internationalen Terrorismus* (Berlin: Links, 2002); Colin Smith, *Carlos: Portrait of a Terrorist* (New York: Holt, Rinehart and Winston, 1977).

Fuerzas Armadas Revolucionarias de Colombia (FARC) had also stud-ied at Lumumba.

While these cases were exceptions, they kept a certain fear of returning alumni alive. Most of them, however, went home and did not have revolution on their mind, but careers as engineers, doctors, academics or civil servants. The group that experienced the least persecution were the engineers. The Brazilian student returned in 1979 and had 'no problem at all! To the contrary!'[109] in his home country, at the time already under military rule for fifteen years. The student from Panama worked on a hydroelectric power plant after his return, and later for a state institute for hydro-energy, as a professor and a journalist. Only in the very beginning did he have to justify his Soviet education occasionally in a country that was under the firm rule of strongman Omar Torrijos.[110]

Also for the majority of other students, it was their professional skills that finally calmed the waves. 'In the beginning it was a bit rocky; they saw us as Russian spies. But thanks to my good education, I later never experienced any difficulties', the Dominican explained. He eventually worked in several state ministries and even as an envoy to the United States.[111] Others found work easily when they returned, but got into trouble again whenever the military took power, as happened regularly in many Latin American states. 'I went back as a mathematician in 1970, a profession that did not exist in Bolivia at the time. I was the first mathematician in Bolivia. Those who taught mathematics were usually engineers and taught at an academic level of the nineteenth century. I had to start a revolution in the university where I began my work ... But I again and again had problems with my Soviet diploma; they considered me a Marxist, a *guerrillero*. They persecuted me, they expelled me from work, every time there was a new right-wing coup. But, in the end, I had a career and became head of department in several universities because I was the best mathematician in Bolivia.'[112] Others faced similar problems and found similar solutions: 'I had a very good education; it helped me achieve things that would have been impossible as a woman in Uruguay. But for having studied in the USSR I had to leave Uruguay in

[109] Interview with a male Brazilian alumnus, middle-class background, student in Soviet Union 1973–9, economics, university professor, no political affiliation.
[110] Interview with a male Panamanian alumnus, petty bourgeois background, student at Moscow State University 1970–7, engineering, engineer and civil servant, member of non-specified political party.
[111] Interview with a male Dominican alumnus, peasant background, student in Kharkov and Odessa 1973–9, engineering, engineer and civil servant, trade union activist.
[112] Interview with a male Bolivian alumnus, working-class background, Quechua, student at Lumumba University 1965–70, mathematics, university professor, no political affiliation.

the 1970s ... I easily found work in other Latin American countries though.'[113] The Chileans, after Pinochet's putsch in 1973, seem to have had the severest difficulties. Several Lumumba alumni are among the *desaparecidos*, people who disappeared especially in the early days of the dictatorship and were most likely murdered by order of the regime. Many Chilean students who were in the Soviet Union during the putsch could not return back to their home country. Some went to other Latin American states, others went back to the country of their summer jobs: the largest and most active group of Lumumba alumni operates today from Sweden. Many returning students who stayed in Latin America started to work in academia, a traditionally very liberal milieu all over Latin America. 'People here would still associate "Moscow" with Russian high culture rather than communist subversion', a Colombian put it. As long as there was no political interference, they had their undisturbed careers, and many became professors. In Colombia, where, according to Russian embassy estimates, some 10,000 alumni from Soviet and Russian universities live, a large proportion of faculty staff in both private and public universities have a Soviet degree. As history had not been taught as a separate subject at Colombian universities until the 1960s, the Soviet alumni filled a gap and today represent up to half of the teaching staff in some departments. The Universidad Nacional alone has employed more than twenty professors with a Soviet degree, while at the Faculdad de História of the Universidad Autónoma almost half of the teaching staff came from Lumumba University.[114] And being trained in Marxism helped some of them in their careers as social historians.[115] Alumni from Soviet universities dominate the diplomatic service of all Latin American states in the former Soviet republics today, while some made their careers in high politics: Henry Ruiz joined the Sandinista movement after his studies in Moscow and in the 1990s became Nicaragua's minister of foreign trade. His fellow student at Lumumba, Ernesto Tablada, acted as minister of health in the same cabinet.[116] The author Jan Carew had described the mixed experiences of Third World students in Moscow in the 1960s; in the 1990s, Bharrat Jagdeo, who had

---

[113] Interview with a female Uruguayan alumnus, peasant background, student at Lumumba University 1964–70, chemistry, university professor, member of non-specified political party.

[114] Interview with a male Colombian alumnus, middle-class background, student at Lumumba University 1979–85, history, journalist, no political affiliation.

[115] Interview with a male Chilean alumnus, middle-class background, student at Lumumba University 1976–82, history, university professor, no political affiliation.

[116] 'Yo me diplomé en Rusia: 42. aniversario de la Universidad de la Amistad de los Pueblos', Radio broadcast by Voice of Russia, 2002, www.vor.ru/Spanish/Diplome/dipl-com1.html (last accessed 3 Sep. 2009).

studied at Lumumba University during perestroika, became president of his home country Guyana.

The successes and shortcomings of Soviet internationalism in the field of education

Jan Carew's *Green Winter* was not the only literary account of the life of Third World students in the USSR. While Carew showed both sides of the story and did criticise some aspects of how foreigners were treated in the Soviet Union, another author entirely and uncritically celebrated Soviet lavishness. The Dominican historian and novelist Ramón Alberto Ferreras is perhaps best known for having inspired Mario Vargas Llosa to write his *The Feast of the Goat*, an accusatory novel about the dictator Rafael Trujillo. In 1981, Ferreras, who, like Carew, had never been to the Soviet Union himself, wrote a semi-autobiographical novel about the life of Latin American students in Moscow.[117] As even the title *¿Infierno?* (Hell?) suggests, he questioned the negative depiction of student life in Moscow and of the Soviet Union in general. Although not a communist, Ferreras, in a foreword to the novel, conceded his great admiration for the Soviet state and deplored the impact of US propaganda on his fellow Latin Americans. Even the highly regarded Gabriel García Márquez had fallen for it: the final inspiration to write the book, Ferreras revealed, came from García Márquez's critical travelogue from the Soviet Union (as discussed in Chapter 3). While the latter sounded to him like Ronald Reagan or Joseph McCarthy when describing the USSR, all his Dominican acquaintances had assured him how wonderful life was in the socialist camp.

Based on interviews with returning students, the novel told the story of Josue and Samuel, two youngsters from the Dominican Republic, and a nameless Venezuelan girl during their studies at Lumumba and Moscow State University. The Dominican boys came from deprived backgrounds and, before they went to Moscow, had lived rough lives: hard physical labour in the morning paid for their studies in the afternoon. When a member of the Dominican Communist Party offered them Soviet scholarships, they initially declined out of fear of anti-communist persecution, but finally accepted them anyway and secretly left for Moscow. They both were given preparatory classes at Moscow State University, struggled a bit with the Russian language, made friends from all over the world, played folklore music in a band and thoroughly enjoyed their

---

[117] Ferreras, *¿Infierno?*

time. They travelled around the country, marvelled at Azerbaijan and Central Asia, and basked in their popularity among their Soviet acquaint-ances, whom they usually told they were Cubans: 'this way I avoid having to explain over and over what the Dominican Republic is – and I immediately have people's sympathies, as they all love Fidel Castro', Josue explained.

By way of contrast, Ferreras, after quoting these students, their friends and parents, and after giving some rather superficial and even faulty information on Russian and Soviet history, related the sad story of another Dominican youngster who went to study in the United States. He had to work for a living during the day, studied at night, hardly slept or ate until he returned to the island, exhausted and without a diploma. Not only did US universities ostensibly not pay scholarships to their students, they also created blinkered specialists, Ferreras explained, quoting Marcuse. The Venezuelan girl in the next chapter, also from a humble family background, worked in the Caracas city administration and could not afford the post-graduate studies she wanted to undertake, but one day learnt of the Soviet offer from a newspaper article. Ferreras painted her life in the Soviet Union in a very rosy light, too; the only problem she ever encountered was some bureaucratic disorganisation in the Latin American territorial association. She studied the production of children's television programmes and was impressed by the progressive gender roles, the free kindergartens and schools and the health care system in the Soviet Union.

Full of idealism, the Dominicans and the Venezuelan returned to their home countries, but all found themselves in a difficult situation. 'Here we need personal contacts, elbows and servility. None of that have we learned at our socialist university.' Besides being paid very low wages, they all heard reproaches from their superiors that they were *izquierdistas*, unwanted leftists. The happy tale of Josue and his friends in the Soviet Union thus ended with a sad outlook for their further lives back home in their underdeveloped home country.[118]

Like Carew, Ferreras wrote his book as a collective memoir, based on interviews he conducted in the Dominican Republic. What he believed to have found out about Latin American students in the Soviet Union seems lopsided, but is actually very much in line with the tenor of many of the interviews quoted in this chapter. While Carew still found fault with certain aspects of Soviet reality (without being as critical as it

[118] *Ibid.*, pp. 110, 295–6, 479–522.

sounded in the *New York Times* review), the overwhelming majority of Latin American students perceived their stays in the Soviet Union very positively. A tendency has become clear: the poorer the country that students came from and the lower the social background, the more students were impressed by Soviet living standards, quality of education and their hosts' generosity. Interestingly, their memories are much closer to the Soviet official representation than to western depictions. Some did complain about small nuisances, but many students spent, on their own admission, 'the best time of their lives' in the Soviet Union of the 1960s and 1970s.

From a western student's point of view, the grey and dismal USSR was a backward place with a living standard well below the western one. There were hardly any bars and restaurants, and a political system prevailed that sent critics to Siberia and banned modern art and international newspapers. For students from the Third World, however, things looked quite different. They usually came from a background with a living standard below the Soviet one. Moreover, higher education was often indeed not accessible for them where they came from. The Soviet Union, with the lavish scholarships it provided, offered stunning possibilities to them that were unobtainable or unaffordable in their home countries. The students lived, ate and studied for free. For very little money, they could go to theatres, museums, operas and cinemas. They could play sports, travel and meet people from all over the world. Or they simply had the opportunity to take a hot shower at any time of the day – an asset many alumni remembered.[119] Western students could hardly be impressed by that – for many Third World students, it was a revelation.

Gathering information on the basis of interviews decades after the experience requires some constraint and vigilance, as nostalgia tends to blur what people of an advanced age recall from their youth; the memories from the Soviet Union during the Cold War are bound up with personal factors. Most interviewees, upon request, did mention hardships of their lives in the Soviet Union, but played them down. Rigid control, rude behaviour in public, poor living conditions, an extremely harsh climate and the unwonted diet may have faded more into the background of the alumni's memories than would have been their perception while they were there. However, the few contemporary sources used in this section, letters home from students and reports from foreign travellers to the Soviet Union, completely coincide with the picture given in the interviews.

---

[119] Derostas *et al.*, *Un crisol de experiencias.*

Another analytical limitation should be considered: the students' memories allow the reconstruction of a subjective perception of Soviet reality. They do not represent Soviet reality. That the students did not experience racism in the Soviet Union – and every single memoir, recollection and enquiry suggests that they indeed did not – does not mean that racism was absent from Soviet society. It certainly existed, but it was not a regular experience for the majority of Latin American students. The great enthusiasm and gratitude not necessarily towards the entire Soviet state, but at least towards Soviet society as they encountered it – teachers, friends, acquaintances and internationalist institutions – were not simply a stereotype of Soviet propaganda. Many students indeed felt this way, and their non-western, internal view of the Soviet Union gives a sense of the fascination and the respect towards the USSR that prevailed in many parts of the Third World.

Students from Latin American middle-class families, a group that lived a very European or western lifestyle, were less impressed with Soviet realities and it was usually they who got into conflict with Soviet authorities – for reading western journals, smoking hashish or having liberal views on sexual relations. The contingents from richer Latin American countries, such as Argentina, Brazil and Mexico, always had a larger group of political students. About one-third of those students were members of communist youth organisations, while many others were active in other leftist groups. Their views of the Soviet Union were of course very benevolent, too, but more for ideological reasons than due to their actual experience in the USSR. An important corollary is what has been said already about Latin American intellectuals: the view of the Soviet Union depended not only on the political orientation of the beholder, but also on his geographical origin. The Soviet Union looked fundamentally different from the South than from the West.

There were, to be sure, many shortcomings of free higher education in the Soviet Union. In order to not endanger political goals, students were also given degrees when their academic performance was poor. For that reason, and due to anti-communist fears, many students had problems getting their diplomas acknowledged and finding work back home. Quantitatively, the Soviet Union could not keep pace with the numbers of Third World students in the West. Nevertheless, the opening of Soviet universities to foreigners was a success story of Soviet internationalism after Stalin. While it built on experience with the training of international communist cadres in the 1920s and 1930s, this programme set and met the different objective of creating a sympathetic stance towards the Soviet Union by giving complimentary higher education to youngsters from the Third World who in their home countries would not have had the opportunity to study. For that matter, the Soviet offer operated more in the context of quite similar endeavours in west European countries and the United States. The tremendously increased student exchange and scholarship programmes, on both sides of the Iron Curtain, were an integral part of cultural internationalism from the 1950s.

From a Soviet internationalist's perspective, the impact foreign students had on the Soviet population was quite a success, too. Foreigners, at least in the 1960s, were still an exotic rarity in the USSR. For Soviet citizens, the presence of thousands of foreign students was 'one of the most tangible effects of the Cold War on daily life in the USSR'.[120] Research on the students' impact usually focused on their acts of resistance against Soviet bureaucracy, on racist discrimination and the undermining of Soviet values through their contacts with the West. However, the first reaction these exotic young men (and to a much smaller extent women) from the South aroused was often enormous curiosity and sympathy. The large effort and expense of the education programme drew criticism among some Soviet citizens, but among many more it was a sense of paternalistic superiority towards their guests. If all these people underwent all this hardship to come to the cold other side of the globe, leaving their families and friends for six years, how much better must life be in the Soviet Union than in these countries they came from?

This chapter, as much as the one before it, has looked at the Soviet Union after Stalin from a southern point of view and has approached the question of what Soviet internationalism meant for Latin American intellectuals and students. Well into the 1970s, the majority of both groups returned to their home countries with rather positive impressions from the Soviet Union; tens of thousands of them spread their view, through their writing and individual accounts, to all countries in Latin America. As an element of Soviet internationalism after Stalin, the offer of free education for Third World foreigners proved to be a rather successful initiative, towards the Soviet population as much as towards the Third World. The fifth and last chapter returns to the Soviet perspective and introduces those men and women who designed and organised most Soviet internationalist activities. Tracing their careers, their views of the world and their initiatives with foreigners helps us understand Soviet internationalism after Stalin not only as a geo-political strategy, but also as a conviction on the part of many individuals that lasted through the 1980s and the disintegration of the Soviet state.

---

[120] Hessler, 'Death of an African Student in Moscow', 34.

5   Desk revolutionaries: Soviet Latin Americanists and internationalism in the late Soviet Union

In Soviet times, we entered academia like people used to enter convents: in order to get a maximum distance from the demands and vicissitudes of political and social life. It was not completely safe, but it was indeed a sanctuary.

Nikolaj Leonov[1]

We wanted to do things completely differently.

Sergo Mikojan[2]

Between 'gorillas' and guerrillas: Soviet area studies in the Cold War

Soviet internationalism after Stalin had its high point around 1960, when both the upper echelons of the CPSU and the majority of the Soviet artistic and literary intelligentsia revelled in the global prospects of a de-Stalinised socialism. In the aftermath of the Cuban Crisis, and especially with Brezhnev and Kosygin in power from 1964, romanticism disappeared from political decision making. Nor did most cultural figures still idealise 1920s socialist art and internationalism. Their hopes for the reforms of the Thaw were disappointed when Khrushchev sharply denounced modern art; his successors choked off what was left of socialist idealism among artists with renewed show trials against writers, and finally the invasion of Czechoslovakia in 1968. The artistic intelligentsia retreated into private life, emigrated to Israel or found a new spiritual home in Russian nationalism.

Nonetheless, an idealistic notion of Soviet internationalism lingered also through the Era of Stagnation and up until the disintegration of the USSR. While many political and cultural elites moved towards much more pragmatic, and often outright cynical, stances on the ideological foundations of the Soviet state, a separate group carried further their

---

[1] Leonov, *Licholet'e*, p. 36.
[2] Sergej Mikojan, 'Neuželi tridcat' piat' let?', *Latinskaja Amerika* 7 (2004), 29.

concept of internationalist solidarity out of conviction: academic specialists from Soviet area studies. These scholars, called *meždunarodniki* (a
term that superseded that of the synonymous *internacionalisty*), were
specialists in one specific world region – including all parts of the global
South – and they were to supply the Soviet state and CPSU organisations
with reliable information on political, social, economic and cultural
developments of that area. Their intellectual work and world-view are
proof of the on-going relevance of ideology in the late Soviet Union, and
their influence on Soviet politics and culture helps explain a series of
paradoxes in Soviet relations with the Third World in the late 1960s and
throughout the 1970s.

Soviet foreign policy under Brezhnev was, on the one hand, characterised by increasing international integration. The Soviet foreign ministry
pushed for the expansion of a conventional diplomatic network, and the
USSR collaborated in ever more international organisations. This 'normalisation' of Soviet behaviour in world affairs laid the foundation of
détente with the United States. But the Kremlin, in the course of the
1970s, again expanded its sphere of influence all around the Third World,
as it supported, with considerable financial and military means, communist regimes from the Horn of Africa and the Arabian peninsula to Vietnam.
This contradiction between integration and ideological imperialism was to
do with the fact that Soviet interactions with the world were always based
on two internally competing channels, diplomatic relations on the one
hand, and the international communist network on the other.

This tension was also reflected in relations with Latin America. As this
book has illuminated so far, Soviet self-representation underplayed the
communist character of the USSR and presented the country as a peace-
loving, modern state that played by the rules of the international political
system. The majority of non-communist visitors from the Americas
commented very benignly on the USSR; tens of thousands of Latin
American students who returned to their home countries mostly spread
a rather positive image of the Soviet Union, too. In the same integrative
line, the Soviet Union expanded its diplomatic network: by 1971, ambassadors had been exchanged with all major countries of the hemisphere
except the Dominican Republic, Haiti, Honduras and Paraguay – and
this meant that the motherland of socialism now maintained relationships with a whole series of anti-communist military dictatorships.

The Thaw-era optimism, which led the Soviets to support nationalist
developmentalist regimes in the Third World, was gone, and so were
charismatic leaders from Nasser in Egypt to Sukarno in Indonesia and
Goulart in Brazil. The USSR now actually acquired a liking for several
military regimes. The Brazilian coup in 1964 was publicly condemned by

the Soviet leadership but, in fact, a continuing collaboration with the ruling generals proved beneficial for both sides.[3] Similarly, when the military took power in Panama (1968), Bolivia and Peru (both 1969), Soviet media initially denounced them as 'fascist take-overs' but, before long, coverage of the Andean military regimes, and of the Panamanian *caudillo* Torrijos, became very favourable. The Soviets developed close relations with the Peruvian military dictator Velasco: they sold him large amounts of heavy-duty weaponry, distributed many scholarships for Peruvian students, sent doctors and medical care after an earthquake in 1970, and applied the usual programme for states considered 'friends of the Soviet Union'.[4]

The 'gorillas', as the military dictators came to be called all over the Americas, offered some advantages to Soviet foreign policy: they were occasionally critical of the United States and – most importantly – unlike socialists, never asked for financial help from Moscow. 'At that time, revolutions worried the Kremlin more than the reactionaries', Nikolaj Leonov recalled, 'for when a revolution succeeded, requests for help, credits and money quickly followed. A stable conservative government, however, ... offered normal relations, without problems, without concerns.'[5] The Soviet foreign ministry and its boss Gromyko were now openly contemptuous of further Third World adventures: 'not even the Central Committee could get him to travel to the Middle East, Africa or Latin America', Leonov believed.[6] Gromyko did eventually travel to Cuba with Party boss Brezhnev in 1974; the chairman of the Council of Ministers, Kosygin, had already been there in 1967 and, throughout the 1970s, several high-ranking Soviet state representatives visited many other Latin American countries. Yet these official state visits had little to do with internationalist solidarity or socialist romanticism. They were much more signs of an adaptation of Soviet politicians to international customs of diplomacy. With their foreign trade, too, the Soviets participated in the world economic system – in Latin America, remarkably, they traded mostly with the military regimes in Brazil and Argentina.

This rapprochement to 'fascist' dictators put pro-Moscow communist parties to an even more painful acid test than 'peaceful coexistence' with

[3] Rupprecht, 'Socialist High Modernity and Global Stagnation'.
[4] Juan Cobo, 'Die sowjetische Hilfe für Peru', *Neue Zeit* 43 (1970), 16–17; Michail Kruglow, 'Die peruanische Überraschung', *Neue Zeit* 8 (1969), 15; *Izvestija*, 22 Nov. 1969; Juan Cobo, 'Der Militärputsch in Peru', *Neue Zeit* 41 (1968), 18.
[5] Nikolai Leonov, Eugenia Fediakova and Joaquin Fermandois, 'El general Nikolai Leonov en el CEP', *Estudios Públicos* 73 (1999), 78.
[6] Leonov, *Licholet'e*, p. 141.

the 'imperialist' West. Many political forces in the USSR were now indeed so unenthusiastic about revolutionary, or even only reform-oriented, leftists that many 'friends of the Soviet Union' complained of being neglected in letters to Moscow. Members of the Soviet–Uruguayan Friendship Society asked for more Soviet activity in Montevideo in a 1967 report – other countries such as West Germany and the United States now constantly offered free or very cheap concerts and art exhibitions, they complained.[7] The Soviet–Bolivian Friendship Society, too, wrote several times to Moscow in 1971, disappointed that their letters remained unanswered and that they were never again invited to the Soviet Union.[8]

At a time when Marxist thought was on the rise at universities all over Latin America, Soviet-style communism lost further ground. Indigenous Marxism had existed in parallel all along, and Trotskyism was a challenge still, while ever more socialists abandoned the Soviet Union and turned to Castroism and Maoism. As early as 1962, the pro-China PCdoB had seceded from the old Brazilian Communist Party PCB. Similar break-aways occurred now in Bolivia and Colombia, and several happened even in Peru: after a trip to China during the Cultural Revolution, the philosophy professor Abimael Guzmán split the Maoist Sendero Luminoso (Shining Path, or more formally Partido Comunista del Perú – por el Sendero Luminoso de José Carlos Mariátegui) from the traditional Peruvian Communist Party. Castroites and Maoists both advocated violent struggle; the former realised it as *guerrilleros* against dictators and their armies, as in Argentina, Bolivia and Brazil. The Maoists in Peru unleashed a spiral of violence against the entire population, above all against precisely the indigenous population of rural Peru they claimed to be fighting for. While Cuba did support some groups (albeit not the Sendero Luminoso) with weapons and training, Beijing's activities remained at a symbolic level. With the economic reforms in late 1970s China, the Latin American Maoists turned away from this role model, too, and found their last friend in Enver Hoxha's Albania.[9] But these guerrilla groups, which formed in many Latin American states and regions, now operated mostly without support, or even against the explicit will, of traditional Soviet-oriented communist parties. Che Guevara was forsaken by the Partido Comunista de Bolivia, and executed by the Bolivian army in 1967.

[7] Undated, GARF f.9518 op.1 d.1015 ll.17–19.
[8] 25 Jan. 1971, GARF f.9576 op.10 d.141 l.7; 5 Jun. 1971, GARF f.9576 op.10 d.141 ll.102–103.
[9] Löwy and Pearlman (eds.), *Marxism in Latin America from 1909 to the Present*, pp. xiii–lviii.

However, all this new pragmatism, increased professionalism and 'normalisation' of Soviet foreign policy notwithstanding, the Soviets, throughout the Brezhnev period and thereafter, continued their support for those communist parties that stayed faithful to Moscow and tolerated the support of guerrilla units by their ally Cuba. The Communist Party of Chile alone received US$ 200,000 in 1963 and US$ 645,000 in 1973, while Soviet foreign policy was very restrained towards the Popular Front-governed Chile.[10] This money was taken in cash to Latin America from Moscow and distributed via the KGB network, which was interwoven with the Soviet embassies. While not inciting revolutions, the KGB was now, after the end of Khrushchev's reign, allowed to be much more active in Third World politics than the Kremlin and especially the foreign ministry.[11]

There are several reasons for this contradictory policy. For one thing, even the most Realist pragmatists in the Kremlin and the foreign ministry had to acknowledge that the Latin American radical left, a potentially pro-Soviet group, had not only turned to Cuba, but were also increasingly flirting with Chinese-Maoist ideas. This was considered a problem, and concessions were made to keep them interested in the Soviet model.[12] Secondly, the two-track foreign policy had its roots in a rivalry between the foreign ministry and the International Department of the Central Committee. In this controversy, the civil servants in the ministry campaigned, firstly, for restrictions in Third World adventures and, secondly, for more political power for themselves, while members of the International Department pushed for more 'revolutionary' activity in the Third World.[13]

All but one member of the International Department (as of 1983) were scholars from the area studies institutes; all but one were *doktory nauk*, the highest academic degree in the Soviet system. These 150 *meždunarodniki*, on the one side, taught and researched and, on the other side, influenced the conception of Soviet foreign policy. Many of them had supported Khrushchev's internal reforms and his Third World endeavours and were unhappy with the retrenchment under the new Soviet leadership. From the 1970s, some 7,400 *meždunarodniki* surrounded

---

[10] These were huge amounts of hard foreign exchange, whose numbers must be multiplied by more than ten to give today's value, for the ever badly off Soviet Union; see Arturo Fontaine Talavera, 'Estados Unidos y Unión Soviética en Chile', *Estudios Públicos* 72 (1998).

[11] Andrew and Mitrokhin, *The World Was Going Our Way*, p. 40; Leonov *et al.*, 'El general Nikolai Leonov en el CEP', 78; Benjamin Welles, 'Soviet Intelligence Role in Latin America Rises', *New York Times*, 7 Dec. 1970.

[12] Prizel, *Latin America through Soviet Eyes*, p. 136.   [13] Westad, *The Global Cold War*.

the nerve centre of Soviet foreign policy making. Using their connections to the influential Central Committee, it was they who pushed for more Soviet activities in the Third World, not only to strengthen the USSR's geo-political position, but also out of socialist internationalist conviction.[14]

This fifth and final chapter will track the idea of internationalism in the late Soviet Union. Ideas do not exist in and of themselves; they need people who carry them, and they need to be communicated from generation to generation. The personal history of individuals and groups determines, to a great extent, whether an idea continues to live or dies out. The chapter thus looks at lifelines and self-conceptions of selected *meždunarodniki* in Latin American studies. Mostly born in the 1920s, they had experienced, as young men, Stalinist state terror and the war against Germany. They received their higher education during late Stalinism and began their professional careers in Soviet academe during the Thaw. The *meždunarodniki* shared Khrushchev's idealism for the prospects of a de-Stalinised socialism and spread this spirit in state and Party organisations well into the 1980s.

The international experts in the Soviet Union have received little attention from historians. Most of what is known about them was gathered and interpreted by US Sovietologists during the Cold War, who analysed their publications not out of a purely academic interest in the area studies, but in a sort of political exegesis. Information on Soviet political internal debates was hard to come by, and the Kremlinologists thus read academic writing just as they interpreted the symbolic politics of the inner circle of Soviet leadership: as a reflection or a testing probe on Soviet foreign policy stances.[15] In a variant thereof, western observers divined secret deviance and criticism of the communist regime between the lines of Soviet academic writing. Both views had in common that they

---

[14] Richmond, *Cultural Exchange and the Cold War*, p. 81; Rose E. Gottemoeller and Paul Fritz Langer, *Foreign Area Studies in the USSR: Training and Employment of Specialists* (Santa Monica: Rand, 1983), p. 93.

[15] Prizel, *Latin America through Soviet Eyes*; Elizabeth Kridl Valkenier, *The Soviet Union and the Third World: An Economic Bind* (Westport: Praeger, 1983), pp. 40–51; Oded Eran, *Mezhdunarodniki: An Assessment of Professional Expertise in the Making of Soviet Foreign Policy* (Ramat Gan, Israel: Turtledove Publications, 1979); Joseph Gregory Oswald and Robert G. Carlton (eds.), *Soviet Image of Contemporary Latin America: Compiled and Translated from Russian. A Documentary History 1960–1968* (Austin: University of Texas Press, 1970). Some of these authors, especially during times of high political tension, displayed a strong political bias and sometimes rather crudely exaggerated Soviet ambitions to conquer the world by all means possible, e.g. Tyrus W. Cobb, 'National Security Perspectives of Soviet "Think Tanks"', *Problems of Communism* 30/6 (1981), 52; P. Urban, 'Los estudios iberoamericanos en la URSS', *Estudios sobre la Unión Soviética* 3 (1962), 27–40.

saw Soviet academia only as a reflection of political phenomena, of Soviet foreign and domestic policy. The interest was not so much in the academics themselves, but in their writing, in order 'to find information that could help answer [questions about the Soviet Union] and, in the process, to enhance our ability to predict world affairs'.[16]

Soviet academics in area studies were indeed linked closely to Soviet foreign policy, and, occasionally, scholars found cryptic ways to cautiously criticise conditions in the country or actions of their government. However, while there cannot be talk of a free scientific community in the Soviet Union, science not only reflected high politics. It also had a story of its own. The *meždunarodniki* were often the fulcrum of internationalist activities, not merely subordinated numb executers of Politburo orders. They themselves drafted and implemented programmes of Soviet internationalism after Stalin until the end of the Cold War. An institutional history and a collective biography will prove that the *meždunarodniki*, drawing their socialist convictions from those internationalists who survived the Stalinist purges, were actually the last true believers in Soviet internationalism after Stalin. Their debates about Salvador Allende's raise and fall as Chilean president will make clear that the *meždunarodniki* developed a rather diversified knowledge on the world abroad from the early 1970s – and did not always comply with official Soviet foreign policy stances. They carried their ethos of internationalism, their sense of a mission to help the global South develop along its own lines, into Soviet politics. The *meždunarodniki*'s calls for solidarity with Sandinista Nicaragua around 1980, finally, will illustrate that it was usually they who rallied – if often in vain – for more Soviet support of worldwide leftist movements.

Niches and nooks of internationalism during late Stalinism

Scholars in the social sciences and humanities were always considered important for the legitimisation of the Soviet regime, and the last generation with pre-revolutionary socialisation had therefore been severely hit by Stalinist terror campaigns. The same fate befell many socialist internationalists, scholars or not, and especially those who had fought in the Spanish Civil War. They suffered extensively in two waves of purges, one

---

[16] It was surmised, for example, that Soviet studies on China in the late 1970s actually debated the future of the USSR itself; see Gilbert Rozman, *A Mirror for Socialism: Soviet Criticisms of China* (London: Tauris, 1985), p. 3. Studies that do look at individual scholars have not included the international experts; see Beyrau, *Intelligenz und Dissens*.

in the Soviet Union in the late 1930s and another in the whole of Soviet-controlled eastern Europe in the late 1940s. A look at the lives of some of those who survived this persecution helps us understand the intellectual roots of Soviet internationalism after Stalin. To that end, it is worthwhile surveying an institution where many of the future *meždunarodniki* were trained by those old internationalists: the Moskovskij Gosudarstvennyj Institut Meždunarodnych Otnošenij (Moscow Institute for International Relations, MGIMO).

Founded as a branch of Moscow State University in 1943, MGIMO was attached as the diplomatic school to the foreign ministry the year after. Unlike in traditional university curricula, students were educated in history, political science, economy and law at the same time, and they had to choose a geographical, linguistic and thematic major according to their career plans.[17] MGIMO was considered a highly elite cadre school, which trained the bulk of Soviet diplomats, area studies experts, international correspondents and decision makers in foreign policy. Before the war, no Soviet institution – besides the short-lived Ispano-Amerikanskoe Obščestvo in Leningrad – had dealt exclusively with Latin American affairs, which were left to 'solitary enthusiasts'.[18] Those who now taught the new generation at MGIMO in Latin American affairs had developed their own expertise on the Hispanic world from their careers as professional internationalists and academics during the 1920s and 1930s.

Three of these 'father figures' of Soviet Latin Americanists, Ivan Majskij, Lev Zubok and Iosif Grigulevič, each represent a different trajectory of this 'old' socialist internationalism.[19] Ivan Majskij (1884–1975) was an early Menshevik who spent the greater part of his younger life alternating between tsarist prisons and western Europe. In Soviet Russia, he had become a member of the CPSU in 1921, chief editor of the journal *Zvezda* (The Star) and began a diplomatic career that led him, as ambassador, to Finland, Japan and Great Britain during the war. Majskij was the Soviet representative on the Transnational Committee for Non-Interference into the Spanish Civil War (in which

[17] Anatolij Torkunov (ed.), *MGIMO Universitet: tradicii i sovremennost' (1944–2009)* (Moscow: Moskovskie Učebniki, 2009).

[18] Académia de las Ciencias de la URSS (ed.), *Estudios Latinoamericanos soviéticos de hoy* (Moscow: Nauka, 1987), pp. 5–6.

[19] The sources of the biographical data, unless otherwise stated, are obituaries and congratulatory addresses from the last pages of the journal *Latinskaja Amerika*. Vladislav Zubok shared information on his grandfather, and some additional information is taken from the *Great Soviet Encyclopaedia* and MGIMO's alumni website (www.alumni.mgimo.ru; last accessed 15 Mar. 2011).

the Soviets actually did interfere) and, as Soviet deputy foreign minister from 1943, participated in the Yalta and Potsdam conferences. After the war, he began his academic career as a historian at the Soviet Academy of Sciences and at MGIMO, where he researched and wrote about the history of nineteenth-century and republican Spain.

The life history of Lev Zubok (1894–1967) resembled Majskij's in many respects: born into a working-class Jewish family from Odessa, Zubok emigrated to the United States before the First World War. As a historian at the University of Pennsylvania, he became active in the US labour movement and subsequently a member of the CPUSA. He returned to Russia after the Civil War, enrolled in the CPSU, worked with the old Bolshevik internationalist Solomon Lozovskij in the Profintern and began a successful career as a historian with a focus on US imperialism in Latin America and the worldwide workers' movement. Just like Majskij, Zubok taught classes at MGIMO from the late 1940s, where Lozovskij, by now deputy foreign minister and head of the Sovinformbjuro, was widely read, and even came to give talks at least once a month, as one student remembered.[20]

It was from this old guard of internationalist professors that students at MGIMO absorbed their anti-Stalinist socialist ideals and internationalist spirit, as well as from a childhood memory: members of an informal 'Spanish' circle at MGIMO recalled their romanticism for the Spanish Civil War as the main motive for focusing their studies on the Hispanic world. 'All the boys in class were enthusiastic', a student of international journalism remembered; 'we dreamt of the Ebro and of Madrid. At night in school, we saw the *Kinokronika* and our rector would give us the latest news from Spain ... It was for sentimental-romantic reasons that I picked Spanish as my foreign language, which I associated with internationalist solidarity.'[21] Another 'Spaniard' confirmed: it was 'out of sympathy for the internationalist fighters of the Spanish Civil War' that he chose the Spanish-speaking world as his regional field.[22] Before long, the 'Spanish group' focused much more on Latin America than Spain, which added another attraction to some prospective students: he chose this field, another student later explained, because of the 'exoticism of these far-away countries ... the prospect of travelling there was just too tempting'.[23]

---

[20] Torkunov (ed.), *MGIMO Universitet*, p. 15.
[21] Karen Chačaturov, *Zapiski očevidca* (Moscow: Novosti, 1996), pp. 67–9.
[22] Leonov, *Licholet'e*, p. 20.
[23] B. Martynov, 'Molodoj čelovek', *Latinskaja Amerika* 7 (2006), 140.

Before the future *meždunarodniki* made it to Latin America personally, the lack of recent first-hand information on their subject of study and political interference were serious limitations on the academic training at MGIMO until the end of Stalinism. Academic writings in Russian on the Third World were still very rare at the time. 'You cannot imagine how difficult it was to get any information,' one of them recalled; 'books were such a rarity in the libraries!'[24] Another alumnus from the 'Spanish group' remembered how he, after getting his degree from MGIMO, was sent abroad in the mid 1950s, but 'had no clue of many things [about Latin America] that today every first-former knows'.[25] By Soviet standards, however, the young future Latin Americanists got a good general education thanks to the individual abilities of several academic teachers.

One of the few 'solitary enthusiasts' who had written about Latin America in the 1930s was the geographer and historian Ivan Vitver (1891–1966), who joined MGIMO in the late 1940s. The Indonesia expert Aleksandr Guber, too, had done some, if not much, research on Latin America at Moscow State University before the war, enough for someone from the younger generation to declare him the 'patriarch of Soviet Latin Americanists'. Several other outstanding academics from different fields kept alive a tradition of serious scholarship at MGIMO. Evgenij Tarle had already been a respected historian before the October Revolution and had secured Stalin's clemency with an ostentatious account of Napoleon's Russia campaign. As one of the founders of MGIMO, he taught there from the beginning and was later considered to be the 'teacher of the *šestidesjatniki*', the romantic socialist generation of the 1960s. The orientalist Grigorij Erenburg (cousin of the writer Ilya Ehrenburg), the historian of the ancient world Anatolij Bokščanin, the Arabist Charlampij Baranov and the philosophers Michail Lifšic and Mark Rozental were remembered by their students as other remarkable and influential intellectuals, as was the jurist Sergej Krylov, one of the authors of the UN Charter and a judge at the International Court of Justice.[26]

'In the very early days of the institute, only academic performance and not bribery or nepotism decided admission', recalled an alumnus.[27] 'Initially, there was a very democratic spirit', a student from the first

---

[24] Viktor Vol'skij, 'Sovetskaja latinoamerikanistika: nekotorye itogi i zadači', *Latinskaja Amerika* 3 (1971), 6–16.

[25] Chačaturov, *Zapiski očevidca*, pp. 10–25.

[26] Kutejščikova, *Moskva-Meksiko-Moskva*, p. 153; Viktor Vol'skij, 'I. A. Vitver – odin iz osnovatelej sovetskoj latinoamerikanistiki', *Latinskaja Amerika* 5 (1971), 160–72.

[27] Leonov, *Licholet'e*, pp. 8–22.

generation remembered in the same vein; 'it was only a bit later that all the sons and daughters of rank-and-file Party members, statesmen and diplomats came ... Classes at MGIMO were broad and intensive; there were regional studies, politics, economy, but also literature on the schedule ... Most teachers were outstanding in their field.' His Spanish-language teacher was a refugee from the Civil War; modern history was taught by Al'bert Manfred, a specialist on Russian–French relations, who had done time in the Gulag for three years in the 1930s.[28]

Another student recalled the seminars as a 'laboratory of interdisciplinary research' and the education at MGIMO 'the best thing that could have happened to me ... a fantastic humanistic education that opened up an interesting and fulfilling life for me'.[29] Less impressive were the obligatory 'grey lecturers of Marxism-Leninism' and classes by retired diplomats who also taught at MGIMO. And lingering as downright appalling and very burdensome in the Latin Americanists' memoirs was the 'moral terror' instigated by some Komsomol activists against Jewish professors and students on campus in any way 'deviant' or 'suspicious'.

'There were three sorts of students', one of them explained: firstly, the offspring of the Party and state elite; secondly, young and talented but inexperienced boys from provincial Russia, often with parents from the lower intelligentsia; and thirdly the veterans from the Second World War. The latter received preferential treatment and were admired by the younger ones, but had often difficulties in keeping up with academic standards in class. Many of the second group became good journalists and diplomats, the alumni recalled, but they were consumed by careerism from early on. And then there were those who had the same ambition, but no talent. They tried to make up for their academic deficits with special commitments to 'social work': 'this was not only bothersome, but outright dangerous. Unfortunately these people, albeit a minority, dominated the atmosphere at MGIMO at that time.' He summed up: 'it was an oppressive atmosphere ... not a church of the sciences, but a career springboard'.[30]

The renewed state terror of late Stalinism had made itself palpable also within academe. Serious research and publications had almost come to a standstill and were replaced by 'axioms ... that, at most, were allowed to be illustrated, yet not to be discussed' and couched in an 'ideological

---

[28] Chačaturov, *Zapiski očevidca*, pp. 67–9.
[29] A. Šestopal and N. Anikeeva, 'Iberoamerikanistika v MGIMO: tradicii i sovremennost'', *Latinskaja Amerika* 4 (2001), 24–9.
[30] Leonov, *Licholet'e*, pp. 8–22.

bellicose language'.[31] For Jewish students, it was very difficult to get admitted to MGIMO before the death of Stalin. In private conversations between professors and students, some criticism seems to have been voiced on these restrictions: a student recalled that one professor cursed Stalin as a *staryj čert* (old devil) in front of him, courage that – at least in retrospect – impressed him deeply.[32] When the last wave of the anti-cosmopolitan campaign hit the Soviet Union, it spilled into MGIMO, too: Majskij was arrested, and Lozovskij even sentenced to death and executed in 1952, while Zubok merely lost his job as a professor at Moscow State University and his position at the Vysšaja Partijanja Škola (Higher Party School), the Central Committee's research institute.

A third important 'father figure' of Soviet Latin Americanists spent these leaden years of late Stalinism mostly abroad in official missions. The turbulent life of Iosif Grigulevič (1913–88) justifies some extra lines here: born to a Karaite Jewish family in Lithuania, Grigulevič, after being imprisoned and deported from tsarist Russia for being a member of the illegal Polish Communist Party, studied at the Sorbonne in Paris. He spent much time in Argentina, where he worked for French communist front organisations and the Comintern. In 1936, he travelled to Spain, where he made friends with the *Izvestija* and *Pravda* correspondents Ilya Ehrenburg and Michail Kol'cov, with TASS envoy Ovadi Savič, with the Latin American left radical intelligentsia, and with a young Catalan communist by the name of Ramón Mercader. Under the command of the NKVD general Aleksandr Orlov, Grigulevič (under his *noms de guerre* 'Max' and 'Filipe') organised the arrest and execution of several left deviants in Spain. Most infamously, Andreu Nin, head of the anti-Stalinist Partido Obrero de Unificación Marxista (Workers' Party of Marxist Unification, POUM), was kidnapped from a Falange prison in 1937, put on trial by Grigulevič and shot by a 'mobile group' two days later.

Summoned to Moscow himself in 1939, Grigulevič feared the worst, but was in fact only given training as a secret agent. Unlike his brother-in-arms, *Pravda* correspondent and NKVD informer Kol'cov, he survived the purges, partly because he was important to Stalin for another task: in 1940, he travelled (now as 'Južek') to Mexico City, where he joined a group around Pablo Neruda and David Siqueiros in a first and unsuccessful attempt to assassinate Leon Trotsky.[33] For a second assault,

---

[31] Beyrau, *Intelligenz und Dissens*, p. 47.

[32] Chačaturov, *Zapiski očevidca*, p. 70; Leonov, *Licholet'e*, pp. 18–20.

[33] Neruda always disavowed his participation, but probably did help at least with visa issues as Chilean consul to Mexico at the time, and was also good friends with everyone else in

Grigulevič only did the organising and left the execution to his young friend from Spain, Ramón Mercader, who killed Trotsky in August that year. Grigulevič (now as 'Artur') remained in Latin America for several years as an undercover NKVD agent, supplied Moscow with information on the continent, wove a net of acquaintances and planted bombs where German representatives tried to propagate Nazism among European immigrants.

In 1949, Grigulevič moved to Rome (as 'Teodoro B. Castro'), established an import/export business with Central America and succeeded in the biggest exploit of his career as a spy: with the help of the writer and diplomat Joaquín Gutiérrez (see Chapter 3), he managed to become the Costa Rican ambassador to the Vatican and, in 1952, to Italy and to Yugoslavia as well. The Soviets needed information on the politics of the Holy See, as they now occupied Catholic territories in eastern Europe; and they needed information on international opinion on the Italian–Yugoslav dispute over the future of Trieste. Grigulevič, now awarded Soviet citizenship and a CPSU membership card, developed a friendship with the pope and with the Italian prime minister Alcide de Gasperi; he represented Costa Rica at the 6th General Assembly of the United Nations, was a well-known and popular man in Rome's intellectual and diplomatic scene, and had a close friendship with the female US ambassador to Italy.

Grigulevič's task was not only to keep Moscow informed. After years of planning, he was finally able to arrange meetings with high officials in Yugoslavia, as he was the one chosen to assassinate Tito. The execution was planned for April 1953, but was aborted, on the orders of Lavrentij Berija, after Stalin died in March. In the same year, Grigulevič's superior in the Spanish Civil War, Aleksandr Orlov, defected to the United States (which actually went unnoticed by the US authorities for many years), and the identity of Mercader, who served twenty years in a Mexican prison without ever giving his name, was revealed by his mother. The cover of Castro, the Costa Rican diplomat, was in danger, and fundamental political changes were taking place in Moscow – Grigulevič was ordered back to the USSR in December 1953.[34]

Grigulevič was the archetype of the revolutionary internationalist militant: born to a national minority of the Russian empire, highly educated,

---

the group, including the hitman Vittorio Vidali. Siqueiros vigorously defended his own – very physical – participation in the first attack, but later claimed 'this was only to scare [Trotsky], not to kill him'. See Siqueiros, *Me llamaban el Coronelazo*, p. 369.

[34] For a more detailed account of Grigulevič's life, see Marjorie Ross, *El secreto encanto de la KGB: las cinco vidas de Iósif Griguliévich* (San José, Costa Rica: Grupo Editorial Norma, 2004).

smart, cultured and worldly. He was fluent not only in Yiddish, Lithuanian, Russian and Spanish (the latter to the extent that he convinced Costa Ricans he was their compatriot), but also spoke Polish, English, French, Italian and Portuguese. He was an expert in Latin American literature and European ancient history, about which he gave lectures at the Italian Academy of Sciences during his time in Rome. At the same time, he was a hyper-ideologised communist cadre, ruthless when it came to eliminating real or perceived adversaries in *mokrye dela* (wet business), subordinate to any and every order of the Stalinised Communist International.

Iosif Grigulevič, the internationalist militant, had his intellectual roots in the communist world movement, as had the other 'father figures' of Soviet Latin Americanists. Each in their own way, they were convinced and active socialist internationalists: Majskij was an internationalist politician, Zubok an internationalist academic. All of them influenced a younger generation of *meždunarodniki*, through their positions as academic teachers from the late 1940s. It was people like Zubok, Majskij and Grigulevič who again raised the banner of internationalism in the Soviet Union as soon as this became possible when the isolation and nationalism of late Stalinism ended.

New Thaw-era institutions and a new generation of professional internationalists

When the Third World appeared on the Soviet horizon from the mid 1950s, knowledge of the global South was still very limited. At the time of Stalin's death, there was no Soviet correspondent in the entire Third World, and hardly any recent information on these vast areas of the world was available in libraries. The romanticising Soviet imagery and political conception of Latin America in the 1950s and early 1960s, as described in Chapter 2, was still based on this kind of schematic perception of the world abroad. In order to interact with the global South more successfully in its own interest, the Soviets urgently needed more expertise on global affairs in the Party and state organs. To that end, they established an ever-expanding network of 'area studies' from the late 1950s. These new research centres, organised around universities and branches of the Soviet Academy of Sciences, trained and employed an increasing number of specialists on all world regions.

The institutional framework to develop foreign expertise after 1953 was based on two trajectories: firstly, as far back as the nineteenth century, Russian *vostokovedenie* (orientalism) had dealt academically with the geography, languages, history and cultures of Asia, both within and outside the empire. As alluded to earlier in this book, the Soviets' view of the emerging Third World from the mid 1950s was shaped by the experience they had had with the inner periphery in Central Asia and the Caucasus. In 1954, MGIMO incorporated the Moskovskij Institut Vostokovedenija (Moscow Institute of Oriental Studies). The second trajectory was an external inspiration, to which Anastas Mikojan referred during his speech at the 20th Party Congress in 1956: 'in the United States, there are more than fifteen scientific institutes that study the Soviet economy alone ... and we snore and close down old research centres!'[35] The establishment of think tanks of the Rand Corporation type in the United States had not gone unnoticed in Moscow; thus the Soviets started to establish their own. The most notable foundation concerned with the intellectual conquest of the world abroad was actually a re-establishment: the Institut Mirovogo Chozjajstva i Mirovoj Politiki (Institute of World Economy and Politics) had been shut down in 1947 because its Hungarian director Jenö Varga was a foreigner and, just as unfashionable at that time, had predicted the economic convergence of capitalism and socialism. In 1956, shortly after Mikojan's speech, the institute reopened with the more modern sounding name Institut Mirovogo Ekonomiki i Meždunarodnych Otnošenij (Institute of World Economy and International Relations, IMEMO). As a branch of the Soviet Academy of Sciences, it was led initially by the Armenian Anušavan Arzumanjan and, from 1959, Nikolaj Inozemcev headed an agency that eventually employed 700 high-profile researchers in its own tower building in Moscow's Novye Čeremuški district. At IMEMO, they conducted research in all branches of the social sciences and provided Soviet organs with information on global economic, political and social developments. Like all foreign institutes in the USSR, it had to contribute to foreign propaganda and public relations.[36]

Besides IMEMO, the Soviet Academy of Sciences established several regional study centres that eventually covered the whole world. The Institut Narodov Azii (Institute of the Peoples of Asia, INA) developed several subdivisions from Japan to Pacific studies and the Middle East). An independent Institut Afriki (Africa Institute, IAF) came into being in 1959; one for the USA and Canada followed some years later. The Institut Latinskoj Ameriki (Institute of Latin America, ILA) opened its

---

[35] Quoted in Gerhard Duda, *Jenö Varga und die Geschichte des Instituts für Weltwirtschaft und Weltpolitik in Moskau 1921–1970: Zu den Möglichkeiten und Grenzen wissenschaftlicher Auslandsanalyse in der Sowjetunion* (Berlin: Akademie-Verlag, 1994), p. 284.

[36] Duda, *Jenö Varga und die Geschichte des Instituts für Weltwirtschaft und Weltpolitik in Moskau 1921–1970*; Rose, *The Soviet Propaganda Network*, p. 269.

doors, in the spring of 1961, in a vast former military building in central Bol'šaja Ordynka street in Moscow. More than a hundred researchers and an expanding special library with international literature and journals (much of it western) made it one of the largest research facilities of its kind on Latin America worldwide. Seven departments gathered and processed information on the economy, foreign policy, workers and social movements, culture, geography, history and agrarian problems of all states and cultures south of the Rio Grande. The recently 'discovered' and cherished revolutionary Cuba got its own department.[37]

Within already existing structures of the Academy and many more scientific and political institutions, too, regional offices now gathered worldwide regional expertise. The Moscow State Institute of History opened a Latin American section in 1953. Several departments of the Soviet Academy of Sciences followed: in 1957, IMEMO split its department of the Americas into a northern branch for the United States and Canada, and a Latin American one; the Gorky Institute of World Literature, the Institute of General History and the Institute of Philosophy had completed the same restructuring by 1961.[38] Smaller Latin America centres opened at universities all over the Union: in Leningrad and Kiev, and also in Voronezh, Alma-Ata, Frunze, Dushanbe, Lvov, Tbilisi, Baku and Kishinev. But most resources for this expanded research on the Third World were allocated to Moscow, where the old internationalists filled the many newly created research and teaching positions.

Ivan Majskij, released from the Gulag in 1955, now supervised a young generation of historians of the modern Hispanic world at Moscow State University. Lev Zubok, rehabilitated after Stalin's death, kept teaching at MGIMO until 1961. In parallel, he was a senior researcher at the Institute of History in the Soviet Academy of Sciences, where he finished his *magnum opus*, a grand two-volume history of the Second International.[39] Iosif Grigulevič was dismissed from the secret service in 1956 and given positions at the Institute of Ethnography at the Soviet Academy of Sciences, and was a founding member of the ILA, where he worked for the remaining twenty-seven years of his life. In addition, he was an advisor to the Latin American department of VOKS and the GKKS, and he was appointed vice-president of the friendship society with Venezuela. He was awarded a *doktor nauk* for his study of the Cuban

[37] Viktor Vol'skii, 'The Study of Latin America in the USSR', *Latin American Research Review* 3/1 (1967), 85.
[38] E. Larin, 'Centr latinoamerikanskich issledovanij Instituta vseobščej istorii', *Latinskaja Amerika* 4 (2001), 46–8.
[39] Lev Zubok, *Istorija vtorogo internacionala* (Moscow: Nauka, 1966).

cultural revolution and became an editor of a number of journals and a member of the Soviet Academy of Sciences. His hopes for socialism were still alive in an interview he gave on his 70th birthday: 'the French Revolution needed a hundred years, too, to be established in Europe. Latin America will not need that much time to reach socialism.'[40] Grigulevič knew probably every single rank-and-file person in the Spanish and Latin American left and communist movements, and he was well connected to the highest positions within the Soviet Union. Through his classes on Latin American history (and, while his past remained secret, on spying techniques to KGB cadets), and through an impressive output of academic writings, Grigulevič conveyed both his knowledge and his internationalist ideals to a younger generation.[41]

Knowledge exchange, knowledge expansion

Thanks to the quick build-up of area studies, and contacts re-established with international academe, the Soviet gap in knowledge of the outside world gradually filled. In 1946, Soviet scholars had published one book on Latin America; in 1953 the number had risen slightly to twelve. Seven years later, even before contacts with Cuba were established, sixty volumes a year informed Soviet readers about all aspects of life in and history of Latin America.[42] In 1955, the first cautious scientific contacts had been established with Latin America, building on a book-exchange agreement with Mexico. A year later, Soviet researchers had been allowed, for the first time, to travel to Brazil for a geographical congress. In 1958, the first scholars from Argentina arrived at the Academy in Moscow.[43] From these tender beginnings, the number of exchanges, personal as much as intellectual, soon rose significantly. After years of Stalinist introspection, Soviet academics read and analysed 6,900 international scientific journals, a Chilean visitor reported in 1959.[44]

---

[40] Anon., 'Odin iz starejšich sovetskich Latinoamerikanistov: beseda s členom-korrespondentom AN SSSR I. R. Grigulevičem', *Latinskaja Amerika* 5 (1983), 141–3.

[41] Grigulevič, who now occasionally used the new pseudonym Iosif Lavreckij, published fifty-eight books on the history of the Catholic Church and several best-selling biographies of Latin American liberation heroes from Bolívar to Che Guevara.

[42] Moisej Al'perovič, *Sovetskaja istoriografija stran Latinskoj Ameriki* (Moscow: Nauka, 1968), p. 17; Institut Latinskoj Ameriki (ed.), *Latinskaja Amerika v Sovetskoj pečati* (Moscow: ILA RAN, 1964).

[43] S. Korneev, 'Svjazy Akademii nauk SSSR s Latinskoj Amerikoj', *Latinskaja Amerika* 8 (1974), 137–40.

[44] Aldunate, *En Moscú*, p. 68.

Somewhat ironically, reading early Cold War US assessments of Latin America led many Soviet Latin Americanists initially to the same – if perhaps more cheerful – belief in imminent revolutions all across the Americas.[45]

From its foundation in 1961, the ILA, too, sent its researchers abroad, starting with a series of *komandirovki* to Cuba. By 1966, it was exchanging books and maintaining personal contacts with scientific centres in twenty-five countries, most closely with those in eastern Europe and with the Cuban Academy of Sciences.[46] Universities all over the Americas, western Europe and China and the states of Argentina, Mexico, Brazil and Cuba signed reciprocal agreements, too. As an institutional member of several UN bodies, the ILA sent researchers to UNESCO, to the United Nations Economic Commission for Latin America and the Caribbean (CEPALC) and the United Nations Industrial Development Organisation (UNIDO). The economist Lev Kločkovskij (1927–), founding researcher of the ILA and professor at MGIMO, was the Soviet representative in CEPALC; Anatolij Glinkin (1926–2006), a 1952 MGIMO graduate, led the UNESCO department of social sciences in Paris from 1968 to 1972.[47] The deputy director of the ILA, Marklen Lazarev (1920–2008), had been a lawyer for the lend-lease programme and, for that purpose, had lived in the United States from 1944 to 1946, and was a permanent member of the International Court of Justice in The Hague for fifteen years.[48]

By the same token, international academics and representatives of international organisations were received within the institute's walls: as head of the United Nations Conference on Trade and Development (UNCTAD), Raúl Prebisch went to the ILA in 1963, 1966 and 1967, where his theories of structuralist economics (a precursor of dependency theory) evoked heated discussion among Soviet researchers. The ILA regularly organised congresses at which Soviet academics debated with staff of Latin American embassies, with Latin American students from Moscow universities and with Latin American leftist writers and politicians, but also with apolitical researchers from all over the world. Roland

---

[45] Rabe, *The Most Dangerous Area in the World*, p. 197; Al'perovič, *Sovetskaja istoriografija stran Latinskoj Ameriki*.

[46] Hugo Fazio Vengoa, 'América Latina Vista por los Académicos Soviéticos: preámbulo de las relaciónes Ruso-Latinoamericanas', *H-Critica* 15 (2003), 35; A. Maevskij, 'Meždunarodnye naučnye svjazi Instituta Latinskoj Ameriki', *Latinskaja Amerika* 7 (1974), 148–52; Vol'skii, 'The Study of Latin America in the USSR', 84–6.

[47] Anatolij Nikolaevič Glinkin, obituary in *Latinskaja Amerika* 9 (2006), 105–6; Cole Blasier, 'The Soviet Latin Americanists', *Latin American Research Review* 16 (1981), 109–10.

[48] Marklen Ivanovič Lazarev, obituary in *Latinskaja Amerika* 2 (2009), 108–9.

Ely, an Argentine professor at the Universidad Nacional de Buenos Aires, conducted research at the ILA in 1965 as a guest scholar. In 1966, eighteen Soviet researchers spent several weeks each in different Latin American countries, and as many as seventy-five Latin Americans went as guests of the ILA to Moscow. The US Latin Americanist Russell Bartley was the first western historian to conduct fieldwork in Moscow in 1967/8. And, when Radio Free Europe organised a conference on Soviet Latin Americanists in Munich in 1968, the head of the ILA, Viktor Vol'skij, himself participated. In the late 1960s, the ILA had contacts with 450 institutes, libraries and universities all over the world. By 1973, an impressive number of 350 guest scholars had been received, most of them Latin Americans.[49]

From 1969, the ILA distributed its own popular scientific journal internationally: *Latinskaja Amerika* combined news, articles, essays and debates on Latin America in a colourful and innovative format. Sergo Mikojan was editor in chief, and Juan Cobo (a child refugee during the Spanish Civil War who became a Soviet citizen and prominent journalist in the Soviet Union) oversaw its Spanish-language edition *América Latina*. A decade later, the Russian and Spanish edition were both appearing monthly at 140 pages in print runs of 15,000 and 8,000 copies respectively in 54 countries worldwide, an quantity that reflected the editors' ambition to be more than a purely academic journal. Leftist Latin American authors wrote occasionally for the journal, and many issues were dedicated to a guest of the institute with a long interview. Many a Latin American left intellectual and politician, from Jorge Amado and Mario Vargas Llosa to Mexico's president José Lopez and Nicaragua's minister of culture, the leftist Catholic Ernesto Cardenal, accepted invitations; Gabriel García Márquez went four times for interviews and chats with the Soviet Latin Americanists.[50]

Privileges and limits of academic work in the late Soviet Union

The *meždunarodniki*'s lives were glamorous by Soviet standards. They could travel abroad and had access to international literature and contacts with foreigners. While they were not 'free of competition and

---

[49] Otčet o rabote po linii meždunarodnych naučnych svjazej Instituta Latinskoj Ameriki AN SSSR v 1966 godu, undated, GARF f.9518 op.1 d.1021 ll.2–25; Blasier, *The Giant's Rival*, p. 180; Bekopitov, 'Raul' Prebiš'; Maevskij, 'Meždunarodnye naučnye svjazi Instituta Latinskoj Ameriki', 152; Vol'skii, 'Sovetskaja latinoamerikanistika', 13; Roland T. Ely, 'El panorama interamericano visto por investigadores de la URSS', *Journal of Inter-American Studies* 8/2 (1966), 294–317.

[50] Mikojan, 'Neuželi tridcat' piat' let?', 36.

responsibility for good work' as a critical western observer believed, they – as long as they did not dissent too obviously from the official Party line – lived secure lives protected from unemployment and with many publishing opportunities.[51] In Soviet society, their prestige was high and so were their salaries: the Portuguese communist Francisco Ferreira, who worked for the Brazilian radio programme in Moscow, recalled that his *meždunarodnik* colleagues at the station not only had an enjoyable job, a good reputation and privileges such as dachas and many holidays; they also earned ten times more than the best engineers in the Kharkov factory, where he had worked previously.[52] The Chilean liberal parliamentarian Raúl Aldunate, during his visit to the USSR in 1959, remembered the same ratio between intelligentsia and workers' wages.[53]

It is therefore unsurprising that the offspring of many high-ranking state and Party officials, banned from Party careers according to an unwritten Soviet rule, were among this group. In the early days, the daughters of Vjačeslav Molotov and Aleksej Kosygin as well as Georgij Žukov's son studied at MGIMO.[54] Jurij Brežnev was Soviet trade representative in Switzerland, his sister Galina an official for Novosti. Andrej Gromyko's son Anatolij firstly went as special envoy to Great Britain and was later head of the Africa Institute. Ljudmila Kosygina became a researcher at the Institute of Scientific Information and director of the All-Union Library for Foreign Literature.[55] Not without justification, western scholars considered the *institutniki* and especially the *meždunarodniki* a 'privileged caste'.[56]

The newly founded area studies were run mostly by loyal social scientists, but, because of their novelty and the relatively liberal intellectual atmosphere of the Thaw, they benefited from a degree of academic freedom. In their professional and personal lives, the *meždunarodniki* enjoyed privileges that went way beyond what an average Soviet citizen could expect. That said, they were not given free rein, and they had no carte blanche for their writings or public speech. The highest authority on academic questions remained the Central Committee. Only government and CPSU institutions and the Academy of Sciences were allowed to publish political analysis. In social studies and political journals,

---

[51] Apollon Davidson and Irina Filatova, 'African History: A View from behind the Kremlin Wall', in Maxim Matusevich (ed.), *Africa in Russia, Russia in Africa: Three Centuries of Encounters* (Trenton: Africa World Press, 2007), p. 118.
[52] Ferreira, *26 años na União Soviética*, pp. 105–6.   [53] Aldunate, *En Moscú*, p. 67.
[54] Chačaturov, *Zapiski očevidca*, pp. 67–9.
[55] Leonov, *Licholet'e*, p. 258; Gottemoeller and Langer, *Foreign Area Studies in the USSR*, p. 23.
[56] Eran, *Mezhdunarodniki*, p. 183.

editors had to be members of the CPSU, their editors appointed by higher authorities, and those in significant positions had to be confirmed by the Central Committee or the Politburo.

Editorial boards for journals covering the outside world always included high officials from the International Department of the Central Committee, and every book published within the organisation of the Academy had to be reviewed by the Academy Council. Finally, all books and all journal issues had to be counter-checked by the state censor Glavlit, which did not care much about ideological debates, but usually only made sure no unwanted information on the Soviet military or economy was revealed. Criticism of political leaders or the Party was explicitly forbidden.[57] Neither was the choice of research topics completely free: maxims for Soviet area studies were *partijnost'* (partisanship), *konkretnost'* (relevance) and *sovremennost'* (topicality).[58] When the Central Committee wanted a topic researched or political line followed in academia, they placed – authorless – prefaces in academic journals.[59] The closer a research topic was to current affairs, the stricter were the rules. A *meždunarodnik* writing on recent developments in a certain area of the contemporary world was under much closer surveillance than, say, historians of the eighteenth century or ethnographers, who were rather free in their expression.[60]

As for their travels abroad, most *meždunarodniki* still had to pass through a complicated screening process before they could leave the country. Exit visas were given only upon recommendation of the work place, the local Party branch and, ultimately, the KGB. The latter, in need of linguistic and regional expertise, actually became an important employer of *meždunarodniki* itself, just like the diplomatic service, which had an entire department that was responsible purely for the surveillance of its own employees abroad.[61]

A prosopography of the first generation of 'Mgimovci'

The massive expansion and differentiation of institutionalised expertise on Latin America in the USSR provided hundreds of lucrative and

---

[57] Jerry F. Hough, *The Struggle for the Third World: Soviet Debates and American Options* (Washington, DC: Brookings Institution Press, 1986).

[58] Eran, *Mezhdunarodniki*, pp. 135–6.

[59] E.g. anon., 'Postanovlenie CK KPSS: O zadačach partinoj propagandy v sovremennych uslovijach i istoričestkaja nauka', *Voprosy Istorii* 6 (1960), 3–9.

[60] Gottemoeller and Langer, *Foreign Area Studies in the USSR*.

[61] Zubok, *Zhivago's Children*, pp. 88–120; Gottemoeller and Langer, *Foreign Area Studies in the USSR*, p. 100.

prestigious positions for specialists. Along with academic institutions, the International Department of the Central Committee of the CPSU, its affiliated Institute of Social Sciences, the foreign ministry, the KGB, and the military secret service GRU also all founded their own regional, including Latin American, departments. Initially, leading positions in these newly created institutions and departments were filled with functionaries; Sergej Michajlov, formerly Anastas Mikojan's secretary in the foreign trade ministry and a dutiful diplomat, was appointed head of the ILA.[62] The founding director of the Latin American department at the Institute of History of the Academy of Sciences was Nikolaj Lavrov (1915–89), like Michajlov a bureaucrat, a highly decorated officer in the Red Army, a member of the state board for the Lenin Peace Prize and a 'loyal officer and patriot', as he was remembered by his colleagues.[63] The next generation of professional internationalists did not share these military virtues to any great extent. These younger *meždunarodniki* were well educated and very ambitious and breathed new life into Soviet academic and political institutions. Many of them had diplomas from MGIMO and, from the mid 1950s, began their careers in the newly created positions in the internationalist academic and political institutions.

Some of the graduates from the 'Spanish group' at MGIMO have already made their appearance in this book: Vasilij Čičkov (1925–), the author of several novels and children's books was sent, after his graduation, to Mexico and Central America as correspondent for *Pravda* and was the very first Soviet to set foot in revolutionary Cuba in January 1959.[64] Genrich Borovik (1929–), the Minsk-born Soviet star journalist who wrote the first reportage from Cuba, and later reported from New York as Novosti correspondent for many years, had been his classmate at MGIMO. A third member of their group, the future KGB agent Nikolaj Leonov, has already featured on several occasions, too.

In what could be called a prosopography of Soviet internationalism after Stalin, this section will present the professional biographies of selected members of their cohort of alumni from MGIMO. Leonov, and his colleagues Anatolij Šul'govskij, Karen Chačaturov, Sergej (Sergo) Mikojan and Viktor Vol'skij, albeit from very different social

---

[62] Korneev, 'Svjazy Akademii nauk SSSR s Latinskoj Amerikoj', 138.

[63] N. Kalmykov and E. Larin, 'Oficer, patriot, latinoamerikanist', *Latinskaja Amerika* 4 (2001), 46–7; Nikolaj Matveevič Lavrov, obituary in *Latinskaja Amerika* 8 (1989), 141–2.

[64] Mikojan, *Anatomija Karibskogo krizisa*, p. 49.

backgrounds, all had similar political convictions that characterised their generation of academic intellectuals. Better than any institutional history could, their individual careers exemplify how these regional specialists, all born in the 1920s, carried their spirit of anti-Stalinist socialist internationalism into the newly founded institutions and departments, where they began their careers in the mid 1950s.

Nikolaj Leonov (1928–), born to a family of peasants in Rjazan' oblast, had graduated from MGIMO in 1952. Briefly in the firing line of the anti-cosmopolitan campaign, he was, although an excellent student, assigned the least prestigious position for a *meždunarodnik*: an underpaid administration job in the publishing house Editorial Progreso.[65] The majority of the staff there were Spanish refugees, whom Leonov befriended, and from whom he picked up his fluency in authentic everyday *castellano*. As the work proved very unsatisfying, he happily grabbed the first opportunity to escape. Shortly after Stalin's death, the foreign ministry sent young experts for language training all over Europe. Leonov applied and was accepted. However, Spain under dictator Francisco Franco did not issue visas to Soviet citizens at the time, so Leonov was sent for language studies to the Universidad Nacional Autónoma de México (UNAM) and later to a traineeship at the Soviet embassy in May 1953. On the ship that took him across the Atlantic, he began a lifelong friendship with a young Cuban of a similar age, who was returning from the preparatory meetings for the World Youth Festival in Bucharest: Raúl Castro.

Leonov stayed in Mexico for three years, studied philology at UNAM and acquired a full position at the embassy. He made friends with Raúl's brother Fidel and a young Argentine medical student by the name of Ernesto Guevara, who addressed everyone around him with an Argentine expression that would soon stick as his nickname: ¡*che!* ('hey!'). The group around the Castro brothers had, in a burst of juvenile megalomania, attempted to stir a revolt by attacking barracks in eastern Cuba. After some time in prison, they went into Mexican exile, and planned yet another attempt to topple the Cuban *caudillo* Batista. When they were arrested in the summer of 1956, the Mexican authorities found Leonov's visiting card from the Soviet embassy in Che Guevara's pocket. Leonov was dismissed from the foreign service and had to return to the publishing house in Moscow. Still unfulfilled with his work there, he settled on an academic career as a historian of Latin America at the Soviet Academy of Sciences under Nikolaj Lavrov.

---

[65] Leonov, *Licholet'e*, pp. 8–22.

Shortly after the Cuban Revolution in early 1959, Leonov was summoned to the KGB headquarters on Lubjanka Square. The reception was heartier than he had feared: the secret service had learnt that he knew the Castro brothers from Mexico. Desperate for information on what was happening in the Caribbean, the secret service offered Leonov a position as a KGB agent. All too aware of the repressive past of the Soviet secret service, Leonov hesitated, but finally agreed, convinced that, some years after Stalin's death, things had changed for the better. 'It was a time of great optimism and confidence', he recalled; 'we had won the war, Stalin's repressions were over, we had conquered the cosmos, the consumer situation was getting better, and Khrushchev's optimism was catching ... Even though I still had bad associations with the building, I entered the Lubjanka.'[66]

When, in late 1959, Anastas Mikojan went to Mexico and Cuba to open the Soviet exhibitions (see Chapter 1), Leonov went along as translator. In Havana, they met his old Cuban friends, who had succeeded in their apparently forlorn cause of revolution on the island. Leonov now stayed in Mexico and replaced Aleksandr Alekseev as the KGB's man in Latin America. At the same time, he was an associated founding member of the Institute of Latin America, where colleagues and friends remembered him as 'a bright, clever, serious and experienced man ... whose general's shoulder straps did not spoil his character'.[67] With great nostalgia, Leonov recalled from these days his friend and patron, the master-spy-turned-historian, Iosif Grigulevič.[68] Following his role model, Leonov continued his academic writing throughout his life as secret agent and published a series of books on the history of Central America and of the Catholic Church in Latin America, and a very gentle biography of the Panamanian *caudillo* Omar Torrijos. 'In science', he recalled from the time of Brezhnev's stagnation, 'a certain democratic spirit continued.'[69] When he returned to Moscow in 1968, Leonov made a career in the KGB administration; he became head of the foreign espionage department in 1971 and, in the 1980s, head of the analytical department and deputy head of the chief directorate, the second most important post within the KGB structure.[70]

Leonov's boss at the ILA, and successor of the functionary Sergej Michajlov, was Viktor Vol'skij (1921–99). From a Lithuanian white-collar family, he had been accepted to the first generation of students at

[66] *Ibid.*, pp. 40–1, 85, 93, 286.   [67] Mikojan, *Anatomija Karibskogo krizisa*, pp. 49–50.
[68] Leonov et al., 'El general Nikolai Leonov en el CEP', 77, 87, 91.
[69] Leonov, *Licholet'e*, p. 36.
[70] Leonov et al., 'El general Nikolai Leonov en el CEP', 72.

the newly established MGIMO. He gained a reputation as a talented economist and expert on capitalist countries firstly at MGIMO and, from 1959, also as a professor at Moscow State University. In 1966, he was made director of the ILA, a position he would keep until after the dismantling of the Soviet Union. Vol'skij was considered the 'founder of the modern school of Soviet Latin Americanists' and wrote, among more than 300 scientific works on Latin America, the standard works on Soviet–Latin American relations.[71] In 1970, he was appointed to the council for developing countries at the Academy and later became a full member of the Academy – the highest award in Soviet academia. Vol'-skij's academic reputation went beyond the USSR: he was a member of the Peruvian, Dominican and Mexican geographical societies, was awarded the Order of the Aztec Eagle, the highest decoration for foreigners in Mexico, and won state prizes in Venezuela, Peru and Cuba. Vol'skij held an honorary doctorate from universities in Barranquilla, Havana and Lima and honorary citizenship of the cities of Jalapa, Guadalajara, Quito and Rio de Janeiro.

The honour of the Mexican Aztec Order was awarded to yet another Soviet historian: Anatolij Šul'govskij (1926–91). Born into a family of Soviet *intelligenty*, he had graduated from MGIMO in 1953. For several years, he worked in the Inostrannaja Literatura publishing house for international literature. Michajlov called him to the newly founded Institute of Latin America in 1961, and he held a parallel position at IMEMO from 1963 as well as one at the Politizdat publishing house. Fluent in Russian, German, Spanish, Portuguese, English and French, Šul'govskij wrote many scientific and popular scientific books on Simón Bolívar, on the proletariat in Latin America, on the Mexican president Lázaro Cárdenas (for which he received the Aztec Order) and especially on the role of the army in Latin American states. For his research, Šul'govskij travelled often and extensively to many parts of the Americas, 'even though the *vlasti* [those in power] time and again directly or indirectly, for this reason or that', thwarted his trips abroad. But Šul'govskij was far from being a dissenter: it was he who made sure ideological premises of the CPSU were followed at the ILA. He was 'a child of the socialist system, a Soviet historian', but one who 'did not try to confuse the desired with reality', a long-time colleague remembered in his obituary.[72]

---

[71] Vol'skii, 'Sovetskaja latinoamerikanistika'; Vol'skii, 'The Study of Latin America in the USSR'.
[72] E. Dabagjan, 'Anatolij Fedorovič Šul'govskij (1926–1991)', *Novaja i Novejšaja Istorija* 5 (2007), 178–91; E. Dabagjan, 'Jarkij i mnogogrannyj talant', *Latinskaja Amerika* 4 (2001), 18–27; Anatolij Fedorovič Šul'govskij, obituary in *Latinskaja Amerika* 1 (1992), 140.

At the ILA, Šul'govskij worked for many years with Karen Chačaturov (1927–2005), son of an Armenian intelligentsia family in Tbilisi that was hit hard by the Great Terror of the 1930s.[73] After his graduation from MGIMO, Chačaturov worked as a journalist for the Soviet Army journals *Krasnyj Flot* (The Red Fleet) and *Kraznaja Zvezda* (The Red Star) and wrote his early articles, in best Stalinist pathos, from a Soviet battleship in the Atlantic. In 1953, he covered the violent, CIA-sponsored overthrow of the Guatemalan president Arbenz – and found the topic of his life. US interventions in Latin America became Chačaturov's academic special-isation, and he wrote about them with such passion and fervour that, until perestroika, he was denied visas to the United States and Canada for conferences and to meetings of the Soviet–US society.

In 1957, Chačaturov was appointed press attaché at the Soviet embassy in Uruguay, and he became head of the Sovinformbjuro/ Novosti in Latin America. From Uruguay, he regularly wrote for *Litera-turnaja Gazeta* and local left newspapers. In addition, he organised visits by Soviet journalists – Anatolij Sofronov from *Ogonek*, Adžubej from *Komsomolskaja Pravda*, Nikolaj Gribačev from *SSSR* and Danil Krami-nov from *Pravda* – during their trips through South America (see also Chapter 2).[74] Chačaturov stayed for five years, only interrupted for a few months when he built up the Novosti office in post-revolutionary Cuba, and summed up his experience of Uruguay for a broad Soviet readership in a colourful little book that mixed depictions of the beauty of the country with wild accusations of the local evil-doings of the 'Yankees'.[75]

Once back in Moscow, Chačaturov began an academic career as protégé of another 'father figure', the politician-turned-historian Ivan Majskij, at both the ILA and Moscow State University, where he com-pleted his dissertation in 1969. For his academic endeavours, he travelled to almost all countries of the Americas (except Canada and the United States), and he received awards in Chile and Venezuela. Having long served as head of the Latin American section of Novosti, Chačaturov became deputy president of the entire organisation in 1971, which made him responsible for the activities of Novosti in the entire Third World. As a professor at the diplomatic school of the foreign ministry and as a leading *žurnalist-meždunarodnik*, he was a serious voice among Soviet Latin Americanists. But it was especially thanks to his position in the

---

[73] Chačaturov, *Zapiski očevidca*, p. 57.   [74] *Ibid.*, pp. 10–25.
[75] Karen Chačaturov, *Urugvaj Segodnja* (Moscow: Izdatel'stvo Instituta Meždunarodnych Otnošenij, 1962).

International Department of the Central Committee that this voice was also heard at highest levels of politics.[76]

The last representative of this generation covered here is Sergo Mikojan (1929–2010). He graduated from MGIMO in 1952, and, after a dissertation on India and Pakistan, joined IMEMO as scientific assistant and editor of the journal *Mirovaja Ekonomika i Meždunarodnye Otnošenija* (World Economy and International Relations). In early 1960, he travelled with his father, the Armenian Old Bolshevik Anastas Mikojan, to Cuba. Enthralled with the tropical revolution, young Mikojan became friends with Che and Fidel, and decided to change the focus of his scientific work to Latin America and especially Cuba. Sergo recalled his own father as inspiration: 'he was an internationalist of the old school, it was part of his conception of himself . . . He belonged to a generation in which many internationalist Jews were killed in Stalin's purges, but he himself stayed true to the cause.'[77]

Sergo Mikojan, after his conversion in Cuba, entered the ILA and later edited the institute's monthly journal *Latinskaja Amerika*. His background in the highest Soviet elite and his friendship with influential members of the *nomenklatura* provided him with a security that allowed him to be very experimental and open-minded in his editorial and scientific work and enabled him to survive several attempts of both the Propaganda Department of the Central Committee and the presidium of the Academy to oust him as chief editor. One of the most reform-oriented of the Soviet Latin Americanists, Sergo Mikojan was an outspoken critic of Stalin, whose terror had affected his family, too: his father-in-law, Aleksej Kuznecov, had been the first secretary of the CPSU in Leningrad and had been shot during the second Leningrad affair in 1950. But Sergo was nonetheless a convinced socialist internationalist. Even in his post-Soviet recollections, he hailed the Cuban revolutionaries and the *comprometidos* Pablo Neruda and David Siqueiros as the great heroes of his life.[78]

Jews in Soviet area studies

The bulk of future leading *meždunarodniki* received their education from MGIMO. Numerous Jewish students, however, no matter how talented, were not accepted to its study programme. After 1953, many of them

---

[76] Sergej Kisljak, 'K ego sovetam prislušivalsja MID Rossii', *Latinskaja Amerika* 9 (2005), 7; Chačaturov, *Tri znaka vremeni*; Blasier, *The Giant's Rival*, p. 202.

[77] Mikojan, *Anatomija Karibskogo krizisa*, p. 151.

[78] Mikojan, *Anatomija Karibskogo krizisa*, p. 50; Mikojan, 'Neuželi tridcat' piat' let?'

found their way into Latin American studies anyway, where they joined an older generation of internationalists such as Zubok, Majskij and Grigulevič – who were all from different Jewish backgrounds themselves. Indeed, a large proportion of Latin Americanists in the Soviet Union came from Jewish families, as is often evident from their father's names: the historian Boris (Moiseevič) Merin (1932–2007), at the ILA from 1963, was an expert on social movements in Latin America and a leading member of the Soviet solidarity committee with Latin American countries. The anthropologist Abram (Davidovič) Dridzo (1926–2003) was a researcher with a talent for poetry at the Academy of Sciences; and Lev (Samojlovič) Ospovat (1922–2009) was the author of several biographies of Latin American artists.

Two other Jewish historians stand out from the Thaw generation of Soviet Latin Americanists: Moisej Al'perovič (1918–), son of a Jewish insurance company agent from Moscow, graduated from Moscow State University in 1941. After fighting in the Red Army for four years, and working for the Soviet Military Administration in Germany, Al'perovič finished a dissertation on Mexican–US relations. But as a Jew in the Soviet Union in 1949, he was not allowed an academic position in Moscow. The Soviet ministry of education sent him to the provincial town of Rjazan' instead, where he taught at the local pedagogical university until he could return to the Soviet capital in 1954. He became an expert on liberation movements in sixteenth- to nineteenth-century Latin America at the Academy's Institute of History. Al'perovič was decorated with the Aztec Order, as well as with the title of honorary doctor of the UNAM.[79] He established his reputation with a series of books on the history of Mexico and the United States and one on the whole of Latin America, *From Ancient Times to the Early Twentieth Century*. The latter book, co-authored with Lev Slezkin (1920–2012) became a standard reference for all scholars. Slezkin himself had grown up in Moscow's bohemia of the 1920s in a Jewish intelligentsia household, where his father, the author Jurij Slezkin, hosted illustrious friends such as Mikhail Bulgakov, Vladimir Mayakovsky and Anatolij Lunačarskij. Lev studied history at Moscow State University, finished his *kandidatskaja* in 1953 and found a position with Lavrov and Al'perovič at the Academy's section for the Americas. Al'perovič and Slezkin were rather latitudinarian academics: both got into trouble several times with the authorities for their writings on Latin American liberation movements.

[79] Anon., 'Jubilej Moiseja Samuiloviča Al'peroviča', *Novaja i Novejšaja Istorija* 2 (2009), 214–16; Boris Koval', 'Korifej otečestvennoj latinoamerikanistiki: k 90-letiju Moiseja Samuilovia Al'peroviča', *Latinskaja Amerika* 9 (2008), 92–6.

They had their problems with Party dogma and hypocritical cowardice, which still prevailed in Soviet academia, but they were convinced socialist internationalists, 'Soviets in the non-official sense', as a colleague remembered.[80]

The high ratio of Jews in Soviet Latin Americanists is remarkable, and so is the fact that almost all of them were purely academics, without the ties to political institutions that most of their Slavic and Caucasian colleagues had. Open discrimination and exclusion stopped after 1953, but Jewish *meždunarodniki* were still obstructed from careers in more influential positions. This subtle anti-Semitism went hand in hand with an increasing rehabilitation of Stalin from the late 1960s, and Al'perovič found a shrewd way to comment on this tendency. His book on the nineteenth-century Paraguayan strongman José Gaspar Rodríguez de Francia was clearly a parable on the recent history of the Soviet Union and its dictator.[81]

Stalinist repression until 1953, and the remnants of Stalinism and anti-Semitism throughout the 1960s and 1970s, did keep many Jews from following higher careers in Soviet administrative jobs. It did not, however, result in a loss of their socialist ideals, as is shown by the life and work of another Jewish-Soviet Latin Americanist, Kiva Majdanik (1929–2006). He graduated from Moscow State University with a specialisation in Latin American history in 1951, with top grades, but at a bad moment; the son of a renowned Jewish lawyer from Moscow did not get a recommendation for an *aspirantura*. He was sent to provincial Ukraine as a high school teacher. Only after the 20th Party Congress was he allowed to return and begin his dissertation on the Spanish Civil War, at the Academy of Sciences, under supervision of Ivan Majskij, who had just been released from the Gulag.

From 1963, Majdanik lived in Prague as Latin America expert for *Problemy Mira i Socializma*. The editing board of this international, multi-language, communist journal, founded to replace the disbanded structures of the Cominform, was a hub where Soviet intellectuals could debate comparatively freely with socialists from all over the world – and where they were sometimes inspired to express criticism of their own state. Majdanik built up contacts and friendships with many Latin American leftists during his work in Prague. In exchanges with the Salvadorans Schafik Handal and Roque Dalton, and with the Dominican Narciso Isa Conde, Majdanik developed a distinct revolutionary idea of

---

[80] Boris Koval', 'K jubileju L'va Jur'eviča Slezkina', *Novaja i Novejšaja Istorija* 3 (2010), 250–1.

[81] Moisej Al'perovič, *Revoljucija i diktatura v Paragvae* (Moscow: Nauka, 1975).

socialism, often very critical of the Latin American communist parties and the CPSU, which earned him the nickname of the 'Soviet Che Guevara'. For a while, Majdanik's solo runs were tolerated, even though Latin American communist parties time and again demanded he be fired – which he was, after he publicly criticised the Soviet invasion of Czechoslovakia in 1968.

Highly educated, worldly and fluent in Spanish, Portuguese, French, English, Italian, German, Czech and Russian, Majdanik found a position as a historian and political scientist at IMEMO afterwards. In his academic work, which was very unconventional by Soviet standards, he dealt with Brazil, Cuba, Mexico, Nicaragua and Venezuela, and with workers' and liberation movements all over the continent from an unorthodox Marxist perspective. Majdanik even dared to use Trotskyist terminology in his sharp criticisms of the rehabilitation of Stalin, and, in the course of the 1970s, got increasingly into trouble with the authorities. Some of his publications never made their way through the censors: a foreword for his friend and fellow historian Michail Gefter was pulped, along with the entire edition of the book on orders of the Central Committee. A booklet on *Ultra-Left Liberation Movements in Asia, Africa, Latin America*, which Majdanik circulated with a warning note 'only for internal use', was nonetheless considered so dangerous that the leadership of the Academy decided to burn it right away. What saved him from worse was his network of friends, especially Sergo Mikojan, and prominent communist foreigners in Moscow and Prague, including Dolores 'La Pasionaria' Ibárruri, the exiled head of the Partido Comunista de España (PCE), who at the time was developing from a hard-core Stalinist into a more moderate socialist.

The *meždunarodniki*'s march through the Soviet institutions

The massive expansion of Soviet area studies on Latin America from the mid 1950s, initiated in order to strengthen Cold War competitiveness, provided hundreds and ultimately thousands of scholars with privileged and well-funded workplaces. The members of the first generation of these post-Stalin professional internationalists were male and born in the 1920s. The *meždunarodniki* who later focused on Latin America had experienced, during their childhood, the Spanish Civil War as a great romantic cause for altruistic revolutionaries in a faraway and exotic country, which was suddenly, through media and refugees, very present in the lives of many of this generation. At the same time they lived through the dread of Stalinist state terror at home, and they experienced, soon thereafter, the horrors of the Second World War, either fighting themselves as very young men, or witnessing their fathers and older brothers fight, be wounded or die. Imperialism was no abstract threat to them. During the late 1940s and early 1950s, they, as talented students, got their higher education, most of them at the newly founded MGIMO. Those with a Jewish family background were barred there until 1953 and experienced an institutionalised anti-Semitism also in the years thereafter. These restraints notwithstanding, many Jewish students also managed to get a good education and academic positions.

All *meždunarodniki*, Jewish or not, were multi-lingual, and they had – in the Soviet Union a rarity at the time – experience of life abroad. Chačaturov had spent many years living in Uruguay, Leonov more than a decade in Mexico. Several others were born to Russian parents abroad and moved to the Soviet Union to work for internationalist organisations.[82] All of them were critical of Stalin, whose repression most of them had felt among their family and friends. They thus welcomed Khrushchev's reforms and the denunciation of the dictator's crimes. 'Kiva had a high estimation of the 20th Party Congress', remembered Majdanik's friend and biographer Narciso Isa Conde.[83] Viktor Vol'skij recalled that he finally convinced the censors to publish his dissertation, which proposed a new look at the developing countries, thanks to a reference to Khrushchev's speech.[84] Nikolaj Leonov, too, still admired Khrushchev in his post-Soviet memoirs: 'back in that day as today, I feel great sympathy for this man, and I am sure that, with him, Russia lost its last political leader of stature'.[85]

Relieved by the end of Stalinism and infected by Khrushchev's politicking and his swashbuckling optimism, all the *meždunarodniki* joined the Communist Party. Sergo Mikojan criticised Stalin remarkably openly, but never lost faith in the Party, whose ranks he joined in 1953, shortly after the death of the dictator. Vol'skij was a member, and so were Chačaturov and Šul'govskij, the latter not merely nominally, like anyone in any relevant position in the USSR, but as an active politician. Even the bustling Majdanik was in the Party – until he was thrown out. To be sure, being a member of the CPSU was quasi-indispensable for any Soviet citizen who wanted to travel abroad. But many young and well-educated Soviets, the first generation born under the Soviet regime, did not join the ranks of the CPSU after 1953 for these pragmatic reasons: at least

[82] Pavel Nikolaevič Bojko, obituary in *Latinskaja Amerika* 6 (2007), 140; Chačaturov, *Zapiski očevidca*, p. 45.
[83] Narciso Isa Conde, *Kiva Maidanik: humanidad sin límites y herejía revolucionaria* (Santo Domingo: Editora Tropical, 2007), p. 57.
[84] A. Glinkin, 'Slovo o druge', *Latinskaja Amerika* 4 (2001), 11–17.
[85] Leonov, *Licholet'e*, p. 93.

until the mid 1960s, many of them thought of themselves as a 'vanguard of a fair and egalitarian society' and shared a sense among them of a need to improve the Party from within.[86]

Leonov was – at least in hindsight – highly critical of Stalinism and Soviet deficiencies such as the bureaucracy, the influence of the military, careerism, nepotism and denunciation. Nonetheless, he was a dedicated socialist and enrolled with the Komsomol and later the Party. Reflecting on his relations with the Soviet powers in his post-Soviet memoirs, Leonov claimed to have been always judicious, critical and without ideological limitations. But he considered himself a convinced patriot and communist, which were interchangeable terms for him: 'my appreciation of the Party and power structures was based on the fact that I considered them my state, therefore my *rodina* [homeland]'.[87] If the Soviet Union followed a 'revolutionary-imperialist' paradigm, as Vladislav Zubok claimed, then Leonov can be considered the embodiment of this principle: a loyal and career-oriented civil servant to an empire, whose geo-political interests he safeguarded by all means necessary. Yet this imperialist stance was based on his political conviction, an almost romanticist socialist internationalism: 'I was an orthodox communist and a loyal servant', Leonov described himself in retrospect, and claimed for his generation: 'we were led by the belief that the fate of the global conflict between capitalism and socialism would be decided in the Third World'.[88]

From their teachers and father figures, socialist internationalists from the 1920s, the *meždunarodniki* inherited their ideals. During their march through old and new Soviet institutions, they carried this conviction with all its initial romantic connotations, and their academic work often reflected this stance. In Latin American history and politics, they found a huge range of stories of national liberation movements, revolutions, anti-western thought, anti-US struggle and workers' movements, and they included countless biographies of liberation heroes from José Martí to Fidel Castro.[89] The unconditional enthusiasm for the latter and for the socialist prospects of Cuba and Latin America shows that, thanks to the *meždunarodniki*, Soviet knowledge of Latin American past and present had grown tremendously in the decade after 1953, but was still based on clear ideological leanings and full of glorifying romanticism.

---

[86] Zubok, *Zhivago's Children*, pp. 34–6; Chačaturov, *Zapiski očevidca*, p. 72.
[87] Leonov, *Licholet'e*, p. 22.
[88] Zubok, *A Failed Empire*; Leonov, 'La inteligencia soviética en América Latina', 53, 85.
[89] Al'perovič, *Sovetskaja istoriografija stran Latinskoj Ameriki*.

Cold War profiteers: the *meždunarodniki* and Soviet humanities

This resumption of socialist internationalism was a specifically Soviet trend, but the institutionalisation of expertise on world regions was not. The expansion of area studies was a northern-hemisphere phenomenon in the 1950s and 1960s, when a rather similar culture of experts emerged in the United States and, to some extent, in western and eastern Europe at a similar time. The Cold War led governments on both sides of the Iron Curtain not only to massively increase their military expenditure, but also to stimulate technological development and invest in research and education. The Soviets, as Mikojan's references exemplify, took inspiration for these institutes from the enemy camp, but influences also happened in the other direction.

The contest with the Soviet Union, especially after its translocation from Europe to the Third World, made government officials in Washington realise how little they themselves actually knew about many areas of the world. Just as in the Soviet Union, centres of research were founded in the United States, which brought together specialists from different fields, historians, social scientists, linguists, anthropologists and economists, who all had, or developed, specific knowledge on one area of the world. For the first time, scholars participated in the making of US foreign policy. Most urgently, the United States needed to know more of the USSR itself and built up, more or less from scratch, an academic armada of Sovietologists, who, more often than not, blurred the distinction between academic scholarship and politically partisan intelligence analysis.[90] But many other world areas were studied closely now, too, and, most conspicuously, Latin American studies expanded tremendously after the Cuban Revolution and the first Soviet inroads into the region.[91]

In the United States as in the Soviet Union, a global foreign policy needed expertise, and, to that end, the two countries expanded scientific institutions and funded research in fields that had hitherto been

---

[90] David C. Engerman, *Know Your Enemy: The Rise and Fall of America's Soviet Experts* (Oxford: Oxford University Press, 2009).

[91] Michael Adas, *Dominance by Design: Technological Imperatives and America's Civilizing Mission* (Cambridge, MA: Belknap Press of Harvard University Press, 2006); Nils Gilman, *Mandarins of the Future: Modernization Theory in Cold War America* (Baltimore: Johns Hopkins University Press, 2003); Christopher Simpson (ed.), *Universities and Empire: Money and Politics in the Social Sciences during the Cold War* (New York: New Press, 1998), p. 68; Laura Nader, 'The Phantom Factor: Impact of the Cold War on Anthropology', in Noam Chomsky (ed.), *The Cold War and the University: Toward an Intellectual History of the Postwar Years* (New York: New Press, 1997), pp. 107–46; Immanuel Wallerstein, 'The Unintended Consequences of Cold War Area Studies', in Chomsky (ed.), *The Cold War and the University*, p. 202.

neglected. In both, the political leadership considered academe a tool to be used for their own advancement, but its professors sometimes saw things differently. Even in the Soviet Union, some branches of the humanities and the social sciences, without any obvious geo-political relevance, were actually able to profit from the Cold War rivalry. The lavish funds given to amass regional knowledge provided the liberal arts, in particular those with a certain distance from ideology, with good working conditions. Soviet anthropologists, geographers, art historians and literary scholars were able to conduct research that was often on par with that of their colleagues from the best western universities.

Rostislav Kinžalov (1920–2006), a scholar of the folklore of indigenous America, was an internationally renowned and published expert on the pre-Columbian art of Central America, which he presented in a series of exhibitions to the Soviet audience from 1956. After a joint research project with the linguist Jurij Knorozov (1922–99), who had laid the foundation for the deciphering of the language of the ancient Maya, and the mathematician Jurij Kosarev, who had contributed early computer models, the team published a Russian–Maya dictionary in 1960.[92] A precise cartography of Latin America was undertaken by Jakov Mašbic (1928–97).[93] Vladimir Kuz'miščev (1925–88), a cultural historian at the ILA and professional internationalist at VOKS and the SSOD, translated Latin American literature and wrote a series of best-selling historical novels on the Maya (see Chapter 2).[94] His colleague Jurij Zubrickij (1923–2007), an expert on the pre-Columbian cultures of the South American Andeans, was the first Russian to learn fluent Quechua, which, as the Peruvian writer Francisco Miró Quesada recalled, always made an incredible impression on people from that region.[95] 'Iuri el Grande', as he was called by his South American acquaintances, was able to conduct his research on Bolivia, Ecuador and Peru thanks to the positions he held at the ethnological department of the Academy of Sciences. In addition to his research, he taught at Lumumba University, gave language classes, wrote in Soviet popular magazines about his trips and, from 1965, organised radio broadcasts in Quechua, Aymara and Guaraní. Zubrickij was awarded honorary doctorates from two Peruvian universities and was given the freedom of the city of Cuzco, former

---

[92] Rostislav Vasil'evič Kinžalov, obituary in *Latinskaja Amerika* 9 (2006), 107–9; Al'perovič, *Sovetskaja istoriografija stran Latinskoj Ameriki*, p. 24; E. Evreinov, Ju. Kosarev and V. Ustinov, *Primenenie elektronnych vyčislitel'nych mašin v issledovanim pis'mennosti drevnich Majja* (Novosibirsk: Izdatel'stvo Sibirskogo Otdelenija AN SSSR, 1961).
[93] Torkunov (ed.), *MGIMO Universitet*, pp. 216–26.
[94] Vladimir Aleksandrovič Kuz'miščev, obituary in *Latinskaja Amerika* 7 (1988), 143.
[95] Miró Quesada, *La otra mitad del mundo*, p. 31.

capital of the Inca empire, and the state order of Peru. As well as his academic feats, Zubrickij, an 'in all respects non-mediocre human being ... a poet and dreamer, full of creativity', as he was called in *Latinskaja Amerika*'s normally rather sober obituaries, was an avid poet himself and, thanks to an impressive linguistic knowledge, translated poetry from languages that many people inside and outside the Soviet Union had not even heard of, among them Georgian, Lithuanian, Aymara, Guaraní, Quechua and Mapudungun.[96]

Other arts of modern Latin America also found advocates in the 1960s Soviet Union thanks to the originally geo-political consideration of knowledge expansion: the architect Vladimir Chajta (1933–2004), after his graduation from the Moscow Institute of Architecture, took an interest in Latin American construction methods and, as an affiliate to the ILA, introduced the Brazilian architect Oscar Niemeyer to the Soviet Union.[97] Georgij Stepanov (1919–86), a surviving veteran of the Spanish Civil War, and head of the language and literature department of the Academy of Sciences, became an internationally renowned linguist with an expertise on the regional varieties of the Spanish language. Latin American folk music got its own Soviet expert with Pavel Pičugin (1932–) from the Institute of World Literature, who wrote regularly in *Sovetskaja Muzyka* about the latest trends in Latino tunes, and published sheet music and analyses of Latin American music.

The enormous popularity of Latin American literature in the Soviet Union was due in no small part to Vera Kutejščikova (1919–2012). The literary critic had begun her career at the department of the Americas at VOKS in the 1940s. From 1956, she introduced and promoted Latin American authors to a Soviet readership from her position at the Institut Mirovoj Literatury imeni Gor'kogo (Gorky Institute of World Literature) at the Academy of Sciences, where she, after a trip to Mexico in the same year, organised the Latin American section and published her standard work *The Latin American Novel in the Twentieth Century*.[98] At the same time, Kutejščikova occupied the position of editor at the newly founded Spanish section of Progress publishing house, where she laid the foundation for the boom in Latin American literature in the Soviet Union in the 1960s.[99] Kutejščikova, too, found international recognition for her work and was awarded the Aztec Order as well as an honorary degree of

[96] Jurij Aleksandrovič Zubrickij, obituary in *Latinskaja Amerika* 6 (2007), 142–4.
[97] Pamjati V. L. Chajta, obituary in *Latinskaja Amerika* 10 (2004), 92–3.
[98] Vera Kutejščikova, *Roman Latinskoj Ameriki v XX. veke* (Moscow: Nauka, 1964).
[99] V. Zemskov, 'Ot izučenija literaturnogo processa k osmysleniju civilizacionnoj paradigmy: latinoamerikanistika v Institute mirovoj literatury', *Latinskaja Amerika* 4 (2001), 30–45; Kutejščikova, *Moskva-Meksiko-Moskva*.

UNAM. Like many intellectuals of her generation, during the Thaw she harboured an idealised notion of 1920s socialism and internationalism, which they believed was still unsoiled by Stalin's crimes. It was Eisenstein's fascination for Mexico, Kutejščikova later remembered, that kindled her interest in Latin America.[100]

By the late 1960s, the yawning Soviet gap in knowledge on Latin America of the decade before was by and large closed. True, much Soviet writing on contemporary history and political relations was embedded in an 'ideological framework ... that annoys deeply',[101] as the US historian Russell Bartley described it. But in other fields Soviet scholars delivered highly qualified research that impressed him to the extent that he conceded: 'Soviet research on Latin America is at such an elevated level that experts in the field who do not read Russian are in an unfortunate position.'[102] The ILA historians proudly quoted him in resumes of their own work, but preferred not to echo the less enthusiastic comment.[103]

The return of open academic debate to Soviet area studies and the fall of Allende

Ideological bias notwithstanding, the Soviet view of Latin America in the late 1960s and early 1970s was significantly less stereotypical and homogenising than it had been a decade before. Researchers continuously published ever more detailed studies on many aspects of the past and present of most states of the subcontinent. This included political movements, their stances towards the Third World, the Catholic Church, the armed forces and the trades unions as well as the great variations between countries and social strata within them. This differentiation of knowledge brought back a degree of cautious debate into Soviet academe. Always within a Marxist-Leninist conception of history, Soviet scholars now offered competing interpretations of Latin American developments. Scientific journals published articles that still used cautious wording and never directly opposed an individual scholar or a policy, but, for an informed reader, clearly argued against other opinions.[104]

---

[100] Kutejščikova, *Moskva-Meksiko-Moskva*, pp. 20–2, 90.
[101] Russell H. Bartley, 'A Decade of Soviet Scholarship in Brazilian History: 1958–1968', *Hispanic American Historical Review* 50/3 (1970), 465.
[102] Russell H. Bartley, 'On Scholarly Dialogue: The Case of US and Soviet Latin Americanists', *Latin American Research Review* 1 (1970), 60; Oswald, 'Contemporary Soviet Research on Latin America', 91.
[103] Vol'skii, 'Sovetskaja latinoamerikanistika', 13; Al'perovič, *Sovetskaja istoriografija stran Latinskoj Ameriki*, pp. 64–5.
[104] Prizel, *Latin America through Soviet Eyes*.

Two episodes confirm that the obsequiousness of Soviet academe had given way to a cautiously critical stance. In 1965, the director of the ILA was redeployed, and the academic staff was afraid of being allocated a clueless *nomenklatura* man as successor. So they voted for one themselves and suggested him to the Central Committee, which sent a representative, who sharply rebuked this insubordination. But the upshot was that they got the director they asked for, Viktor Vol'skij.[105] In addition, the *meždunarodniki*'s reactions to the Soviet invasion of Czechoslovakia in 1968 were not all in line with the regime. Vera Kutejščikova recalled: 'my contemporaries would never again forget that day; we were overwhelmed by feelings of shame and despair'; and she compared the crushing of the Prague Spring with the violence against protesting students in Mexico City the same year.[106] Kiva Majdanik, in Prague during these events, criticised the Soviet course of action publicly – and lost his job for this insolence. And even the conservative Anatolij Šul'govskij, within the walls of the ILA, made no secret of his sympathies for Alexander Dubček and his disapproval of the invasion.[107]

Increased self-awareness among academics fomented discussion, at the level of politics as much as academically, as did another factor: institutional competition. The expansion of area studies created a rivalry between historians of the ILA and the Academy's history department, each group indirectly claiming to be more professional and modern than the other.[108] With the end of the somewhat naive enthusiasm in the Third World for the Thaw, experts sometimes felt the need to validate their *raison d'être* and to justify their further existence. Nikolaj Leonov recalled that his Latin American department of the KGB often took initiatives only 'to prevent being aborted'.[109] By the same token, the ILA also made sure officials knew of the advances the Cold War enemy was making in the field of area studies and, in 1970, published an anthology of Latin American studies abroad.[110]

The substantially increased knowledge, cautious criticism and an atmosphere of competitiveness brought something back to academic life in the Soviet Union that had been severely restricted during Stalinism: relatively open academic debate. While differentiation and qualitative improvement happened everywhere in Soviet area studies, none of the

---

[105] Glinkin, 'Slovo o druge'.   [106] Kutejščikova, *Moskva-Meksiko-Moskva*, p. 213.
[107] Dabagjan, 'Anatolij Fedorovič Šul'govskij (1926–1991)'; Dabagjan, 'Jarkij i mnogogrannyj talant'.
[108] Oswald and Carlton (eds.), *Soviet Image of Contemporary Latin America*.
[109] Andrew and Mitrokhin, *The World Was Going Our Way*, p. 65.
[110] Vol'skii, 'Sovetskaja latinoamerikanistika'; Institut Latinskoj Ameriki (ed.), *Zarubežnye centry po izučenuju Latinskoj Ameriki* (Moscow: ILA RAN, 1970).

published Soviet debates on the outside world was more sophisticated than the one dealing with Latin America. The quick establishment of a hitherto hardly existing field gave many young scholars academic opportunities that they took up with enthusiasm and optimism. Moreover, since Latin America had only minor relevance in geo-political terms to the Soviet Union, academics were relatively free of direct political responsibility.[111]

Progressive vs conservative scholars

By the late 1960s, there were differing opinions in Soviet academia on the stage of development that capitalism had reached in Latin America. Based on these interpretations, there were different stances towards the support of left populists, left military regimes, communist parties and alternative socialist movements. Two lines of thought evolved in the Soviet debate, represented by two groups of scholars, who, for lack of better terms, will be called here 'conservatives' and 'progressives'. Conservatives were those who were most loyal to the Soviet state and its official policies; progressives instead took a stand for international socialism, and, for that matter, Latin American revolutionary movements. In the centre of all debates on the Third World in general and Latin America in particular was the question of violent revolutionary struggle: the official Soviet position condemned it, and being associated with 'left extremism' or even 'Maoism' could still bring people serious trouble in the late 1960s. However, there was the successful example of Cuba, which gave some Latin Americanists leverage to openly and publicly propose revolutionary struggle on the continent. Anything remotely critical of Soviet policies still had no chance of getting published, so the discussants always referred to foreign groups with a certain leaning; if scholars wanted to express their condemnation of support for revolutionary groups, they would not point fingers at the International Department of the CPSU, but instead criticised the left radicalism of foreign socialists such as Régis Debray. By the same token, criticism of Soviet support for anti-communist populists was expressed only indirectly, as through the repudiation of an article in a foreign newspaper.

The *meždunarodniki* of the ILA were usually in the conservative camp in these debates, and Šul'govskij and Vol'skij, as the leading historians of the institute, were its spokesmen. In a speech at a 1969 Third World conference in Frunze, Šul'govskij summed up his rather conformist

---

[111] Jerry F. Hough, 'The Evolving Soviet Debate on Latin America', *Latin American Research Review* 16/1 (1981), 125.

political stance: the main road to socialism was still 'non-capitalist development' (see Chapter 1). Central Asia, certainly not coincidentally the venue for the event, was still to serve as a role model. The revolution had won in a highly developed country (in his view, Soviet Russia); backward countries, by implication, could leapfrog the phase of capitalism by being inspired and helped by the socialist motherland ('Marxism-Leninism, that is the sentiment of historical optimism plus the experience of the peoples of the Soviet Union'). This was only possible via the working class, represented by the respective communist parties, which did not exclude the possibility that, in the first place, a national liberation movement or military rule might lead the way (as in Cuba and Peru respectively). Many paths were possible: whoever denied that, like the left extremists, only played into the hands of imperialism. Šul'govskij drew parallels between the collaboration with different 'anti-imperialist forces' and the (actually rather short-lived) support for Muslim movements in early 1920s Central Asia. He denounced Maoist theories of an urban vs rural opposition, called dependency theory 'far from objective reality' and 'latently racist' and said Che Guevara's *foco* theory was 'refuted by history'.[112]

In the 1970s, Šul'govskij no longer considered Latin America a part of an imperialism-stricken Third World and compared it to southern Europe rather than Asia and Africa. In a book co-written with his ILA colleagues Boris Koval' and Sergej Semenov, he suggested the concept of *zavisimyj kapitalizm* (dependent capitalism) for the further study of Latin America.[113] This was apparently too conservative even for the ILA. For a while, Vol'skij did not allow the book to leave the walls of the institute; later, the authors got into trouble with the censors at the publishing house. When the book finally came out, however, it did establish a new theory 'from below' that was discussed rather openly in the Soviet scientific community.

On the progressive side of the debates, scholars discussed dependency theory and later liberation theology with more goodwill. Ostensibly generally condemning certain foreign groups, they criticised the support of populists and military regimes, as in Brazil or Peru, and hinted at the revolutionary potential in some Latin American regions.[114] These progressives, with Majdanik and Al'perovič the most latitudinarian amongst them, not only proposed more active support for Latin American

---

[112] Šul'govskij, 'Latinskaja Amerika i opyt respublik Sovetskogo Vostoka', 86–8.

[113] Boris Koval', Sergej Semenov and Anatolij Šul'govskij, *Revoljucionnye processy v Latinskoj Amerike* (Moscow: Nauka, 1974).

[114] Hough, 'The Evolving Soviet Debate on Latin America', p. 89.

'liberation movements', but they also complained about the prevailing constraints within Soviet academia: in 1968, Al'perovič, after outlining the successes of Soviet area studies, could cautiously criticise the 'mechanical interpretation of historical processes' by more conventional Soviet historians – again without giving names – and their lack of dialogue with non-Marxist historians.[115]

The debate on Allende's fall

The end of the Chilean Frente Popular under Salvador Allende in 1973 caused the biggest clash between 'conservatives' and 'progressives' in Soviet academe. Official foreign policy towards Allende had been contradictory. Three years before, he had become the world's first democratically elected Marxist president. On the one hand, his victory seemed to finally prove what the Soviets had been preaching to the worldwide left for more than a decade: a peaceful path to socialism was feasible. Ponomarev, the head of the International Department, saw the election as a 'revolutionary blow to imperialism'.[116] Allende was celebrated in the Soviet press accordingly, headlined in the newspapers and hailed on Soviet television.[117] There was a coming and going of representatives of Chilean government members to Moscow. In 1972, a contract was signed that arranged exchanges in the fields of public health, education, media, sports and arts, and Aeroflot scheduled a weekly flight to Santiago, the first one to South America.[118] Yet the enthusiasm was a far cry from the Cuban craze a decade earlier. Most importantly, there was hardly any financial support.

Allende went himself later that year, together with the head of the communist party, Luis Corvalán; again, they were celebrated as great socialist heroes, but they had to return almost empty-handed. Although they bargained with their contacts with China, their requests for sorely needed credits were met only with restraint – the Soviets gave a one-off US$ 20 million loan, but could never have afforded yet another tremendously expensive friend like Castro's Cuba.[119] Scholars as much as politicians harboured serious doubts from the beginning as to whether the regime could prevail. Economically, Chile was irrelevant for the Soviets: the main export material, copper, was abundant in the USSR.

[115] Al'perovič, *Sovetskaja istoriografija stran Latinskoj Ameriki*, p. 31.
[116] Quoted in Prizel, *Latin America through Soviet Eyes*, p. 163.
[117] *Izvestija*, 27 Oct.–5 Nov. 1970.   [118] *Pravda*, 4 Mar. 1972.
[119] *Pravda* and *Izvestija*, 10 Dec. 1972; Theodore Shabat, `Allende Arrives in Soviet, Seeks New Aid for Chile', *New York Times*, 7 Dec. 1972.

For Soviet foreign policy, cautious not to disturb *détente* with the United States, Chile offered no advantages either – hence there was only mild disappointment in the Soviet foreign ministry when Allende was over-thrown and killed himself. Massive economic difficulties and attacks from leftist guerrillas had debilitated the Frente Popular, and it had lost the support of the majority of Chileans by the time that, in 1973, the supreme commander of the Chilean army, General Augusto Pinochet, led a putsch and installed himself as new president.

Interestingly, officials in the Soviet Union found no fault with the United States for these events. US media had been reporting for two weeks on the active role of the CIA and the State Department in the putsch, before *Pravda* tepidly mentioned 'allegations concerning US involvement'.[120] Brezhnev called the events a 'bloody fascist coup',[121] but did not refer to external influences. Ponomarev reminded his com-rades that the Bolsheviks, unlike the Frente Popular, survived their revolution because they managed to get the economy running. Šulgovskij blamed Allende for being too straightforward with his reforms and defended the cautious Soviet position towards Chile. Michail Kudačkin, head of the Latin American department of the Central Committee, found fault with the left radicals and their lack of discipline, which had pushed the middle classes into the camp of the reactionaries.[122] East European and Soviet scholars agreed at a conference at the Academy: Allende's Frente Popular was unprepared, and its own domestic policy caused its demise. Tellingly, the only ones in Soviet debates who blamed the United States for Allende's fall were not Soviets: Cheddi Jagan, founding father of Guyana and long-time admirer of the Soviet Union, and the Bolivian communist Nina Tadeo, in an issue of *Problemy Mira i Socializma*.[123]

Those inside and outside the Soviet Union who still believed in the prospects of world socialism learned a momentous lesson: a peaceful path to socialism was possible, but to stay in power socialists needed to be able to defend themselves. Among 'progressive' and 'conservative' Soviet academics, heated debates broke out in the wake of the Chilean putsch. For the first time, divergent opinions were discussed publicly. Majdanik, the 'Soviet Che Guevara', wrote an article that criticised the reluctant Soviet foreign policy towards Chile. In order to get this reproach published, he had to disguise it: the *New York Times* had written

---

[120] Prizel, *Latin America through Soviet Eyes*, p. 164.   [121] Quoted *ibid.*, p. 27.
[122] Michail Kudačkin, 'Algunas enseñanzas de la revolución chilena', *Latinskaja Amerika* 1 (1975), 80–8.
[123] Prizel, *Latin America through Soviet Eyes*, p. 166.

that the nationalisation of banks and industries had brought about Allende's downfall; Majdanik protested that, on the contrary, the deferential inclusion of 'bourgeois circles' had proved fatal for Chile's socialism – clearly a criticism more of Soviet foreign policy than of US journalists. At the ILA, during the preparations for a Chile special edition of *Latinskaja Amerika*, 'conservatives' and 'progressives' could not agree on a common position, which, in Soviet tradition, they were expected to take in any publication. Mikojan remembered: 'we had problems from the very beginning with the press administration . . . it was dominated by a generation of ideological dogmatists. I was told once in the Central Committee: "is it worth debating questions, about which we still have no established opinion?". . . Back then, discussion usually looked like this: "comrade X is correct to say. . . I come round to the opinion of comrade Y" . . . We wanted to do things completely differently.'[124]

In the aftermath of the Chilean putsch, Majdanik denounced not only Soviet passivity, but also Allende for not being determined enough against his adversaries. His colleague Evgenij Kosarev, by contrast, argued in his paper 'Against Revolutionary Romanticism and Illusions' that the Chilean socialists had shown a lack of patience and discipline and had acted hastily. Mikojan, his colleagues' qualms and the censors' initial 'Nyet' notwithstanding, now called for what was a complete novelty in Soviet sciences: in the very same edition of the journal, two articles were to be published that held completely opposite opinions on the same issue. 'The editorial team protested vehemently,' Mikojan recalled, 'but I wanted to create an interesting and newsworthy issue and present arguments to the reader that allowed him to form his own opinion.'

Until he managed to follow through with this first pinch of pluralism in Soviet press, Mikojan had had to endure long debates and fights with his bosses at the ILA and with the directory of the Academy of Sciences, threaten resignation and continue the struggle with the Propaganda Department of the Central Committee and the Glavlit censors at the printing plant. His friend Nikolaj Leonov, the KGB's man for Latin America, helped him over these hurdles. Finally, as with any ILA publication, the issue still had to be approved by the Central Committee's Latin American department, 'the court of last resort', as Mikojan called it. Luckily for him, the historians Vasilij Ermolaev and Michail Kudačkin were in charge there. Both were relatively unorthodox scholars – and close friends of Mikojan. Thanks to his perseverance and

---

[124] Mikojan, 'Neuželi tridcat' piat' let?', 29–31.

his excellent contacts with high-ranking Party members, Sergo Mikojan won through, and the issue appeared.[125]

The animated debate around Allende, and in particular around his fall, shows just how much the Soviet perception of Latin America had changed. The enormous, and still somewhat naive, enthusiasm for the Cuban Revolution and the ostensible prospects of socialism in continental Latin America around 1960 had given way to a diversity of rather well-informed voices that drew different conclusions of the Chilean events. The Allende discussion, and Sergo Mikojan's role in it, also shows that the tolerance towards diverging opinions that could be uttered publicly in the late Soviet Union depended significantly on the personal network of the one uttering them.

The political impact of Soviet area studies and support for the Sandinistas in Nicaragua

Occasional tolerance of diverging opinions in smaller circles of academics notwithstanding, the autocratic Soviet leaders persisted in a state ideology that claimed a predominance of politics over all other aspects of society including the sciences. It is an unresolved and difficult question of whether, under these circumstances, the *meždunarodniki* had any impact on Soviet foreign policy making at all. As has been propounded, the original motivation for building up a refined system of area studies and acquiring knowledge of the world abroad was a political one: in times of global conflict, Soviet foreign policy decision makers needed expertise on distant world regions. The academic institutions had to deliver this knowledge, and they were given lavish funds and good working conditions to this end. It was institutions such as the ILA and IMEMO which supplied the Central Committee, the foreign ministry and the KGB with – secret – briefings on world areas.[126] First-hand information on world affairs was a rare commodity in the USSR. The *meždunarodniki*, thanks to their travels, personal connections and access to different sources of information, often knew their countries of study much better than political decision makers and could thus, through their representation of the outer world, manipulate what the decision makers thought of certain conflict situations.[127]

[125] Mikojan, *Anatomija Karibskogo krizisa*, p. 50; anon., 'Vokrug urokov Čili', *Latinskaja Amerika* 5 (1974).
[126] Leonov et al., 'El general Nikolai Leonov en el CEP', 72; Cobb, 'National Security Perspectives of Soviet "Think Tanks"', 53–4.
[127] Fazio Vengoa, 'América Latina Vista por los Académicos Soviéticos', also argues along these lines.

This power factor should not be overestimated. Soviet foreign policy was formulated within a very small circle of Politburo members, and scholars would be unlikely to present opinions that were too controversial directly to the top decision makers. This hierarchy was just as pronounced between the KGB and academe: Leonov recalled how difficult it was to work with the professors from IMEMO, simply because they were deeply afraid of the secret service.[128] Some western observers thus drew the conclusion that: 'academics are very seldom contacted by officials ... [they] were perceived as party propagandists and often willingly acted as such'.[129] Others stated that Soviet academics had 'hardly any influence on politics'.[130]

A look at the Soviet Latin Americanists suggests, however, that the *meždunarodniki* did influence the Soviet stance towards the world to some extent, if not so much at highest levels of foreign policy making. It was not their briefing of the most important decision makers, and certainly not their books and articles, that left a political mark. Those Latin Americanists who confined themselves to purely academic work had very little impact outside universities, and it is probably safe to assume that their research was not acknowledged by anyone in the Politburo. Yet, due to their constant fluctuation between different academic institutions and bodies of the Soviet state, the *meždunarodniki* carried their internationalist esprit into higher levels of the Soviet administration.

Academics from Moscow State University and IMEMO often turned to broader area studies at the ILA, and taught at MGIMO, Moscow State University or Lumumba University. Others moved from area studies into international journalism. Furthermore, the bulk of *meždunarodniki* shared their internationalist expertise with other Soviet organisations and were involved in, or contributed out of conviction to, Soviet political and economic activities. All state and Party organs that dealt with cultural diplomacy drew on the staff of area studies and their network of contacts. The old master spy Grigulevič now held positions at the ILA and the Latin America sections of both the GKKS and the SSOD. Aleksandr Alekseev came originally from the secret services, too. From 1958, he headed the Latin American section of the GKKS and, as a correspondent for TASS, reported from the Cuban Revolution as one of the first Soviets in the country, and entered the diplomatic service. Many more Soviet *meždunarodniki* provided counselling, contacts and translations for Soviet–Latin American business transactions and political

---

[128] Leonov, *Licholet'e*, pp. 138–9.   [129] Davidson and Filatova, 'African History', p. 118.
[130] Blasier, 'The Soviet Latin Americanists'.

relations: the historian Anatolij Glinkin, head of the foreign policy section of the ILA, and Marklen Lazarev, the deputy director of the ILA, were both lecturers at MGIMO, at Moscow State University and Lumumba University – and they were both counsellors to the Soviet foreign ministry.[131]

The interchange of expert staff between the different internationalist organs and institutes was indeed impressive. Most *meždunarodniki* had their academic jobs, but worked as well for media, for government agencies, for the Party organisation, the military and intelligence services and in missions abroad, commercial enterprises and international exchange organisations. Some of the Latin Americanists forged careers that took them into elevated posts in the Soviet administration. It was through these power positions and their personal contacts that some made their voices heard. Chačaturov, in parallel with his academic work at ILA and MGIMO, pursued a career in the Sovinformbjuro/Novosti; he eventually became the deputy director of the news agency TASS and worked in the Latin American section of the International Department of the Central Committee. Others held positions in the academic branches of the CPSU, such as the History Department of the Central Committee, and had therefore at least an indirect influence on how future decision makers would perceive the world.[132]

Leonov worked his way up from being an assistant in a publishing house for international literature to serving as a historian at the Academy, finally to deputy head of the KGB, head of its strategic department and a member of the Soviet defence council. Through such positions, some of the *meždunarodniki* exercised a certain influence on Soviet politics. Yet, while someone like Chačaturov certainly had considerable influence on the Third World strategies of TASS (and others on their respective organisations), their impact on the highest realms of Soviet foreign policy was still limited; more often than not, their calls for more internationalist activities fell on deaf ears. Leonov recalled writing countless suggestions on how to improve Soviet Third World policy in reports 'that never made it beyond [KGB boss] Jurij Andropov's desk'.[133]

---

[131] Torkunov (ed.), *MGIMO Universitet*, pp. 216–26; Mikojan, *Anatomija Karibskogo krizisa*, pp. 18–19; Chačaturov, *Zapiski očevidca*, pp. 37–8; Blasier, 'The Soviet Latin Americanists', 109–10; anon., *ILA. Instituto de América Latina: 30 años 1961–1991* (Moscow: ILA, n.d.).

[132] Anon., '"O vremeni i o sebe": k 75-letiju Borisa Iosifoviča Koval'ja', *Latinskaja Amerika* 6 (2005), 72–9; Vasilij Ermolaev, *Nacional'no-osvoboditel'noe i rabočee dviženie v stranach Latinskoj Ameriki posle vtoroj mirovoj vojny: lekcii, pročitannye v Vysšej partijnoj škole pri CK KPSS* (Moscow: Vysšaja Partijnaja Škola pri CK KPSS, 1958).

[133] Leonov et al., 'El general Nikolai Leonov en el CEP', 72, 83.

The politically most influential Soviet Latin Americanist was Michail Kudačkin, and he, too, like Leonov, succeeded not through his academic writing, but due to his institutional involvement. He was the head of the Central Committee's Latin American department, where he was in charge of more than thirty regional experts. Academically, Kudačkin never reached the fame of others in the field. Yet politically, he was *the* crucial person for everyone writing about and dealing with Latin America. Thanks to his position in the Central Committee, he sat directly at the interface of science and politics. In the strictly hierarchical Soviet system of governance, he was the highest-ranking expert about the continent, the source of information for everyone in the Central Committee and, through personal contacts, linked to decision makers in the Politburo, whose members were briefed personally by representatives of the International Department on the fields of their respective expertise. Sources on Kudačkin's interactions with the power brokers are scarce, unfortunately, but it is clear that, through his access to the inner circle of Soviet foreign policy making, Kudačkin had more influence than any other *meždunarodnik* on Soviet policies towards Latin America.[134]

A fine case through which to study the attempts of other internationalist-minded academics to exert influence on Soviet politics, and the limits thereof, are the political upheavals in Central America and the Caribbean in the late 1970s and early 1980s. Without any interference from Moscow, the Nicaraguan dictator Anastasio Somoza, whose clan had been ruling and exploiting the small and impoverished republic since the 1930s, was toppled in 1979. The Marxist Frente Sandinista de Liberación Nacional (FSLN) under Daniel Ortega emerged as the strongest force in the anti-Somoza coalition and established a revolutionary government. From the same year, the ideologically similar Frente Farabundo Martí para la Liberación Nacional (FMLN) in neighbouring El Salvador started fighting its own provisional government. The Soviet government harboured serious doubts about the endurance of both revolutionary movements, and, aware of the proximity of the United States, initially restrained from any direct interference.

The more 'progressive'-oriented *meždunarodniki*, however, remembered the Chilean case – and this time they not only started the usual cultural exchange programme and Sunday speeches, but also spoke up for sending weapons, technicians and military advisers. Leonov immediately travelled to Managua and, upon return to Moscow,

---

[134] Michail Fedorovič Kudačkin, obituary in *Latinskaja Amerika* 11 (2010), 104; www.warheroes.ru/hero/hero.asp?Hero_id=12404 (last accessed 22 Nov. 2011); Blasier, *The Giant's Rival*, p. 71.

canvassed Soviet foreign policy makers for more substantial support. The Sandinistas Humberto Ortega and Tomás Borge went to the Soviet Union in 1981 and asked for more help, as did FMLN leader Schafik Handal. Majdanik, his old friend from Prague, put Leonov in contact with decision makers, and even collected and donated his own money for the revolutionary cause. Yet when the Soviet government finally did send support to Nicaragua, it was only a fraction of what the *meždunarodniki* and their Latin American comrades had demanded.[135]

To save resources, the Kremlin delegated some tasks to its east European satellites: GDR experts trained and supplied Nicaraguan secret service personnel, Czechoslovakia sent money and equipment, Bulgaria provided aircraft training, Poland donated helicopters.[136] Yevgeny Yevtushenko was sent to Managua for some poetic expressions of solidarity, and Soviet school children collected donations for their young Central American comrades. Alarms went off in Washington, but the extent of assistance from the eastern bloc actually never came close to a substantial level that would have approached the support that Ronald Reagan had the CIA send to the Contra rebels.[137] The amount of support for the New Jewel Movement, a heterogeneous group of leftists in Grenada, a small Caribbean island-state, was also negligible. Contacts with the Soviet Union served more as a pretext for a full-blown US invasion and regime change in Grenada in 1983.[138]

While they occasionally managed to initiate Soviet endeavours in the Third World, the *meždunarodniki* just as often rallied in vain for their ideals. At the political level, internationalism was tamed and subordinated to geo-political interests of an often very pragmatic leadership. But as a conviction among academics, Soviet internationalism after Stalin

---

[135] Westad, *The Global Cold War*, pp. 339–48; Isa Conde, *Kiva Maidanik*; Leonov, *Licholet'e*; Prizel, *Latin America through Soviet Eyes*, p. 147.

[136] Michael Radu, 'Eastern Europe and Latin America', in Mujal-León (ed.), *The USSR and Latin America*, pp. 261–2.

[137] Nicola Miller, *Soviet Relations with Latin America, 1959–1987*, p. 202; Richard Feinberg, 'Central America: The View from Moscow', *Washington Quarterly* 2 (1982), 173.

[138] These cases were the last ones in which the Soviet Union had a large impact on Latin America; over decades, they had provided the United States with justification for most of its interventions in the region. In Guatemala in 1954, in Brazil in 1964 and in the Dominican Republic the year after, in Chile in 1973 and, finally, in Grenada in 1983, the United States actively participated in the violent overthrow of legitimate regimes – to mention only those that took place during the Cold War. It tried but failed in Cuba in 1961, in Guyana in 1963, in Chile in 1970 and in Nicaragua in the early 1980s. The cruel civil war in Guatemala, on a related note, no longer got much attention from either the United States or the Soviet Union by that time. Instead, pariah states such as the military junta-ruled Argentina and apartheid South Africa supported the anti-communist fight. See Grow, *US Presidents and Latin American Interventions*.

persisted until the Soviet Union imploded. Occasionally, this socialist idealism even became a nuisance for the Soviet state. Majdanik's activities had long raised suspicion among the authorities, who regularly wire-tapped his telephone. During Handal's 1980 visit, Majdanik met him together with two of his young scholars from IMEMO, Andrej Fadin and Tatjana Vorožejkina. Handal delivered a blazing speech about the prospects for socialism in El Salvador, on which Fadin, even more a leftist than his academic mentor, commented trenchantly: 'this is all very well with your heroic struggle, but I may ask Comrade Schafik: all these sacrifices, these values, these political possibilities, all this heroism – only to finally live in the same shit system as we do here in the USSR??' Majdanik later made the mistake of mentioning this incident in a phone call to Handal. Fadin was arrested and sentenced for being part of the *molodye socialisti* (young socialists), a group taking inspiration from the western New Left and Eurocommunism. Majdanik was excluded from the CPSU on the grounds of 'unauthorised contacts with foreigners' (with Handal, the head of a communist party) and anti-Soviet conspiracy. He also lost his position at IMEMO until he was readmitted after Brezhnev's death two years later; he was however, never appointed professor and lost his permission to travel abroad.[139]

The *meždunarodniki* as banner-bearers of Soviet internationalism after Stalin

With the revival of Soviet internationalism after Stalin, and parallel with very similar endeavours in the West, the USSR built up a refined system of area studies. It had two major impacts on science, politics and the higher administration: firstly, it expanded tremendously what the Soviets knew about the rest of the world and replaced the hyper-ideologised and schematised global mental map of late Stalinism with detailed regional expertise and a fair knowledge of world affairs; secondly, it provided the institutional framework for the survival of internationalist ideas in the late Soviet Union. The professional biographies of the Latin Americanists demonstrated that many scholars, having drawn their inspiration from an older generation of socialist internationalists, conveyed their renewed spirit of internationalism into both newly founded and old Soviet institutions. The *meždunarodniki* thus became the banner-bearers of Soviet internationalism in the late Soviet Union.

---

[139] Isa Conde, *Kiva Maidanik*, pp. 50–1.

Restrictions on academia were palpably loosened in the Soviet Union after Stalin, and the Russian ethno-centrism of late Stalinism all but ended. Notably, many of the Latin Americanists had a non-Russian family background: Sergo Mikojan and Karen Chačaturov were Russian-raised Armenians, Viktor Vol'skij was Lithuanian. Jews had not been able to enrol as students at the elitist MGIMO during late Stalinism, but a remarkable number nonetheless found their way into area studies later. In the optimistic atmosphere of the early Thaw, the young and ambitious *meždunarodniki* began their careers as academics, journalists, diplomats or secret service agents. They enjoyed lavish salaries, a good reputation and had the great privilege of being able to travel abroad. Good research was done at least in fields with a certain distance from ideology, and scholars made contact again with the academic world outside the eastern bloc. At least within these small circles of elites, the Soviet Union became cosmopolitan again.

Some of the *meždunarodniki* who went to western countries received impressions that did not match the ideological image spread within the Soviet Union, and this view behind the facade led some of them to distance themselves from the Soviet system in the long run. But especially those who devoted themselves to the Third World were staunch anti-imperialist socialist internationalists in the first place, and their experiences abroad only confirmed this view. 'Progressive circles in Latin America', Šul'govskij believed he had discovered on one of his many trips, 'take the USSR as an inspiration for the solution of the national question and economic independence, which they still need to achieve long after their political independence, ... they see the Soviet Union as the future of the world.'[140] As for their political orientation, the director of the Institute of Latin America in Moscow left no doubts: 'our research is built on the granite bedrock of Marxist-Leninist methodology ... a creative Marxism ... is our internationalist obligation'.[141]

Some regional experts came into conflict with the Soviet state occasionally. Yet dissidents, as they emerged from the late 1960s, were usually *institutniki* from the natural sciences, while the bulk of *meždunarodniki* of that generation remained committed socialist internationalists. Things looked different with a younger generation. Some developed into stalwart anti-Soviet socialists. Others adapted to the prevailing pragmatism, or even cynicism, which had replaced the optimism of the Thaw among the Soviet elites. Many who started their careers only in the 1970s became excellent regional experts, too, but did not all develop into desk revolutionaries. This detachment between the generations sometimes

[140] Šul'govskij, 'Opyt rešenija nacional'nogo voprosa v SSSR', 13, 34.
[141] Vol'skii, 'Sovetskaja latinoamerikanistika', 7, 16.

happened quite literally within families: Lev Slezkin's son Yuri firstly was trained as Portuguese translator, but, after some time in Mozambique in the late 1970s, emigrated to the United States and became a historian of the Soviet Union. Lev Zubok's grandson Vladislav, trained at the Academy's Institute of the USA and Canada, likewise pursued an academic career in the United States. Yet theirs were stories of the late 1970s and 1980s, and their deviations should not be projected back on to the generation before them.

The impact of the *meždunarodniki* on Soviet foreign policy is difficult to measure. A look at experts from other fields and source material from the – barely accessible – archive of the Russian/Soviet foreign ministry, could give more detailed insights into the interactions of academic experts and the inner circles of Soviet politics. The biographical assessment of Soviet Latin Americanists has suggested that the *meždunarodniki* did influence to some extent the Soviet stance towards the world, but not so much through their writings, and not so much at the highest levels of foreign policy making, either. It was through a constant interchange of staff between different academic institutions and bodies of the Soviet state that the Latin America experts brought their internationalist spirit into many official organs and institutes. Some of the Latin Americanists also made careers as scientific functionaries or reached influential positions in the administration and the Party. From these powerful positions and through their personal contacts, some advocated a more active role for the Soviet Union in Third World matters, if often in vain.

Soviet internationalism, this book should have made clear by now, did not lose all relevance in the course of the 1970s. The number of Third World students actually rose during that decade; popular culture from Asia or Latin America was more widespread than ever before. Soviet solidarity with Salvador Allende, more rhetorical than substantial, proved that internationalist sentiments were still retrievable among at least parts of the intelligentsia. And the common Soviet man or woman was also still expected to display a degree of internationalism. 'Whoever did not know how the Communist Party in Chile was doing', Boris Groys noted, 'and which baneful adventures US imperialism was undertaking again, risked not getting a new flat, a pay rise or a travel permit, because one needed a recommendation of the local party branch – which gave that recommendation only when it sensed that the person concerned was a genuine Soviet being, *id est* that he thought sufficiently philosophically, by putting his personal needs in the context of the whole world.'[142] This

---

[142] Boris Groys, *Das kommunistische Postskriptum* (Frankfurt am Main: Suhrkamp, 2006), p. 58.

expectation of the state was obviously an invitation to bigotry and hollow repetition of empty rhetoric. A Soviet joke tells of the worker at a political meeting that was to condemn the 1973 putsch in Chile. Assiduously he steps to the speaker's desk and declares: 'I don't know who arrested Pinochet and why, but if they don't release Luis for the carnival, they'll get into trouble with us!'[143] The dutiful worker-activist had picked up the names of putschist dictator Augusto Pinochet and the arrested communist leader Luis Corvalán, but jumbled up the empty words in an attempt to say what he was expected to say.

Occasionally, during this period of Soviet pragmatic imperialism, the rhetoric of internationalism was also used against their own originators. 'The *šestidesjatniki*', Vajl' and Genis wrote about the young romantic socialist Russians of the 1960s, 'took Cuba as a weapon against their enemies within … The bureaucrats and apparatchiks were against modern art – Fidel made abstract painting accessible to his people. They read out boring monologues – Fidel gave rousing speeches without a script … At home, *Krokodil* [the Soviet satirical magazine] made fun of long-haired and bearded men, and Komsomol brigades harassed them – here even the head of state himself wore a beard.'[144] Their critical idealism however, and with it their use of internationalist language, had faded out by the end of their decade. Small illegal groups of radical leftists occasionally used the names and theories of Latin American revolutionary heroes, as did the Moscow Otrjad Če Gevary (Che Guevara Squad) in the late 1970s.[145] But most other examples of this creative adaptation were less romanticising and were found not so much in Russia proper as on the peripheries of the communist empire: Armenian nationalists used the concept of people's friendship in an attempt to gain support from Moscow for their own interests against Azerbaijan and Turkey.[146] Some east Europeans identified with anti-imperialist national independence movements in the global South – because they felt like colonial subjects of the Soviet Union. Whenever the Polish travel writer Ryszard Kapuściński indicted Third World despots in his hugely popular books, readers back home read them as clever criticism of their own authoritarian rulers.[147] And the East German singer-songwriter Wolf Biermann contrasted the selfless socialist

[143] A. Golubev (ed.), *Istorija SSSR v anekdotach* (Smolensk: Smjadyn', 1991), p. 139.
[144] Vajl' and Genis, *60-e*, pp. 52–64.
[145] A. Tarasov, G. Čerkasov and T. Šavšukova, *Levye v Rossii: ot umerennych do ekstremistov* (Moscow: Izdatel'stvo Institut Eksperimental'noj Sociologii, 1997), p. 15.
[146] Maike Lehmann, *Eine sowjetische Nation: Nationale Sozialismusinterpretationen in Armenien seit 1945* (Frankfurt am Main: Campus, 2012), pp. 250–93.
[147] Ryszard Kapuściński, *The Emperor: Downfall of an Autocrat* (London: Penguin Books, 2006).

Che Guevara (*Jesus mit der Knarre*, Jesus with the gun) with the over-indulged communist bureaucrats in the GDR.

In the late Soviet Union, internationalist rhetoric was not so much used to criticise the communist system but, to the contrary, in order to thwart a more pragmatic type of foreign policy. The endurance of ever-ageing Soviet foreign policy makers exacerbated a frustration among more idealist socialists: Foreign Minister Gromyko was in office from 1957 to 1986; Ponomarev headed the International Department of the Central Committee from 1955 to 1986 – to be followed by Anatolij Dobrynin, who had been ambassador to the United States continuously since 1962. When, in 1978, García Márquez's *Otoño del patriarco* (The Autumn of the Patriarch) appeared in the USSR, many Soviet readers immediately drew parallels with their own leaders.[148] The old guard of Soviet apparatchiks and the Latin American 'gorillas', with their fantasy uniforms, jingling from an armada of medals, with their senile stubbornness and their caricatured sclerotic appearance, had a lot more in common than either would have admitted.[149] In the course of the early 1980s, both disappeared from the political stage.

The energetic reformer Mikhail Gorbachev, from the same generation as the first *meždunarodniki*, shared their socialist internationalist values. In his first years in office, he expanded Soviet activities in the Third World and, scaling up the economic support for the Sandinistas by 40 per cent, declared to the West: 'never will we leave Nicaragua at the mercy of the imperialists'.[150] The internationalist academics thus whole-heartedly supported perestroika. Majdanik popularised the Soviet reform programme in the Spanish-speaking world with his 1988 book *Revolución de las esperanzas* (Revolution of Hopes).[151] These hopes were not ful-filled. The ambitious economic reform programme failed miserably, living standards sank rapidly and Soviet internationalism came under fierce attack from all sides as a waste of Russian money.

On Soviet television, the parodist Aleksandr Ivanov, rather humour-lessly, complained: 'and we frittered away our money on Sandinista Nicaragua for ten years, on those dilettantes with the same useless ideology as ours'.[152] Intellectuals and poets, including those who had

[148] Kutejščikova, *Moskva-Meksiko-Moskva*, p. 326.
[149] Volpi, *El insomnio de Bolívar*, p. 58.
[150] Westad, *The Global Cold War*, p. 370; Michail Gorbatschow, *Perestroika: Die zweite Russische Revolution* (Munich: Droemer Knaur, 1987), pp. 221–46.
[151] Marta Harnecker (ed.), *Perestroika: la revolución de las esperanzas. Entrevista a Kiva Maidanik* (Buenos Aires: Dialéctica, 1988).
[152] Aleksandr Snitko, 'Skol'ko stoit naša sovest' v Latinskoj Amerike? Zametki ešče bolee neravnodušnye', *Latinskaja Amerika* 4 (1991), 39.

praised the Sandinistas in their works only few years before, now publicly jumped on the bandwagon. The Latin Americanist Michail Beljat demanded in *Literaturnaja Gazeta*: 'Give me back my credit, Comandante Fidel!' Even Yevgeny Yevtushenko spoke in the same vein as a delegate to the Supreme Soviet.[153] By the end of the 1980s, the popular tune 'Kuba – ljubov' moja' was heard with new bitter and hateful lyrics:

> Kuba, otdaj naš chleb!
> Kuba, voz'mi svoj sachar!
> Nam nadoel tvoj kosmatij Fidel'.
> Kuba, idi ty na cher![154]

In concession to both these popular sentiments and to the economic chaos in the USSR, Gorbachev cut Soviet support for Latin American communist parties as well as leftist movements and governments in the late 1980s. Diplomatic relations and interactions were expanded at the same time; several high-ranking non-socialist Latin American statesmen made official state visits to the USSR. Gorbachev himself scheduled a trip to Argentina, Brazil and Uruguay in 1987, but in the end – in accommodation to the United States – sent his foreign minister Eduard Shevardnadze, and he himself went only to Cuba in 1989.

This meant that, as long as the Soviet Union existed, no Soviet head of state, government or Party ever visited mainland Central or South America. At the level of high politics, they had always remained low priority for the Kremlin, and were mostly of interest as antipode to the United States. Economically, the entire subcontinent was hardly ever relevant for the USSR throughout its existence – with the notable exception of the import of grain from Argentina, which did not join a western embargo in the wake of the invasion of Afghanistan; as return service, the Soviets declared Argentina's aggression against the Falkland Islands to be an act of anti-imperialism. Other than that, the Soviet market proved incompatible with the raw-material-exporting Latin American states, and Soviet commodities were usually not competitive on the open market. Soviet trade with the area did not even match the humble exchange with Africa. For Soviet socialists by conviction, however, Latin America was a haven of a romanticised socialist revolution, just as it was for the western New Left at the same time. The Soviet desk revolutionaries from the area studies made sure that communist parties and leftist movements constantly received large sums of money directly from the Moscow Party

---

[153] *Ibid.*

[154] 'Cuba, give back our bread; Cuba, keep your sugar; we are fed up with your shaggy Fidel; Cuba, go fuck yourself!': Vajl' and Genis, *60-e*, p. 59.

apparatus. With the end of the Soviet Union, all these parties – except the Cuban one – sank into obscurity.

Most Soviet citizens, by that time, had very different sorrows than the fate of global socialism. Aleksandr Snitko, the Belorussian *meždunarodnik*, indignantly reported a view he encountered in conversations with many ordinary Russians at that time: 'whenever I argue in support of the anti-fascist movement in Chile, I hear the answer: "Pinochet – that is good! We need our own Pinochet, to put the country in order. Under Stalin, there was order" ... I speak of the foreign debt, the lack of food, the infant mortality, the political repression in many Latin American countries, and the answer is: "enough of feeding these wogs. They are ungrateful cattle. Remember Indonesia – we fed them, fed them; Egypt, we fed them, fed them, and then they all showed us their arses"... All of my opponents had the same solid conviction: the lack of sausage at our shop counters is to blame on the Cubans, the Vietnamese, the Ethiopians and all the other scum from the Third World.'[155]

Sorely shocked at this widespread attitude, Snitko nostalgically summed up what Soviet internationalism had meant for him: 'Now and in the near future, nothing distinguishes the Soviet Union from the Third World. But our help for its anti-colonial, anti-imperialist struggle might remain the brightest side of our gloomy history.' The most ardent proponents of Soviet internationalism after Stalin, those who saw it as more than an instrument of Soviet geo-politics, were also those who supported Gorbachev's reforms longer than anyone else – and were deeply disappointed to see the Soviet Union, their motherland of socialism, fall apart as a consequence.[156]

---

[155] Snitko, 'Skol'ko stoit naša sovest' v Latinskoj Amerike?', 38–9.   [156] *Ibid.*, 42.

Conclusion: Soviet internationalism after Stalin and its domestic and foreign audiences

In 1972, the Soviet film-maker Roman Karmen travelled to Latin America and shot a long documentary on the 'blazing continent'. *Pylajuščij kontinent* was a grand panorama of Soviet internationalism after Stalin as it has been presented in this book. Karmen drew parallels between the Mexican and Russian Revolutions, painting a picture of a continuous fight of staunch socialists against the evils of imperialism from the Spanish Civil War and the Soviet Great Patriotic War to the struggle against foreign interference in Latin America. The nexus between the inner Soviet periphery and the Third World was taken up again, as the film compared contemporary Venezuela with Azerbaijan before the October Revolution. Exoticism, which made Soviet internationalism attractive to a wide audience at home, appeared once more in the form of beautiful landscapes and racy *Latinas*, underlined with catchy folklore music and Spanish revolutionary slogans that no longer needed translation into Russian. Leftist Latin American intellectuals explained the connections between old European fascists and capitalist imperialists in Latin America. Chilean alumni from Lumumba University expressed their gratitude towards the Soviet Union (one of the youths presented in the film, Lenin Díaz, would be among the first *desaparecidos* of the Pinochet dictatorship only a year after his interview). Karmen even involved the *meždunarodniki* in his film and relied on Viktor Vol'skij, the head of the Institut Latinskoj Ameriki, as his scientific adviser.

The United States figured in the film as an evil-doer on a grand scale. Harrowing pictures showed freight trains full of foodstuffs leaving for the North while starving children cried. Imperialism was presented as the culprit for widespread illiteracy and poverty. Yet 300 million Latin Americans, Karmen made his viewers believe, were full of optimism that, ultimately, socialism would prevail. The people, the revolutions, the imperialist puppet-masters and the fascist dictators – all those heroes and villains of the Cold War from the Soviet perspective – made their appearance in Karmen's film, and it all came in a nice package of tropical eroticism and catchy rhythms. Latin America, in this depiction, was a world arena in which the Soviet perception of the world was proven.[1]

In the just under two decades between Stalin's death and the time Karmen shot his film, the Soviet Union gave up its rigid isolation from the world beyond the control of its army and (re-)established contacts at various levels with states and individuals in the non-communist world, including those in the Cold War enemy's own 'back yard'. Soviet internationalism after Stalin was a crucial element of the relaunch of the Soviet project under Nikita Khrushchev. Based on the ideals of old socialist internationalism, it was both confrontational (against 'the West', 'capitalism', 'imperialism' etc.) and integrative (towards 'progressive forces', 'the wretched of the Earth', 'friends of the Soviet Union' etc.). This conglomeration of revolutionary and inclusive ideals was the specifically Soviet way of participating in an increasingly interconnected world from the mid 1950s.

Soviet Internationalism after Stalin challenges a view that sees the cautious opening up of Soviet society after 1953 as a history of a gradual Westernisation and an undermining of Soviet values and self-confidence. Internationalism was rekindled as a political means to promote the Soviet model of modern society. Displaying a somewhat paternalistic attitude towards the global South, the Kremlin no longer advocated the violent overthrow of governments; it sought to win over anti-imperialist politicians in office, intellectuals of different political leanings, and future elites as friends of the Soviet state. All the findings in this book corroborate that, measured against their own more modest claims, Soviet advances in Latin America were a rather successful and self-affirming endeavour until at least late into the 1970s.

With regard to its domestic targets, Soviet internationalism was even a greater success. This new political backdrop enabled a considerable number of Soviet individuals – intellectuals, artists, musicians and scholars – to leave their country and reconnect to the global discourses and the cultural world community they had been excluded from for many years. While mostly still barred from physically leaving their country, ordinary Soviet citizens were now confronted with foreign visitors, and with a flood of representations and cultural products from abroad. These provided the domestic audience with a systematic and meaningful, if politically biased, world-view, one that presented their own state as an advanced, benevolent and much-admired trail-blazer of modern society. Performed, written and sung by Soviet and Latin American artists alike,

[1] Roman Karmen: *Pylajuščij kontinent* (1972), RGAKFD #24461.

popular culture conveyed internationalism to a willing mass audience. The ordinary Soviet man, while still very much limited in his freedom of movement, was indeed expected to be internationalist, and it was through the consumption of this often politicised culture that the majority of ordinary Soviet citizens developed their idea of the outside world. Based on the positive stereotypes of post-war exoticism, many of them absorbed their own interpretation of the ideals of international solidarity. What Soviet citizens got to hear and to see from Latin America were prime examples of imperialist exploitation and consequent underdevelopment.

The appropriation of the official discourse through popular culture took various forms. Some Soviet artists, such as the bard Jurij Vizbor, popularised solidarity with Latin America without having any connection to state authorities. And many Soviets actually fell in love with Cuba or Paraguayan folklore or fancied Che Guevara, but perhaps did so for other reasons than those officially favoured. Politically endorsed internationalism had opened up spaces of interaction that went beyond the control of the state, but contacts with representatives from the Third World did more to confirm the official Soviet self-image in the world than to undermine it. They confirmed the ostensible superiority of the Soviet system – morally over the West, economically, technologically and culturally over the rest of the world.

The grand narrative of Soviet history after 1953 tells us that contacts with the world abroad fostered the spread of western products and values in the USSR and thus, in the long run, undermined the belief in the superiority of the domestic system. This study of Soviet internationalism, however, has presented Soviet interactions with the Third World much more as an integrative moment. Contacts with underdeveloped countries of the global South and the admiration for the USSR expressed by many of the visitors confirmed to many Soviet politicians, intellectuals and the wider public their perception of the world. Soviet internationalism after Stalin was a source of legitimisation for the new Soviet political elite and reaffirming for Soviet society during the turmoil of de-Stalinisation and through much of the period under the rule of Leonid Brezhnev that has been labelled the Era of Stagnation. The victory in the Second World War, the successes of the space programme and other technological feats have been identified as the basis of a 'Soviet identity' that came into being, from below, in the post-Stalin USSR. Internationalism, this book has argued, had a similar effect as it constructed a self-image of an economically and morally superior, well-meaning superpower.

Using Latin America as a case study raises the question of how much these findings are representative for Soviet Third World advances overall. In economic and geo-political terms, relations with India and the Middle East were more extensive and fruitful for the Soviet state. The spread of state socialism, not initiated by the Kremlin but substantially supported with Soviet weapons, continued much more successfully in Africa. But the Soviet fascination with Latin America confirms, better than any other, one of the main claims of this book: Soviet internationalism was not only a geo-political instrument, but a conviction shared and actively sponsored by many Soviet political and cultural figures. Arguing against purely materialist assessments, this study of Soviet internationalism after Stalin and its entanglements with Latin America thus underlines the relevance of ideas and ideology in the history of the late Soviet Union.

The somewhat naive enthusiasm for the new Third World adventures, among politicians as much as intellectuals around 1960, had already given way to more sober assessments in the later phases of Khrushchev's Thaw. Close relations with Cuba continued after the missile crisis, but the 'island of love and freedom' now caused not simply excitement, as it constantly reminded the Soviet leadership of the financial and political burden and the potential military risk of such endeavours. Nevertheless, internationalism remained an ideal for Soviet socialists, and it was mostly professional internationalists, the *meždunarodniki*, who carried this ideal well into the 1980s. Area studies expanded tremendously what the Soviets knew about the rest of the world and replaced the hyper-ideologised and schematised global mental map of late Stalinism with detailed regional expertise and a fair knowledge of world affairs. Through a constant interchange of staff between different academic institutions and bodies of the Soviet state, the Latin America experts took their internationalist spirit, inspired by early Soviet internationalists from the 1920s and 1930s, into many official organs and institutes. They conceptualised and organised the programmes of Soviet internationalism after Stalin and did so not only as complacent executers of political orders, but actively and out of conviction.

Telling the history of Soviet internationalism after Stalin as an entangled history with selected groups from abroad has provided for a new perspective on the history of both the USSR and Latin America in the Cold War. Studies of international relations have ascertained the relative irrelevance of Latin America in Soviet foreign policy; comparative assessments have outlined many parallels between Soviet and Latin American societies, though still seeing them as independent, self-contained units. The trans-national perspective employed here has amended this picture with many exchange and cultural transfer phenomena between Latin America and the Soviet Union, most of them ignored by scholars so far, at times when both belonged to different, and ostensibly isolated, camps of the Cold War. This new angle has revealed that the Soviet Union looked rather different from a southern perspective as compared to a western one.

Time and again, Western observers have underlined the shortcomings, faults and inner contradictions and conflicts within the Soviet Union to an extent that makes it difficult to understand why this system actually prevailed for so long. Much better than these stories of failure and deficiency, a view from the South helps us understand the attractive and thus cohesive factors of the Soviet system. Compared to west European standards of living, rising to hitherto unknown levels through the 1960s and 1970s, Soviet society was in all respects backward. In the eyes of many Latin Americans from different political and social backgrounds, however, many traits of the Soviet state still commanded respect. Intellectuals found the Soviet emphasis on high-brow art and music, and the reverence shown to their Soviet colleagues, appealing, and they were impressed by the politico-military and scientific prowess of the Soviet Union: as the only European great power, it had (at least in its self-representation and in Third World perception) no colonial past and had resisted western imperialist attacks. It had apparently managed to find a solution to the national question of the multi-ethnic state. And it had managed to turn a by and large pre-modern agrarian society into an industrialised superpower, erasing illiteracy on the way.

Soviet internationalist organisations were rather successful in creating a positive stance towards their state both with their activities abroad and with foreign visitors in the USSR. The tenor of almost all Latin American travelogues from the Soviet Union is predominantly positive. Those who lost their faith in the Soviet Union did not do so during their journey, but in reaction to Soviet higher politics or, if they were leftists, to quarrels within their own political movements or parties. Conversely, many who visited to the Soviet Union with no stable opinion went back home with a rather positive stance towards the USSR. So did the bulk of the Latin American students who received their higher education in the Soviet Union. The Latin American views of the Soviet Union presented extensively in this book shed light on the fact that the USSR looked fundamentally different from the South than from the West. While few Latin Americans maintained the uncritical admiration for the Soviet project we know from western leftists of the 1920s and 1930s, many Latin Americans found positive things to say about the USSR as well as inspiration to draw for their own countries from its example.

The dominant East–West axis in much Cold War literature has tended to over-emphasise the differences between societies on the two sides of the Iron Curtain and blocked the view on many commonalities. The southern perspective on the Soviet Union has offered a new angle of vision. It has revealed that, in many respects, the Soviet Union after Stalin followed global, or at least northern-hemisphere, trends, in culture even more than in politics and economics. Historians have written extensively about what it meant for someone from the West to live through the subsequent period of the Cold War. Two factors defined the general view of geo-politics: there was a confrontation with an ideological foe which represented a looming threat of mutual annihilation. At the same time, ordinary people experienced an increasingly interconnected world at political, cultural and intellectual levels. Decolonisation, the developing Third World and its cruel proxy wars brought the global South ever more to the attention of the populace in western Europe as much as North America.

This book has demonstrated that basically the same processes as in the West took place on the eastern side of the Iron Curtain. For Soviet citizens, too, the Cold War now meant both geo-political confrontation with the West and increased interaction with the rest of the world. Indeed, many of the phenomena of Soviet internationalism after Stalin in relation to Latin America had their parallels in western developments and thus indicate that the Soviet Union, from the mid 1950s, was again in tune with many global cultural trends. The Soviet craze for all of Latin America had its roots in an old pan-European romanticising of the Hispanic world. Soviet cinema reflected a longing for authenticity, as did western art-house cinema at the time. Latin American music – or local music with a dash of 'Latin American' flair – was a very noticeable element of popular entertainment everywhere in the northern hemisphere from the 1950s, where it served a demand for escapism after the hardships of war and the post-war era.

The contrast of this folklorisation to the Soviets' own cultural self-representation towards Latin Americans reveals another, very pan-European aspect: in their attempt to appear modern, civilised and cultivated, the USSR sent only high-brow artists abroad. In doing so, they constructed a cultural gradient between Soviet representatives of classical European high culture and the – selectively invited – folkloristic groups from Latin America. This practice shows a sense of cultural superiority that many Europeans maintained towards the rest of the world, be they from the East or the West of the old continent. A decade later, both in the USSR and in the West, socio-critical Latin American folk music and the leftist literature of the Latin American boom fostered the enthusiasm for an apparently romantic revolution; rebellious youngsters on both sides of the Iron Curtain cherished Cuba and the modern Jesus, Che Guevara.

The establishment of area studies, too, was a common northern-hemisphere development. East and West built up a refined system of research on the South. The *meždunarodniki* acted as banner-bearers of internationalism until the end of the Soviet Union. Their biographies endorse another of the book's principal arguments: the inspiration for Soviet internationalism after Stalin came from socialist internationalism of the 1920s, but it stood in a context of rather similar developments in Europe and North America at the same time.

These parallel phenomena of eastern and western views of Latin America are not be confused with an adaptation of the Soviet Union to western standards. Similarly to the Russian confrontation with 'backward' Central Asia during its colonisation in the nineteenth century, the Third World of the 1950s and 1960s provided for a newly won sense of superiority and was a source of self-confirmation, an encounter in which, unlike with the West, the Soviets seemed to be the more 'advanced' civilisation.

The story of Soviet internationalism after Stalin illustrates the important role that the USSR played in the global history of the late twentieth century. 'Global connections and comparisons', as Christopher Bayly called integrative processes in the nineteenth century, again reached, from the 1960s, the levels from before the First World War and finally surpassed them in scope and extension. No longer was this so much a western-only endeavour under western control. At the cultural, intellectual and scientific levels, the Soviet Union reintegrated into global discourses from the mid 1950s, and this came as a result of Khrushchev's rekindling of internationalism. The end of Soviet isolation from the world began with Stalin's death and, for a while, did more to contribute to the cohesion of the Soviet Union rather than anticipating its disintegration. Even early perestroika witnessed a final upsurge of pro-Third World sentiments. Political ideologies in global geo-politics remained confrontational until the end of the Cold War; the methods and types of international exchange, however, were – qualitatively if not quantitatively – rather similar. These connections had long been marginalised in a Cold War historiography that tended to underline the particularities of an isolated communist world. A trans-national perspective on the history of the Soviet Union, by contrast, sheds light on the understudied links and commonalities that the Soviet state shared with other world regions. As the editors of *Kritika* put it: 'Another road to the "normalisation" of Russian history may well pass through Madrid and Mexico City.'[2]

---

[2] *Kritika* 1 (2011), 4.

Postface: legacies of Soviet internationalism in Latin America and Russia

This being Russia, a nation of busybody peasants thrust into an awkward modernity, some idiot will always endeavour to spoil your good fun. And so the neighbouring biznesman, a sunburned midlevel killer standing next to his pasty girlfriend from some cow-filled province, starts in with 'Now, fellows, why do you have to sing like African exchange students? You both look so cultured' – in other words, like vile-looking Yids – 'why don't you declaim some Pushkin instead? Didn't he have some nice verses about the White Nights? That would be very seasonal.'

'Hey, if Pushkin were alive today, he'd be a rapper,' I said. 'That's right,' Alyosha-Bob said. 'He'd be M.C. Push.'   Gary Shteyngart,
                                                                        Absurdistan

Zjuzja: Do you know, Čubajka, what Russian history was like in the twentieth century? For seventy years, the country built this lokhotron *[scam], even though no one knew what it was and how it should work. Then some smart guy said, 'lets break it into pieces, flog it off and we share the money.*

Čubajka: Could it be that not everything in our history was dark and meaningless, Zjuzja? Could it be that you just missed the moment when the lokhotron *actually once worked for a while?*   Viktor Pelevin,
                          Dialectics of the Transition Period from Nowhere to Nowhere

Soviet internationalism after Stalin faded out in the late 1980s. No longer did the Soviets claim to have a superior model of modern society to spread over the rest of the planet. No longer was the Third World particularly interested in the Soviet experience. Latin American intellectuals, for the longest time leftists almost *per definitionem*, now spoke out in favour of liberalism. During the disintegration of the Soviet Union, Octavio Paz invited writers and intellectuals to Mexico City to discuss the events for the journal *Vuelta*. Mario Vargas Llosa, Jorge Edwards and Carlos Franqui participated, and they rejoiced at the developments in Russia.[1] Their generation's socialist romanticism was gone and so was

---

[1] Kutejščikova, *Moskva-Meksiko-Moskva*, pp. 359–63.

their *latinoamericanidad*: 'for Mexicans today', according to the novelist Jorge Volpi, 'Bolivia is as exotic as Kazakhstan'.[2]

But a younger generation of Latin American writers has retained a fascination for the Soviet Union as a social and political experiment, and traces of Soviet internationalism of the Cold War can be found all over Latin America. The exiled Cuban poet and translator José Manuel Prieto (1962–), who studied in Novosibirsk and worked for *Sovetskaja Literatura*, has dedicated most of his successful literary work to topics on Russia and the USSR. His 1998 novel *Livadia* (translated into English as 'Nocturnal Butterflies of the Russian Empire') was considered by Volpi one of the 'most indispensable literary works in the Latin American twentieth century'.[3] Volpi himself gave a balanced view of the history of the late Soviet Union from the two points of view of a veteran of the Afghanistan conflict and *Ogonek* reporter, and a female employee of the International Monetary Fund, in his 2006 novel *No será la tierra* (published in English as 'Season of Ash'). Ignacio Padilla, co-founder of the Mexican anti-magic realism movement Crack together with Volpi, did the same in his 2003 novel *Espiral de artillería* (Artillery Spiral), from the perspective of a doctor and forced informant before and after the fall of the communist regime.

It was not only in literature that Soviet advances towards the global South left a trail of relics. Soviet panel buildings can be found all over Cuba and Chile; a replica of one such apartment won the Chileans a Silver Lion at the 2014 Venice Biennale of Architecture. As for the Soviet attempts at spreading a positive image of themselves in Latin America, there is other evidence for its success, which is convincing and lasting: the extent of respect that many Latin Americans paid to the Soviet Union is reflected in the popularity of Russian given names. The baseball stars Iván Rodríguez and Vladimir Guerrero, as well as heavy metal drummer Igor Cavalera, were all born and baptised in the early 1970s, when the Soviets still enjoyed a good standing in Latin America. A generation before, the Venezuelan lawyer José Altagracia Ramírez had called his three sons Vladimir, Ilich, and Lenin; Ilich gained global notority, after his studies at Lumumba University, as the terrorist Carlos the Jackal. Another of about his age, Lenín Cerna, was a leading Sandinista and shares his first name with Lenín Morena, vice president of Ecuador, with Lenin Guardia, a Chilean sociologist, and countless other men born before the 1990s all across Latin America.

---

[2] Volpi, *El insomnio de Bolívar*, p. 31.   [3] *Ibid.*, p. 197.

Proofs of the success of Soviet internationalism after Stalin in the realm of higher education are associations of alumni from Soviet universities – and of their Russian or Ukrainian wives who joined them. They exist in most countries in Latin America and nostalgically recall their student days in the USSR at regular, including pan-Latin American, meetings. Their members work, or worked, as doctors, professors and engineers and in the public administration of most Latin American states – or, as one alumnus does after a career as a salesman, run a Russian café in the centre of Bogotá. Two former Latin American students of Lumumba University later became presidents of their home countries, Bharrat Jagdeo of Guyana and Porfirio Lobo Sosa of Honduras. Only a tiny minority fought violently for their political ideas, and even fewer still do so today; among the few are Timoleón 'Timochenko' Jiménez and Joaquín Gómez of the current leadership of the Colombian guerrilla troops FARC.

Some of the real estate of the Soviet friendship societies was taken over by the Russian foreign ministry; the SSOD became the Rossijskij Centr Meždunarodnogo Naučnogo i Kul'turnogo Sotrudničestva (Russian Centre of International Scientific and Cultural Collaboration, Rossotrudničestvo) in 1992, which now runs these institutes, in the style of the 'Cervantes' or 'Goethe' cultural diplomacy institutes, in Argentina, Chile, Mexico and Peru. Many others lost support from Moscow in the 1990s; they either shut down or have survived independently through their members – or through piano lessons that Russian expatriates give to local children. Arguably the most curious relic of this kind is the Instituto León Tolstoi in Bogotá's old centre La Candelaria, a rundown but atmospheric Soviet island in South America with a Russian library and a cinema with a huge collection of Soviet films.

Soviet flotsam and jetsam are, as I have alluded to in the preface, most visible in Cuba, from Minsk refrigerators in relatively well-off households to the abandoned construction site of a Soviet nuclear power plant in Juragua. And unlike what tourism catalogues have potential visitors believe, it is not mostly US Chevrolets from the 1950s, but rather the less picturesque Ladas, Moskvichs and GAZ lorries from the 1980s which predominate in the streets of Havana to this day.[4]

At a political level, a new wave of left governments in Latin America has taken office since the early 2000s, a development that has become acceptable only with the end of the Cold War. They have their roots much more in indigenous Marxism than in Soviet communism but,

---

[4] Jacqueline Loss and José Manuel Prieto, *Caviar with Rum: Cuba–USSR and the Post-Soviet Experience* (New York: Palgrave Macmillan, 2012).

nonetheless, have strengthened their links with the successor states of the USSR. 'We take as a premise that Russia should return to Latin America, and that is why [we] are positively seeking to expand diplomatic, economic, and trade relations with Moscow', the Bolivian president Evo Morales said after he met with Russian prime minister Vladimir Putin and the late Venezuelan president Hugo Chávez in Caracas in April 2010.[5] Beyond the usual arms sales, there are plans for Russian engineers to build an airport, a nuclear power plant and even a space centre in Bolivia. Chávez had established strong ties during several state visits to Moscow, has had a nuclear power plant built by Russia, has held joint Russian–Venezuelan military manoeuvres in the Caribbean and signed an agreement on student exchange, scientific collaboration and a petroleum deal with the Belorussian leader Alexander Lukashenko.[6] Nicaragua, where Daniel Ortega returned to the presidential office in 2007, and Venezuela are the only states besides Russia (and some bribed South Sea islands) that have recognised the Russian-imposed independence of South Ossetia and Abkhazia from Georgia. Brazil and Argentina have become important suppliers of meat for the Russian market and will probably expand this position: just as Argentina had not followed a western economic boycott after the Soviet invasion of Afghanistan, South American states did not join western sanctions against Russia after its relapse into imperialist reflexes and the invasion of Crimea and eastern Ukraine in 2014.

The support that Putin's Russia was given by European conservative and nationalist parties during this crisis had its precursors in the admiration of Latin American conservatives for the anti-modern, anti-pluralistic Soviet Union with its ostensibly intact traditional family values and healthy patriotism. Other ironic volte-faces had been taking place, in the 1990s, on the Russian side, too: human rights activists now held meetings in Moscow that denounced Fidel Castro as a totalitarian dictator, and reports of a 'tropical Gulag' appeared in the press.[7] Russian liberal economists, by contrast, hailed the Chilean dictator Pinochet, who had allegedly saved his country from socialism and defended free markets thanks to his authoritarian rule. 'Many in Russia today feel that we need a Pinochet', Nikolaj Leonov reported to Chilean colleagues,

[5] 'Bolivian Ministers to Visit Moscow in Late April', Ria Novosti, 4 Apr. 2010.
[6] 'Chávez Says Venezuela and Russia Will Build a Nuclear Reactor in Oil-Rich Zulia', *Latin American Herald Tribune*, 19 Nov. 2008.
[7] A. Cipko, 'Iz vystuplenij na meždunarodnoj konferencii "Rossija–Kuba: ot totalitarisma k demokratii"', *Latinskaja Amerika* 10–11 (1992), 27–32; I. Zorina, 'Uznik kubinskogo GULAGa', *Latinskaja Amerika* 5–6 (1992), 36–40; A. Blinova, 'Moja Kuba', *Latinskaja Amerika* 5–6 (1992), 41.

'a strong man who stops the decay of the country . . . In Russia, they think that Chile is a capitalist paradise.'[8]

Large parts of the Russian population were shocked at the collapse of their familiar world and of the economy. In the course of the 1990s, a small, excessively rich new upper class confronted impoverished masses of the population. Political instability, high foreign debt, social insecurity, a continuously low life expectancy, new extents of corruption, drug abuse, violence, and open and organised crime marked the era. People sought a spiritual crutch in religion and esoteric movements, and were looking for someone to blame for their misery. Many internal and external observers were reminded of typical Third World problems. The term 'Latin Americanisation of Russia' was doing the rounds in political debates of the 1990s.

Most African, South Asian and Latin American students had their scholarships cancelled at that time, and many returned to their home countries. Others, often because they could not afford the flight, followed a contemporary Russian trend and took their chance in sometimes shady *biznes*. Many suffered attacks from violent Russian nationalist youths, a sad development that had begun when people began looking for scapegoats for the economic disaster of perestroika. In the 1990s, Russian racists murdered several African and Asian students. Even in 2008 and 2009, when I began my research on Third World students in Moscow, I witnessed an appalling ritual that takes place every year on 20 April. Celebrating Hitler's birthday, Russian neo-Nazis stroll around Moscow, and especially the campus of the University of the Friendship of the Peoples, looking for non-white foreigners to beat up. Police seem unable, or unwilling, to cope with these thugs; hence a helpless university administration has imposed the resolution that all foreign students must not leave their dormitories on that day.

While many Russians sought ideological sanctuary in the Orthodox Church and Russian nationalism, Russian popular culture became heavily influenced by US and west European forms of expression. But Latin America has retained a special position it. Brazilian and Mexican television soap operas such as *A escrava Isaura* (The Slave Isaura) or *Los ricos también lloran* (The Rich Also Cry), which had already enjoyed enormous success all across the eastern bloc in the 1980s, consoled many Russians through the hardships of the 1990s. Boris Yeltsin allegedly ordered the Brazilian telenovela *Tropicalente* to be specially scheduled during the 1996 presidential elections in order to dissuade people from

---

[8] Leonov, *Licholet'e*, pp. 313–14.

leaving town on polling day.[9] One of the most popular contemporary Russian writers, Victor Pelevin, is fundamentally influenced by magic realism and in particular by Jorge Luis Borges.[10] Revolutionary romanticism has not faded out completely in the post-Soviet space: in 2004, it was Violeta Parra's *Gracias a la Vida* that became the anthem of the Ukrainian Orange Revolution. And contemporary Russian hip-hop music is full of references to Che Guevara and co.: '*Viva la revolución, viva comandante*', shouted Kasta feat. Noggano in 2010 from the Russian rap stronghold Rostov-on-Don.

Guevara's popularity has prevailed until today in many other spheres of the post-Soviet space. The semantics of the iconic symbol were frayed enough to offer a link between very contrary discourses. During excursions to several former Soviet republics during research for this book, I met an Armenian, born in the early 1980s, by the name of Ernesto; I was bid goodbye by a Kyrgyz acquaintance (who did not know about my research) with the words: '*Hasta la victoria siempre!*', and I saw a government-run PR-company in the Slavic-populated Moldovan separatist republic of Transnistria juxtaposing Che and Vladimir Putin in their pro-Russia campaign.

Among Russian intellectuals and artists, Che Guevara has retained his rebellious image. The *comandante*'s portrait, reimported from western Europe's New Left, is a popular motif in state-critical art by painters such as Aleksandr Barkovskij and Aleksandr Šaburov.[11] In his 1999 novel *Generation P*, Pelevin uses the ghost of Guevara as an esoteric adviser to the main character Tatarsky, an advertisting copy writer during the first post-Soviet years in Russia. Even in 2009, for the celebration of the fiftieth anniversary of the Cuban Revolution, a flood of Russian publications glorified the romantic revolutionary heroes Guevara and Fidel Castro. The image still evokes positive associations and, while it is used in different strands of Soviet nostalgia, plain commercial advertisements in Russia use it to emphasise their products' 'revolutionary' prices.

For the *meždunarodniki*, too, Che remained a source of inspiration, irrespective of their further careers. The late Kiva Majdanik became an outspoken critic of the new Russian leadership and of liberal economics in general. He participated in the World Social Forums in Porto Alegre, and the last book he wrote shortly before his death in 2006 was a very favourable biography of his personal idol Che Guevara. The historian Zoja Sokolova

---

[9] Kutejščikova, *Moskva-Meksiko-Moskva*, p. 19.
[10] Dina Odnopozova, 'Russian–Argentine Literary Exchanges', Ph.D thesis, Yale University, 2012.
[11] See www.art4.ru (last accessed 18 Sep. 2009).

continues in Majdanik's spirit with emphatic books on Cuba, written from her position at the still-functioning Institut Latinskoj Ameriki.[12]

Nikolaj Leonov, during perestroika, had still contrasted 'Che's ascetic-moral ethics' to the rampant debauchery in the mouldering Soviet Union. After the trauma of the chaotic 1990s, Leonov, just as so many of his compatriots, found solace in his newly discovered Orthodox faith and joined the left-nationalist Rodina party. Using his KGB networks, he supported his former protégé Vladimir Putin on his way into politics.[13] Putin notoriously mourns the disintegration of the Soviet Union, less for its communist ideology than as a global power that, at least in his view, was tightly organised within and commanded respect abroad. His retrogressivity and the reactionary domestic and foreign policies of his administration have seriously hindered Russia's necessary modernisation and, as I am finishing this typescript, threaten to bring Russia back into a period of isolation. What is even sadder is that the majority of Russians, including many of those who had protested against election fraud and corruption in the governing party until recently, seem to haven fallen for this old Macchiavellian strategy of inventing a hostile world abroad in order to close ranks at home.

The end of Stalinist isolation sixty years before, to end on a more optimistic note, is still remembered nostalgically in Russia today, too. A great example is Stolovaja No. 57. On two floors of the pricy GUM shopping mall on Red Square in Moscow, a huge Soviet-style canteen is designed in the style of the 1957 Youth Festival. With the USSR being literally sealed off from the rest of the world for many years, the festival had been a remarkable event and is today considered a formative experience of the so-called Gorbachev Generation. The song 'Moscow Nights', written on the occasion of the festival, is even today one of the most famous and popular Russian tunes (sung in Spanish as 'Noches de Moscú'). How much the festival was linked to the guests from the Third World in popular perception is evident from the iconography of the canteen, which features many original watercolours, painted in 1957 by the Soviet people's artist Nikolaj Žukov: in no way do they relate to a western impact, but they depict stereotypical youngsters from Asia and Africa along with the inevitable guitar-playing *muchacho* from Latin America. Future researchers of Soviet internationalism after Stalin should consider the Stolovaja as an affordable and pleasant lunch place during research at the Russian Archive of Contemporary History nearby.

[12] Zoja Sokolova, *Vsja pravda o Fidel'e Kastro i ego komande* (Moscow: Astrel', 2009); Maksim Makaryčev, *Fidel' Kastro* (Moscow: Molodaja Gvardija, 2008).
[13] Leonov, 'La inteligencia soviética en América Latina'; Leonov, *Licholet'e*, pp. 313–14.

Bibliography

ARCHIVES

Gosudarstvennyj archiv Rossijskoj Federacii (GARF, State Archive of the
Russian Federation), Moscow
Fond 5283: Vsesojuznoe obščestvo kul'turnoj svjazi s zagranicej (VOKS,
All-Union Organisation for Cultural Contacts)
Fond 6903: Gosteleradio (State Television and Radio)
Fond 9518: Gosudarstvennyj komitet kul'turnych svjazej (GKKS, State
Committee for Cultural Relations)
Fond 9576: Sojuz sovetskich obščestv družby (SSOD, Union of Friendship
Societies)
Rossijskij gosudarstvennyj archiv novejšej istorii (RGANI, Russian State Archive
of Contemporary History), Moscow
Fond 5: Obščij otdel Central'nogo Komiteta KPSS (General Department of
the Central Committee of the CPSU)
Rossijskij gosudarstvennyj archiv social'no-političeskoj istorii (RGASPI, Russian
State Archive of Socio-Political History), Moscow
Fond 1M: Central'nyj Komitet VLKSM (Central Committee of the Komsomol)
Fond 3M: Komitet molodežnych organizacij SSSR, 1956–1991 (Commitee of
Youth Organisations)
Fond 5M: Dokumenty BMMT 'Sputnik' (Documents of the Bureau of
International Youth Tourism 'Sputnik')
Rossijskij gosudarstvennyj archiv literatury i iskusstva (RGALI, Russian State
Archive of Literature and Art), Moscow
Fond 631: Sojuz pisatelej SSSR (Moskva 1932–1991) (Union of Soviet Writers)
Fond 1204: Il'ja Grigor'evič Erenburg (1891–1967)
Fond 2989: Roman Lazarevič Karmen (1906–1978)
Rossijskij gosudarstvennyj archiv kinofotodokumentov (RGAKFD, Russian State
Archive of Film- and Fotodocuments, Krasnogorsk
Arquivos do Ministério das Relações Exteriores, Itamaraty (AMRE, Archive of
the Brazilian Ministry of Foreign Affairs, Itamaraty), Brasília
Archive of the Instituto Cultural Colombo-Soviético, Bogotá

LIBRARIES

Archivo y Biblioteca Nacional, La Paz
Biblioteca del Archivo General de la Nación, Lima
Biblioteca Luis Ángel Arango, Bogotá
Bibliothek des Osteuropa-Instituts, Tübingen
Gosudarstvennaja publičnaja istoričeskaja biblioteka (State
    Public Historical Library), Moscow
Iberoamerikanisches Institut, Berlin
Library of the European University Institute, Florence
Rossijskaja Gosudarstvennaja Biblioteka (Russian State
    Library), Moscow
Universitätsbibliothek der Humboldt-Universität zu Berlin

LIST OF JOURNALS AND NEWSPAPERS

African Diaspora
Agitator
American Economic Review
American Political Science Review
Aus Politik und Zeitgeschichte
Boletín del Instituto Cultural Colombo-Soviético
Cahiers du Monde Russe
Central Asian Survey
Cold War History
Comparativ
Cuadernos Americanos
Cuadernos de la Fundación Pablo Neruda
Daedalos
Dekorativnoe Iskusstvo SSSR
Diálogo Científico
Diplomatic History
Družba Narodov
Estudios Públicos
Estudios sobre la Unión Soviética
Foreign Policy
Forum für osteuropäische Ideen-und Zeitgeschichte
H-Critica
Hispanic American Historical Review
History and Theory
Inostrannaja Literatura
International History Review

Iskusstvo Kino
Izvestija
Jahrbücher für Geschichte Osteuropas
Journal of Cold War Studies
Journal of Global History
Journal of Inter-American Studies
Journal of Interamerican Studies and World Affairs
Journal of Latin American Studies
Journal of Modern European History
Journal of World History
Kommunist
Kritika
Kuba
Kultur und Leben (Cultura y Vida, Kul'tura i žizn')
Laboratorium
Latin American Research Review
Latinskaja Amerika
Marxismo Militante
Mesoamerica
Moderne Welt
Molodaja Gvardija
Molodež' Mira
Le Monde Diplomatique
Moscow News (Novedades de Moscú)
Moskva
Muzykal'naja Žizn'
Die neue Ordnung in Kirche, Staat, Gesellschaft, Kultur
Neue Zeit (New Times, Novoe Vremja, Tiempos Nuevos)
New York Times
Novaja i Novejšaja Istorija
Nueva Frontera
Ogonek
Oktjabr'
Osteuropa
Pravda
Presencia
Problemas del Paz y el Socialismo (Problemy mira i socializma,
     World Marxist Review)
Razón y Fábula
Revolutionary Russia
Slavic Review
Smena

Sovetskaja Fotografija
Sovetskaja Literatura
Sovetskaja Muzyka
Sovetskaja Pečat'
Sovetskaja Ženščina
Sovetskij Cirk
Soviet Studies
Sowjetunion Heute
Stavropol'e
Studies on the Soviet Union
Survey
Teatr
Time
Tvorčestvo
Ultima Hora
Vestnik Vysšej Školy
Vnešnjaja Torgovlja
Vokrug Sveta
Voprosy Istorii
Vsemirnye Studenčeskie Novosti
Washington Quarterly
Za Rubežom
Zeitschrift für Weltgeschichte
Znamja

BOOKS AND ARTICLES

Académia de las Ciencias de la URSS (ed.), *Estudios Latinoamericanos soviéticos de hoy* (Moscow: Nauka, 1987).

Adas, Michael, *Dominance by Design: Technological Imperatives and America's Civilizing Mission* (Cambridge: Belknap Press of Harvard University Press, 2006).

Adshubej (Adžubej), Aleksej, *Gestürzte Hoffnung: Meine Erinnerungen an Chrustschow* (Berlin: Henschel, 1990).

Adžubej, Aleksej, *Kueka i modern-meščane* (Moscow: Pravda, 1959).
Na raznych širotach (Moscow: Pravda, 1959).

Agudelo Villa, Hernando, *La revolución del desarrollo: origen y evolución de la Alianza para el Progreso* (Mexico City: Roble, 1966).

Aguilar, Manuela, *Cultural Diplomacy and Foreign Policy: German–American Relations 1955–1968* (New York: Peter Lang, 1996).

Aldunate, Raúl, *En Moscú* (Santiago de Chile: Ultramar, n.d.).

Alexander, Robert J., *Communism in Latin America* (New Brunswick: Rutgers University Press, 1957).

'Soviet and Communist Activities in Latin America', *Problems of Communism* 10/1 (1961), 8–13.

Al'perovič, Moisej, *Revoljucija i diktatura v Paragvae* (Moscow: Nauka, 1975).

Sovetskaja istoriografija stran Latinskoj Ameriki (Moscow: Nauka, 1968).

Alted, Alicia, Nicolás, Encarna and Roger González, *Los niños de la guerra de España en la Unión Soviética: de la evacuación al retorno (1937–1999)* (Madrid: Fundación Largo Caballero, 1999).

Amado, Jorge, *Navegação de cabotagem: apontamentos para um livro de memórias que jamais escreverei* (Lisbon: Editora Record, 1992).

O mundo da paz: União Soviética e democracias populares (Rio de Janeiro: Editorial Vitória, 1951).

Amar, Andrew Richard, *Als Student in Moskau* (Stuttgart: Seewald, 1961).

Anciferov, Nikolaj and Sergej Polikarpov (eds.), *Tebe, Kuba! Stichi* (Moscow: Sovetskij Pisatel', 1961).

Andrew, Christopher and Vasili Mitrokhin, *The World Was Going Our Way: The KGB and the Battle for the Third World* (New York: Basic Books, 2005).

Annenkov, Julij, *Šachterskij senator* (Moscow: GosIzDetLit, 1962).

Anon., '21,000 Foreign Youth Attending Universities in Soviet Union', *New York Times*, 13 Jan. 1965.

'Argentina, Russia Sign: Trade Agreement Is Renewed as Soviet Opens Big Exhibit', *New York Times*, 20 May 1955.

'Auf Freundschaftsbahnen', *Kultur und Leben* 12 (1971), 38.

'Bolivian Ministers to Visit Moscow in Late April', *Ria Novosti*, 4 Apr. 2010.

'Chávez Says Venezuela and Russia Will Build a Nuclear Reactor in Oil-Rich Zulia', *Latin American Herald Tribune*, 19 Nov. 2008.

Čile–Rossija: 100 let diplomatičeskich otnošenij 1909–2009 (Moscow: [Embassy of Chile], 2009).

'Escuche diariamente Radio Moscú', *Boletín del Instituto Cultural Colombo Soviético* 5–6 (1974), 7.

Grafika Kuby: katalog vystavki (Moscow: Sovetskij Chudožnik, 1960).

'Grupo de parlamentarios bolivianos visita Rusia', *Presencia*, 3 Jul. 1960.

ILA. Instituto de América Latina: 30 años 1961–1991 (Moscow: ILA, n.d.).

'Im Namen von 40 Millionen', *Kultur und Leben* 11 (1971), 18–20.

'Jubilej Moiseja Samuiloviča Al'peroviča', *Novaja i Novejšaja Istorija* 2 (2009), 214–16.

'Kogda poliaki srazhalis'za svobodu Kuby', *Inostrannaja Literatura* 12 (1960), 260.

'Lateinamerikanische Literatur', *Kultur und Leben* 12 (1961), 16–18.

'Lateinamerikanische Literatur in der Sowjetunion', *Kultur und Leben* 3 (1958), 46.

'Das lateinamerikanische Seminar in Moskau', *Kultur und Leben* 4 (1969), 32.

'A Longing for Truth: Russia's New Generation', *Time*, 13 Apr. 1962.

'Melodie Mexikos und Gedichte Perus', *Kultur und Leben* 2/8 (1958), 55–6.

'Mikoyan Leaves Mexico for Home: His Trip Is Generally Held a Success though Press Comment Was Hostile', *New York Times*, 29 Nov. 1959.

'"O vremeni i o sebe": k 75-letiju Borisa Iosifoviča Koval'ja', *Latinskaja Amerika* 6 (2005), 72–9.
'Odin iz starejšich sovetskich Latinoamerikanistov: beseda s členom-korrespondentom AN SSSR I. R. Grigulevičem', *Latinskaja Amerika* 5 (1983), 141–3.
'Parlamentarios colombianos en la URSS', *Boletín del Instituto Cultural Colombo Soviético* 3–4 (1967), 3.
'Postanovlenie CK KPSS: o zadačach partinoj propagandy v sovremennych uslovijach i istoričestkaja nauka', *Voprosy Istorii* 6 (1960), 3–9.
'Prekrasnaja vosmožnost': beseda s kubinskim poetom Gil'enom', *Molodež' Mira* 4 (1957), 15.
'El presidente A. Sukarno afirmó que existe similtud de espíritu entre los pueblos de Bolivia e Indonesia: cordial bienvenida tributo la población paceña al mandatorio visitante', *Presencia*, 8 May 1961.
'Reglamento para la adjudicación de becas en la Universidad de la amistad de los pueblos "Patricio Lumumba" de Moscú en 1967', *Boletín del Instituto Cultural Colombo Soviético* 1 (1966), 4–5.
'Reiz des Exotischen, Fernen', *Kultur und Leben* 4 (1965), 36–7.
'Sombrero', *Kultur und Leben* 8 (1960).
'Soviet Exposition Opened in Brazil: Diversified Show Is Russia's Biggest in Latin America', *New York Times*, 4 May 1962.
'Trio "Los Mechikanos"', *Sovetskaja Muzyka* 21/8 (1957), 126.
Viva Kuba! Vizit Fidelia Kastro Rus v Sovetskij sojuz (Moscow: Pravda, 1963).
'Vokrug urokov Čili', *Latinskaja Amerika* 5 (1974).
Živopis' Kuby: katalog vystavki (Moscow: Sovetskij Chudožnik, 1962).
Anweiler, Oskar and Karl-Heinz Ruffmann (eds.), *Kulturpolitik der Sowjetunion* (Stuttgart: Kröner, 1973).
Ardao, Arturo, *Génesis de la idea y el nombre de América Latina* (Caracas: Centro de Estudios Latinoamericanos Rómulo Gallegos, 1980).
Ashby, Timothy, *The Bear in the Back Yard: Moscow's Caribbean Strategy* (Lexington, MA: Lexington Books, 1987).
Asturias, Miguel Angel, 'Die russische Literatur in Lateinamerika', *Kultur und Leben* 3 (1958), 46–9.
Aust, Martin (ed.), *Globalisierung imperial und sozialistisch: Russland und die Sowjetunion in der Globalgeschichte 1851–1991* (Frankfurt am Main: Campus, 2013).
Ball, Alan M., *Imagining America: Influence and Images in Twentieth-Century Russia* (Lanham, MD: Rowman & Littlefield, 2003).
Barghoorn, Frederic C., *Soviet Foreign Propaganda* (Princeton: Princeton University Press, 1964).
Bark, Dennis L., *The Red Orchestra* (Stanford: Hoover Institution Press, 1986).
Barnet, Enrique Pineda, 'Ein sowjetisch-kubanischer Film', *Neue Zeit* 10 (1962), 16–17.
Bartley, Russell H., 'A Decade of Soviet Scholarship in Brazilian History: 1958–1968', *Hispanic American Historical Review* 50/3 (1970), 445–66.
'On Scholarly Dialogue: The Case of US and Soviet Latin Americanists', *Latin American Research Review* 1 (1970), 59–62.

Batal, Georges, Dawagsuren, Zerewijn and Pedro Motta Lima, 'Oktoberrevolution und Fortschritt', *Probleme des Friedens und des Sozialismus* 11 (1966), 845–51.

Behrends, Jan C., *Die erfundene Freundschaft: Propaganda für die Sowjetunion in Polen und in der DDR* (Cologne: Böhlau, 2006).

'Vom Panslavismus zum Friedenskampf: Außenpolitik, Herrschaftslegitimation und Massenmobilisierung im sowjetischen Nachkriegsimperium', *Jahrbücher für Geschichte Osteuropas* 56/1 (2008), 27–53.

Bekopitov, I., 'Raul' Prebiš: v poiskach al'ternativ', *Latinskaja Amerika* 5 (1976), 200–5.

Bell-Villada, Gene, *García Márquez: The Man and His Work* (Chapel Hill: University of North Carolina Press, 1990).

Belmonte, Laura, *Selling the American Way: US Propaganda and the Cold War* (Philadelphia: University of Pennsylvania Press, 2008).

Berg, Walter Bruno and Michael Rössner, *Lateinamerikanische Literaturgeschichte* (Stuttgart and Weimar: Metzler, 2007).

Berner, Wolfgang, 'Die Sowjetunion und Lateinamerika', in Dietrich Geyer (ed.), *Osteuropa-Handbuch: Sowjetische Außernpolitik Band II* (Cologne: Böhlau, 1976), pp. 844–78.

Berríos, Ruben and Cole Blasier, 'Peru and the Soviet Union 1969–1989: Distant Partners', *Journal of Latin American Studies* 23 (1991), 365–84.

Besrodny (Bezrodnyj), Igor, 'Von Argentinien bis Kuba', *Neue Zeit* 51 (1956), 28–31.

Bessonov, Sergei, 'Soviet Basketballers in South America', *Moscow News* 58 (1956), 8.

Bethell, Leslie (ed.), *Latin America: Politics and Society since 1930* (Cambridge: Cambridge University Press, 1998).

Bethell, Leslie and Ian Roxborough, 'The Impact of the Cold War on Latin America', in Melvyn Leffler (ed.), *Origins of the Cold War: An International History* (New York: Routledge, 2007), pp. 293–316.

(eds.), *Latin America between the Second World War and the Cold War: Crisis and Containment, 1944–1948* (Cambridge: Cambridge University Press, 1997).

Beyrau, Dietrich, *Intelligenz und Dissens: Die russischen Bildungsschichten in der Sowjetunion 1917–1985* (Göttingen: Vandenhoeck & Ruprecht, 1993).

Bezrodny (Bezrodnyj), Igor, 'Seventy-Five Days in Latin America', *Moscow News* 94 (1956).

Bikčentaev, Anver, 'Ad'jutanti ne umirajut', *Oktjabr'* 5 (1963), 7–34.

'Trudno čeloveku bez borody', *Družba Narodov* 5 (1960), 105–8.

Birjukov, Vadim, 'Doč' solnca', *Ogonek* 47 (1960), 29.

Blasier, Cole, *The Giant's Rival: The USSR and Latin America* (Pittsburgh: University of Pittsburgh Press, 1983).

'The Soviet Latin Americanists', *Latin American Research Review* 16 (1981), 107–23.

Blinova, A., 'Moja Kuba', *Latinskaja Amerika* 5–6 (1992), 41–9.

Bluth, Christoph, Plaggenborg, Stefan and Manfred Hellmann, *Handbuch der Geschichte Russlands: 1945–1991. Vom Ende des Zweiten Weltkriegs bis zum Zusammenbruch der Sowjetunion* (Stuttgart: Hiersemann, 2003).

Boden, Ragna, *Die Grenzen der Weltmacht: Sowjetische Indonesienpolitik von Stalin bis Brežnev* (Stuttgart: Steiner, 2006).

Boeckh, Andreas, 'La modernización importada: experiencias históricas con importaciones de conceptos de desarrollo en América Latina', *Diálogo Científico* 14/1–2 (2005), 37–55.

Bol'šakov, Ivan, 'Uspech sovetskich vystavok v stranach Latinskoj Ameriki', in Ivan Bol'šakov (ed.), *Na vsech kontinentov mira* (Moscow: Pravda, 1962), pp. 87–100.

Borovik, Genrich, *Kak eto bylo na Kube* (Moscow: Pravda, 1961).

'Pervye šagi po Sovetskoj zemle', *Ogonek* 19 (1963), 28–9.

Povest' o zelenoj jaščerice (Moscow: Molodaja gvardija, 1963).

'Pylajuščij ostrov', *Ogonek* 7 (1960), 4–5.

Brands, Hal, *Latin America's Cold War* (Cambridge, MA: Harvard University Press, 2010).

Brown, Archie, *Seven Years That Changed the World: Perestroika in Perspective* (Oxford: Oxford University Press, 2007).

Brun, Ellen and Jacques Hersh, *Soviet–Third World Relations in a Capitalist World: The Political Economy of Broken Promises* (New York: St Martin's Press, 1990).

Buckmiller, Michael and Klaus Meschkat (eds.), *Biographisches Handbuch zur Geschichte der Kommunistischen Internationale: Ein deutsch-russisches Forschungsprojekt* (Berlin: Akademie-Verlag, 2007).

Campo, Héctor, 'Das 6. Weltjugendfestival: Die Jugend trifft sich in Moskau', *Neue Zeit* 15/26 (1957), 18–19.

Campusano, J., 'Die Kommunisten und die Jugend', *Probleme des Friedens und des Sozialismus* 1 (1962), 69–71.

Canal Ramírez, Gonzalo, *La Unión Soviética: reto moral* (Bogotá: Imprenta y Rotograbado, 1969).

Carbonell, Néstor, *And the Russians Stayed: The Sovietization of Cuba. A Personal Portrait* (New York: William Morrow & Co., 1989).

Carew, Jan, *Moscow Is Not My Mecca* (London: Secker & Warburg, 1964).

Carmagnani, Marcello, *L'altro Occidente: l'America Latina dall'invasione europea al nuovo millennio* (Turin: Einaudi, 2003).

Carranza, Maria Mercedes, 'El discreto encanto del socialismo', *Nueva Frontera* 127 (1977), 23–4.

Carter, James Richard, *The Net Cost of Soviet Foreign Aid* (New York: Praeger, 1969).

Castañeda, Jorge, *Compañero: The Life and Death of Che Guevara* (New York: Vintage, 1997).

Utopia Unarmed: The Latin American Left after the Cold War (New York: Vintage, 1994).

Caute, David, *The Dancer Defects: The Struggle for Cultural Supremacy during the Cold War* (Oxford: Oxford University Press, 2003).

The Fellow Travellers: Intellectual Friends of Communism (New Haven: Yale University Press, 1988).

Chačaturov, Karen, *Tri znaka vremeni: polveka v meždunarodnoj žurnalistike* (Moscow: Meždunarodnye Otnošenija, 2002).

Urugvaj Segodnja (Moscow: Izdatel'stvo Instituta Meždunarodnych Otnošenij, 1962).

Zapiski očevidca (Moscow: Novosti, 1996).

Chejfec, L., '"Čtoby rasskazat' pravdu o SSSR": pervye latinoamerikanskie delegacii v Sovetskom Sojuze', *Latinskaja Amerika* 12 (1982), 73–83.

Chruščev (Khrushchev), Nikita, 'Poslanie k posetiteljam sovetskoj vystavki v Rio-de-Žanejro', *Vnešnjaja Torgovlja* 42/6 (1962), 3–5.

Čičkov, Vasilij, *Buntujuščaja zemlja: putešestvija i vstreči* (Moscow: DetGiz, 1961).

Mal'čiški iz Gavany (Moscow: DetGiz, 1963).

Pepe, malen'kij Kubinec: povest' (Moscow: DetGiz, 1961).

Pod sozvezdiem južnogo kresto (Moscow: DetGiz, 1960).

'V vysokich Andach', *Ogonek* 24 (1959), 14–16.

Zarja nad Kuboj (Moscow: Izdatel'stvo Instituta Meždunarodnych Otnošenij, 1960).

Cipko, A., 'Iz vystuplenij na meždunarodnoj konferencii "Rossija–Kuba: ot totalitarisma k demokratii"', *Latinskaja Amerika* 10–11 (1992), 27–32.

Clementi, Hebe, *María Rosa Oliver* (Buenos Aires: Planeta, 1992).

Clissold, Stephen (ed.), *Soviet Relations with Latin America, 1918–1968: A Documentary Survey* (London: Oxford University Press, 1970).

Cobb, Tyrus W., 'National Security Perspectives of Soviet "Think Tanks"', *Problems of Communism* 30/6 (1981), 51–9.

Cobo, Juan, 'Der Militärputsch in Peru', *Neue Zeit* 41 (1968), 18.

'Die sowjetische Hilfe für Peru', *Neue Zeit* 43 (1970), 16–17.

Cooper, Frederick and Jane Burbank, *Empires in World History: Power and the Politics of Difference* (Princeton: Princeton University Press, 2010).

Courtois, Stéphane, Wert, Nicolas and Jean-Louis Panné (eds.), *Le Livre noir du communisme: crimes, terreur, répression* (Paris: Éditions Robert Laffont, 1997).

Crossley, Pamela Kyle, *What Is Global History?* (Cambridge: Polity Press, 2008).

Cull, Nicolas, *The Cold War and the United States Information Agency: American Propaganda and Public Diplomacy, 1945–1989* (Cambridge: Cambridge University Press, 2008).

Dabagjan, E., 'Anatolij Fedorovič Šul'govskij (1926–1991)', *Novaja i Novejšaja Istorija* 5 (2007), 178–91.

'Jarkij i mnogogrannyj talant', *Latinskaja Amerika* 4 (2001), 18–27.

Dahlmann, Dittmar, *Land und Freiheit: Machnovščina und Zapatismo als Beispiele agrarrevolutionärer Bewegungen* (Stuttgart: Steiner, 1986).

Dal'nev, Oleg, '"Kuba" – novyj žurnal', *Sovetskaja Pečat'* 9 (1964), 56.

Dangond, Alberto, *Mi diario en la Unión Soviética: un conservador en la URSS* (Bogotá: Ediciones Suramerica, 1968).

David-Fox, Michael, *Orientalism and Empire in Russia* (Bloomington: Slavica, 2006).

Showcasing the Great Experiment: Cultural Diplomacy and Western Visitors to Soviet Union, 1921–1941 (Oxford: Oxford University Press, 2012).

Davidson, Apollon and Irina Filatova, 'African History: A View from behind the Kremlin Wall', in Maxim Matusevich (ed.), *Africa in Russia, Russia in Africa: Three Centuries of Encounters* (Trenton: Africa World Press, 2007), pp. 111–31.

de Holanda, Nestor, *Como seria o Brasil socialista?* (Rio de Janeiro: Editôra Civilização Brasileira, 1963).

Diálogo Brasil–URSS (Rio de Janeiro: Editôra Civilização Brasileira, 1962).

O mundo vermelho: notas de um repórter na URSS (Rio de Janeiro: Editora Pongetti, 1962).

de Moraes, Eneida, *Caminhos da terra: URSS, Tchecoslováquia, China* (Rio de Janeiro: Antunes, 1959).

'Mein Brasilien', *Neue Zeit* 25 (1959), 19.

Denisov, N., 'Na orbite mira i družby', *Sovetskaja Pečat'* 10 (1961), 38–42.

Derostas, Daniela, Poch, Maria Jesus and Carmen Winter, *Un crisol de experiencias: Chilenos en la Universidad de Amistad de los Pueblos Patricia Lumumba* (documentary film, Chile, 2008).

Dinerstein, Herbert, 'Soviet Policy in Latin America', *American Political Science Review* 1 (1967), 80–90.

Dirnecker, Bert, 'Die "Patrice Lumumba-Universität für Völkerfreundschaft" in Moskau', *Moderne Welt* 3 (1961/2), 211–24.

Dmiterko, Ljubomir, *Pod južnym krestom* (Moscow: Sovetskij Pisatel', 1958).

Dobson, Miriam, *Khrushchev's Cold Summer: Gulag Returnees, Crime, and the Fate of Reform after Stalin* (Ithaca: Cornell University Press, 2009).

Dorenski, S.,'In Brasilien', *Kultur und Leben* 1 (1960), 53–5.

Dubinina, Iu., 'Sovetskij Sojuz v Rio-de-Žanejro', *Ogonek* 20 (1962), 2.

Duda, Gerhard, *Jenö Varga und die Geschichte des Instituts für Weltwirtschaft und Weltpolitik in Moskau 1921–1970: Zu den Möglichkeiten und Grenzen wissenschaftlicher Auslandsanalyse in der Sowjetunion* (Berlin: Akademie-Verlag, 1994).

Dülfer, Jost, *Europa im Ost–West-Konflikt: 1945–1990* (Munich: Oldenbourg, 2004).

Ehrenburg, Ilja (Ilya), *Menschen, Jahre, Leben: Memoiren* (Berlin: Volk und Welt, 1977).

Ehrenburg, Ilya, Khachaturian, Aram and Vladimir Pomerantsev, 'Three Soviet Artists on the Present Needs of Soviet Art', *Soviet Studies* 4 (1954), 412–45.

Ely, Roland T., 'El panorama interamericano visto por investigadores de la URSS', *Journal of Inter-American Studies* 8/2 (1966), 294–317.

Engerman, David C., *Know Your Enemy: The Rise and Fall of America's Soviet Experts* (Oxford: Oxford University Press, 2009).

'The Second World's Third World', *Kritika* 1 (2011), 183–211.

Eran, Oded, *Mezhdunarodniki: An Assessment of Professional Expertise in the Making of Soviet Foreign Policy* (Ramat Gan, Israel: Turtledove Publications, 1979).

Ermolaev, Vasilij, *Nacional'no-osvoboditel'noe i rabočee dviženie v stranach Latinskoj Ameriki posle vtoroj mirovoj vojny: lekcii, pročitannye v Vysšej partijnoj škole pri CK KPSS* (Moscow: Vysšaja Partijnaja Škola pri CK KPSS, 1958).

Estrada, Rafael, 'Moe mnenie o VI Festivale', *Molodež' mira* 7 (1957), 6.

Evreinov, E., Kosarev, Ju. and V. Ustinov, *Primenenie elektronnych vyčislitel'nych mašin v issledovanim pis'mennosti drevnich Majja* (Novosibirsk:Izdatel'stvo Sibirskogo Otdelenija AN SSSR, 1961).

Evtušenko, Evgenij (Yevtushenko, Yevgeny), 'Ja – Kuba: poema v proze', *Znamja* 3 (1963), 3–89.

Nežnost' (Moscow: Sovetskij Pisatel', 1962).

'Stichi', *Sovetskaja Literatura* 10 (1962), 147–52.

Fadeicheva, Margarita, 'Friends from All Countries Meet Here', *Moscow News* 26 (1962), 8–9.

Fazio Vengoa, Hugo, 'América Latina Vista por los Académicos Soviéticos: preámbulo de las relaciónes Ruso-Latinoamericanas', *H-Crítica* 15 (2003), 31–49.

Feinberg, Richard, 'Central America: The View from Moscow', *Washington Quarterly* (1982), 171–5.

Fel'cman, Oskar, 'Gosti iz Brazilij', *Muzykal'naja Žizn'* 14 (1958), 21.

Ferraz, Vicente, *Soy Cuba, o mamute siberiano* (2005).

Ferreira, Francisco, *26 años na União Soviética: notas de exilio do Chico da CUF* (Lisbon: Edições Afrodite, 1975).

Ferreras, Ramón Alberto, *¿Infierno? 1974–1980: vida estudantil en la URSS* (Santo Domingo: Editorial del Nordeste, 1981).

Fonseca, Carlos, *Un nicaragüense en Moscú* (Managua: Secretaría Nacional de Propaganda y Educación Política, 1980).

Fontaine Talavera, Arturo, 'Estados Unidos y Unión Soviética en Chile', *Estudios Públicos* 72 (1998).

Fradkine, Alexandre (ed.), *Le monde sous un même toit: documents sur les études et la vie des étudiants de l'Université de l'amitié des peuples Patrice Lumumba à Moscou* (Moscow: Novosti, 1973).

Franco, Jean, *The Decline and Fall of the Lettered City: Latin America in the Cold War* (Cambridge, MA: Harvard University Press, 2002).

Frank, Andre Gunder, *Capitalism and Underdevelopment in Latin America: Historical Studies of Chile and Brazil* (New York: Monthly Review Press, 1969).

Freitag, Ulrike (ed.), *Globalgeschichte: Theorien, Ansätze, Themen* (Frankfurt am Main: Campus Verlag, 2007).

Fursenko, Aleksandr, *Prezidium CK KPSS: 1954–1964* (Moscow: Rossijskaja Političeskaja Enciklopedija, 2003).

Fürst, Juliane, 'The Arrival of Spring? Changes and Continuities in Soviet Youth Culture and Policy between Stalin and Khrushchev', in Jones (ed.), *The Dilemmas of De-Stalinization*, pp. 135–53.

Gaddis, John Lewis, *We Now Know: Rethinking Cold War History* (Oxford: Oxford University Press, 1998).

Galeano, Eduardo, *Las venas abiertas de América Latina* (Montevideo: Editorial Universidad de la República, 1971).

Ganzelka, Jiri and Miroslav Zikmund, *Ot Argentiny do Meksiki* (Moscow: Izdatel'stvo Detskoj Literatury, 1961).

García Márquez, Gabriel, *De viaje por los países socialistas: 90 días en la 'Cortina de Hierro'* (Bogotá: La Oveja Negra, 1982).

Gelman, Juan, 'U Lolity Torres', *Ogonek* 48 (1957), 28.

Geršber, A., 'Kubinskaja revoliucija v fotografijach', *Sovetskaja Fotografija* 23/2 (1963), 5.

Gestwa, Klaus, 'Kolumbus des Kosmos: Der Kult um Jurij Gagarin', *Osteuropa* 10 (2009), 121–51.

Die Stalinschen Großbauten des Kommunismus: Sowjetische Technik-und Umweltgeschichte, 1948–1967 (Munich: Oldenbourg, 2010).

Geyer, Martin H. and Johannes Paulmann, *The Mechanics of Internationalism: Culture, Society, and Politics from the 1840s to the First World War* (Oxford: Oxford University Press, 2008).

Ghioldi, Rodolfo, *Uzbekistan: el espejo* (Buenos Aires: Editorial Fundamentos, 1956).

Gilman, Claudia, *Entre la pluma y el fusil: debates y dilemas del escritor revolucionario en América Latina* (Buenos Aires: Siglo Veintiuno, 2003).

Gilman, Nils, *Mandarins of the Future: Modernization Theory in Cold War America* (Baltimore: Johns Hopkins University Press, 2003).

Glinkin, A., 'Slovo o druge', *Latinskaja Amerika* 4 (2001), 11–17.

Goehrke, Carsten, *Sowjetische Moderne und Umbruch* (Zürich: Chronos, 2005).

Goldenberg, Boris, *Kommunismus in Lateinamerika* (Stuttgart: Kohlhammer, 1971).

Goldhamer, Herbert, *The Foreign Powers in Latin America* (Princeton: Princeton University Press, 1972).

Goldmann, Kjell, *The Logic of Internationalism: Coercion and Accommodation* (New York: Routledge, 2001).

Golomštok, I. and I. Karetnikova, *Iskusstvo stran Latinskoj Ameriki* (Moscow: Iskusstvo, 1959).

Golubev, A. (ed.), *Istorija SSSR v anekdotach* (Smolensk: Smjadyn', 1991).

Gómez Valderrama, Pedro, *Los ojos del burgués: un año en la Unión Soviética* (Bogotá: Oveja Negra, 1971).

Gorbatschow (Gorbachev), Michail, *Perestroika: Die zweite Russische Revolution* (Munich: Droemer Knaur, 1987).

Gorjunov, Dmitri, *Zdrastvui, Kuba!* (Moscow: Pravda, 1961).

Gottemoeller, Rose E. and Paul Fritz Langer, *Foreign Area Studies in the USSR: Training and Employment of Specialists* (Santa Monica: Rand, 1983).

Gould-Davies, Nigel, 'The Logic of Soviet Cultural Diplomacy', *Diplomatic History* 27/2 (2003), 193–214.

Goure, Leon and Morris Rothenberg, *Soviet Penetration of Latin America* (Miami: Center for Advanced International Studies, University of Miami, 1975).

Grandin, Greg, *The Last Colonial Massacre: Latin America in the Cold War* (Chicago: University of Chicago Press, 2004).

Granin, Daniil, *Ostrov molodych: rasskazy o Kube* (Leningrad: Lenizdat, 1962).

Greco, Jorge, '"Moe serdce s vami" pišet Lolita Torres čitateljam Smeny', *Smena* 34/4 (1957), 22–3.

Greiner, Bernd (ed.), *Heiße Kriege im Kalten Krieg* (Hamburg: Hamburger Edition, 2006).

Gribačev, Nikolaj, *Dym nad vulkanom: očerki o stranach Latinskoj Ameriki* (Moscow: Molodaja Gvardija, 1959).

Grigulevich, Iosif, 'Ilya Ehrenburg y América Latina', *América Latina* 2 (1976), 181–96.

Gromyko, Andrej and Hermann Kusterer, *Erinnerungen* (Düsseldorf: Econ, 1989).

Grow, Michael, *US Presidents and Latin American Interventions: Pursuing Regime Change in the Cold War* (Lawrence: University Press of Kansas, 2008).

Groys, Boris, *Das kommunistische Postskriptum* (Frankfurt am Main: Suhrkamp, 2006).

Grün, Leopold, The Red Elvis: The Dean Reed Story (film, 2007).

Gruško, Pavel, 'Licom k Kube: stichi', *Družba Narodov* 1 (1965), 139–45.

Guevara, Ernesto, 'Kuba und der Kennedy-Plan', *Probleme des Friedens und des Sozialismus* 2 (1962), 119–20.

Guillén, Abraham, *El capitalismo soviético: última etapa del imperialismo* (Madrid: Queimada Ediciones, 1979).

Guillén, Nicolás, *Páginas vueltas: memorias* (Havana: Unión de Escritores y Artistas de Cuba, 1982).

Gukasov, A., 'Sovetskij balet v stranach Južnoj Ameriki', *Teatr* 19/5 (1958), 164–5.

Guljam, Chamid, *Kontinenty ne spjat* (Moscow: Sovetskij Pisatel', 1961).

Gutiérrez, Joaquin, *La URSS tal cual* (Santiago de Chile: Nascimento, 1967).

Gvozdev, Iurij, 'Gork'ij kofe Kolumbii', *Ogonek* 51 (1962), 28–9.

Haddow, Robert H., *Pavilions of Plenty: Exhibiting American Culture Abroad in the 1950s* (Washington, DC: Smithsonian Institute Press, 1997).

Hangen, Welles, 'Soviet Makes Bid to Latin America for Economic Tie: Bulganin Offers Trade Deals and Aid on Pattern Set in Asia and Mideast. Foothold Believed Aim', *New York Times*, 17 Jan. 1956.

Harnecker, Marta (ed.), *Perestroika: la revolución de las esperanzas. Entrevista a Kiva Maidanik* (Buenos Aires: Dialéctica, 1988).

Hayward, Max, *Proceso a los escritores: el estado soviético contra Siniavski y Daniel* (Buenos Aires: Editorial Americana, 1967).

Hershberg, James, '"High Spirited Confusion": Brazil, the 1961 Belgrade Non-Aligned Conference, and the Limits of an "Independent Foreign Policy" during the High Cold War', *Cold War History* 7/3 (2007), 373–88.

Hessler, Julie, 'Death of an African Student in Moscow: Race, Politics, and the Cold War', *Cahiers du Monde Russe* 47/1–2 (2006), 33–63.

Hilger, Andreas (ed.), *Die Sowjetunion und die Dritte Welt: UdSSR, Staatssozialismus und Antikolonialismus im Kalten Krieg 1945–1991* (Munich: Oldenbourg, 2009).

Hixson, Walter L., *Parting the Curtain: Propaganda, Culture, and the Cold War, 1945–1961* (New York: St Martin's Griffin, 1998).

Holbraad, Carsten, *Internationalism and Nationalism in European Political Thought* (New York: Palgrave Macmillan, 2003).

Hollander, Paul, *Political Pilgrims: Western Intellectuals in Search of the Good Society* (Piscataway, NJ: Transaction, 1997).

Holthusen, Johannes, *Russische Literatur im 20. Jahrhundert* (Tübingen: Francke, 1992).

Hopkins, Anthony, *Global History: Interactions between the Universal and the Local* (Basingstoke: Palgrave Macmillan, 2006).

Hopkins, Mark W., *Mass Media in the Soviet Union* (New York: Pegasus, 1970).

Hough, Jerry F., 'The Evolving Soviet Debate on Latin America', *Latin American Research Review* 16/1 (1981), 124–43.

The Struggle for the Third World: Soviet Debates and American Options (Washington, DC: Brookings Institution Press, 1986).

Ignat'ev, Oleg, 'Skripka barabanščika', *Vokrug Sveta* 9 (1960), 13–16.

Ot Argentiny do Venesuely (Moscow: Pravda, 1961).

Ilchenco, V., *A la URSS por los conocimientos* (Moscow: Progreso, 1971).

Ilic, Melanie (ed.), *Soviet State and Society under Nikita Khrushchev* (London: Routledge, 2009).

Ilic, Melanie, Reid, Susan Emily and Lynne Attwood (eds.), *Women in the Khrushchev Era* (Basingstoke: Palgrave Macmillan, 2004).

Institut für Auslandsbeziehungen (IfA) Stuttgart (ed.), *Exotische Welten, europäische Phantasien: Ausstellungskatalog* (Stuttgart: Edition Cantz, 1987).

Institut Latinskoj Ameriki (ed.), *Latinskaja Amerika v Sovetskoj pečati* (Moscow: ILA RAN, 1964).

(ed.), *Zarubežnye centry po izučenuju Latinskoj Ameriki* (Moscow: ILA RAN, 1970).

Intourist, *Moscú: Intourist* (Moscow: Intourist, n.d.).

Iriye, Akira, *Cultural Internationalism and World Order* (Baltimore: Johns Hopkins University Press, 1997).

Global Community: The Role of International Organizations in the Making of the Contemporary World (Berkeley: University of California Press, 2004).

Irnberger, Harald, *Gabriel García Márquez: Die Magie der Wirklichkeit* (Frankfurt am Main: Fischer, 2005).

Isa Conde, Narciso, *Kiva Maidanik: humanidad sin límites y herejía revolucionaria* (Santo Domingo: Editora Tropical, 2007).

Isaev, N. (ed.), *Dokumenty proletarskoj solidarnosti: sbornik dokumentov o sodružestve trudjaščichsja Sovetskogo Sojuza s trudjaščimisja stran Azii, Afriki i Latinskoj Ameriki v 1918–1961 godach* (Moscow: Profizdat, 1962).

Ivanov, G., 'Na pylajuščem ostrove: pisma s Kuby', *Stavropol'e* 3 (1962).

Ivanov, Jurij, *Kurs na Gavanu* (Kaliningrad: Kaliningradskoe Knižnoe Izdatel'stvo, 1964).

Ivanova, E., 'Cuban Carnival', *Moscow News* 43 (1962), 12.

Jewtuschenko, Jewgeni (Yevtushenko, Yevgeny), *Der Wolfspass: Abenteuer eines Dichterlebens* (Berlin: Volk und Welt, 2000).

Jones, Polly (ed.), *The Dilemmas of De-Stalinization: Negotiating Cultural and Social Change in the Khrushchev Era* (London: Routledge, 2007).

Jostock, Paul, 'Die Lumumba-Universität in Moskau', *Die neue Ordnung in Kirche, Staat, Gesellschaft, Kultur* 16/1 (1962), 62–5.

Kachurin, Pamela, 'The ROCI Road to Peace: Robert Rauschenberg, Perestroika and the End of the Cold War', *Journal of Cold War Studies* 4/1 (2002), 27–44.

Kalesnik, Stanislav, *Po Brazilij: putevye očerki* (Moscow: Gosizdat Geografičeskoj literatury, 1958).

Kalmykov, N. and E. Larin, 'Oficer, patriot, latinoamerikanist', *Latinskaja Amerika* 4 (2001), 46–7.

Kanet, Roger E., 'The Superpower Quest for Empire: Cold War and Soviet Support for "Wars of National Liberation"', *Cold War History* 6/3 (2006), 331–52.

Kapuściński, Ryszard, *The Emperor: Downfall of an Autocrat* (London: Penguin Books, 2006).

Karetnikova, I., 'Po Meksike', *Tvorčestvo* 10 (1960), 17.

Kasack, Wolfgang, 'Kulturelle Außenpolitik', in Anweiler and Ruffmann (eds.), *Kulturpolitik der Sowjetunion*, pp. 345–92.

Katsakioris, Konstantin, 'Soviet Lessons for Arab Modernization: Soviet Educational Aid to Arab Countries after 1956', *Journal of Modern European History* 1 (2010), 85–106.

Kaufman, Edy, *The Superpowers and Their Spheres of Influence: The United States and the Soviet Union in Eastern Europe and Latin America* (London: Croom Helm, 1976).

Kelly, Catriona and David G. Shepherd (eds.), *Russian Cultural Studies: An Introduction* (Oxford: Oxford University Press, 1998).

Kerov, V., '30 let Universitet Družby Narodov im. Patrisa Lumumby', *Novaja i Novejšaja Istorija* 5 (1990), 227–9.

Kisljak, Sergej, 'K ego sovetam prislušivalsja MID Rossii', *Latinskaja Amerika* 9 (2005), 7.

Klauß, Cornelia and Frank Böttcher (eds.), *Unerkannt durch Freundesland: Illegale Reisen durch das Sowjetreich* (Berlin: Lukas Verlag, 2011).

Koebner, Thomas and Gerhart Pickerodt (eds.), *Die andere Welt: Studien zum Exotismus* (Frankfurt am Main: Athenäum, 1987).

Koenen, Gerd, *Traumpfade der Weltrevolution: Das Guevara-Projekt* (Cologne: Kiepenheuer & Witsch, 2008).

Koivunen, Pia, 'The 1957 Moscow Youth Festival: Propagating a New, Peaceful Image of the Soviet Union', in Ilic (ed.), *Soviet State and Society under Nikita Khrushchev*, pp. 46–65.

Korneev, S., 'Svjazy Akademii nauk SSSR s Latinskoj Amerikoj', *Latinskaja Amerika* 8 (1974), 136–43.

Köstenberger, Julia, 'Die Internationale Leninschule 1926–1938', in Buckmiller and Meschkat (eds.), *Biographisches Handbuch zur Geschichte der Kommunistischen Internationale*, pp. 287–309.

Kotek, Joel, *Students and the Cold War* (Oxford: Macmillan, 1996).

Kotkin, Stephen, 'The Kiss of Debt: The East Bloc Goes Borrowing', in Niall Ferguson (ed.), *The Shock of the Global: The 1970s in Perspective* (Cambridge, MA: Belknap Press of Harvard University Press, 2010), pp. 80–93.

Koval', Boris, 'Korifej otečestvennoj latinoamerikanistiki: k 90-letiju Moiseja Samuilovia Al'peroviča', *Latinskaja Amerika* 9 (2008), 92–6.

'K jubileju L'va Jur'eviča Slezkina', *Novaja i Novejšaja Istorija* 3 (2010), 250–1.

Koval', Boris, Semenov, Sergej and Anatolij Šul'govskij, *Revoljucionnye processy v Latinskoj Amerike* (Moscow: Nauka, 1974).

Krasnickij, Gennadij, *Ot Rio-de-Žanejro do Montevideo* (Tashkent: Gosizdat UzSSR, 1964).

Kruglow, Michail, 'Die peruanische Überraschung', *Neue Zeit* 8 (1969), 15.

Kudačkin, Michail, 'Algunas enseñanzas de la revolución chilena', *Latinskaja Amerika* 1 (1975), 80–8.

Kushner, Marilyn, 'Exhibiting Art at the American National Exhibition in Moscow, 1959: Domestic Politics and Cultural Diplomacy', *Journal of Cold War Studies* 4/1 (2002), 6–26.

Kuteishchikova (Kutejščikova), Vera, 'Latin American Literature in the Soviet Union', *Moscow News* 48 (1960), 7.

'Mexican Art Popular in USSR', *Moscow News* 74 (1960), 7.

Kutejščikova, Vera, *Roman Latinskoj Ameriki v XX. veke* (Moscow: Nauka, 1964).

Moskva-Meksiko-Moskva: doroga dlinoju v žizn' (Moscow: AkademProekt, 2000).

Kutejščikova, Vera and Lev Ospovat, 'Progressivnaja Kul'tura Latinskoj Ameriki', *Sovetskaja Literatura* 6 (1956), 212–17.

Lara, Mario, 'Jesús Lara (1898–1980): homenaje', *Marxismo Militante* 24 (1998), 79–83.

Larin, E., 'Centr latinoamerikanskich issledovanij Instituta vseobščej istorii', *Latinskaja Amerika* 4 (2001), 46–8.

Larraín Ibáñez, Jorge, *Identity and Modernity in Latin America* (Cambridge: Polity Press, 2000).

Laserna Pinzón, Mario, 'El Doctor Laserna en la URSS', *Boletín del Instituto Cultural Colombo Soviético* 1 (1966), 9.

'Formas de viajar a la Unión Soviética', *Razón y Fábula* 4 (1967), 57–66.

Lasky, Victor, *The Ugly Russian* (New York: Trident, 1965).

Lavreckij, Iosif, *Ernesto Če Gevara* (Moscow: Molodaja gvardija, 1972).

Lavričenko, Michail, *Ekonomičeskoe sotrudničestvo SSSR so stranami Azii, Afriki i Latinskoj Ameriki* (Moscow: Gosizdat Političeskoj Literatury, 1961).

Lehmann, Maike, *Eine sowjetische Nation: Nationale Sozialismusinterpretationen in Armenien seit 1945* (Frankfurt am Main: Campus, 2012).

Leonov, Nikolai, 'La inteligencia soviética en América Latina durante la Guerra Fría', *Estudios Públicos* 73 (1999), 31–63.

Licholet'e: sekretnye missii (Moscow: Meždunarodnye Otnošenija, 1995).

Leonov, Nikolai, Fediakova, Eugenia and Joaquin Fermandois, 'El general Nikolai Leonov en el CEP', *Estudios Públicos* 73 (1999), 65–102.

Lévesque, Jacques, *The USSR and the Cuban Revolution: Soviet Ideological and Strategical Perspectives, 1959–1977* (New York: Praeger, 1978).

Lindenberger, Thomas (ed.), *Massenmedien im Kalten Krieg: Akteure, Bilder Resonanzen* (Cologne: Böhlau, 2006).

López Moreno, Roberto, *Poema a la Unión Soviética: la tierra y la palabra* (Mexico City: Claves Latinoamericanas, 1986).

Loss, Jacqueline, and José Manuel Prieto (eds.), *Caviar with Rum: Cuba–USSR and the Post-Soviet Experience* (New York: Palgrave Macmillan, 2012).

Löwy, Michael and Michael Pearlman (eds.), *Marxism in Latin America from 1909 to the Present: An Anthology* (Atlantic Highlands: Humanities Press, 1992).

Lukin, Boris, 'La sociedad hispanoamericana en el Leningrado de la preguerra', *América Latina* 3 (1979), 174–82.

Machover, Jacobo and Hainer Kober, *Che Guevara – die andere Seite* (Berlin and Potsdam: Wolbern, 2008).

Maevskij, A., 'Meždunarodnye naučnye svjazi Instituta Latinskoj Ameriki', *Latinskaja Amerika* 7 (1974), 148–52.

Majakovskij, Vladimir, *Ispanija. Okean. Gavana. Meksika. Amerika: stichi* (Moscow: Gosizdat, 1926).

Moe otkrytie Ameriki (Moscow: Gosizdat, 1926).

Meksika: pervye očerki (Moscow: Biblioteka Ogonek, 1933).

Majdanik, Kiva, 'Revoljucioner', *Latinskaja Amerika* 6 (1977).

Major, Patrick and Rana Mitter, 'East Is East and West Is West? Towards a Comparative Socio-Cultural History of the Cold War', *Cold War History* 4/1 (2003), 1–22.

Makaryčev, Maksim, *Fidel' Kastro* (Moscow: Molodaja Gvardija, 2008).

Malia, Martin, *Russia under Western Eyes: From the Bronze Horseman to the Lenin Mausoleum* (Cambridge, MA: Belknap Press of Harvard University Press, 1999).

Mancisidor, José, *Ciento veinte días* (Mexico City: Editorial México Nuevo, 1937).

Marek, Christoph, *Pop/Schlager: Eine Analyse der Entstehungsprozesse populärer Musik im US-amerikanischen und deutschsprachigen Raum* (Vienna: LitVerlag, 2006).

Martin, Terry, *The Affirmative Action Empire: Nations and Nationalism in the Soviet Union, 1923–1939* (Ithaca: Cornell University Press, 2001).

Martynov, B., 'Molodoj čelovek', *Latinskaja Amerika* 7 (2006), 140.

Maslennikow, Gennadi, 'Kuba – meine ganze Liebe', *Kultur und Leben* 12 (1966), 36–7.

Matusevich, Maxim, 'Journeys of Hope: African Diaspora and the Soviet Society', *African Diaspora* 1 (2008), 53–85.

No Easy Row for a Russian Hoe: Ideology and Pragmatism in Nigerian–Soviet Relations, 1960–1991 (Trenton: Africa World Press, 2003).

Mazlish, Bruce, *The New Global History* (New York: Routledge, 2006).

Mdivani, Georgij, *Den' roždenija Terezy* (Moscow: Izdatel'svo Iskusstvo, 1962).

Medvedev, A., 'Poet Ima Sumak', *Muzykal'naja Žizn'* 4/2 (1961), 12.

Mendes, José Guilherme, *Moscou, Varsóvia, Berlim: o povo nas ruas* (Rio de Janeiro: Editôra Civilização Brasileira, 1956).

Mendoza, María Luisa, *Raaa reee riii rooo Rusia: la URSS* (Mexico City: Fondo de Cultura Económica, 1974).

Menzel, Sewall, *Dictators, Drugs and Revolution: Cold War Campaigning in Latin America 1965–1989* (Bloomington: AuthorHouse, 2006).

Meščerjakov, M., 'Sovetskaja vystavka v Meksike', *Vnešnjaja Torgovlja* 30/1 (1960), 5–7.

Meschkat, Klaus, 'Die Komintern in Lateinamerika: Biographien als Schlüssel zum Verständnis einer Weltorganisation', in Buckmiller and Meschkat (eds.), *Biographisches Handbuch zur Geschichte der Kommunistischen Internationale*, pp. 111–26.

Michajlova, N., 'Spektakl' o geroičeskom ostrove', *Sovetskij Cirk* 8 (1962), 1–3.

Michalkov, Sergej, *Sombrero: komedija v 3 dejstvijach, 5 kartinach* (Moscow: Iskusstvo, 1957).

Middell, Matthias and Katja Naumann, 'Global History 2008–2010: Empirische Erträge, konzeptionelle Debatten, neue Synthesen', *Comparativ* 6 (2010), 93–133.

Mikojan, Sergej, *Anatomija Karibskogo krizisa* (Moscow: Izdatel'stvo Academia, 2006).

'Neuželi tridcat' piat' let?', *Latinskaja Amerika* 7 (2004), 25–39.

Miller, Frank, *Folklore to Stalin: Russian Folklore and Pseudofolklore of the Stalin Era* (London: Sharpe, 1990).

Miller, Nicola, *In the Shadow of the State: Intellectuals and the Quest for National Identity in Twentieth-Century Spanish America* (London and New York: Verso, 1999).

Soviet Relations with Latin America, 1959–1987 (Cambridge: Cambridge University Press, 1989).

Miró Quesada, Francisco, *La otra mitad del mundo: treinta años despues* (Lima: Editorial Perla-Perú, 1989).

Mujal-León, Eusebio (ed.), *The USSR and Latin America: A Developing Relationship* (Boston: Unwin Hyman, 1989).

Nader, Laura, 'The Phantom Factor: Impact of the Cold War on Anthropology', in Noam Chomsky (ed.), *The Cold War and the University: Toward an Intellectual History of the Postwar Years* (New York: New Press, 1997), pp. 107–46.

Neruda, Pablo, *Confieso que he vivido* (Barcelona: Plaza & Janés, 2001).

'En la Unión Soviética', *Cuadernos de la Fundación Pablo Neruda* 37 (1999), 29–37.

Nieto Caballero, Agustín, *El secreto de Rusia* (Bogotá: Antares, 1960).

Nogee, Joseph, 'Allende's Chile and the Soviet Union: A Policy Lesson for Latin American Nations Seeking Autonomy', *Journal of Interamerican Studies and World Affairs* 21 (1979), 339–68.

Novikov, L., 'Golos Mira: k 40-letiju radioveščanija na Latinskuju Ameriku', *Latinskaja Amerika* 9 (1972), 140–6.

Odnopozova, Dina, 'Russian–Argentine Literary Exchanges', Ph.D thesis, Yale University, 2012.

Okinsevic, Lev and Robert G. Carlton, *Latin America in Soviet Writings: A Bibliography* (Baltimore: Johns Hopkins University Press, 1966).

Olea, Victor Flores, 'La crisis del stalinismo', *Cuadernos Americanos* 5–6 (1962), 80–108.

Onis, Juan de, 'Soviet Five Balks at Taiwan Game: Russians Rout US Team but Face Loss if They Don't Play Chinese', *New York Times*, 30 Jan. 1959.

Osakwe, Chris, *The Participation of the Soviet Union in Universal International Organizations: A Political and Legal Analysis of Soviet Strategies and Aspirations inside ILO, UNESCO and WHO* (Leiden: Brill, 1972).

Osterhammel, Jürgen, 'The Great Work of Uplifting Mankind', in Boris Barth and Jürgen Osterhammel (eds.), *Zivilisierungsmissionen: Imperiale Weltverbesserung seit dem 18. Jahrhundert* (Konstanz: UVK, 2005).

Die Verwandlung der Welt: Eine Geschichte des 19. Jahrhunderts (Munich: Beck, 2011).

Oswald, Joseph Gregory, 'Contemporary Soviet Research on Latin America', *Latin American Research Review* 1/2 (1966), 77–96.

Oswald, Joseph Gregory and Robert G. Carlton (eds.), *Soviet Image of Contemporary Latin America: Compiled and Translated from Russian. A Documentary History 1960–1968* (Austin: University of Texas Press, 1970).

Oswald, Joseph Gregory and Anthony Strover (eds.), *The Soviet Union and Latin America* (New York: Praeger, 1970).

Otero Silva, Miguel, *México y la revolución mexicana: un escritor venezolano en la Unión Soviética* (Caracas: Universidad Central de Venezuela, 1966).

Palayret, Jean-Marie, *Un'università per l'Europa: le origini dell'Istituto Universitario Europeo di Firenze (1948–1976)* (Rome: Presidenza del Consiglio dei ministri, 1996).

Paleckis, Justas, *V Meksike: putevye zametki* (Vilnius: Vaga, 1964).

Parra, Nicanor, *Canciones rusas* (Santiago de Chile: Editorial Universitaria, 1967).

Paulmann, Johannes (ed.), *Auswärtige Repräsentationen: Deutsche Kulturdiplomatie nach 1945* (Cologne: Böhlau, 2005).

Pavlov, Yuri, *Soviet–Cuban Alliance, 1959–1991* (Miami: North–South Center Press, University of Miami, 1996).

Pavlyčko, Dmytro, *Pal'mova vit'* (Kiev, 1962).

Pechatnov, Vladimir, 'Exercise in Frustration: Soviet Foreign Propaganda in the Early Cold War', *Cold War History* 1/2 (2001), 1–27.

Pičugin, Pavel, 'Ansambl' iz Paragvaja', *Muzykal'naja Žizn'* 7/12 (1964), 23. *Narodnaja muzyka Argentiny* (Moscow: Izdatel'stvo Muzyka, 1971).

Poe, Marshall T., *The Russian Moment in World History* (Princeton: Princeton University Press, 2003).

Poljakov, Jurij, 'Posle rospuska Kominterna', *Novaja i Novejšaja Istorija* 1 (2003), 106–16.

Pomeranz, Kenneth, 'Social History and World History: From Daily Life to Patterns of Change', *Journal of World History* 1 (2007), 69–98.

Ponomarev, Boris, 'O gosudarstve nacional'noj demokratii', *Kommunist* 8 (1961), 33–48.

Popowa, Nina, 'Über die Tätigkeit und die Aufgaben des Verbandes der Freundschaftsgesellschaften', *Kultur und Leben* 4 (1962), 6–9.

Poppino, Rollie, *International Communism in Latin America: A History of the Movement 1917–1963* (Glencoe: Free Press of Glencoe, 1964).

Prebisch, Raúl, *Hacia una dinámica del desarrollo latinoamericano* (Montevideo: Ediciones de la Banda Oriental, 1967).

Prince, Douglas, 'Los intelectuales soviéticos atacan el conformismo en la literatura impuesto por el estado', *Ultima Hora*, 24 Apr. 1961.

Prizel, Ilya, *Latin America through Soviet Eyes: The Evolution of Soviet Perceptions during the Brezhnev Era 1964–1982* (Cambridge: Cambridge University Press, 1990).

Pučkov, R., 'Opyt Sovetskogo Vostok i razvivajuščiesja strany', *Latinskaja Amerika* 6 (1970), 171–5.

Rabe, Stephen G., *The Most Dangerous Area in the World: John F. Kennedy Confronts Communist Revolution in Latin America* (Chapel Hill: University of North Carolina Press, 1999).

Rabelo, Genival, *No outro lado do mundo: a vida na URSS* (Rio de Janeiro: Editôra Civilização Brasileira, 1967).

Radu, Michael, 'Eastern Europe and Latin America', in Mujal-León (ed.), *The USSR and Latin America*, pp. 254–69.

Rajagopalan, Sudha, *Leave Disco Dancer Alone! Indian Cinema and Soviet Movie-Going after Stalin* (New Delhi: Yoda Press, 2008).

Raleigh, Donald, *Russia's Sputnik Generation: Soviet Baby Boomers Talk about Their Lives* (Bloomington: Indiana University Press, 2006).

Rama, Angel, *Los poetas modernistas en el mercado económico* (Montevideo: Universidad de la República, 1967).

Ramos, Graciliano, *Viagem: Tcheco-Eslováquia–URSS* (São Paulo: Martins, 1970).

Rapoport, Mario, 'Argentina and the Soviet Union: History of Political and Economic Relations, 1917–1955', *Hispanic American Historical Review* 2 (1986), 239–85.

Rawnsley, Gary (ed.), *Cold War Propaganda in the 1950s* (Basingstoke: Macmillan, 1999).

Reid, Susan Emily, 'Cold War in the Kitchen: Gender and the De-Stalinization of Consumer Taste in the Soviet Union under Khrushchev', *Slavic Review* 61/2 (2002), 211–52.

Reinaga, Fausto, *El sentimiento mesiánico del pueblo ruso* (La Paz: Ediciones SER, 1960).

Revueltas, José, *Los errores* (Mexico City: Fondo De Cultura Economica, 1964).

Richmond, Yale, *Cultural Exchange and the Cold War: Raising the Iron Curtain* (University Park: Penn State University Press, 2003).

Richter, Dieter, *Der Süden: Geschichte einer Himmelsrichtung* (Berlin: Wagenbach, 2009).

Rivas, Carlos, *América Latina, Unión Soviética: relaciones económicas y comerciales* (Bogotá: Ediciones Librería del Profesional, 1989).

Rivera, Diego and Gladys March, *My Art, My Life: An Autobiography* (New York: Citadel, [1960]).

Riza, Bayram and Catherine Quirk, 'Cultural Relations between the Soviet Union and Latin America', *Studies on the Soviet Union* 2 (1968), 30–9.

Rodionov, N., *V strane Inkov: putevye očerki* (Alma-Ata: Kazgoslitizdat, 1963).

Romanovskij, Sergej (ed.), *Meždunarodnye naučnye i kul'turnye svjazi SSSR* (Moscow: Gosizdat, 1966).

Romero, Federico, *Storia della guerra fredda: l'ultimo conflitto per l'Europa* (Turin: Giulio Einaudi, 2009).

Rose, Clive, *The Soviet Propaganda Network: A Directory of Organisations Serving Soviet Foreign Policy* (London: Pinter, 1988).

Rosen, Seymour, *The Development of the People's Friendship University in Moscow* (Washington, DC: US Department of Health, 1973).

Ross, Marjorie, *El secreto encanto de la KGB: las cinco vidas de Iósif Griguliévich* (San José, Costa Rica: Grupo Editorial Norma, 2004).

Roth-Ey, Kristin, '"Loose Girls" on the Loose? Sex, Propaganda and the 1957 Youth Festival', in Ilic, Reid and Attwood (eds.), *Women in the Khrushchev Era*, pp. 75–95.

Rozman, Gilbert, *A Mirror for Socialism: Soviet Criticisms of China* (London: Tauris, 1985).

Rubinstein, Alvin, 'Friendship University', *Survey* 34 (1960), 8–10.

'Lumumba University: An Assessment', *Problems of Communism* 20/6 (1971), 64–9.

Rumjancev, S., 'Pervyj god universiteta', *Vestnik vyssej skoly* 5 (1961), 108–10.

Rupprecht, Tobias, 'Gestrandetes Flaggschiff: Die Universität der Völkerfreundschaft in Moskau', *Osteuropa* 1 (2010), 95–114.

'Die Liebe der Linken zu Lateinamerika: Vom Radical Chic zur Nikaragua-Solidarität', *Le Monde Diplomatique* 11 (2010), 16–17.

'Musenkuss in Nukus: Sowjetische Avantgarde-Kunst in der usbekischen Provinz', *Osteuropa* 3 (2012), 159–71.

'Socialist High Modernity and Global Stagnation: A Shared History of Brazil and the Soviet Union during the Cold War', *Journal of Global History* 3 (2011), 505–28.

'Die sowjetische Gesellschaft in der Welt des Kalten Kriegs: Neue Forschungsperspektiven', *Jahrbücher für Geschichte Osteuropas* 58 (2010), 381–99.

Ryklin, Michail, *Kommunismus als Religion: Die Intellektuellen und die Oktoberrevolution* (Frankfurt am Main: Verlag der Weltreligionen, 2008).

Sahni, Kalpana, *Crucifying the Orient: Russian Orientalism and the Colonization of Caucasus and Central Asia* (Bangkok: White Orchid Press, 1997).

Said, Edward, *Orientalism* (London: Penguin Books, 2007).

Saítta, Sylvia, *Hacia la revolución: viajeros argentinos de izquierda* (Buenos Aires: Fondo de Cultura Económica, 2007).

Sakharov, Andrei, *Memoirs* (New York: Alfred A. Knopf, 1990).

Salazkina, Masha, *In Excess: Sergei Eisenstein's Mexico* (Chicago: University of Chicago Press, 2009).

Saldívar, Dasso, *García Márquez: el viaje a la semilla, la biografía* (Barcelona: Folio, 2005).

Sanchez-Sibony, Oscar, *Red Globalization: The Political Economy of the Soviet Cold War from Stalin to Khrushchev* (Cambridge: Cambridge University Press, 2014).

Sapata, Carlos and L. Kulidžanov, 'Luče znat' drug druga', *Latinskaja Amerika* 9 (1977), 159–64.

Sarab'yanov, Dmitri and John Bowlt, 'Keepers of the Flame: An Exchange of Art and Western Cultural Influences in the USSR after World War II', *Journal of Cold War Studies* 4/1 (2002), 81–7.

Saunders, Frances Stonor, *Who Paid the Piper? The CIA and the Cultural Cold War* (London: Granta Books, 2000).

Schlögel, Karl, *Terror und Traum: Moskau 1937* (Munich: Hanser, 2008).

Schpetny, A., 'Wir lernen Spanisch', *Kultur und Leben* 10 (1971), 39.

Schröm, Oliver, *Im Schatten des Schakals: Carlos und die Wegbereiter des internationalen Terrorismus* (Berlin: Links, 2002).

Šervašidze, Amiran, *Devuška iz Sant'iago: viva Kuba!* (Moscow: Sovetskaja Rossija, 1963).

Šestopal, A., 'Koncepcii social'no-ekonomičeskogo razvitija stran "tret'ego mira"', *Latinskaja Amerika* 3 (1977).

Šestopal, A. and N. Anikeeva, 'Iberoamerikanistika v MGIMO: tradicii i sovremennost'', *Latinskaja Amerika* 4 (2001), 24–9.

Shabat, Theodore, 'Allende Arrives in Soviet, Seeks New Aid for Chile', *New York Times*, 7 Dec. 1972.

'What They Do at Old Lumumba U', *New York Times*, 18 Apr. 1971.

Shubin, Vladimir, *The Hot Cold War: The USSR in Southern Africa* (London: Pluto Press, 2008).

Simpson, Christopher (ed.), *Universities and Empire: Money and Politics in the Social Sciences during the Cold War* (New York: New Press, 1998).

Siqueiros, David, *Me llamaban el Coronelazo: memorias* (Mexico City: Grijalbo, 1977).

Sizonenko, Aleksandr, *Sovetskij Sojuz i Latinskaja Amerika: sovremennyj etap otnošenij* (Kiev: Politizdat Ukrainy, 1976).

Slepuchin, Jurij, *U čerty zakata* (Leningrad: Lenizdat, 1961).

Slezkine, Yuri, 'The USSR as a Communal Apartment, or How a Socialist State Promoted Ethnic Particularism', *Slavic Review* 53/2 (1994), 414–52.

Slick, Sam L., *José Revueltas* (Boston: Twayne, 1983).

Smirnov, Sergej, *Poezdka na Kubu* (Moscow: Sovetskij Pisatel', 1962).

Smith, Colin, *Carlos: Portrait of a Terrorist* (New York: Holt, Rinehart and Winston, 1977).

Smith, Steve, 'Two Cheers for the "Return of Ideology"', *Revolutionary Russia* 17/2 (2004), 119–35.

Smith, Tony, 'New Bottles for New Wine: A Pericentric Framework for the Study of the Cold War', *Diplomatic History* 24 (2000), 567–91.

Snitko, Aleksandr, 'Skol'ko stoit naša sovest' v Latinskoj Amerike? Zametki ešče bolee neravnodušnye', *Latinskaja Amerika* 4 (1991), 38–44.

Sofinskij, N., 'Pomošč v podgotovke kadrov', *Latinskaja Amerika* 5 (1977), 125–8.

Sofronov, Anatolij, 'Dobro požalovat' v Čili!', *Moskva* 7/5 (1963), 196–204.

'Otkrytie Južnoj Ameriki', *Ogonek* 37 (1958), 9–12.

Sokolova, Zoja, *Vsja pravda o Fidel'e Kastro i ego komande* (Moscow: Astrel', 2009).

Sorensen, Thomas, *The Word War: The Story of American Propaganda* (New York: Harper & Row, 1968).

Sosa, Jesualdo, *Mi viaje a la URSS* (Montevideo: Ediciones Pueblos Unidos, 1952).

Soto, Luis, 'Un verano en Siberia' (unpublished article, 2008; druzhba.se/druzhba/vivencias/unveranoensiberia.pdf).

Spota, Luis, *El viaje* (Mexico City: Joaquin Moritz, 1973).

Stanis, V., 'Kuznica kadrov dlja razvivajuiščichsja stran', *Latinskaja Amerika* 7 (1972), 117–24.

Starr, Frederick, 'The Third Sector in the Second World', in Bruce Mazlish and Akira Iriye (eds.), *The Global History Reader* (New York: Routledge, 2005), pp. 191–200.

Stein, Philip, *Siqueiros: His Life and Works* (New York: International, 1994).

Stites, Richard, 'Heaven and Hell: Soviet Propaganda Constructs the World', in Rawnsley (ed.), *Cold War Propaganda in the 1950s*, pp. 84–103.

Russian Popular Culture: Entertainment and Society since 1900 (Cambridge: Cambridge University Press, 2000).

Stolberg, Eva Maria, 'Transnationale Forschungsansätze in der Osteuropäischen Geschichte', geschichte.transnational.clio-online.net/forum/2005-03-002 (last accessed 9 Mar. 2008).

Stolbov, Valeri, 'Libros Latinoamericanos en la editorial Judozhestvennaya Literatura', *América Latina* 11 (1980), 112–18.

Stöver, Bernd, *Der Kalte Krieg 1947–1991: Geschichte eines radikalen Zeitalters* (Munich: Beck, 2007).

Šul'govskij, A., 'Latinskaja Amerika i opyt respublik Sovetskogo Vostoka', *Latinskaja Amerika* 5 (1970), 82–9.

'Opyt rešenija nacional'nogo voprosa v SSSR i ideologičeskaja bor'ba v Latinskoj Amerike', *Latinskaja Amerika* 8 (1972), 13–34.

Suny, Ronald Grigor, *The Cambridge History of Russia*, vol. III, *The Twentieth Century* (Cambridge: Cambridge University Press, 2006).

Surkov, Alexej, 'Interv'ju', *Sovetskaja Literatura* 8 (1961), 172–5.

Suščenko, Ivan, 'Patria o muerte!', *Ogonek* 47 (1962), 14–15.

Tanner, Henry, 'Soviet Ousts US Cultural Aide as Inciter of African Students', *New York Times*, 12 May 1965.

Taracena, Arturo, 'El camino política de Miguel Angel Asturias', *Mesoamerica* 38 (1999), 86–101.

Tarasov, A., Čerkasov, G. and T. Šavšukova, *Levye v Rossii: ot umerennych do ekstremistov* (Moscow: Izdatel'stvo Institut Eksperimental'noj Sociologii, 1997).

Terán, Oscar, Caetano, Gerardo, Correa Sutil, Sofia and Adolfo Garcé García y Santos, *Ideas en el siglo: intelectuales y cultura en el siglo XX latinoamericano* (Buenos Aires: Siglo Veintiuno, 2004).

Theberge, James, *Latin America in the World System: The Limits of Internationalism* (Beverly Hills: Sage Publications, 1975).

Tichomirnova, Irina, 'Sem'desjat dnej v Latinskoj Amerike', *Muzykal'naja Žizn'* 14 (1960), 13–15.

Tišenko, A., *Konstantin Listov* (Moscow: Sovetskij Kompozitor, 1987).

Toledano, Vicente Lombardo and Victor Manuel Villaseñor, *Un viaje al mundo del porvenir* (Mexico City: Publicaciones de la Universidad obrera de México, 1936).

Torkunov, Anatolij (ed.), *MGIMO Universitet: tradicii i sovremennost' (1944–2009)* (Moscow: Moskovskie Učebniki, 2009).

Torres, Joaquín, *Viaje a Rusia y a otros países socialistas* (Buenos Aires: Edición del Autor, 1962).

Triska, Jan (ed.), *Dominant Powers and Subordinate States: The United States in Latin America and the Soviet Union in Eastern Europe* (Durham: Duke University Press, 1986).

Troitsky, Artemy, *Back in the USSR: The True Story of Rock in Russia* (London: Music Sales, 1987).

Trunina, L., 'Sovetskij balet v Latinskoj Amerike', *Teatr* 23/1 (1962), 182.

Tur, Petr, 'S kameroj po Latinskoj Amerike', *Iskusstvo Kino* 11 (1962), 16–19.

Turrent, Isabel, *La Unión Soviética en América Latina: el caso de la Unidad Popular Chilena, 1970–1973* (Mexico City: Centro de Estudios Internacionales, 1984).

UNESCO, *Statistics of Students Abroad, 1962–1968: Where They Go, Where They Come from, What They Study / Statistiques des étudiants à l'étranger 1962–1968: où vont-ils? D'où viennent-ils? Qu'étudient-ils?* (Paris: UNESCO, 1971).

Urban, P., 'Los estudios iberoamericanos en la URSS', *Estudios sobre la Unión Soviética* 3 (1962), 27–40.

Ustanov, Alexander, 'The First Ball at the Friendship University', *Moscow News* 79 (1960), 2.

Vajl', Petr and Aleksandr Genis, *60-e: mir sovetskogo čeloveka* (Moscow: Novoe Literaturnoe Obozrenie, 2001).

Valcárcel, Gustavo, *Medio siglo de revolución invencible: segunda parte de 'reportaje al futuro'* (Lima: Ediciones 'Unidad', 1967).

Reportaje al futuro: crónicas de un viaje a la URSS (Lima: Perú Nuevo, 1963).

Valkenier, Elizabeth Kridl, *The Soviet Union and the Third World: An Economic Bind* (Westport: Praeger, 1983).

van der Schimmelpenninck Oye, David, *Russian Orientalism: Asia in the Russian Mind from Peter the Great to the Emigration* (New Haven: Yale University Press, 2010).

Vanin, V., 'Review of "Gonzalo Cabal Ramírez: La Unión Soviética: reto moral"', *América Latina* 1 (1973), 182–5.

Varas, Augusto (ed.), *Soviet–Latin American Relations in the 1980s* (Boulder: Westview, 1987).

Varela, Alfredo, *Un periodista argentino en la Unión Soviética* (Buenos Aires: Ediciones Viento, 1950).

Vera, Pedro Jorge, *Gracias a la vida: memorias* (Quito: Editorial Voluntad, 1993).

Veršinina, I., 'Anchela Alonso: geroinia opery', *Ogonek* 15 (1962), 28.

Vinogradov, Vladimir, *Diplomatičeskie memuary* (Moscow: Rossijskaja Političeskaja Enciklopedija, 1998).

Volkov, Vadim, 'The Concept of Kulturnost: Notes on the Stalinist Civilization Process', in Sheila Fitzpatrick (ed.), *Stalinism: New Directions* (London: Routledge, 2000), pp. 210–30.

Volov, Boris, 'Aquí Moscú: con motivo del 50 aniversario de Radio Moscú en español', *América Latina* 9 (1982), 97–111.

Volpi, Jorge, *El insomnio de Bolívar: cuatro consideraciónes intempestivas sobre América Latina en el siglo XXI* (Buenos Aires: Debate, 2009).

Vol'skii (Vol'skij), Viktor, 'The Study of Latin America in the USSR', *Latin American Research Review* 3/1 (1967), 77–87.

Vol'skij, Viktor, 'I. A. Vítver – odin iz osnovatelej sovetskoj latinoamerikanistiki', *Latinskaja Amerika* 5 (1971), 160–72.

'Sovetskaja latinoamerikanistika: nekotorye itogi i zadači', *Latinskaja Amerika* 3 (1971), 6–16.

SSSR i Latinskaja Amerika: 1917–1967 (Moscow: Meždunarodnye Otnošenija, 1967).

Wallerstein, Immanuel, *The Capitalist World-Economy: Essays* (Cambridge: Cambridge University Press, 1979).

'The Unintended Consequences of Cold War Area Studies', in Noam Chomsky (ed.), *The Cold War and the University: Toward an Intellectual History of the Postwar Years* (New York: New Press, 1997), pp. 195–231.

Welles, Benjamin, 'Soviet Intelligence Role in Latin America Rises', *New York Times*, 7 Dec. 1970.

Werner, Michael and Bénédicte Zimmermann, 'Histoire Croisée and the Challenge of Reflexivity', *History and Theory* 45/1 (2006), 30–50.

Westad, Odd Arne, *The Global Cold War: Third World Interventions and the Making of Our Times* (Cambridge: Cambridge University Press, 2007).

Reviewing the Cold War: Approaches, Interpretations, Theory (London: Cass, 2006).

Whitney, Craig, 'Lumumba U: Is It a Soviet Tool?', *New York Times*, 6 Jan. 1980.

Wilford, Hugh, *The Mighty Wurlitzer: How the CIA Played America* (Cambridge, MA: Harvard University Press, 2008).

Wohlforth, William, 'Superpowers, Interventions and the Third World', *Cold War History* 6/3 (2006), 365–71.

Wolfe, Thomas, *Governing Soviet Journalism: The Press and the Socialist Person after Stalin* (Bloomington: Indiana University Press, 2005).

Yarikov, Fyodor, 'Moscow Likes Latin American Music', *Moscow News* 30/6 (1956), 7.

Yurchak, Alexei, *Everything Was Forever, until It Was No More: The Last Soviet Generation* (Princeton: Princeton University Press, 2006).

Zemskov, V., 'Ot izučenija literaturnogo processa k osmysleniju civilizacionnoj paradigmy: latinoamerikanistika v Institute mirovoj literatury', *Latinskaja Amerika* 4 (2001), 30–45.

Zorina, I., 'Uznik kubinskogo GULAGa', *Latinskaja Amerika* 5–6 (1992), 36–40.

Zubkova, Elena, *Russia after the War: Hopes, Illusions, and Disappointments, 1945–1957* (Armonk: Sharpe, 1998).

Zubok, Lev, *Istorija vtorogo internacionala* (Moscow: Nauka, 1966).

Zhivago's Children: The Last Russian Intelligentsia (Cambridge, MA: Belknap Press of Harvard University Press, 2009).

Zubok, Vladislav, *A Failed Empire: The Soviet Union in the Cold War from Stalin to Gorbachev* (Chapel Hill: University of North Carolina Press, 2007).

Zundejas, Adelina, 'Der kulturelle Austausch erweitert sich', *Kultur und Leben* 10 (1973), 28.

Index

20th Party Congress of the CPSU 22, 133, 152, 154, 158, 244, 258, 260
Abkhazia 294
Adorno, Theodor W. 77, 91
Adžubej (Adshubej), Aleksej 43, 96–8 103–4, 112, 114, 177, 255
Aeroflot 269
Afghanistan 5
Africa 7, 23, 64, 91, 101, 106, 115, 120, 201, 216, 232, 244, 276, 282, 287
   African anti-imperialism 11, 58, 141 206
   African students 58, 60, 194, 197–8, 215–17, 291, 295
   Horn of Africa 7, 231
   Portuguese Africa 99, 141, 279
Agenstvo Pečati 'Novosti' (APN) 34, 82, 169, 201, 249, 251, 255, 274
Alarcón, Rolando 93
Albania 189, 233
Alberti, Rafael 94
Aldunate, Raúl 109, 170, 176–7, 181, 249
Aleksandrov, Grigorij 76, 78
Alekseev, Aleksandr 33, 39, 46, 111, 120, 173–4, 253, 273
Alianza Popular Revolucionario de América (APRA) 135
Aliger, Margarita 105
All-Union Organisation for Cultural Contacts (VOKS) 25, 31, 34, 89, 95, 132, 147–9, 156, 187, 245, 264
Allende, Salvador 21, 125, 142, 145, 196, 219, 269–72, 279
Alma-Ata 245
Al'perovič, Moisej 257–8, 268
Amado, Jorge 54, 79, 94, 108, 110, 143, 145, 150–2, 156, 159, 172–3, 190, 248
Amaya Amador, Ramón 151
Anciferov, Nikolaj 114
Andropov, Jurij 274
Angola 141
Anido, María Luisa 90

Anka, Paul 66
Annenkov, Julij 105
Antarctic 7
anti-imperialism 5, 23, 28, 34, 37, 48, 58, 68, 70, 83, 92, 95, 97–8, 102, 104, 106, 110, 112, 114–15, 117, 120, 122, 131, 138, 141, 143, 163, 187, 203, 238, 268, 278–80, 282–5
anti-Semitism 36, 53, 150, 188, 240–1, 256, 258, 260, 278
Apletin, Michail 108
Arafat, Yasser 206
Aral Sea 75
Arbenz, Jacobo 24, 255
Arctic 7
area studies 20, 65, 200, 234–7, 243 249–50, 259, 262, 266, 269, 272–3, 275, 277–8, 287, 290
Arenas, Reinaldo 139
Argentina 10, 24, 30–3, 35, 39–41, 43, 50, 57, 65, 70, 95, 97, 100–1, 105, 129, 131, 139, 142–3, 163, 169, 171, 178, 184, 187, 228, 233, 241, 246–8, 252, 276, 282, 293
   Argentine communists 94, 135, 148, 155, 177, 197
   Argentine culture in USSR 52, 54, 82, 85, 87, 90, 92–3, 109
   economic relations with USSR 24, 28, 49, 232, 282, 294
   Soviet exhibition in Argentina 25, 44
Arguedas, José María 165
Arismendi, Rodney 188, 206
Armenia 31, 41, 64, 89, 98, 106, 172, 187, 244, 255–6, 278, 280, 296
Arzumanjan, Anušavan 244
Asatiani, Guram 82
Asia 7, 9, 11, 64, 76, 101, 106, 141, 243–4, 268, 279
   Asian students 58, 193–4, 197–8, 205, 295
Astrakhan 205

Asturias, Miguel Angel 54, 107, 136–7, 145, 157
Australia 76
Austria 5
Aymara 37, 263
Azerbaijan 76, 83, 89, 172, 175, 226 280, 284
Aztec Order 254, 257, 264

Baku 33, 63–4, 175, 245
ballet 40, 63, 71, 117
Bandung Conference 5, 141
Baranov, Charlampij 239
Barkovskij, Aleksandr 296
Barranquilla 254
Barthes, Roland 77, 91
Batista, Fulgencio 110, 118, 129, 252
Belarus 168
Belgium 58
Beljaev, Aleksandr 85
Benavente, Saulo 145
Benítez, Fernando 164–5
Berija, Lavrentij 242
Berkovskij, Viktor 84, 93
Berlin, Isaiah 1
Bessarabov, Igor' 44, 82
Bezrodnyj (Besrodny), Igor' 39, 82
Biermann, Wolf 280
Bogotá 31, 141, 166, 168, 180–1, 218 221, 293
Bokščanin, Anatolij 239
Bolívar, Simón 134, 136, 246
Bolivia 10, 37, 50, 53–4, 64–5, 98, 103, 120–1, 131, 141, 143, 145, 162–3, 165, 184, 186, 197, 205–6, 208–9, 216, 219, 221–3, 232–3, 270 292, 294
Bolsheviks 1, 10, 28, 63, 135, 193, 238, 256, 270
Bolshoi Theatre 40, 42, 46
Bonavita, Luis Pedro 160
Borge, Tomás 276
Borges, Jorge Luis 138–9, 296
Borisova, Marija 115
Borodin, Michail 36
Borovik, Genrich 83, 111–12, 251
Bovt, Violeta 40
Brasília 49, 99, 105
Bratsk 47, 63, 182
Brazil 10, 29, 36, 40–2, 44, 49–50, 57, 64, 70, 77, 83, 87, 94, 98–100, 102, 129, 131, 137, 139, 141, 143, 145–7, 150, 163, 166, 171–5, 183–4, 187, 189, 206, 223, 228, 231, 233, 246–7, 249, 259, 264, 268, 276, 282

Brazilian communists 29, 42, 66, 79, 90, 94, 99, 150, 152, 172, 175, 188–9, 197, 233
Brazilian culture in USSR 87–8, 90, 93, 108, 110, 146, 173, 295
economic relations with USSR 24 232, 294
Soviet exhibition in Brazil 25, 47–8
Brezhnev, Leonid 3, 156, 169, 182, 230–2, 234, 253, 270, 277
Brežnev, Jurij 249
Brodski, Iosif 143
Bronstein, David 40
Budapest 159
Buenos Aires 30, 32, 36, 38, 40, 44, 57, 73, 82, 85, 96, 105, 152, 163, 248
Bulgaria 194, 276
Buravkin, Gennadij 125
Burma 5
Busch, Ernst 92

Caldas, Silvio 87
Calvimontes, Jorge 145
Campusano, Julieta 66
Canada 5, 10, 16, 245, 255
Canal Ramírez, Gonzalo 169–70
capitalism 1, 3, 23, 34, 45, 48, 65–6, 69, 77, 81, 146, 153, 162, 167, 191 209–10, 220, 254, 261, 267–8, 284–5, 295–6
Caracas 226, 294
Carballido, Emilio 145
Cardenal, Ernesto 170
Cárdenas, Lázaro 145, 254
Carew, Jan 191, 196, 215, 220, 224–6
Caribbean 10, 43, 46, 56, 85, 93, 111–12, 115, 119, 186, 197, 217, 247, 253, 294
Carpentier, Alejo 139, 157
Carranza, María Mercedes 187
Casares, Adolfo Bioy 139
Castañeda, Salvador 222
Castellanos, Rosario 165
Castillo Armas, Carlos 129
Castro, Fidel 16, 46, 71, 82, 102, 106 110–13, 115–17, 119–20, 123, 127, 145, 153–4, 189, 192, 212, 226, 233, 252, 256, 261, 269, 280, 294, 296
state visit to USSR 1963 120
Castro, Raúl 110, 252
Catalonia 114
Catholicism 130–1, 160, 166–71, 173–4, 179, 184, 186, 188–9, 220, 242, 246, 248, 253, 265
Caucasus 37, 50, 53, 63–5, 77, 83, 89, 145, 150, 160, 187, 211, 244

Čebotarev, Vladimir 85
Central America 17, 53, 98, 121, 124, 187, 198, 242, 251, 253, 263, 275–6
Central Asia 26, 37–8, 53, 60, 63–5, 80 83, 87, 89, 173, 192–3, 226, 244 268, 290
Central Committee of the CPSU 30, 33, 35, 69, 103, 149, 202, 232, 234–5, 241, 249, 251, 256, 259, 266, 271–2, 274–5, 281
Chačaturov, Karen 251, 255, 260, 274, 278
Chajta, Vladimir 264
Chalif, Lev 115
Chávez, Hugo 221, 294
chess 40
Chile 13, 32, 36, 39–41, 43, 45, 50, 53, 57, 60, 65–6, 79, 84, 93–5, 97, 105–6, 109, 129, 142–3, 145–6, 155, 161, 165, 170, 176–7, 181, 183–4, 191, 205–9, 211, 216, 218, 220–2, 224, 234, 241, 246, 249, 255, 270–1, 275–6, 283–4, 293–4
  Chilean communists 30, 94, 138, 149, 152, 177, 197, 279
  Chilean culture in USSR 88, 92, 105, 125, 127
  Frente Popular (1970–3) 21, 125 269–70
China 7, 26, 28, 41–2, 61, 120, 122, 133, 140–1, 170, 189, 193–4, 198, 201, 204, 233–4, 236, 247, 269
CIA 21, 24, 102, 114, 166, 187, 270, 276
Čičkov, Vasilij 98–9, 111, 113, 251
Cienfuegos, Camilo 46
cinema 19–20, 24, 32, 38–9, 42, 44, 46–7, 50, 64, 66, 75–7, 81–6, 88–9, 101, 104, 109, 112, 116–19, 123–4, 126, 151, 156, 172, 204, 207, 211, 213, 284, 289, 293
Clavijo, Pedro 169
Cobo, Juan 248
Cold War, definition of 13–14
Colombia 29, 31, 39–40, 45, 49, 54, 61–2, 82, 90, 101, 107–8, 110, 128–9, 138–9, 143, 158, 166–70, 180–1, 186, 196, 201, 204–5, 208–10, 212, 215–22, 224, 233, 293
colonialism 58, 63, 77, 163
Combo, Rafael 110
Cominform 9, 30, 258
Comintern 9, 18, 28–30, 92, 138, 148 193, 241
Comisión Permanente del Congreso Contra la Intervención Soviética en América Latina 129

Communist Party of the Soviet Union (CPSU) 23, 28, 33, 48, 52, 60, 69, 103, 125, 200–3, 209, 213, 230–1, 237–8, 242, 250–1, 254, 256, 259–60, 267, 274, 277, 279, 298
Congo 58, 204
Cortázar, Julio 139, 157
Corvalán, Luis 84, 145, 188, 206, 269, 280
cosmonauts 44, 47, 50, 88, 119, 152 161, 190
cosmopolitanism 1, 35, 74, 94–5, 97 154, 278
Costa Rica 39, 129, 155, 242–3
Crevenna, Alfredo 86
Cruz, Roberto 190
Cuba 16, 18, 33, 36–7, 39–40, 44, 46, 50, 54, 57, 64, 66, 69, 79, 82, 92, 96, 98, 100–1, 106, 126, 129–30, 133–4 139–40, 142–3, 150–1, 153–4, 157, 159, 164, 173, 180, 183, 189, 196, 204, 226, 232–4, 246–7, 251–6, 259, 261, 267–9, 276, 280, 282–3, 286, 289, 293, 297
  Cuban communists 30, 110, 138, 283
  Cuban culture in USSR 78, 88, 110–23, 125
  Cuban Revolution 20–1, 44, 71, 82–3, 85, 99–100, 102, 110, 112–14 116–17, 119, 122, 124, 138, 140, 253, 262, 272–3, 296
  Soviet exhibition in Cuba 25, 46, 111
Cuban missile crisis 14, 21, 47, 71, 119, 133, 230, 287
Cueca 97
Cuzco 263
Czechoslovakia 24, 101, 125, 133, 150, 152, 157, 185, 189, 191, 194, 220, 266, 276

Dalton, Roque 165–6, 190, 258
Danelija, Georgij 76
Dangond, Alberto 90, 167–8, 170
Danilov, Lev 83
de Castro, Antônio Frederico 173
de Gasperi, Alcide 242
de Holanda, Nestor 90, 166, 173, 176, 179
de Moraes, Eneida 66
Debray, Régis 267
del Carril, Hugo 85–6
dependency theory 130, 139–40, 160 247, 268
Depestre, René 161
de-Stalinisation 3, 125, 128, 140, 143 154–6, 182
détente 17, 182, 231

Dmiterko, Ljubomir 95, 144
Dobronravov, Nikolaj 117
Dolmatovskij, Evgenij 121
Dolukhanova, Zara 39
Domingo Silva, Víctor 110
Domínguez, Christopher 188
Dominican Republic 110, 114, 129, 131,
    143, 204–8, 223, 225–6, 231, 254,
    258, 276
Dona, Pedro 145
Dorenskij, Sergej 39
Dorticós, Osvaldo 46
Dridzo, Abram 257
Dubček, Alexander 133, 266
DuBois, W. E. B. 191
Dudincev, Vladimir 74
Dushanbe 245

East Germany (GDR) 56, 60, 144, 211,
    276, 281
eastern Europe 1–2, 8, 13, 17, 30, 38, 61,
    94, 99, 122, 144, 150, 162, 171–2,
    178, 210–11, 242, 247, 262, 276
Echeverría, Luis 142, 182–3
Ecuador 39, 50, 64, 83, 131, 150, 155, 197
education 51, 57–61, 64, 66, 69, 71, 130,
    134, 148–9, 156, 158, 160–3, 166,
    171, 173, 175, 177–8, 181, 184–6,
    190–229, 239, 260, 269
Edwards, Jorge 291
Edwards Bello, Joaquín 109
Egypt 5, 23, 231, 283
Ehrenburg, Ilya 74, 79, 86, 94–5, 106, 111,
    137, 144, 146, 153, 172, 239, 241
Eisenstein, Sergei 78, 83, 85–6, 265
Eisler, Hanns 92
El Salvador 29, 131, 165, 275–7
Erenburg, Grigorij 239
Erevan 63, 187
Erkaj, Nikul 122
eroticism 66, 77, 81, 90, 97, 102, 108, 111,
    115, 117, 119, 167–8, 171, 189, 214,
    228, 285
Erzin, Pavel 214
Estonia 106
Ethiopia 283
Evtušenko, Evgenij, see Yevtushenko,
    Yevgeny
exhibitions 25, 31, 44–8, 52, 54, 64–5, 70,
    82, 111, 115, 233, 253, 263
exoticism 31, 48, 52, 75–8, 80–1, 83–6
    88–9, 91, 93, 100–1, 104–6, 108–9,
    114–15, 117, 122, 124, 126, 182–3,
    186, 189, 206, 216, 229, 238, 243,
    259, 284, 286, 292

Fadin, Andrej 277
Falange 79
Falkland Islands 282
Fallas, Carlos Luis (Calufa) 156
Fernández, Emilio (El Indio) 86
Ferreira, Francisco 146, 249
Ferreras, Ramón Alberto 143, 225–6
Figuereira, Guilherme 110
Figueroa, Gabriel 86
Finland 5, 7, 210, 237
Florida 7
folklore 37, 53–4, 57, 67, 78, 86–91, 100,
    104, 124, 126, 158, 197, 211, 214,
    225, 263, 284, 286, 289
Fonseca, Carlos 55, 163–4
France 10–11, 34, 53, 77, 84, 105, 115,
    132, 134–5, 139, 163, 180, 183
    187, 241
Franco, Francisco 79, 252
Franqui, Carlos 291
French Revolution 246
Frente Farabundo Martí para la Liberación
    Nacional (FMLN) 275
Frente Izquierda de Liberación (Uruguay)
    160
Frente Sandinista de Liberación Nacional
    (FSLN) 55, 125, 164, 196, 224
    275, 281
friendship of the peoples 36, 60, 67
Frondizi, Arturo 49, 96
Frondizi, Risieri 57
Frunze 65, 245, 267
Fuentes, Carlos 109, 136, 139, 157, 162
Fuerzas Armadas Revolucionarias de
    Colombia (FARC) 223, 293
Furceva, Ekaterina 5, 90

Gadžiev, Raúf 33, 64, 117
Gagarin, Yuri 33, 43–4, 47, 59, 71, 116,
    120–1, 152, 161, 185
Galeano, Eduardo 160
Gallegos, Rómulo 107, 136
García Márquez, Gabriel 54, 108, 110,
    128–9, 139, 143–4, 147, 149, 157–9,
    162, 165, 186, 202, 225, 248, 281
Garnett, Norris 195
Gatica, Lucho 90
Gefter, Michail 259
Gelman, Juan 145
gender roles 175, 178, 186, 188, 205
    226, 228
Genoa 163
Georgadze, Michail 50, 64
Georgia 53, 60, 64, 106, 113, 119, 122,
    151, 166, 186, 264, 294

Gerasimov, Aleksandr 154
Germany 24, 53, 77, 86, 91, 105, 115
    132, 135–6, 138, 193, 195, 210, 233,
    242, 280
Ghioldi, Rodolfo 65
Gide, André 128, 143, 166
Gil Gilbert, Enrique 150
Gilardi, Gilardo 54, 145
GKKS, see State Committee for Cultural
    Relations
Glavlit (censor) 250, 271
Glinkin, Anatolij 247, 274
global South 3, 11, 25, 51, 61, 68, 70, 83,
    123, 132, 141, 243, 280, 292
Gómez, Joaquín 293
Gómez Valderrama, Pedro 128, 181
Gonzales, José Luis 150
Gorbachev, Mikhail 281–3
'gorillas' 230, 232, 281
Gorjunov, Dmitrij 112
Goršakov, Viktor 31
Goulart, João 47, 49, 100, 141, 173
    175, 231
Grammatikov, Vladimir 107
Gramsci, Antonio 81
Granin, Daniil 112
Great Britain 132, 141, 249
Grebennikov, Sergej 117
Grenada 83, 93, 276
Gribačev, Nikolaj 96, 104, 255
Grigulevič, Iosif 121, 237, 241–3, 245, 253,
    257, 273
Gromyko, Anatolij 249
Gromyko, Andrej 123, 232, 249, 281
GRU (military secret service) 251
Gruško, Pavel 107, 115
Guadalajara 254
Guantánamo Bay 69, 131
Guaraní 37, 263
Guarany, Horacio 52
Guatemala 10, 24, 45, 69, 96, 105
    129–31, 145, 157, 198, 255, 276
Guber, Aleksandr 239
guerrillas 110, 121, 139, 160, 165, 170,
    189, 222, 233–4, 293
Guevara, Ernesto 'Che' 44, 46, 110–11,
    114, 119–21, 123, 125–7, 139–41,
    165, 233, 246, 252, 256, 268, 270,
    281, 286, 289, 296
Guillén, Abraham 160
Guillén, Nicolás 54, 79, 106–7, 113, 129,
    143, 145, 150–1, 159–60
Guinea-Bissau 141
Gulag 36, 74, 79, 211, 240, 245, 258, 294
Guljam, Chamid 112, 122

Gusev, Sergej 82
Gutiérrez, Joaquín 155, 159, 161, 242
Guyana 191–2, 225, 270, 276, 293
Guzmán, Abimael 233

Haiti 161, 231
Haley, Bill 97
Handal, Schafik 206, 258, 276–7
Hanzelka, Jiri and Miroslav Zikmund 101
Havana 21, 32, 36, 44, 46, 100, 102
    110–11, 113, 115–16, 123, 138, 189,
    253–4, 256, 293
Haya de la Torre, Víctor 134, 137, 165
health care 37, 45, 47, 69, 148–9, 161–3,
    171, 173, 175, 179, 185, 226
Hernandez, Angelo 97
Hikmet, Nazım 193
Ho Chi Minh 155, 193
home fronts 4, 12, 19, 41
homosexuality 171, 219
Honduras 98–9, 131, 231, 293
Honecker, Erich 193
Hoxha, Enver 233
Hungarian uprising 1956 24, 133, 153, 155,
    159, 161, 164, 185
Hurtado, Alváro 168
hydroelectric power plants 42, 47, 60
    63, 69, 132, 152, 168, 175, 182
    186, 223

Ibárruri, Dolores (La Pasionara) 259
Ignat'ev, Oleg 24–5, 69, 99–100, 105, 153
ILA, see Institute of Latin America,
    Moscow
Ilf, Ilja and Evgenij Petrov 83, 105
illiteracy 99, 102, 129–30, 147, 162
    171–3, 178, 181, 184, 187, 284, 288
IMEMO, see Institute of World Economy
    and International Relations
Incas 88, 165, 264
India 5, 7, 23, 91, 193, 204, 256, 287
Indonesia 5, 141, 231, 239, 283
Infante, Guillermo Cabrera 139
infrastructure 124, 159, 171, 173, 176, 185
Ingenerios, José 135
Inozemcev, Nikolaj 244
Institute of Latin America, Moscow (ILA)
    244–5, 247–8, 251, 253, 255–7, 263–8,
    271–4
Institute of World Economy and
    International Relations (IMEMO)
    244–5, 254, 256, 259, 272–3, 277
intellectuals 2–3, 5, 16, 20, 25, 27, 29, 31,
    41–2, 52, 54, 57, 64–6, 68, 71, 75–6,
    79–82, 94–7, 103, 110–12, 117, 119,

123–5, 128–90, 228–9, 239, 252, 258,
    265, 284, 287–8, 291, 296
international organisations 5, 231, 239
    247
international relations 4
Iraq 60, 211
Irkutsk 63, 182, 211
Iron Curtain 13–14, 54, 91, 126, 158, 176,
    229, 262, 289
Isa Conde, Narciso 258, 260
Israel 125, 230
Italy 84, 91, 133, 136, 242–3
Ivanov, Aleksandr 281
Ivanov, Viktor 118
Izvestija 59, 103, 119, 177, 241

Jagan, Cheddi 270
Jagdeo, Bharrat 224, 293
Jalapa 254
Jamaica 40, 43
Japan 130, 237, 244
Jara, Víctor 92–3, 107, 125, 127, 145
jazz music 43, 66, 87, 96, 195
Jerusalem 165, 179
Jiménez, Timoleón 293
Jurandir, Dalcídio 150

Kádár, János 159
Kalatozov, Mikhail 39, 116
Kal'catyj, Aleksandr 117
Kalesnik, Stanislav 98
Kaliningrad 100
Kamchatka 75
Kapuściński, Ryszard 280
Karakalpakstan 75
Karmen, Roman 83, 112, 284
Kazakhstan 37, 64–5, 83, 162, 292
Kazanskij, Gennadij 85
Keres, Paul 40
KGB 42, 55, 68, 95, 111, 121, 183, 187,
    210, 214, 219, 234, 246, 250–1, 253,
    266, 271–4
Khachaturian, Aram 31–2, 37, 39, 46
    64, 74
Kharkov 146, 205, 249
Khrushchev, Nikita 5, 22, 47, 50, 58–9, 64,
    66, 103, 120, 123, 125, 128, 133
    152–3, 155–9, 161, 164, 179, 184,
    201, 215, 230, 234, 253, 260, 285,
    287, 290
Kiev 53, 58, 148, 164, 173, 180, 245
Kim Il-Sung 193
Kinžalov, Rostislav 263
Kipling, Rudyard 93
Kirsanov, Semen 112

Kishinev 245
Klčina, Elena 112
Kločkovskij, Lev 247
Knorozov, Jurij 263
Kobzon, Iosif 42, 117, 121
Kogan, Leonid 39
Kolčina, Elena 107
Kol'cov, Michail 79, 241
Kollontaj, Aleksandra 29
Komsomol 52, 54, 56, 60–2, 120, 122, 193,
    197, 199–200, 202–3, 206, 219, 240,
    261, 280, 298
Kopalin, Ilja 82
Korchnoj, Viktor 40
Korda, Alberto 120
Kosarev, Jurij 263, 271
Kosygin, Aleksej 203, 230, 232, 249
Kosygina, Ljudmila 249
Koval', Boris 268
Kovalev, Dmitrij 115
Kraminov, Danil 255
Krauze, Enrique 139
Krongaus, Anisim 114
Krylov, Sergej 239
Krževskij, Boris 78
Kubitschek, Juscelino 49, 173
Kublinskij, Georgij 83
Kudačkin, Michail 234, 270–1, 275
Kulidžanov, Lev 32
kul'turnost 67
Kutejščikova (Kuteishchikova), Vera 86,
    95, 108, 112, 153, 156, 264, 266
Kuz'min, Evgenij 40
Kuz'miščev, Vladimir 105, 263
Kuznecov, Aleksej 256
Kyrgyzstan 64–5, 151

Lacerda, Carlos 47
Lara, Jesús 162, 164–5
Laserna Pinzón, Mario 180
late Stalinism 1, 5, 14, 21–2, 30, 95, 119,
    123, 132, 148, 150, 156, 179, 240,
    243, 277–8, 287
Latin America, definition of 10–11
Latin American communist parties 24
    29–30, 32, 102, 110–11, 117, 136,
    138, 149, 153–4, 157, 162, 165, 175,
    179, 188–9, 193, 199, 207, 233–4,
    246, 259, 267, 269, 282
Latin American media 25
Latinos, definition of 10
Latinskaja Amerika (journal) 121, 237, 248,
    256, 264, 271
Latvia 101, 106, 188
Lavreckij, Iosif, *see* Grigulevič, Iosif

Lavrov, Nikolaj 251–2, 257
Lazarev, Marklen 247, 274
legitimacy 8
Leipzig 163
Lenin, Vladimir Ilich 1, 6, 38, 42, 48, 119, 132, 136, 165, 169, 179, 181, 190
Lenin, nuclear-powered ice-breaker 47
Leningrad 53, 58, 62–3, 78, 87, 119, 148, 151, 168, 170, 173, 180, 182, 202, 237, 245, 256
León, Carlos Augusto 52, 145
León, María Teresa 94
Leonov, Nikolaj 121, 230, 232, 251–3, 260–1, 266, 271, 273–5, 294, 297
Lermontov, Mikhail 77
liberalism 3, 17, 181
liberation theology 130, 170, 268
Lichačev, Ivan 79
Lifšic, Michail 239
Lima 196
Lisician, Tamara 84
Listov, Konstantin 113, 118
literature 19–20, 24, 27, 32–4, 42, 46, 66, 74, 79, 97, 104–10, 112, 115, 124, 126, 139, 146–7, 151, 178, 182, 184, 207, 212, 240, 243, 245, 248–9, 254, 263–4, 274, 289, 292
Lithuania 105–6, 253, 264, 278
Lizalde, Eduardo 157, 159, 190
Lobo Sosa, Porfirio 293
London, Jack 78
London 73, 191–2
Lopez, José 248
López Mateos, Adolfo 45
López Moreno, Roberto 128, 190
López Pumarejo, Alfonso 31
Los Angeles 179
Lozovskij, Solomon 238, 241
Lučenok, Igor' 125
Lukashenko, Alexander 294
Lumumba University, *see* Patrice Lumumba University of the Friendship of the Peoples
Lunačarskij, Anatolij 257
Lvov 196, 245

Madrid 114, 221, 238, 290
magic realism 107, 157, 292, 296
Magomaev, Muslim 76, 117
Majdanik, Kiva 121, 258–60, 266, 268, 270–1, 277, 281, 296
Majskij, Ivan 237–8, 243, 245, 255, 257–8
Malcolm X 191
Malenkov, Georgij 28
Malinin, Evgenij 39

mambo 81, 88, 91, 117
Managua 164, 275–6
Mancisidor, José 31, 148
Manfred, Al'bert 240
Maoism 61, 65, 120, 136, 198, 201, 233–4, 267–8
Maples Arce, Manuel 135
Mapudungun 264
Marcuse, Herbert 143, 226
Mariátegui, José Carlos 136, 233
Martí, Farabundo 29
Martí, José 92, 134, 261
Marxism 3, 7, 12, 29, 36, 38, 65, 70, 77, 91, 110, 123, 136–8, 140, 163, 165, 168, 185, 209, 217, 223–4, 233, 259, 269, 275, 278, 293
Marxism-Leninism 2, 12, 59, 65, 68, 137, 140, 180, 199, 203, 209, 240, 265, 268, 278
Mašbic, Jakov 263
Maslennikov, Gennadij 115
Mayakovsky, Vladimir 78, 85, 257
Mayas 105, 263
Mdivani, Georgij 113–14
Mehnert, Klaus 143
Mendes, José Guilherme 171–2, 176
Mendoza, María Luisa 183
Mendoza, Plinio 54, 158, 183
Mercader, Ramón 241–2
Merin, Boris 257
meringue 114
mestizaje 15, 106
Mexico 10, 17–18, 29, 31–2, 34–5, 39–40, 43–4, 50, 53, 64, 79, 82, 95, 98, 101, 111, 113, 123, 134–5, 139, 142–3, 145, 148, 150–1, 153–4, 156–7, 164, 182–4, 186, 190, 195–6, 201, 214, 222, 228, 241–2, 246–8, 251–2, 254, 259–60, 264, 293
massacre of Tlatelolco 183
Mexican cinema 86–7
Mexican communists 29, 153–4, 157, 188, 193, 197
Mexican culture in USSR 78–9, 84–6, 109, 117, 295
Mexican Revolution 78, 80, 86, 126, 135, 284
Soviet exhibition in Mexico 25, 45, 64
Mexico City 29, 36, 65, 84, 129, 148, 222, 241, 266, 290–1
meždunarodniki 234, 237, 243, 248–52, 255–6, 258, 260–1, 266–7, 272–5, 278–9, 281, 284, 290, 296
MGIMO, *see* Moscow Institute for International Relations

MGU, *see* Moscow State University
Michajlov, Sergej 90, 251, 253–4
Michalkov, Sergej 84
Middle East 76, 199, 217, 222, 231–2
    244, 287
Migulja, Vladimir 125
Mikojan, Anastas 45–6, 50, 64, 111, 123,
    244, 253, 256, 260, 262
Mikojan, Sergej (Sergo) 230, 248, 251, 256,
    259, 271, 278
military dictators 36, 69, 131, 171, 185,
    189, 232–3
military dictatorships 175
Miller, Arthur 143
Minsk 58, 127, 168, 251, 293
Miró Quesada, Francisco 90, 161, 165,
    170, 177–8, 263
modernism 81, 106
Moiseev, Igor' 40, 103
Moldavia 60, 106
Molotov, Vjačeslav 249
Mongolia 28
Montevideo 28–9, 40, 97, 233
Morales, Evo 294
Morel, Efraín 65, 190
Moscow 23, 40, 49, 51, 54–6, 60, 62–3, 66,
    76, 82, 87, 89–90, 92, 100, 105–7,
    109–10, 113, 118–20, 123, 132
    144–5, 148, 151, 154–5, 158, 160,
    163, 165, 173, 175, 179–80, 182
    190–1, 193, 197, 204, 206, 216, 219,
    244–5, 259
Moscow declaration 23
Moscow Institute for International
    Relations (MGIMO) 237, 239–40,
    244–5, 247, 249, 251, 254, 256, 260,
    273–4, 278
Moscow State University (MGU) 57–8, 93,
    109, 177, 196, 199, 225, 237, 239,
    241, 245, 254–5, 257–8, 273–4
Motyl', Vladimir 76
Movimiénto de Acción Revolucionaria
    (MRA, Mexico) 222
Movimiento Nacionalista Revolucionario
    (MNR, Bolivia) 163
Movsejan, Georgij 126
Mozambique 141, 279
Muños Cota, José 148
music 19–20, 39, 42–3, 52, 54, 57, 60, 66,
    74–7, 80–1, 84–93, 100, 104, 113–14,
    116–17, 121–2, 124–7, 171, 189, 207,
    214, 218, 225, 264, 284–5, 288–9

Nagy, Imre 154
Nasser, Gamal Abdel 141, 231

Nehru, Jawaharlal 141
Neruda, Pablo 32, 54, 79, 94, 96, 105–7,
    112, 128, 136–8, 143, 145–6, 149,
    152–3, 155, 159, 161, 188, 190
    241, 256
Netherlands 10, 141
New Jewel Movement (Grenada) 276
New York Times 41, 46, 111, 191–2, 195,
    227, 270
Nicaragua 29, 55, 125, 129, 134, 163–4,
    170, 184, 196, 198, 224, 248, 259,
    275–6, 281, 294
Niemeyer, Oscar 99, 145, 264
Nieto Caballero, Augustín 43, 166–7, 170
Nikolaev, Andrijan 44
Nikolaeva, Tatjana 39
Nin, Andreu 241
nomenklatura 101, 122, 256, 266
Non-Aligned Movement (NAM) 141–2
non-capitalist path of development 28, 65,
    165, 268
North America 130, 170, 290
North Korea 193, 222
northern hemisphere 2, 91, 126, 289
Novosibirsk 86, 196
Novye Čeremuški 244
Núñez Jiménez, Antonio 54

October Revolution 3, 63, 132, 136
    239, 284
Odessa 58, 90, 148, 205, 238
Odría, Manuel 129
Ogonek (magazine) 96–8, 101, 111–12, 119,
    201, 255, 292
Ojstrach, David 33, 39, 103
Okudžava, Bulat 93
Oliver, María Rosa 54, 96, 145, 155, 159–60
Organisation of American States (OAS) 13,
    129
Orlov, Aleksandr 241–2
Ortega, Daniel 275, 294
Ortega, Humberto 276
Ošanin, Lev 126
Ospovat, Lev 257
Otero Silva, Miguel 145, 170, 179

Pachmutova, Aleksandra 117
Padilla, Heberto 189, 292
Pakistan 256
Palestinian Liberation Organisation (PLO)
    222
Panama 10, 38, 53, 69, 96, 99, 131, 212,
    218, 223, 232, 253
Paraguay 13, 54, 65, 85, 87, 100, 129, 143,
    231, 258, 286

Paris 54, 79, 129, 135, 137, 151, 187, 218, 221, 241, 247
Parra, Nicanor 146, 190
Partido Comunista de Bolivia 233
Partido Indio de Bolivia (PIB) 165
Partido Obrero de Unificación Marxista (POUM, Spain) 241
Partido Revolucionario Institucional (PRI, Mexico) 182
Pasternak, Boris 143, 153, 161, 178
Patoličev, Nikolaj 47
Patrice Lumumba University of the Friendship of the Peoples 58–60, 64, 120, 155, 161, 194–201, 204, 210, 212, 215, 217–19, 222, 273–4, 284, 293
Pavlyčko, Dmitrij 112, 121
Paz, Octavio 137, 139, 148, 291
peaceful coexistence 22, 28, 61, 103, 120, 140, 185, 200, 232
Pelevin, Victor 296
perestroika 3, 17, 21, 225, 255, 281, 297
Pérez, Gustavo 170
Pérez Jiménez, Marcos 100, 105, 129
Perón, Juan 129
Peru 18, 29, 39, 41, 49, 56–7, 61, 65, 83, 88–90, 100, 129, 134, 136, 139, 142, 144, 157, 160, 162, 164–5, 170, 177–8, 189, 196–7, 204, 232–3, 254, 263, 268, 293
Petrosjan, Tigran 40
Pičugin, Pavel 117, 264
Piecha, Edita 76
Pinochet, Augusto 188, 224, 270, 280, 283–4, 294
Pintos, Francisco 96
Pitol, Sergio 184
Poblete de Espinosa, Olga 145, 161
Poland 17, 76, 122, 183, 241, 276, 280
Polikarpov, Sergej 114
Politburo 5, 23, 236, 250, 273, 275
Pomerancev, Vladimir 74
Ponomarev, Boris 30, 269–70, 281
Popovič, Pavel 44
populism in Latin America 15, 130, 140, 172–3, 267
Portugal 10, 115, 134, 141, 146, 249
Posochin, Michail 123
Potechin, Ivan 201
poverty 83, 96–7, 99–100, 102, 104, 123, 138, 151, 159, 181, 183–4, 186–7, 220–1, 284
Prado Junior, Caio 137
Prague 30, 54, 150–1, 157, 206, 252, 258–9, 266, 276

Prague Spring and Soviet invasion 1968 125, 133, 152, 157, 185, 189, 220, 230, 259, 266
Pravda 98, 111–13, 119, 241, 251, 255, 270
Prebisch, Raúl 247
Prestes, Luis Carlos 29, 172, 188, 206
Prieto, José Manuel 292
Problemy Mira i Socializma / World Marxist Review (journal) 30, 258, 270, 275
Profintern 138, 238
Prokofiev, Sergei 39
Prokrovev, Aleksandr 115
propaganda, definition of 27
prostitution 176, 183, 187
Puerto Rico 69, 131, 150
Pugwash Conference 5
Pushkin, Alexander 74, 77, 128, 149, 291
Putin, Vladimir 294, 296–7
Pyongyang 222
Pyr'ev, Ivan 78

Quadros, Jânio 44, 49, 141, 173
Quechua 37, 88, 162, 216, 263–4
Quito 254
Quixote, Don 103

Rabelo, Genival 175–6, 187
racism 134, 163, 191–3, 205, 207, 215–17, 228–9, 268, 295
Radek, Karl 193
radio 5, 25, 33–4, 37–8, 52, 59, 61–2, 64, 101, 104, 120, 146, 155, 169, 188, 197, 213, 248–9, 263
Ramírez, Ariel 54
Ramírez Sanchez, Ilich (Carlos the Jackal) 222
Ramos, Graciliano 145, 150–1
Ravines, Eudocio 137
Realpolitik 12
Reed, Dean 44, 92
Reinaga, Fausto 143, 163–6, 186
religion 48, 52–5, 57, 97–8, 105, 134, 156, 164, 166–7, 169–70, 174–5, 179, 182–3, 199, 203, 220
revolutionary romanticism 79–80, 84, 86, 99, 102, 106, 108, 111, 115, 117, 119–20, 122, 124, 126–7, 186, 189, 232, 259, 271, 282
Revueltas, José 139, 148, 153–4, 156, 159
Reyes, Alfonso 95, 136
Rio de Janeiro 39–40, 47–8, 88, 105, 152, 221, 254
Rivera, Diego 29, 32, 53, 79, 109, 128, 137, 154, 157, 159

Rivera, José Eustasio 107
Rjazan' 252, 257
Rodríguez de Francia, José Gaspar 258
Rojas Pinilla, Gustavo 129
Rolfo, Juan 109
Romania 18
Rome 242–3
Romero, Elvio 143
Roy, Manabendra Nath 193
Rozental, Mark 239
Ruiz, Henry 224
rumba 90
Rumjancev, Sergej 59, 194, 202, 204
Russell, Bertrand 143, 265
Rzakuliev, El'beka 83

Saborit, Eduardo 91
Šaburov, Aleksandr 296
Sagor, Roberto 54
Said, Edward 75, 95
samba 88, 90
San Francisco 7
Sandino, Augusto 134
Santiago de Chile 94, 96, 126, 176
    207, 269
São Paulo 221
Sauvy, Alfred 11
Savič, Ovadi 241
Savickij, Igor' 75
Scandinavia 76
Scorsese, Martin 117
Scorza, Manuel 165
Second Congress of Soviet Writers 74
Second International 245
Second World War 1, 7, 13, 21, 29, 39, 77,
    81, 132–3, 138, 148, 172, 179, 207,
    240, 259, 284
Semenov, Sergej 268
Sendero Luminoso (Peruvian guerrilla
    movement) 233
Senegal 163
šestidesjatniki 6, 122, 239, 280
Shaw, George Bernard 147
Shevardnadze, Eduard 282
Shostakovich, Dmitri 39, 46
Siles Zuazo, Hernán 163
Simón, Victor 88
Simonov, Konstantin 83, 95–6, 103
    144, 146
Sinel'nikov, Boris 93
Sinjavskij, Andrej and Julij Daniel' 143
    154
Siqueiros, David 53, 79, 109, 128, 137,
    145, 148, 154, 159, 186, 188
    241–2, 256

Sirijos-Gira, Vytautas 105
Sixth World Youth Festival, Moscow 1957
    49, 51, 55, 57, 87, 144, 163–5
ska music 43
Skármeta, Antonio 105
Slepuchin, Jurij 105
Slezkin, Lev 257, 279
Smeljakov, Jaroslav 121
Smirnov, Sergej 112
Snitko, Aleksandr 127, 283
socialist realism 74, 108, 157
Sofronov, Anatolij 38, 96–8, 103–4
    201, 255
Solzhenitsyn, Alexander 74, 143, 152, 219
Somoza, Anastasio 129, 275
Sosa, Jesualdo 96, 149–50
Sosa, Susanna 96
South Ossetia 294
Soviet Academy of Sciences 95, 201, 238,
    243–5, 250–2, 254, 257–8, 263–4, 266,
    271
Soviet Army 1, 4, 39, 138, 159, 200, 251,
    255, 257, 274
Soviet Council of Ministers 201, 232
Soviet foreign ministry (MID) 33, 35, 123,
    231–2, 234, 237, 251, 255, 270, 272,
    274, 282
Soviet ministry of culture 5, 90
Soviet ministry of education 201–2, 257
Soviet propaganda 20, 23–4, 26, 55, 84,
    119, 146, 152, 217, 228, 244
Sovinformbjuro 24, 26, 34, 69, 99, 238,
    255, 274
space programme 38, 42–3, 47, 63, 81, 152
Spain 10, 31, 37, 52, 78–9, 85, 92, 94, 106,
    114, 134, 136–7, 139, 143, 146
    162–3, 238, 241, 246, 281
    Spaniards in USSR 79, 95, 132, 158,
    213, 248, 252
    Spanish Civil War 78–80, 83, 85, 92–3,
    106, 113–14, 124, 126, 137, 149
    236–8, 242, 248, 258–9, 264, 284
Spassky, Boris 40
sport 35, 37–8, 40–1, 51, 60–1, 63, 98–9,
    173, 175, 197, 207, 209, 211, 227, 269
Spota, Luis 183, 201
Sputnik 43, 46–7, 70, 111, 152, 163, 166,
    185, 207
Sputnik (youth travel agency) 61–3
SSOD, see Union of Soviet Friendship
    Societies
Stagnation 3, 125, 230, 253, 286
Stalin, Joseph 2, 28, 67, 125, 131, 148–51,
    154, 156, 158, 164, 177, 190, 241,
    258, 260

Stalin/Lenin Peace Prize 107, 145, 150–1, 155, 157, 179, 251
Stalingrad 172
Stalinist aesthetics 154
Stalinist crimes 57, 74, 79, 137, 152–3, 155–6, 235–6, 241, 265
State Committee for Cultural Relations (GKKS) 33, 35, 45, 48–9, 89, 114, 132, 147, 160, 165–6, 173, 245, 273
Stavropol 122
Steinbeck, John 143
Stepanov, Georgij 264
Stolbov, Valerij 108
Stroessner, Alfredo 129
students 20, 26, 31, 38, 51, 53–4, 57–61, 71, 120, 127, 164, 167, 175, 177–8, 183, 191–229, 232, 237–41, 247, 260, 266, 278–9
Sturua, Melor 82, 103
Stuttgart 163
Sukarno 141, 231
Šul'govskij, Anatolij 251, 254–5, 260 266–8, 278
Sultan-Galiev, Mirza 193
Sumac, Yma 88–9
Supreme Soviet 49–50, 64, 104, 282
Svetlov, Mikhail 84, 93
Sweden 210, 219, 224
Switzerland 249

Tablada, Ernesto 224
Tadeo, Nina 270
Tahiti 77, 115
Tajikistan 64, 76, 101, 106
Tarle, Evgenij 239
Tashkent 38, 63–4, 173, 193, 202
TASS, see Telegrafnoe Agenstvo Sovetskogo Sojuza
Tbilisi 63–4, 122, 166, 173, 180, 245, 255
Teitelboim, Volodia 152
Telegrafnoe Agenstvo Sovetskogo Sojuza (TASS) 24, 34, 111–12, 213, 241, 273–4
Tereškova, Valentina 33, 44
Thaw, the, 69, 75–6, 82, 85, 116, 157, 159, 166, 185, 201, 249, 257, 266, 278, 287
Third World, definition of 11
Tichomirovna, Irina 40
Tisse, Eduard 78, 86
Tito, Josip Broz 141, 193, 242
Titov, German 161
Toledano, Vicente 148
Tolstoy, Lev 77, 184
Torres, Camilo 170
Torres, Joaquín 169, 178–9, 187

Torres, Lolita 82, 85, 88
Torres Giraldo, Ignacio 138, 151
Torrijos, Omar 223, 253
Tratado Interamericano de Asistencia Recíproca (TIAR) 13
Trieste 242
Tróccoli, Luís 97
Troickij, Artemij 120, 126
Trotsky, Leon 1, 29, 148, 241
Trujillo, Rafael 129, 225
Tupamaros (Uruguayan urban guerrilla) 160
Turkey 5, 7, 280
Turkmenistan 64, 76, 83
Tursun-Sadeh, Mirso 64

Ukraine 18, 49, 75, 95, 98, 112, 119, 122, 146, 207, 214, 258, 293
Union of Soviet Friendship Societies (SSOD) 6, 31–5, 38–9, 42–3, 59, 61, 64, 89, 96, 107, 132, 147, 199, 207, 233, 245, 273, 293
United Nations 239, 242, 247
United States Information Agency (USIA) 26
United States of America 2–3, 9–10 12–14, 17, 25–6, 29–31, 41–2, 45–7, 66, 71, 76, 83, 86, 88, 91, 94, 96, 99, 102, 113, 115, 122, 126, 130–1 138–9, 142–3, 160, 163, 178–9, 186, 195, 204, 206, 217–18, 223, 226, 229, 231–2, 238, 242, 244–5, 247, 255, 257, 262, 270, 276, 279, 281–2, 284
US popular culture 66
Universidad Nacional Autónoma de México (UNAM) 252, 257, 265
universities 20, 36, 38, 53, 57–61, 93, 132, 136, 149–50, 161–3, 166, 178, 180, 186, 190–229, 233, 237–8, 243, 245, 247–8, 254, 257, 263, 273, 293, 295
University of the Toilers of the East 193
Urrutia, Praxedes 145
Uruguay 10, 25, 29, 31, 36, 39–42, 54, 57, 95–7, 129, 149–50, 160, 188, 197, 205–6, 214, 223, 233, 255, 260, 282
Soviet exhibition in Uruguay 25
Urusevskij, Sergej 117
Uzbekistan 38, 41, 53, 65, 75, 98, 112, 119, 122, 173, 192, 219

Vajl', Petr and Aleksandr Genis 122, 280
Vajnštok, Vladimir 117
Valcárcel, Gustavo 65, 160–2, 164, 190
Valencia 137
Vallejo, César 128, 137

Vanslov, Viktor 118
Varela, Alfredo 85–6, 143, 145, 148, 156, 159
Varga, Jenö 244
Vargas, Getúlio 172
Vargas Llosa, Mario 139, 157, 189, 225, 248, 291
Vasconcelos, José 134
Velasco, Juan 142, 232
Venezuela 39–40, 52, 82, 99–100, 105, 107, 129, 145, 170, 179, 184, 204–5 220–1, 225–6, 254–5, 259, 284, 294
Vera, Pedro Jorge 155, 159, 190
Vidali, Vittorio 242
Vietnam 193, 203, 219, 231, 283
Villafañe, Javier 145
Villaseñor, Víctor Manuel 148
Vinogradov, Vladimir 123
Visión (journal) 24
Vitver, Ivan 239
Vizbor, Jurij 76, 93, 286
Vladimirskij, Sergej 93
Voice of America (broadcaster) 25
VOKS, *see* All-Union Organisation for Cultural Contacts
Volpi, Jorge 292
Vol'skij (Vol'skii), Viktor 248, 251, 254, 260, 267–8, 278, 284
Voronezh 245
Vorožejkina, Tatjana 277
vostokovedenie (Russian Orientalism) 243
Vygodskij, David 78–9
Vysockij, Vladimir 42, 93

Washington, DC, 13, 45, 120, 262, 276
West Berlin 195
western Europe 92, 105, 130, 133, 138, 143, 170, 182, 186, 195, 210–11 247, 296
World Congress of Communist and Labour Parties 23
World Peace Council 144, 153
World Youth Festival, *see* Sixth World Youth Festival, Moscow

Xiaoping, Deng 193

Yevtushenko, Yevgeny (Evtušenko, Evgeny) 44, 76, 93–4, 115–16, 118, 276, 282
youth 51–2, 55, 57, 62, 66, 87, 120, 183, 193, 199, 202, 206
Yugoslavia 5, 18, 193, 242

Zagorskij, Boris 107
Zaid, Gabriel 139
Zakharov, Mark 107
Zapata Olivella, Manuel 54
Ždanov, Andrej 74
Zea, Leopoldo 139
Zetkin, Clara 143
Zinov'ev, Nikolaj 126
Zubok, Lev 237–8, 241, 243, 245, 257, 279
Zubrickij, Jurij 263–4
Žukov, Georgij 114, 249
Žukov, Grigorij 33